AF413379

NEW YORK
BARS
AT DAWN

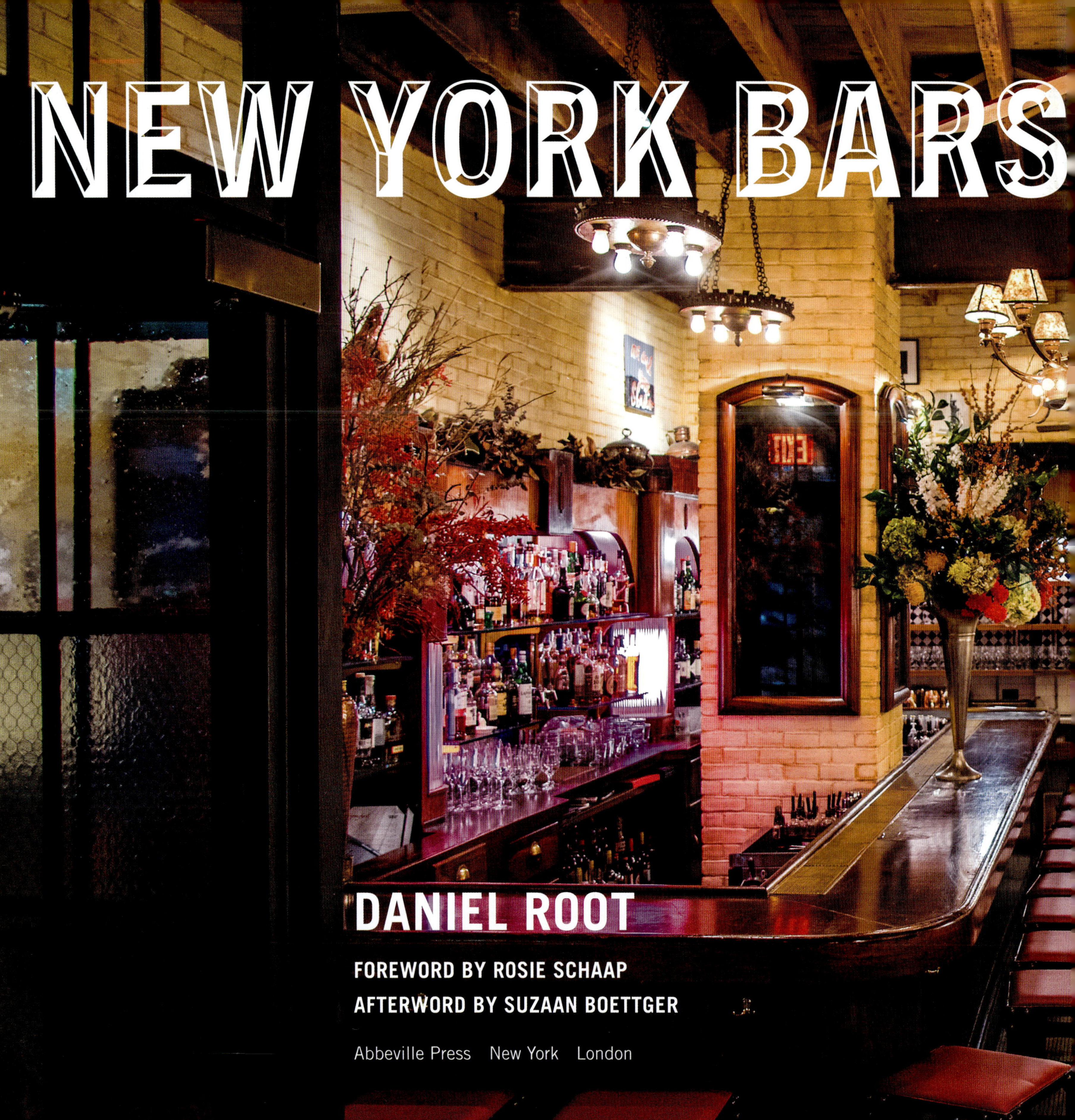

NEW YORK BARS
DANIEL ROOT
FOREWORD BY ROSIE SCHAAP
AFTERWORD BY SUZAAN BOETTGER
Abbeville Press   New York   London

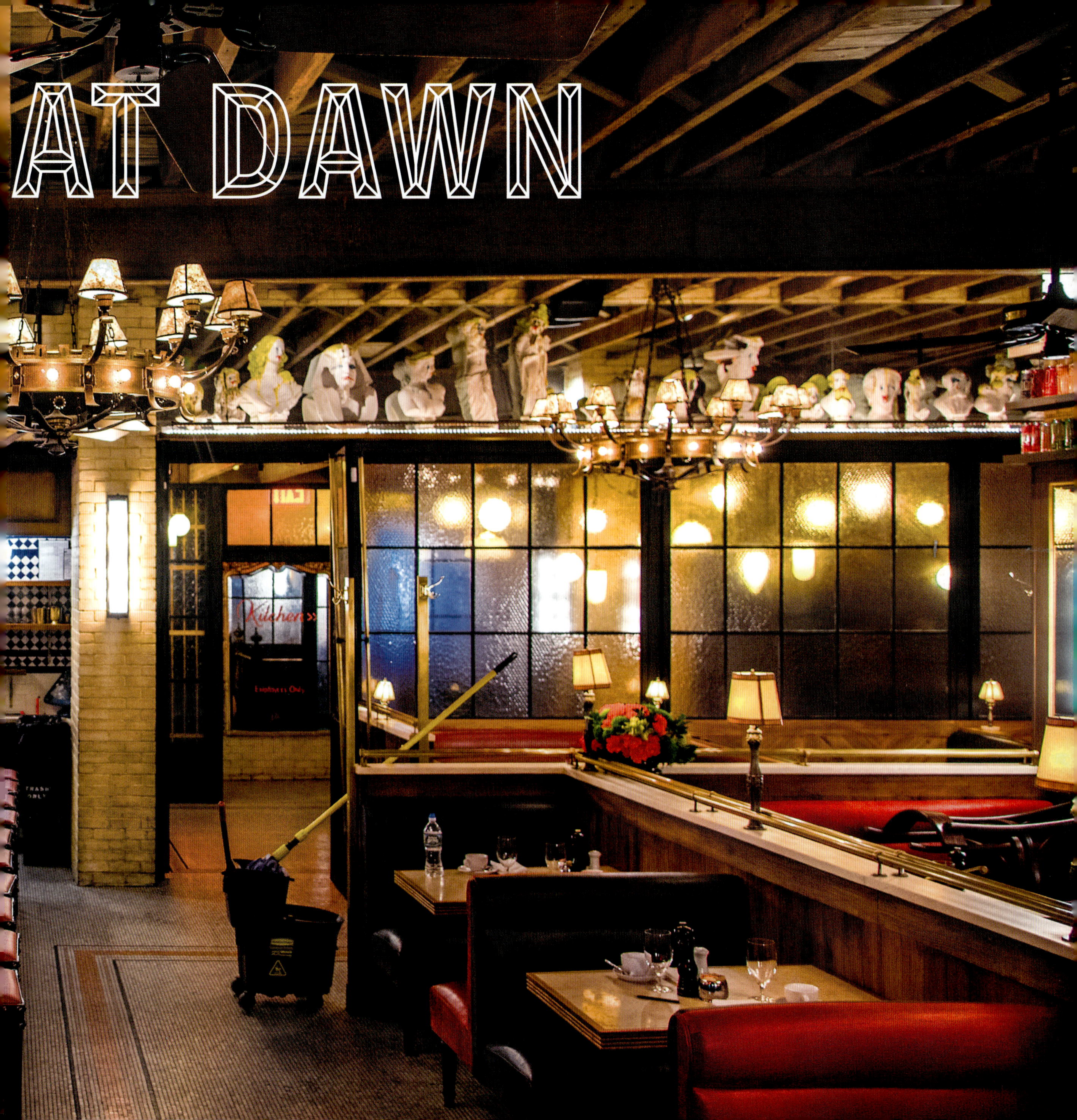
AT DAWN

Daniel Root is a fine art photographer and a principal in the visual arts firm The Root Group. His predawn photographs of Manhattan have attracted a devoted following among bartenders and other night shift workers, and have been featured on NY1. Root lives on the Lower East Side and is a very early riser.

Rosie Schaap is the author of *Drinking with Men*, *Becoming a Sommelier*, and *The Slow Road North: How I Found Peace in an Improbable Country*.

Suzaan Boettger is an art historian and critic, and the author of *Inside the Spiral: The Passions of Robert Smithson.*

Editor: David Fabricant
Designer: Misha Beletsky
Layout: Ada Rodriguez
Production manager: Louise Kurtz

First edition
10 9 8 7 6 5 4 3 2 1

ISBN 978-0-7892-1477-5

Library of Congress Cataloging-in-Publication Data available upon request

For bulk and premium sales and for text adoption procedures, write to Customer Service Manager, Abbeville Press, 655 Third Avenue, New York, NY 10017, or call 1-800-Artbook.

Visit Abbeville Press online at www.abbeville.com.

CONTENTS

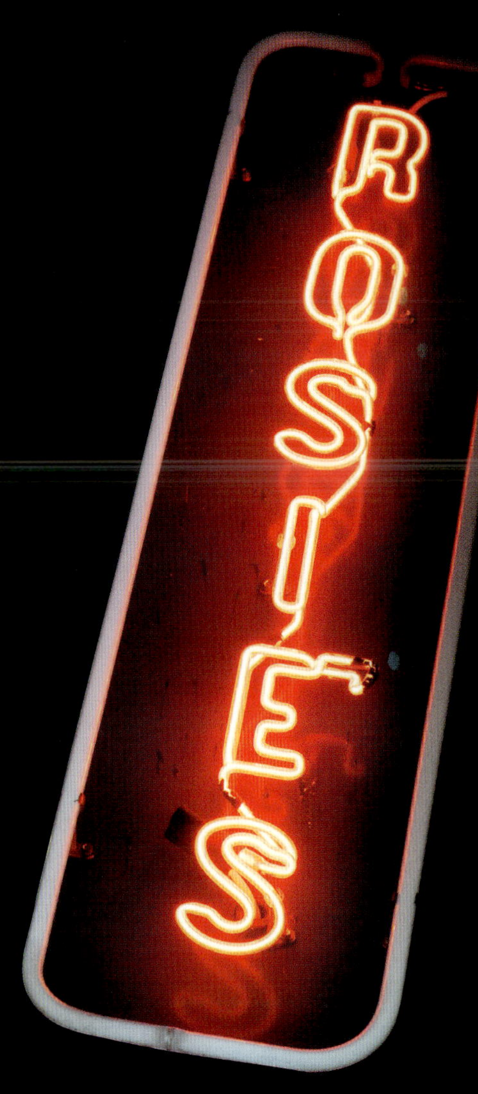

ROSIE'S

FOREWORD

*A Bar is Never Barren: On Daniel Root's
Photographs of New York Bars at Dawn*

By Rosie Schaap

In autumn 2017, a friend emailed to tell me about Daniel Root's photographs
of bars. I was going through a season of change: having spent much of my life
in bars, I had lately observed that I was pulling away from that world, or that
it was pulling away from me. Drinking and I never had a big, bad breakup: it
was more like we saluted each other with a deep, appreciative bow, promised
to check in once in a while, then mostly parted ways.

That year, too, the monthly column about drinking and its pleasures I'd
written since 2011 for the *New York Times Magazine*, in which I regularly cel-
ebrated bars I loved, came to an end. And I had started thinking, hard, about
leaving New York City, for somewhere very different. All this to say: there were
strong signals that my life in bars, such as it was, had wound down.

Still, I was glad my friend had directed me to Dan's photos. I loved them
instantly, because they are so revealing and otherwise remarkable, because
they seem to know exactly why those of us who find bars beautiful feel that
way. I also appreciated Dan's approach, which reflected what I regard as the
essentially democratic, leveling nature of bars: he had sought no special ac-
cess, no special treatment, no special equipment; he walked the streets and
avenues of (mostly lower) Manhattan and looked, and pressed his camera's
lens against windows that could not be counted upon to be crystalline and
unblemished, and then looked again, and closer. He chose that quieter, lim-
inal time, break of day, to capture these spaces—and, in so doing, he com-
pelled even a heretofore bar lifer like me to look more closely, too, and even
to see things differently. I know this territory, and I know these rooms—some
of them intimately. I was a certified regular in three of the places in this book:

the Holiday, Puffy's Tavern, and the Fish Bar, and I made regular appearances at many others, including Kettle of Fish, the Ear Inn, and Milano's.

I have a strong preference for old, and determinedly old-fashioned, neighborhood bars, which are abundantly represented in this collection, and had always considered, for example, Pete's Tavern exceptionally handsome. But had I ever taken a moment to contemplate the clock in the corner until I saw it in Dan's photos? And had I, then, never previously reflected on why there might be something slightly uncanny about the sight of a clock in a pub? Or, take another favorite: Fanelli's. In Dan's photograph of this venerable SoHo saloon, I am immediately drawn to the wounds and scars on that old tile floor. How often I had thoughtlessly stomped across it! What stories it might tell!

There are some bars in these pages that I've never visited (mainly among the fancier spots), but not many. For decades, New York bars were to me sites of comfort, fellowship, easefulness, and respite. If I could spot the Ear's red neon glowing in the distance, or confirm that all the the books and Green Bay Packers mementos were still in place at Kettle of Fish, or catch a glimpse of Jackie, the incomparable day bartender at Milano's, through the window as I walked across Houston Street, or manage to snag a barstool at Jimmy's Corner, my heart rate slowed down, and I grew calmer. Some of these places were almost as familiar to me as my own home—and often more inviting.

But among the many mysterious achievements of Dan Root's photographs is how they make familiar places even more familiar, while defamiliarizing them at the same time. Because—and this is a question I've asked, rhetorically, countless times—what is a bar without people, anyway? And before I was confronted with these images, my rhetorical answer was usually: *nothing*.

A bar, I had always argued, is more than the sum of its bottles and glassware, its woodwork and fixtures and pool tables and booths. A bar is about the people who drink and meet and talk and work in it. I will always believe that, more than anything, what makes a bar an enticing place to be a regular is the people, and the variety of people, it brings together.

The photograph that I return to most is of the Stonewall Inn—a bar I've visted many times, but where I was never a regular. The last time I was there, I couldn't even get through the door: it was June 26, 2015, the day the United States Supreme Court's decision in *Obergefell v. Hodges* made marriage equality the law in all fifty states. As the site of the 1969 riots that galvanized the gay rights movement, Stonewall was where I wanted to celebrate—and thousands of other New Yorkers had the exact same idea.

The previous time I'd been there was in 2013, when I was reporting a story about bar regulars with exceptional skill at various bar pastimes, like darts and pinball. At Stonewall, I went looking for an exceptional pickup artist. It was soon after opening time, and nearly empty. The sharp, young bartender—I think he said he was working on a doctorate in queer studies, if I remember correctly—laughed when I told him what I was up to. "You'll never find that person here," he said. "Our best pickup artists are on the DL. They'd never want to be in a newspaper article." Moments later, a young Irishwoman with long braids stepped inside. She told us she'd been doing a self-guided tour of locations that were important to the Greenwich Village folk scene of the

1960s, and had heard that Bob Dylan had performed at the Stonewall Inn. I didn't think that was true, but I did know that Dave Van Ronk, one of Dylan's early friends and mentors in New York, had been arrested at the Stonewall riots. And that this was the perfect segue for the bartender to tell the folkie tourist what this place was *really* famous for.

As he spoke its history into life, I could envision the room filling with the people at those riots—people who changed the world. And I get the same feeling—both electric and bittersweet—when I look at Dan's photograph of Stonewall: that, even when empty, the people who drank there, loved there, fought there, are still there, still present in the paneled columns, the rainbow flags, the footrail, the Christmas lights. Many of them are now long gone, but they are remembered in this image, even in their absence.

"Where man is not," the artist and poet William Blake wrote in the Proverbs of Hell, "Nature is Barren." It's a provocation, certainly, even if it is also ambiguous: it can say different things to different readers. Among the possibilities: did this mean that what we call nature may exist without us, but "nature" does not exist except as the human *idea* of nature? Or possibly, and more sinisterly, that without human presence in it, nature is empty of meaning? That latter possibility is very close to how I felt, for so long, about bars. But Dan's photos have changed my mind, and have shown me that even without us, the hearts of these places can still hum, still vibrate, still shine. That even without us, we are still there at the bar—vestigially, sometimes spectrally, as stories and even, in some instances, as histories. In their rich-ness, attention, and the surprising intimacy of through-the-window distance, these images show us that bars are never barren. They are replete, in their own skins and on their own terms, even hours before the first pints are pulled

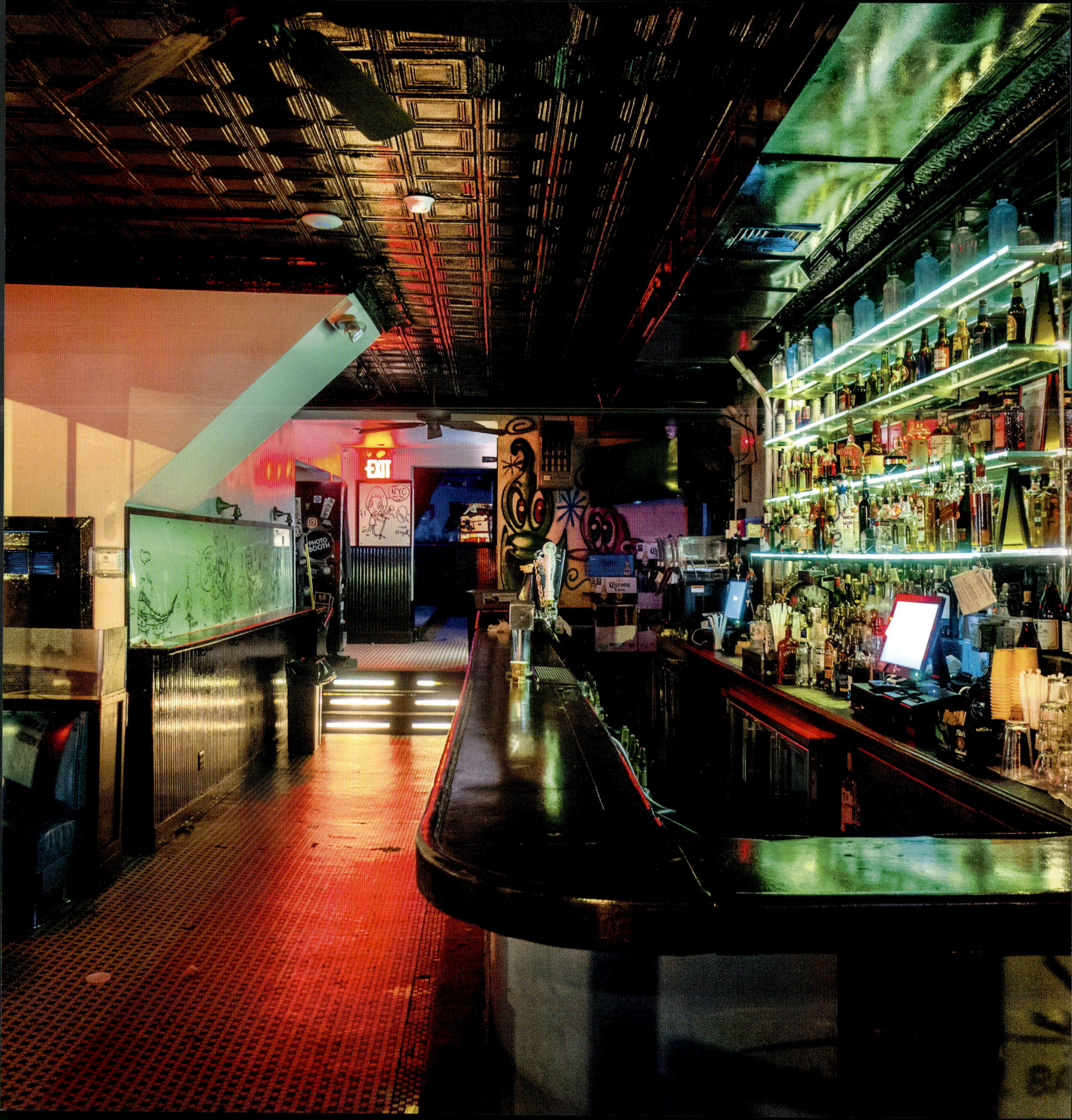

INTRODUCTION

Walking a Perfect Manhattan

My early morning photographic journey began when I walked our dog, Katie, every morning along the East River on the Lower East Side. She lived a long life, but after she died the routine remained essential to my peace of mind. My predawn ambling along the perimeter expanded into downtown Manhattan's maze of streets, lanes, and alleys.

In the calm before the urban hustle, meandering aimlessly on my solitary walk, I noticed unusual lighting at the corner bar, 7B, also known as Horseshoe Bar or Vazac's, a place that I had walked by a million times in the decades I have lived on East 7th Street. The lone light over the cash register, the neon beer signs and their soft glow over the bar, the light of the pinball machine left on overnight. As I continued the walk, with my imagination now piqued, I looked into the next bar, Niagara, and it too had enticing lighting. The horizontal green lines of the glass shelf lighting, the glow of the photo booth from the back room, the red of the traffic light on the corner. That morning as I walked the East Village, a whole world opened up to me.

I knew I had to put the lens directly on the glass to avoid a reflection off the bar's window. Positioning the lens against the pane not only eliminated the reflection but also stabilized the camera, allowing for longer handheld exposures. The longer exposures gather light from the often-dim environments, allowing the camera to see what the eye on its own cannot.

I've spent time in many of these places when they are open, enjoying a refreshment or two, and I can tell you—as you see in my photographs—that looking from a dark street into a deserted tavern evokes a different sort of reverie. Typically, when bars are open they are strikingly lit, aiming to stimulate excitement—and business. When they are quiet till morning, what is left behind is a mix of under-bar strip lighting, an exit sign's red glow, light cascading from a side-room door left ajar, a string of party lights someone forgot to turn off, the radiance of a streetlight, the glare of a DON'T WALK sign on the corner. An acidic glow of conflicting neon colors that combines with the shadows in dark corners to create a mysterious scene.

Once I started noticing bars during the off-hours, I saw an odd jumble of spotty lighting in almost every one of them. Whether it was a dive bar, a restaurant bar, a sports bar, or a hotel bar, each took on a very different look and conveyed a distinct persona.

As I walked the city between four and eight in the morning, noticing the sometimes beautiful, sometimes lurid lighting and the distinctive interiors of these common spaces, a "collection" began to take shape. At first I thought I would limit my photography to my own neighborhood, the East Village. The boundaries soon stretched to include the West Village and the Lower East Side. Then they extended still further into lower Manhattan and, occasionally, even north of 14th Street to Uptown. Ultimately the limit became the distance I could walk from and to home in the early hours.

I find my morning walks and the scenes I observe very relaxing, almost meditative. When I'm alone on the street, the physicality of walking (as well as the occasional fence climbing, but that's rare) allows me to get truly lost in my thoughts. Other times I can be almost without thought and just sensing the street—with all of its sights, smells and sounds—while feeling the ground through the soles of my shoes. At times there is an incredible quiet, a quiet that one would never imagine midday. It's interrupted only by birdsongs, flapping flags, the disturbing rustling of rats in the garbage, and the quiet clinks and clanks of the food truck guy setting up for the day.

What occasionally takes me out of that zone is encounters with people. I must admit that I am on high alert when I run into people at that hour, as those on the street are a mixed bag. Several times people have gotten too close in a pestering way or have gotten in my face, but that is infrequent. For the most part it's the hardworking laborer coming to or from the job, kind of trudging along. The closer to 4 a.m., when "last call" is announced per New York State law and places close for the night, the greater the likelihood of running into the bar set on their way home. I have very few problems with them, or the drug set, as they are easily avoided. Both groups tend to make a lot of noise, so it's easy just to cross the street or turn a corner to avoid a confrontation; as there is almost no traffic, jaywalking is more than all right. As dawn approaches, the dog walkers turn out, along with the occasional person apparently leaving a date (to judge by the evening-wear-at-dawn look) and hailing a cab. The collateral benefit of heightened awareness, keeping my senses on alert, is one I actually enjoy.

While I was walking and letting my mind wander, I would occasionally think about the people I saw. The people who were out on the street at that hour, the people still in the bars, the people who had been in the bars, the people who would be in the bars shortly. Besides people on the street, going to work, coming home from work, the bar and drug sets, there are people just strolling along. Like they have nowhere to get to or nowhere to go.

Then there are those still in the bars. Sometimes through the halfway-down gate one can spot souls just finishing up as the bartender starts the end-of-night cleanup. Other patrons, still imbibing, seem to be making no move to leave. Are they restaurant workers or nightshift people just enjoying their "6 p.m. cocktail" in the early morning? Only once was I invited in as a bartender was closing, and he poured me a drink. It's not my habit to start the day that way, but I was touched by his welcome, so I had a quick one and then got on my way. There are not many bars that open for business at the New York State legal serving time of 8 a.m., but there are a few. (There used to be more.) The people at that hour are as varied as the other times. Night workers, people who can't let the party end, people whose community is the bar.

After several weeks of daily morning walks and photography, I started thinking of the bars as people—bars at rest, bars preparing for the next day. I had anthropomorphized the bars! Amused by this strange logic, I gained further motivation for my walks and began putting a bar a day on Instagram, usually posting around dawn. I was delighted to find how many people were curious about empty bars at dawn.

The people who follow the project are varied as well, starting with friends and friends of friends. I always tag the bar so friends of the bar start paying attention—and friends of one bar tend to have an interest in other bars. People interested in architecture and interiors started following the posts, as well as people whose workday starts early and who were familiar with the same predawn city. I also tagged the neighborhood of each bar, so the friends of the neighborhood started following. It turns out there is vast interest in bars and nightlife, downtown Manhattan, and New York City in general, to the point that I started getting international interest.

As the sun starts to rise, the light changes both the look and the spirit of the city. Once dawn hits, my photographic mission is done for the day. The weird mix of artificial light, with its many sources and different colors, fades into the unified hues of daylight. The street starts filling up, and the magic of 5 a.m. is lost—till tomorrow.

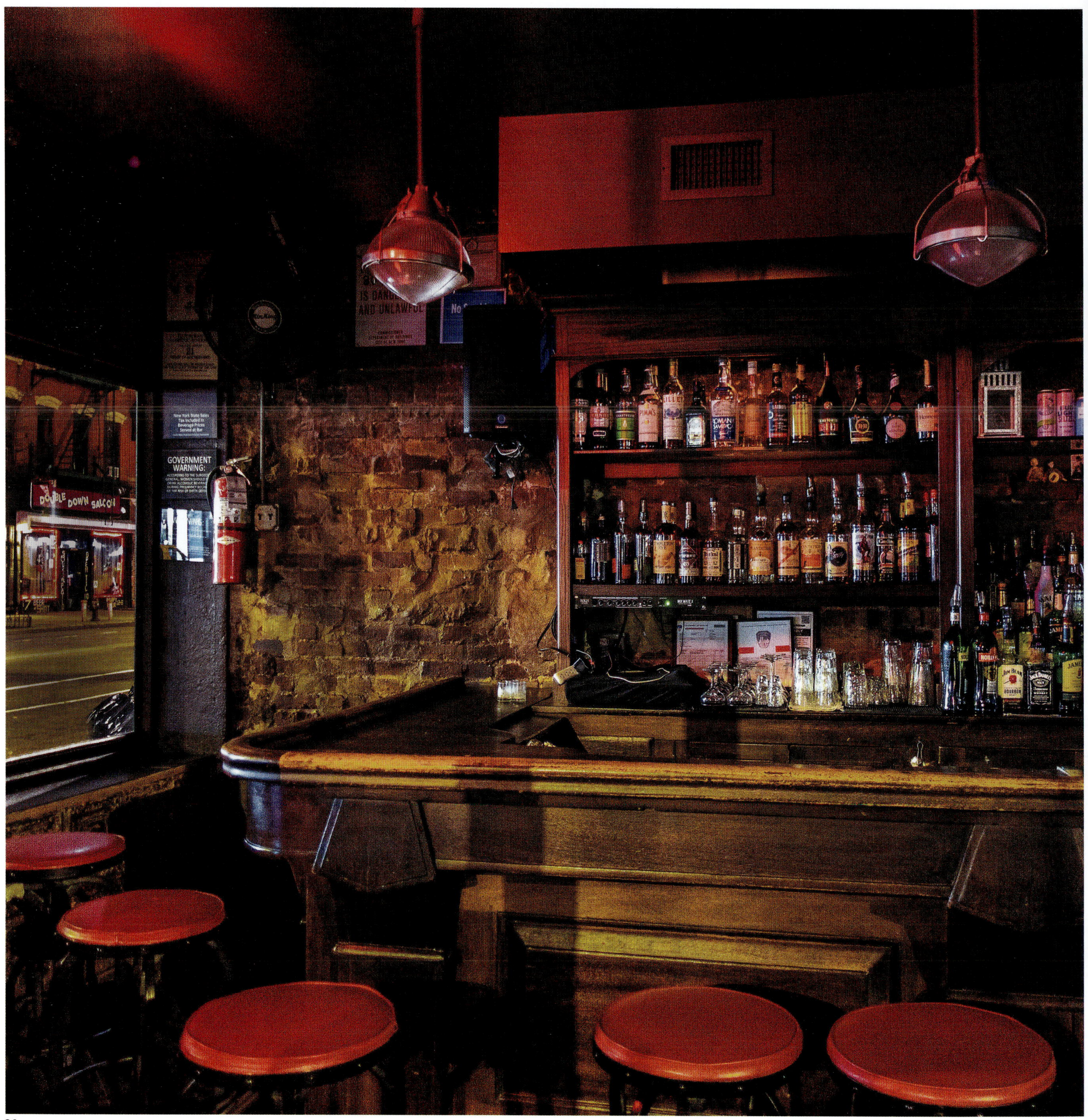
GOVERNMENT
WARNING:
DOUBLE DOWN SALOON

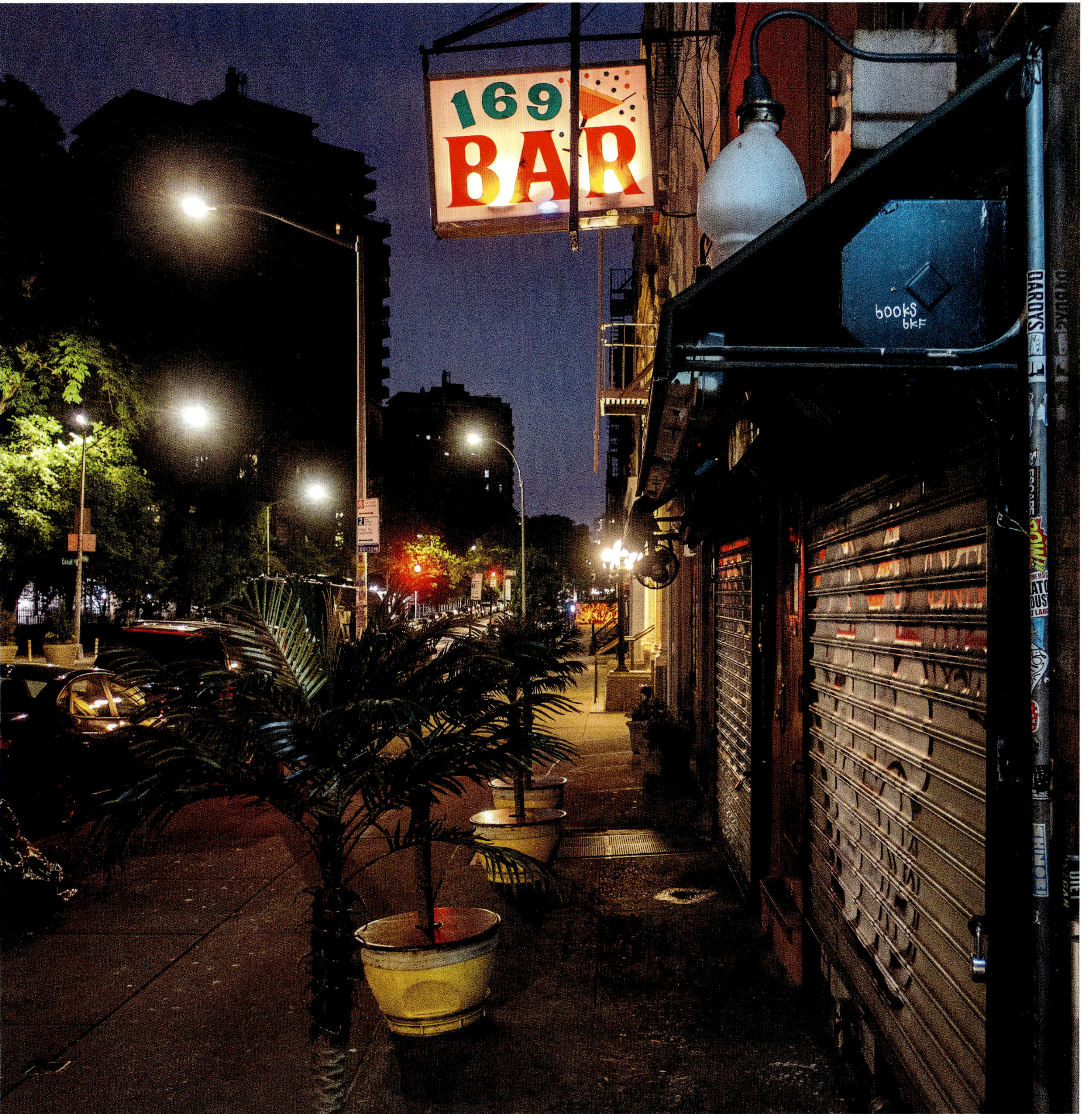

169 Bar

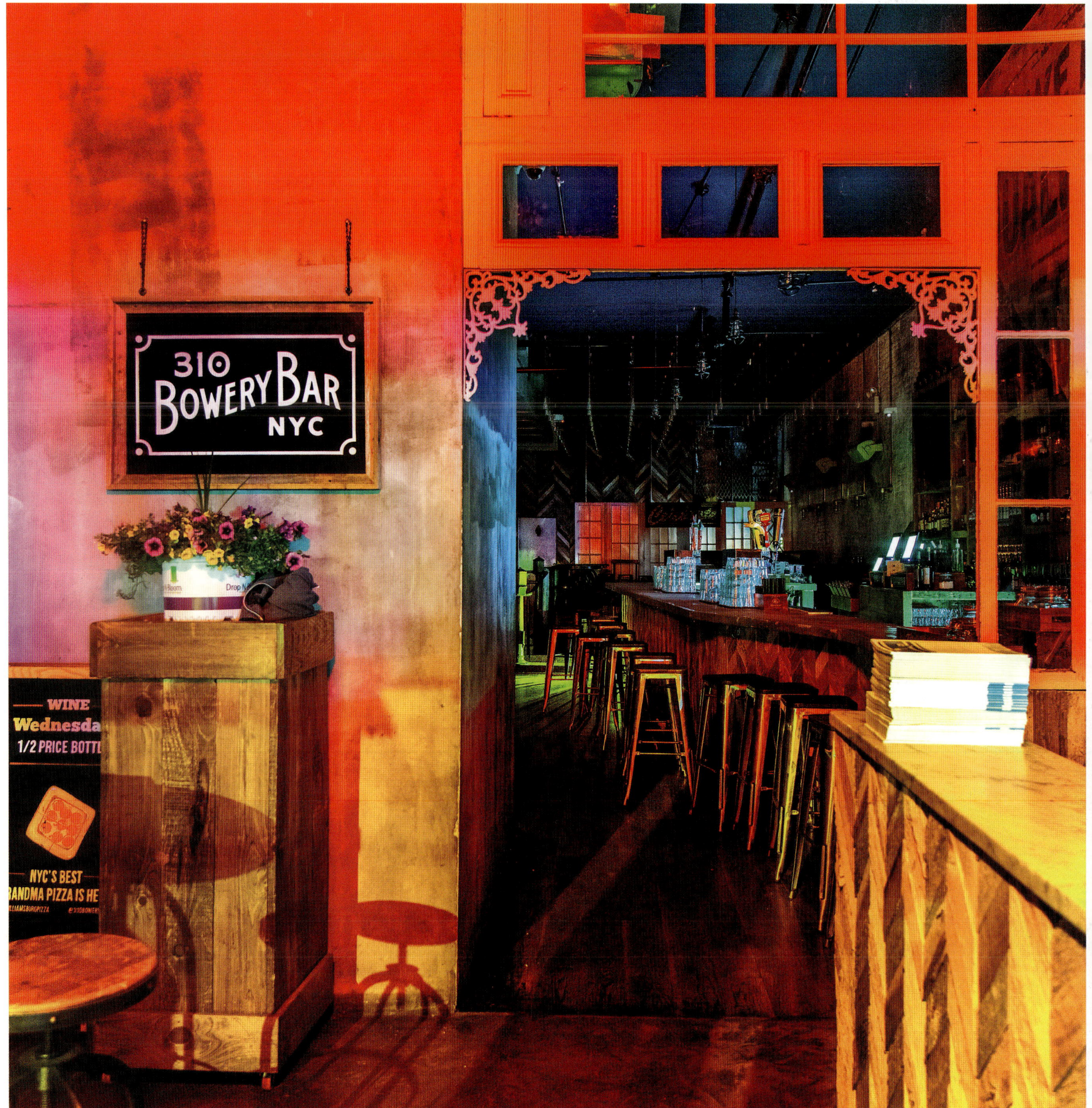

310 Bowery Bar

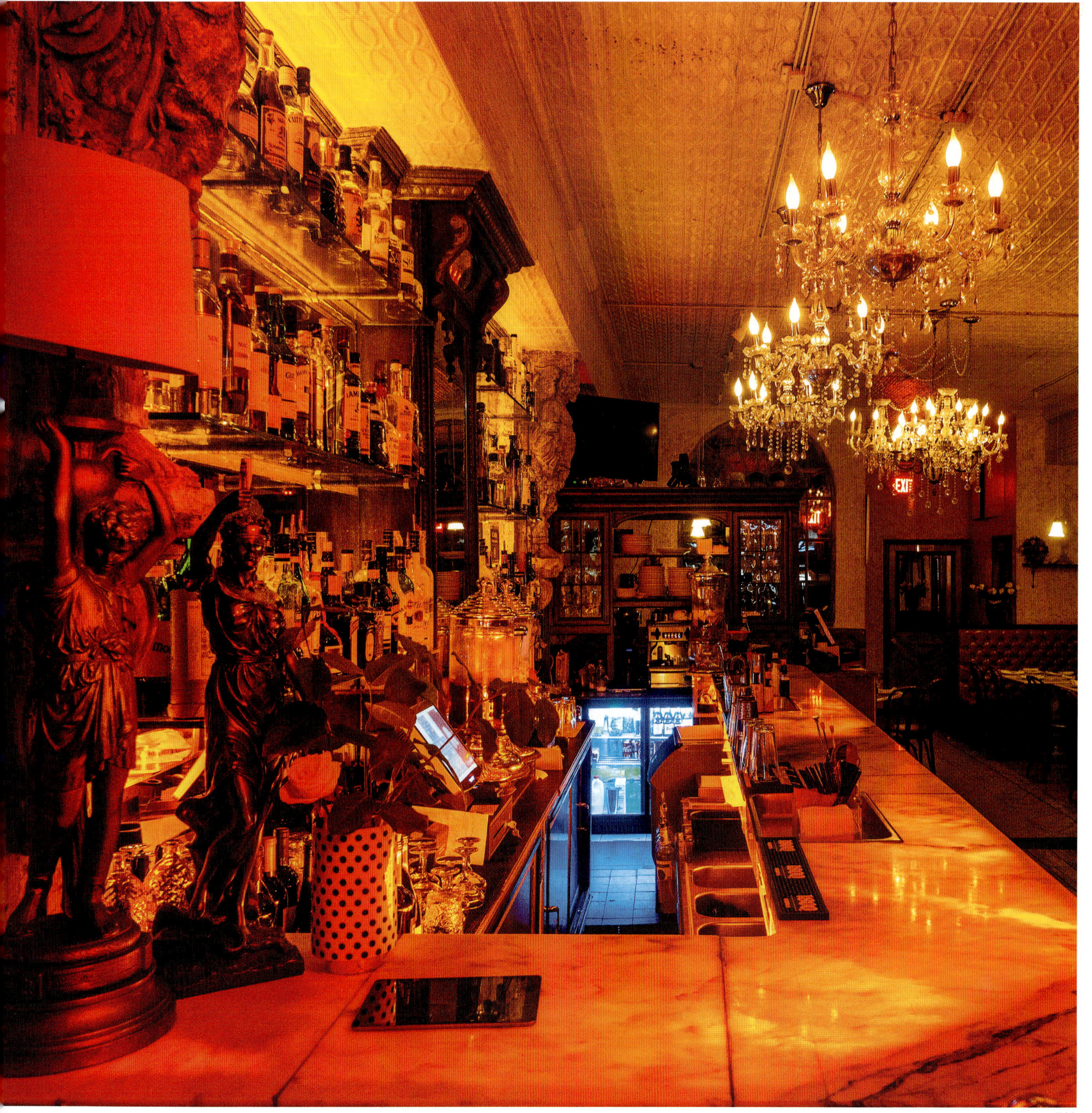

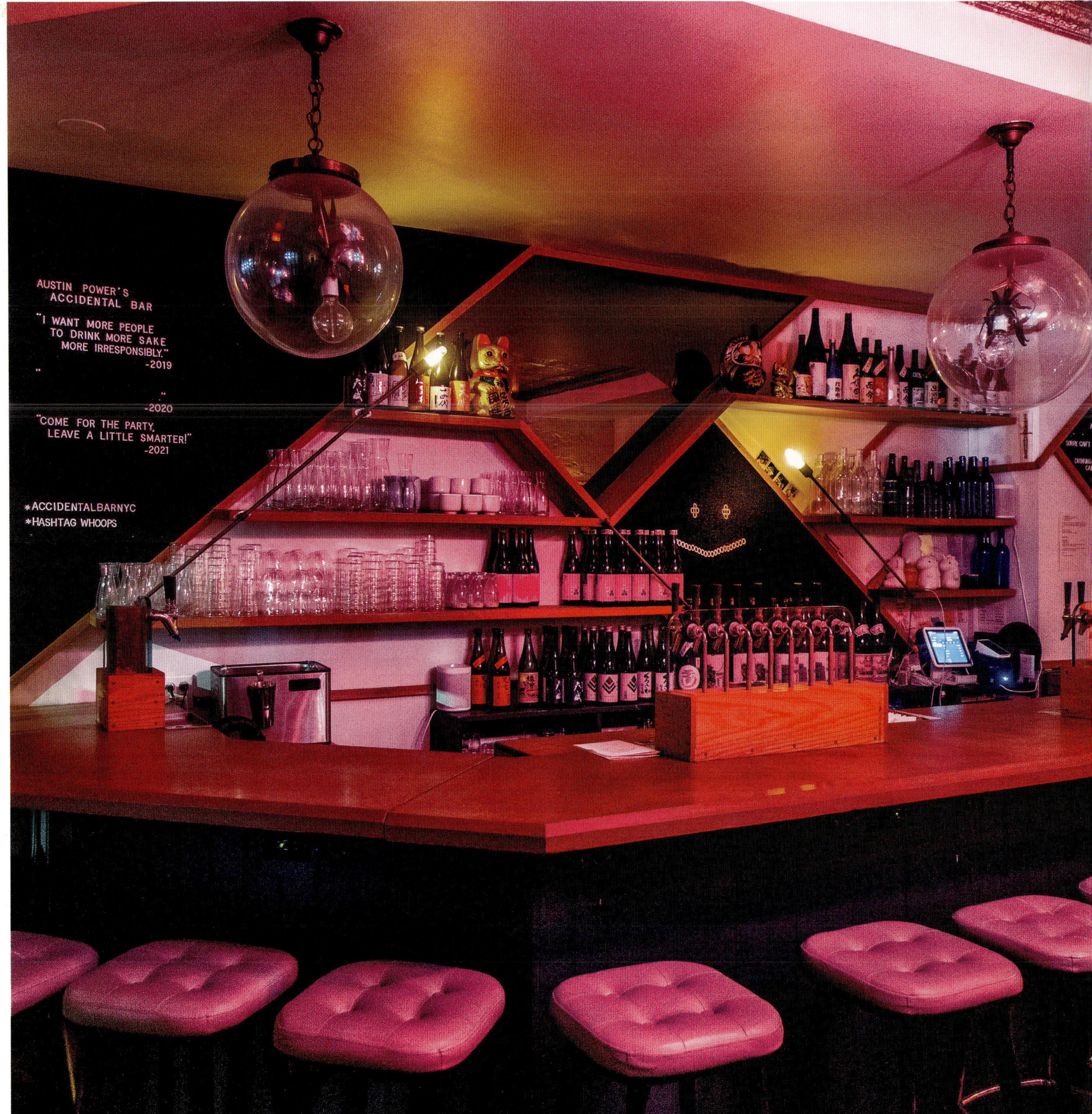

Accidental Bar

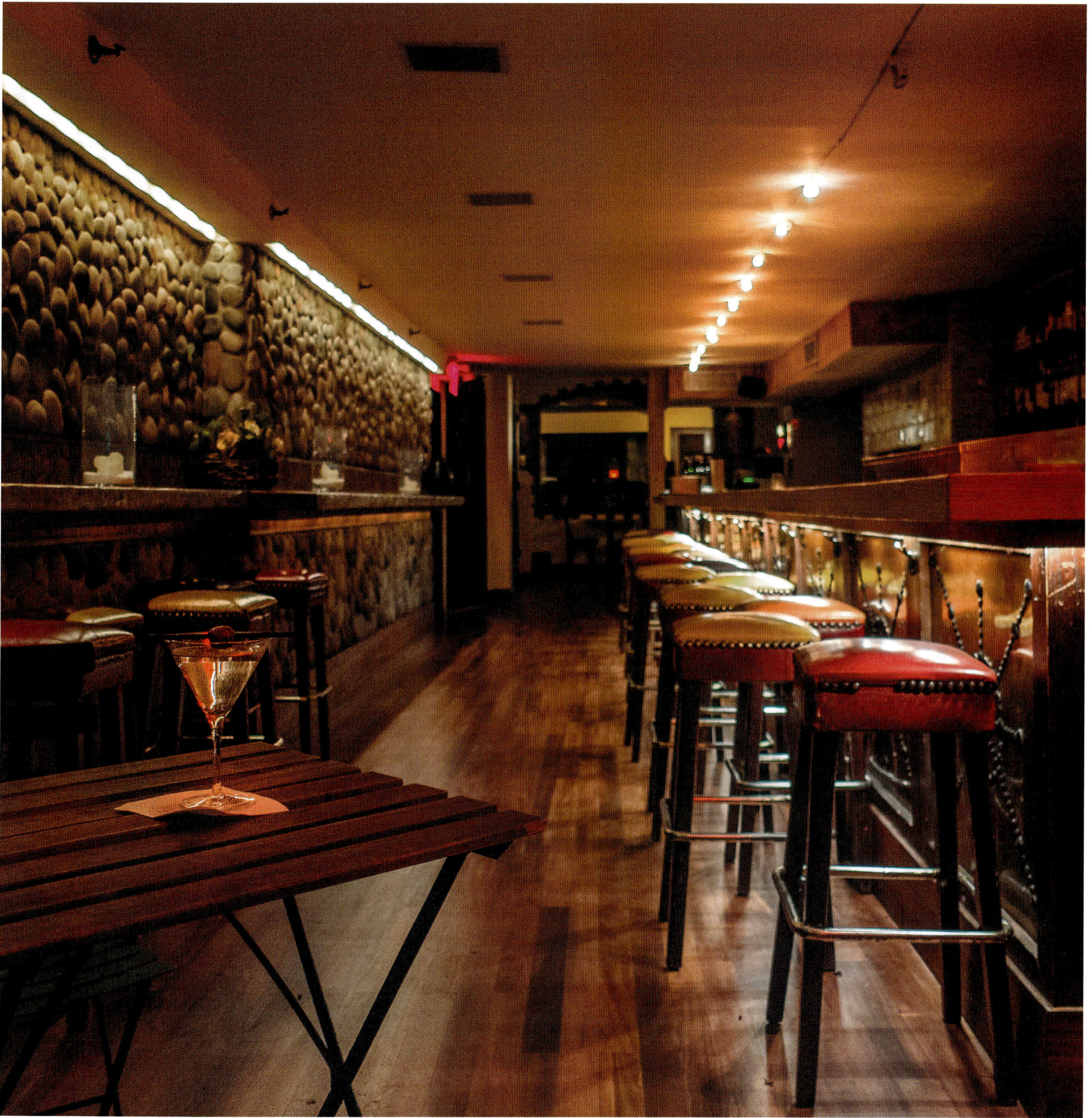

Alta

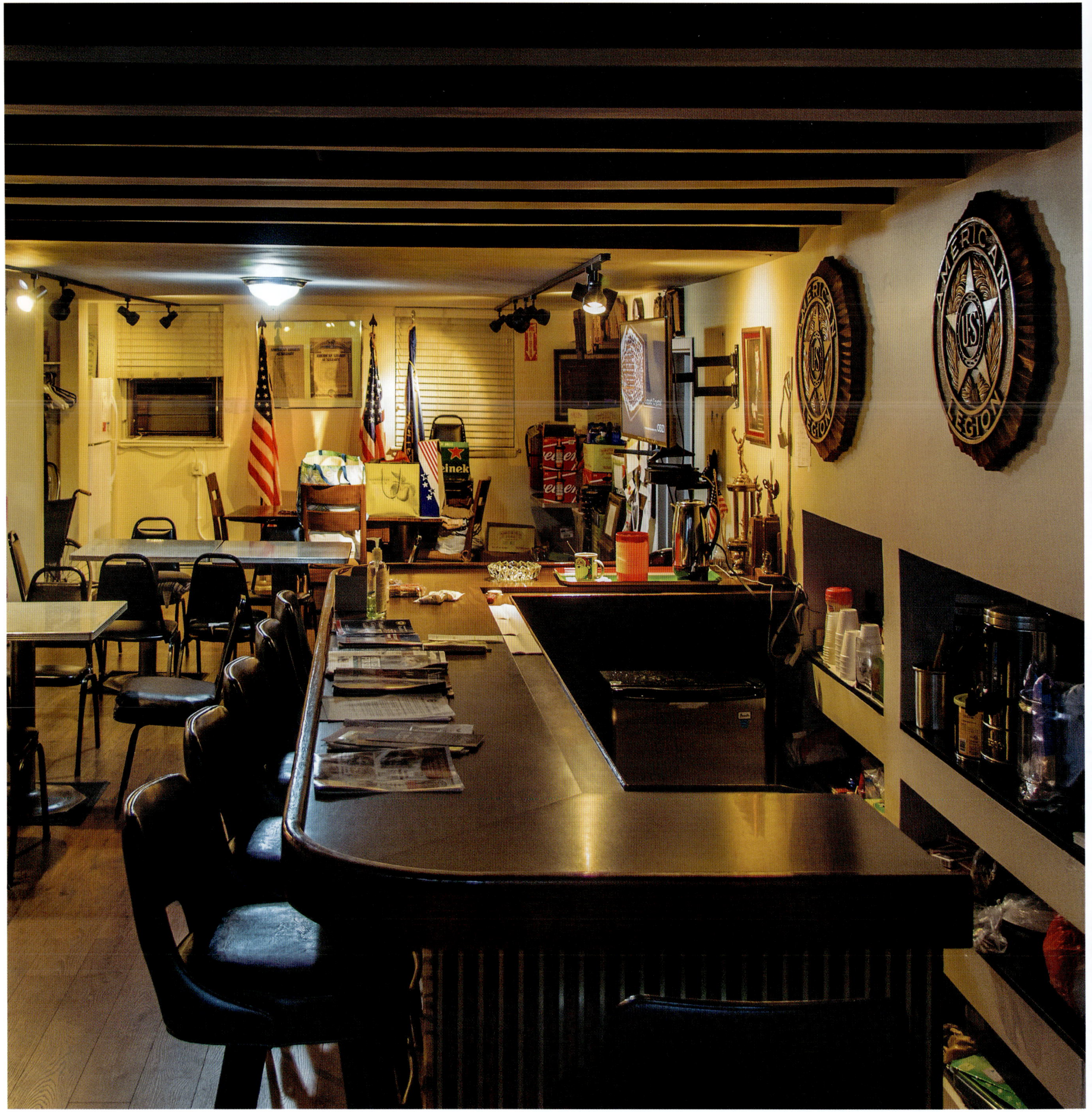

American Legion Post 1212

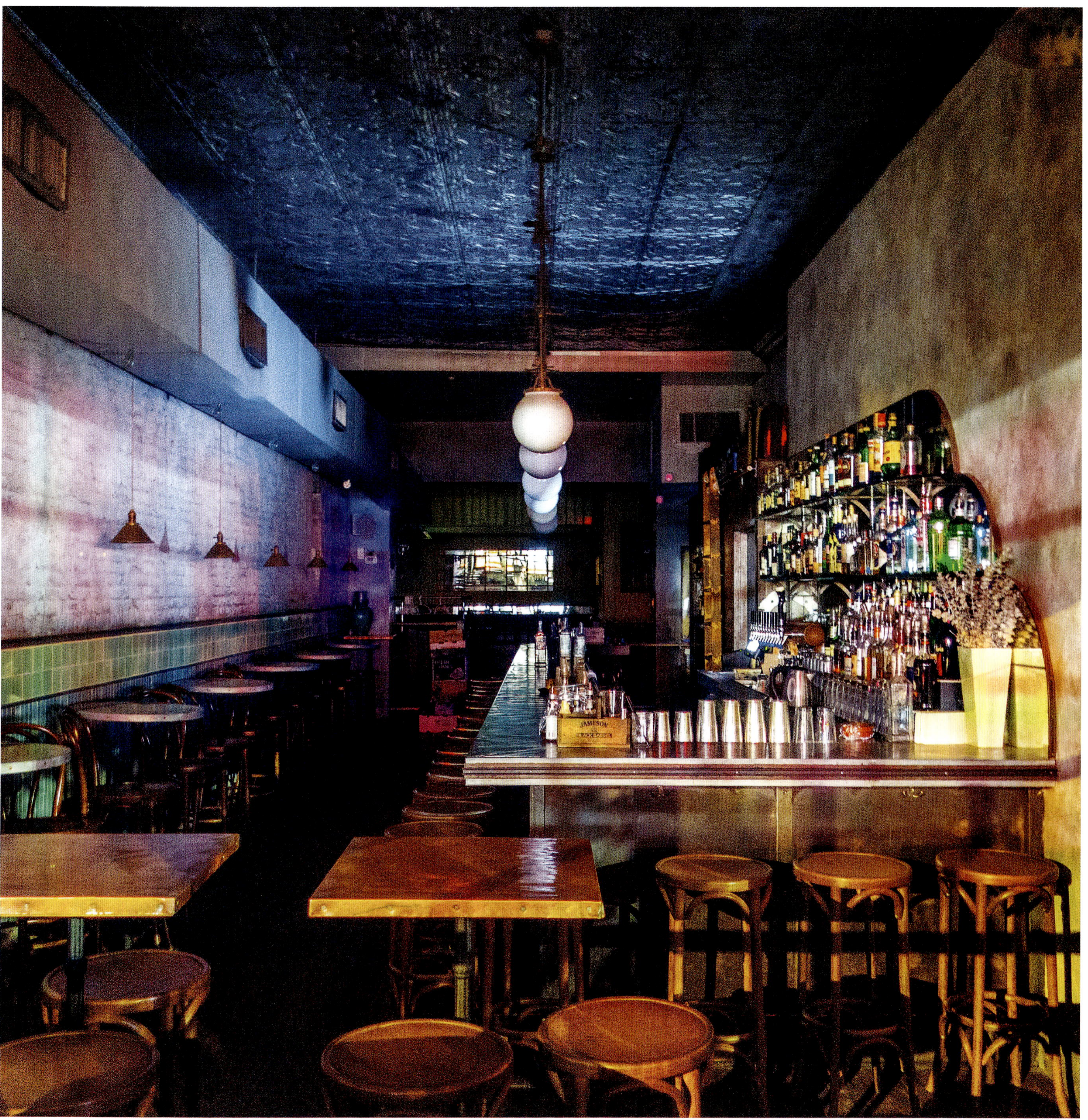

Ampersand

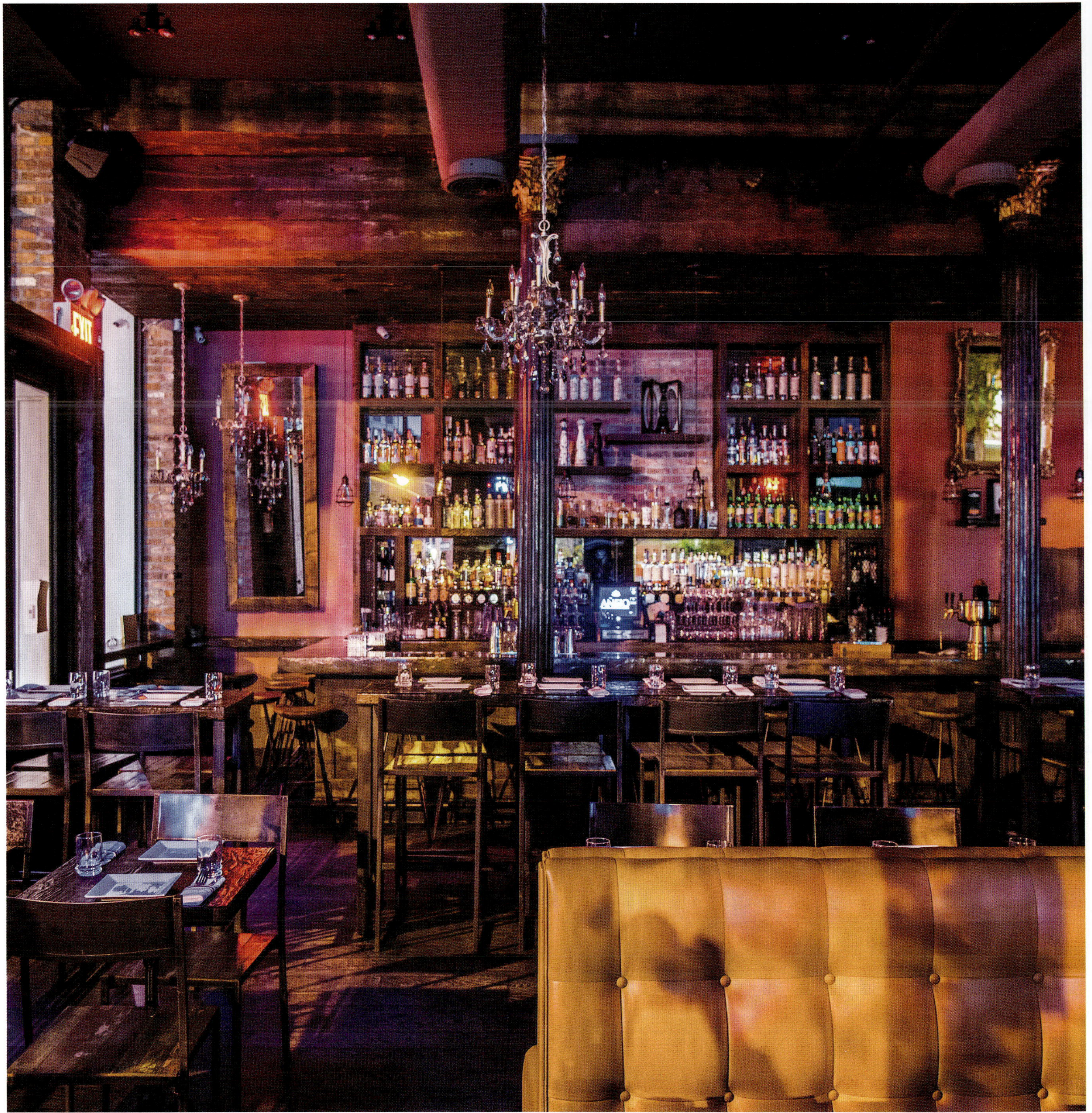

Añejo Tribeca

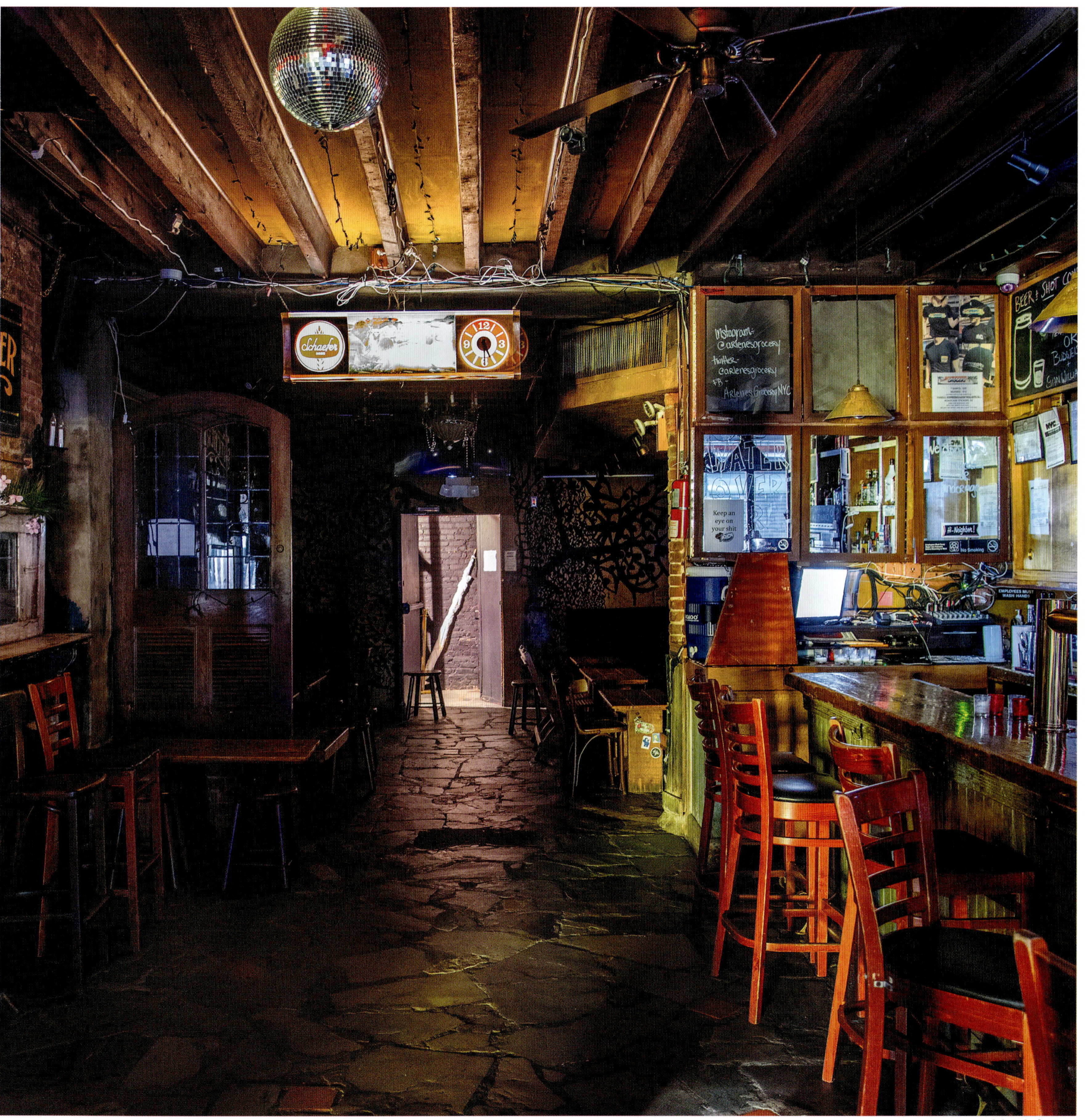

Arlene's Grocery

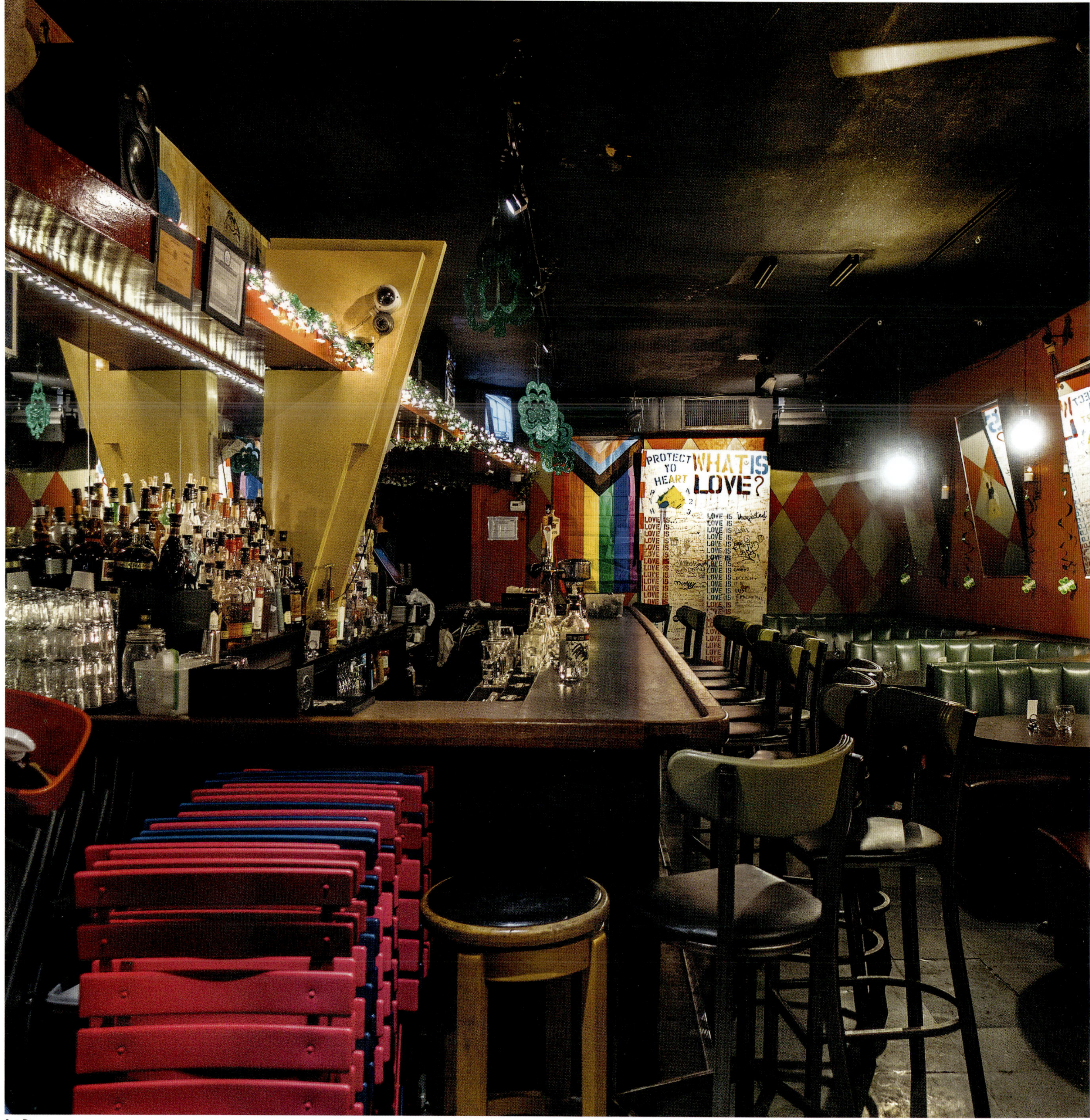

Art Bar

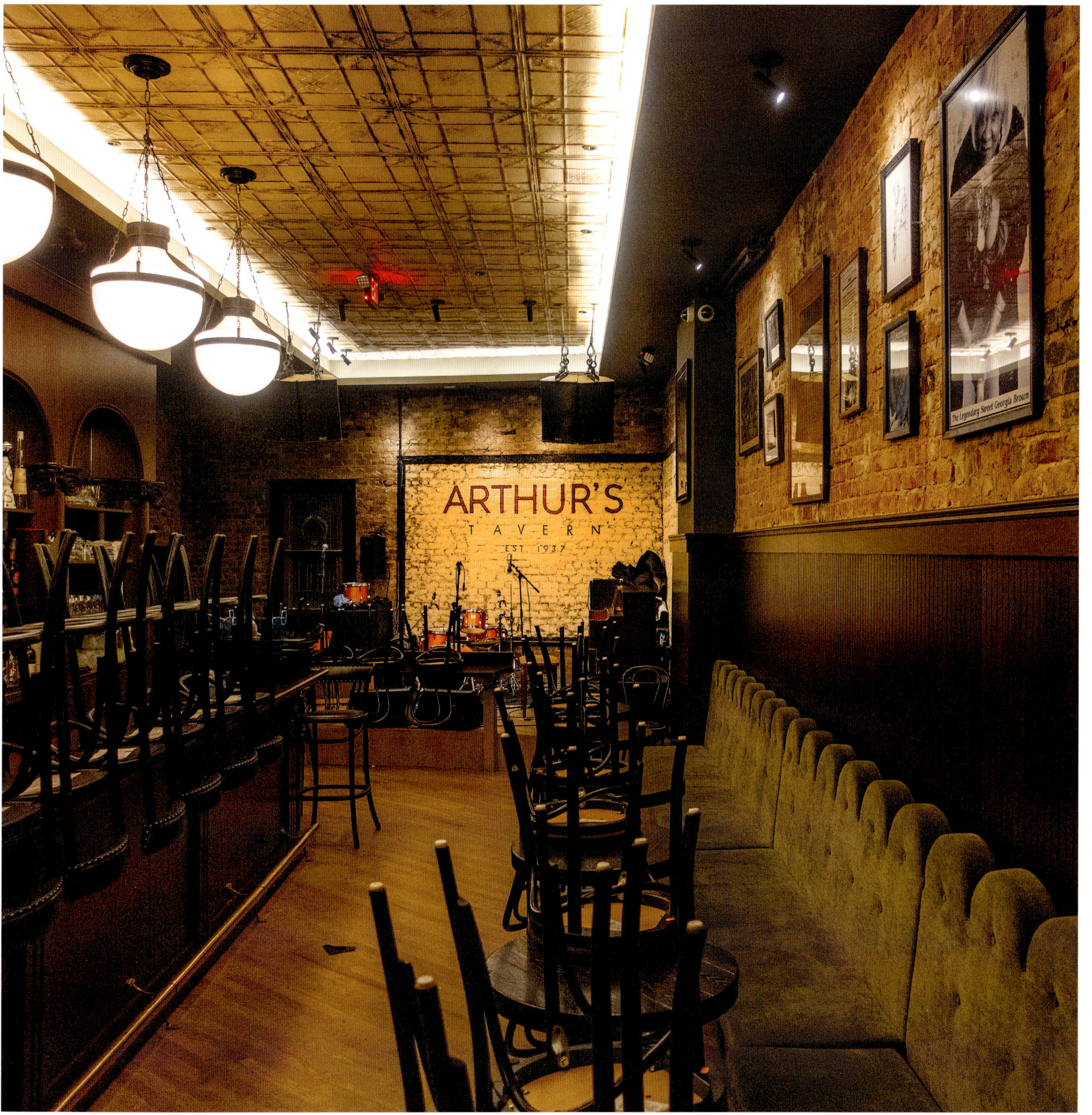

Arthur's Tavern

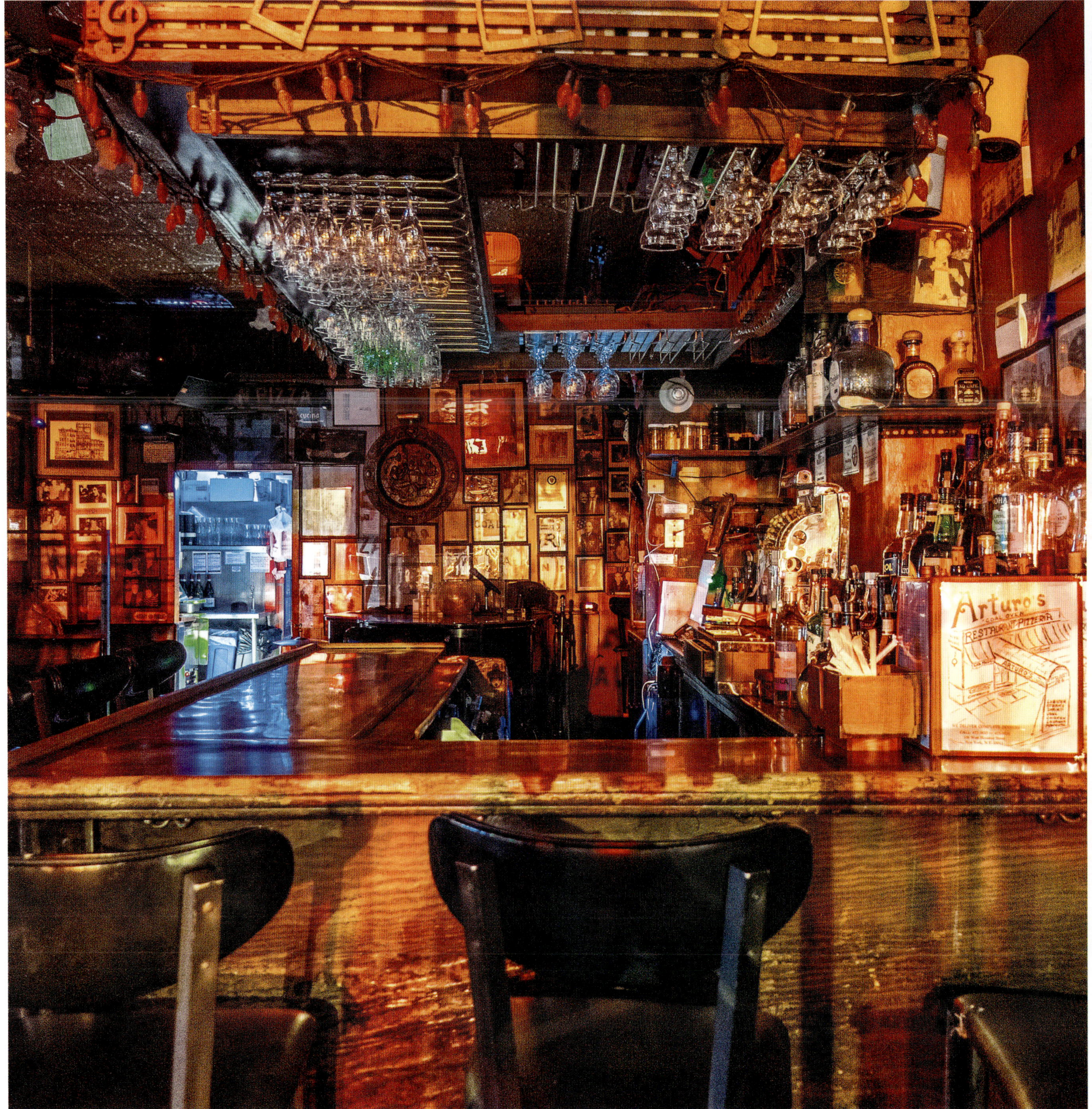

Arturo's

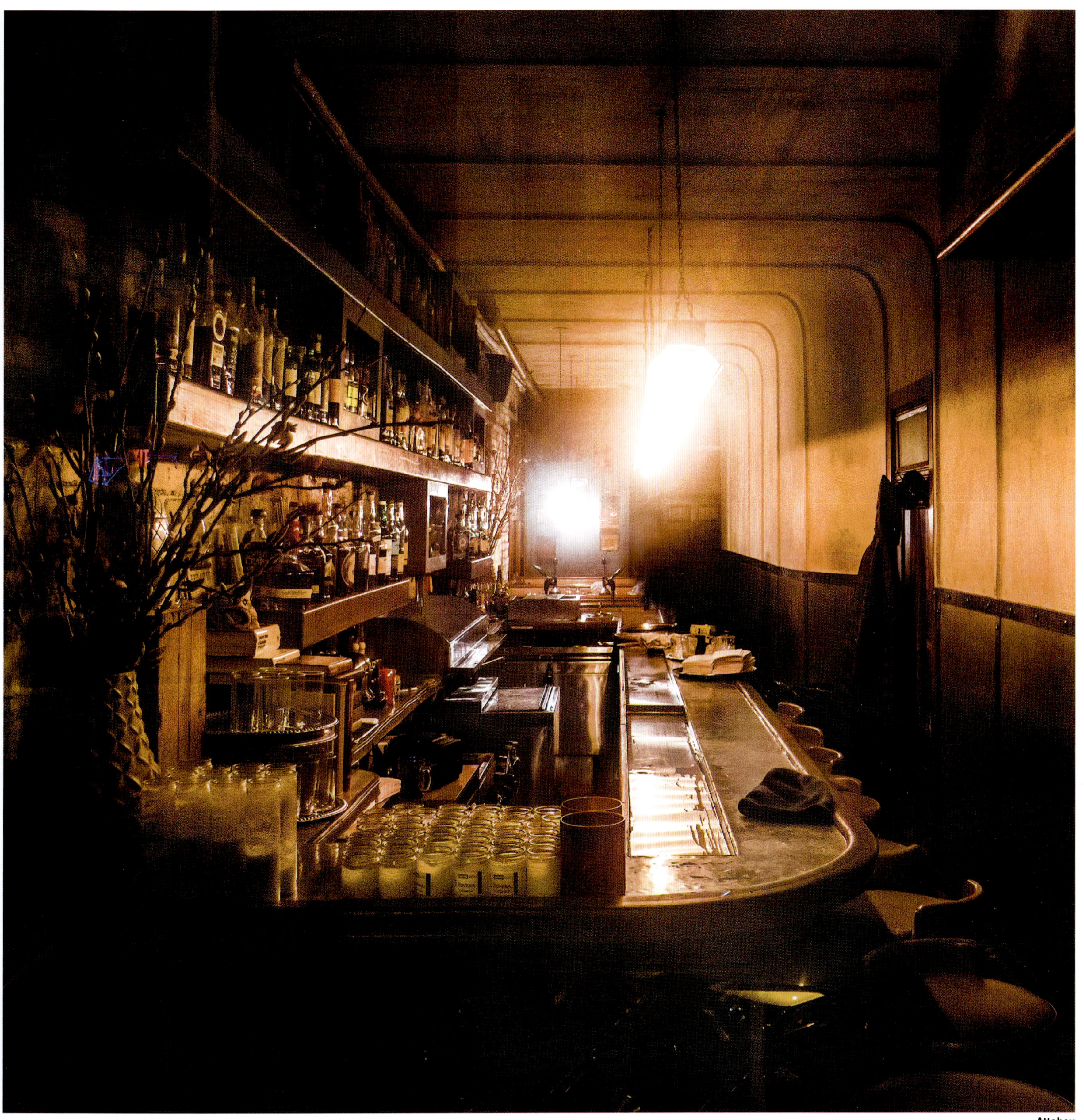

Attaboy

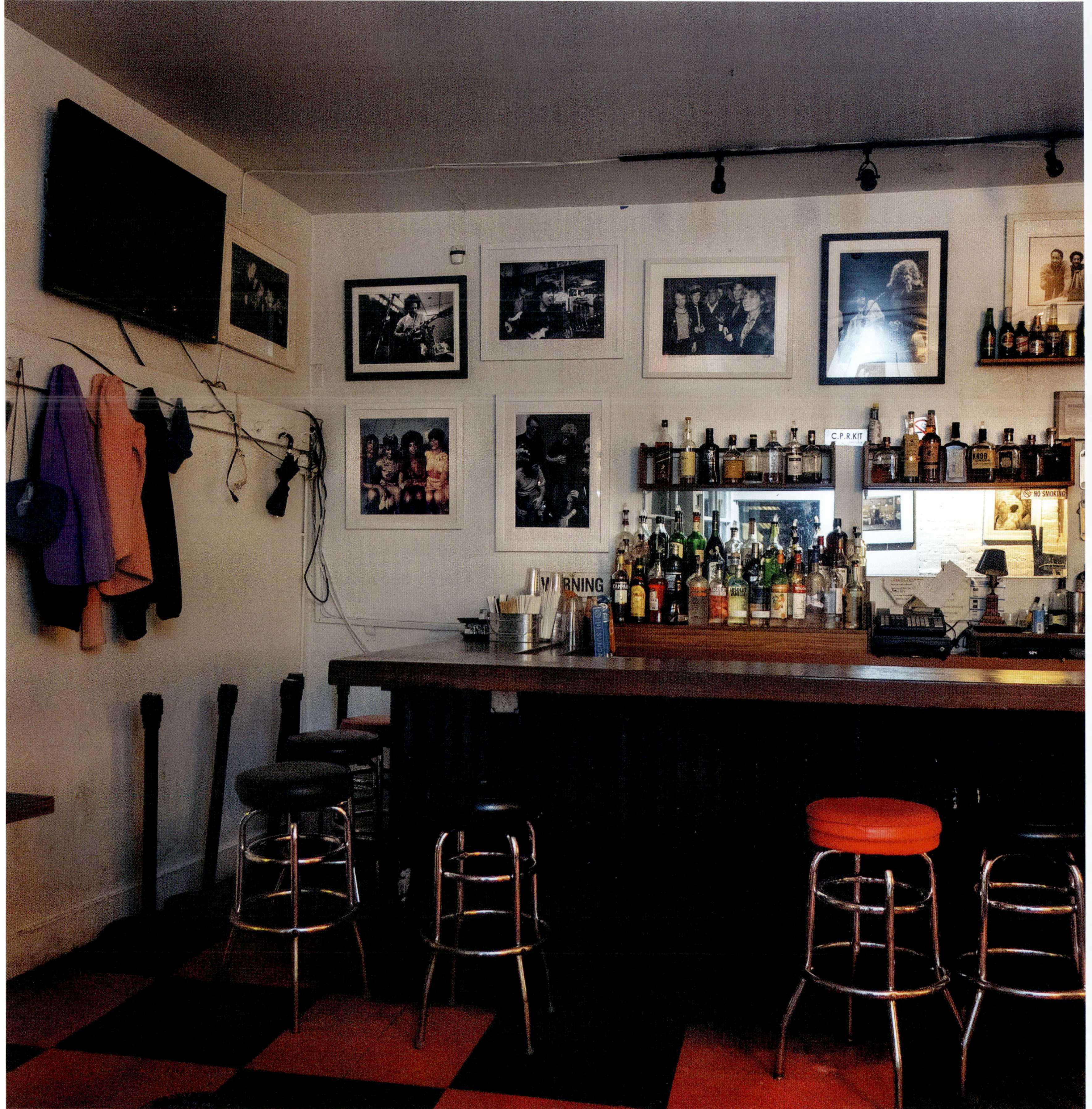

Automatic Slim's

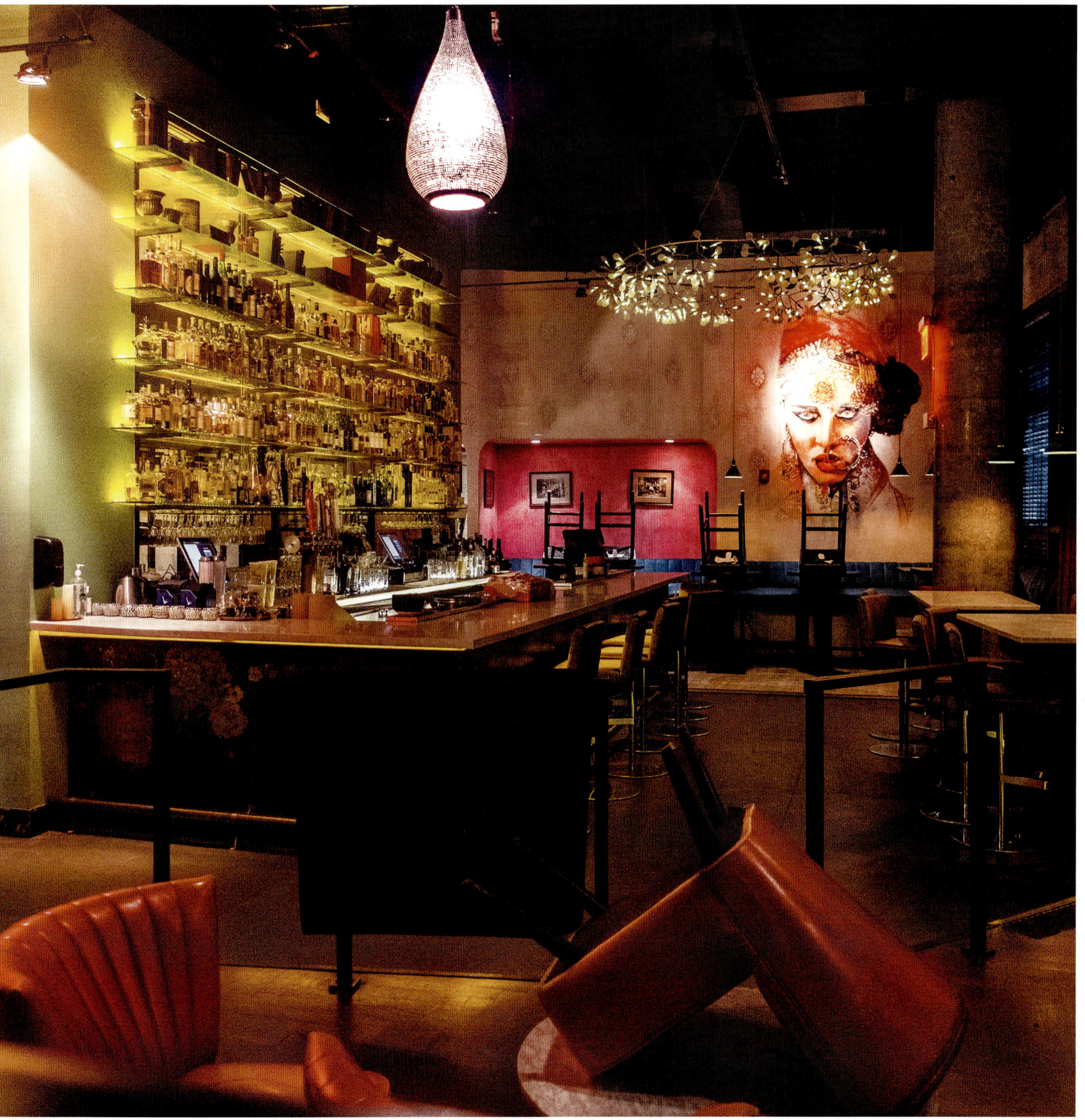

Baar Baar

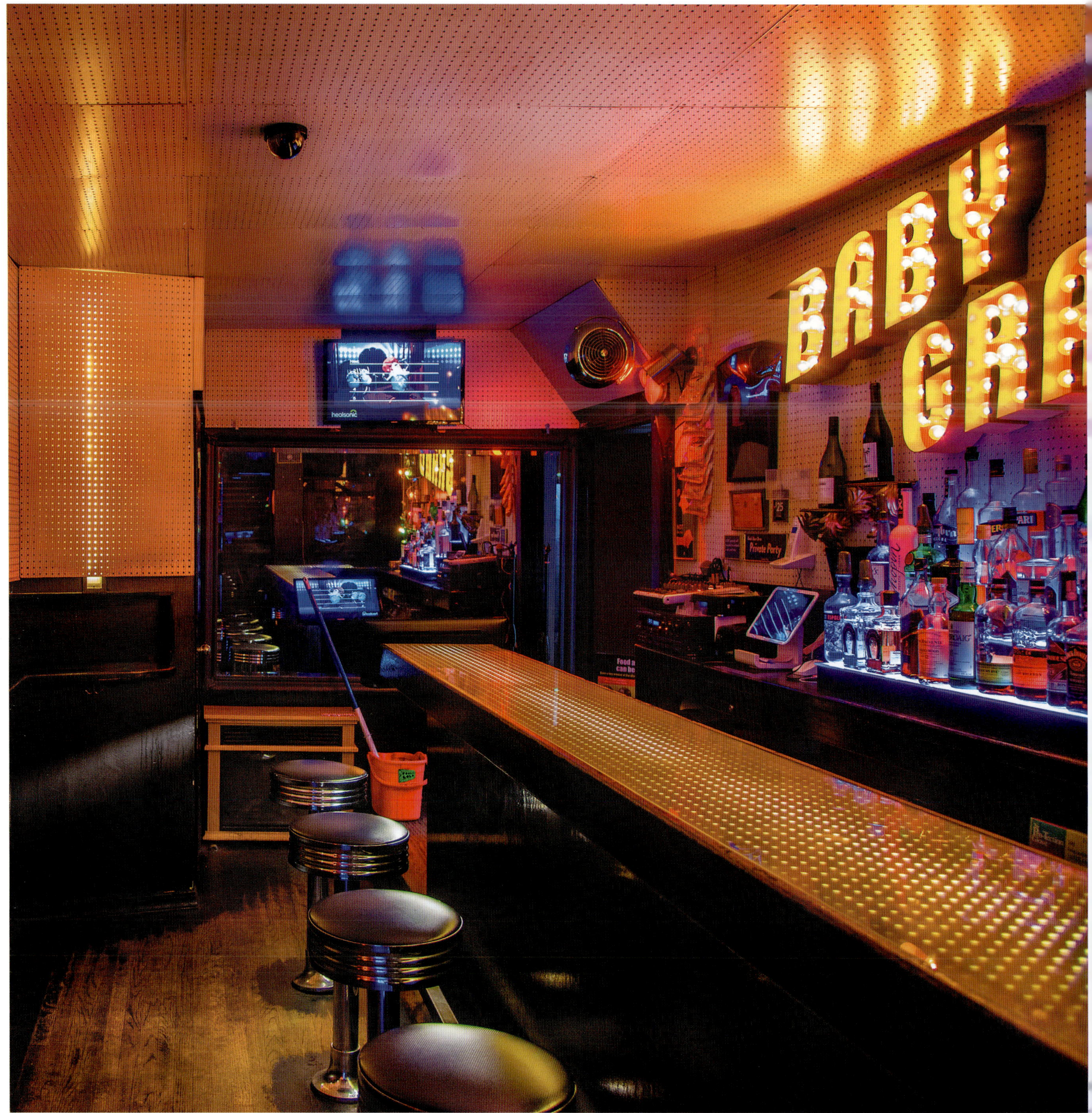

Baby Grand

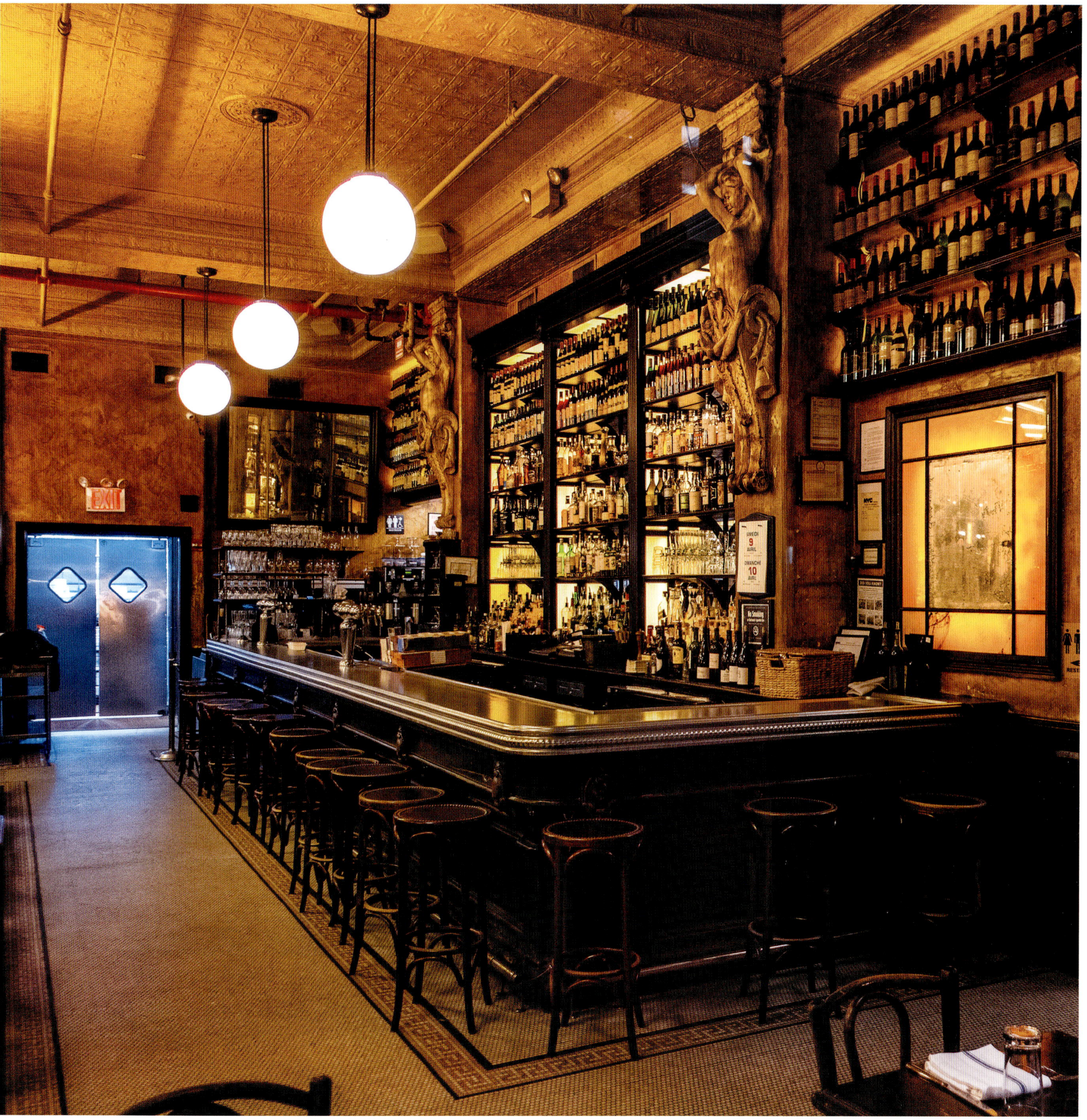

Balthazar

Bandits
COME
STAY FOR A WHILE
BANDITS
COLD BEERS
BANDITS
BANDITS
BANDITS
BANDITS
LATE NIGHT EATS
REAL GOOD COCKTAILS
OKAY PEOPLE TOO

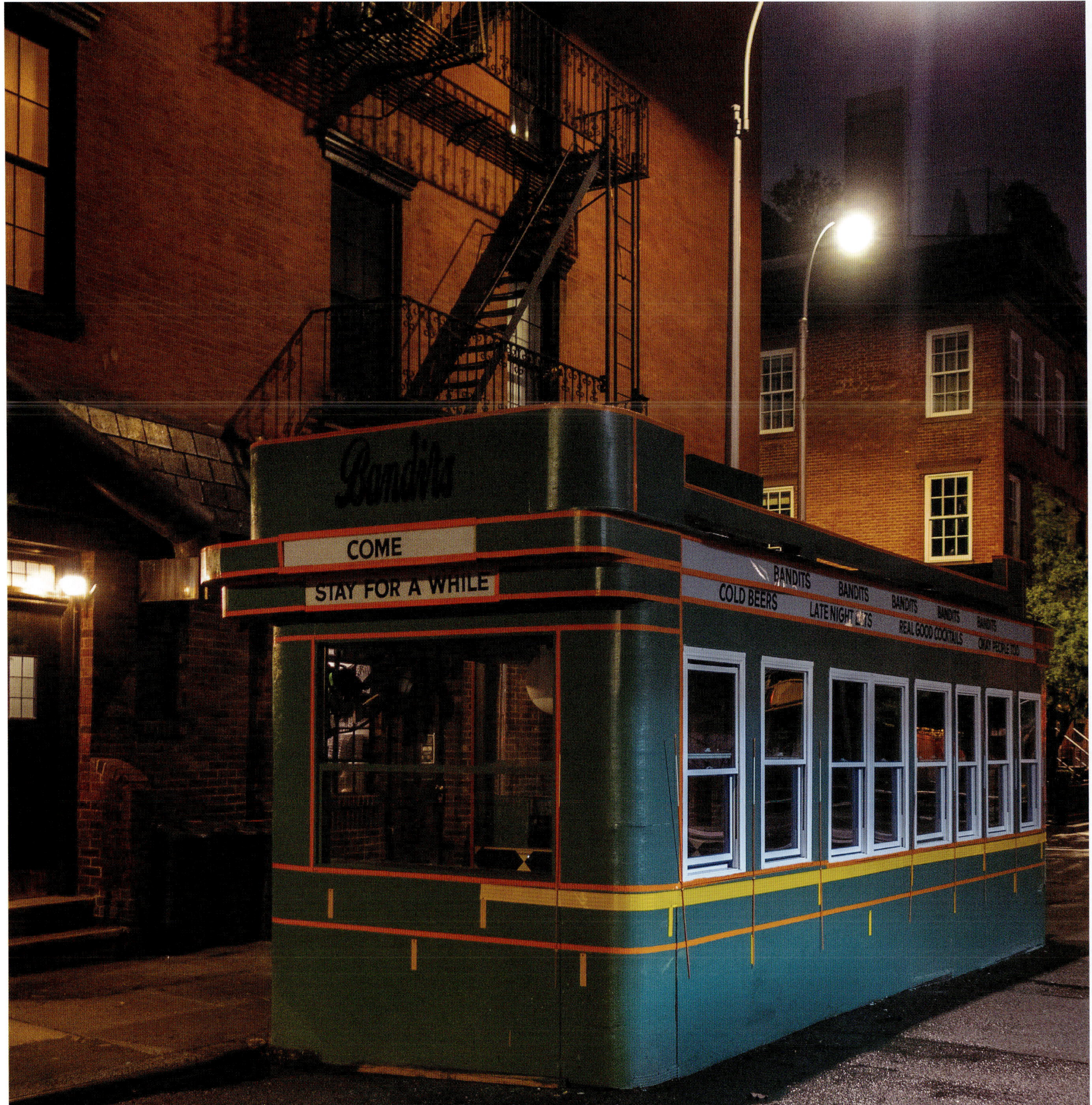

Bandits

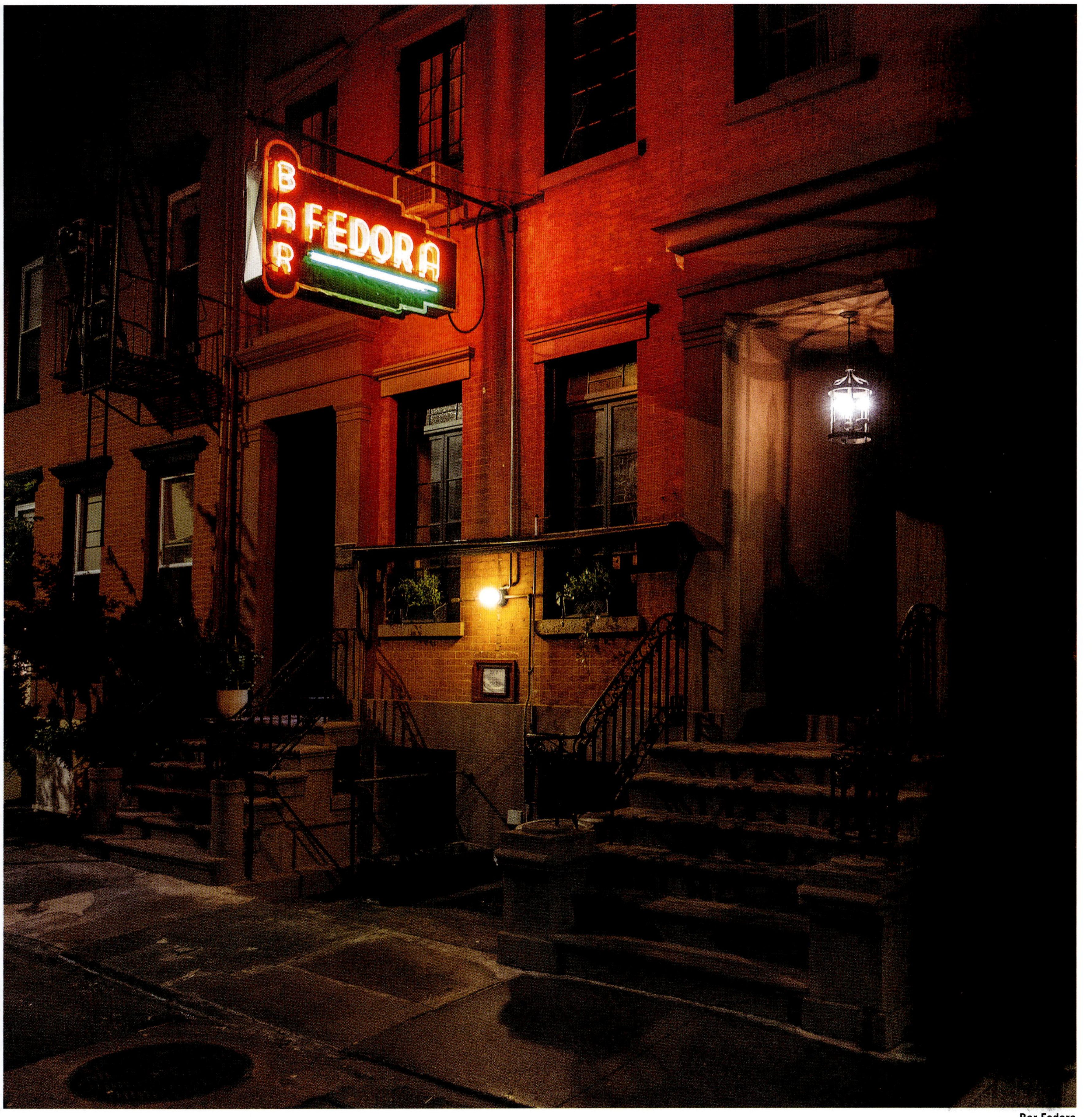

Bar Fedora

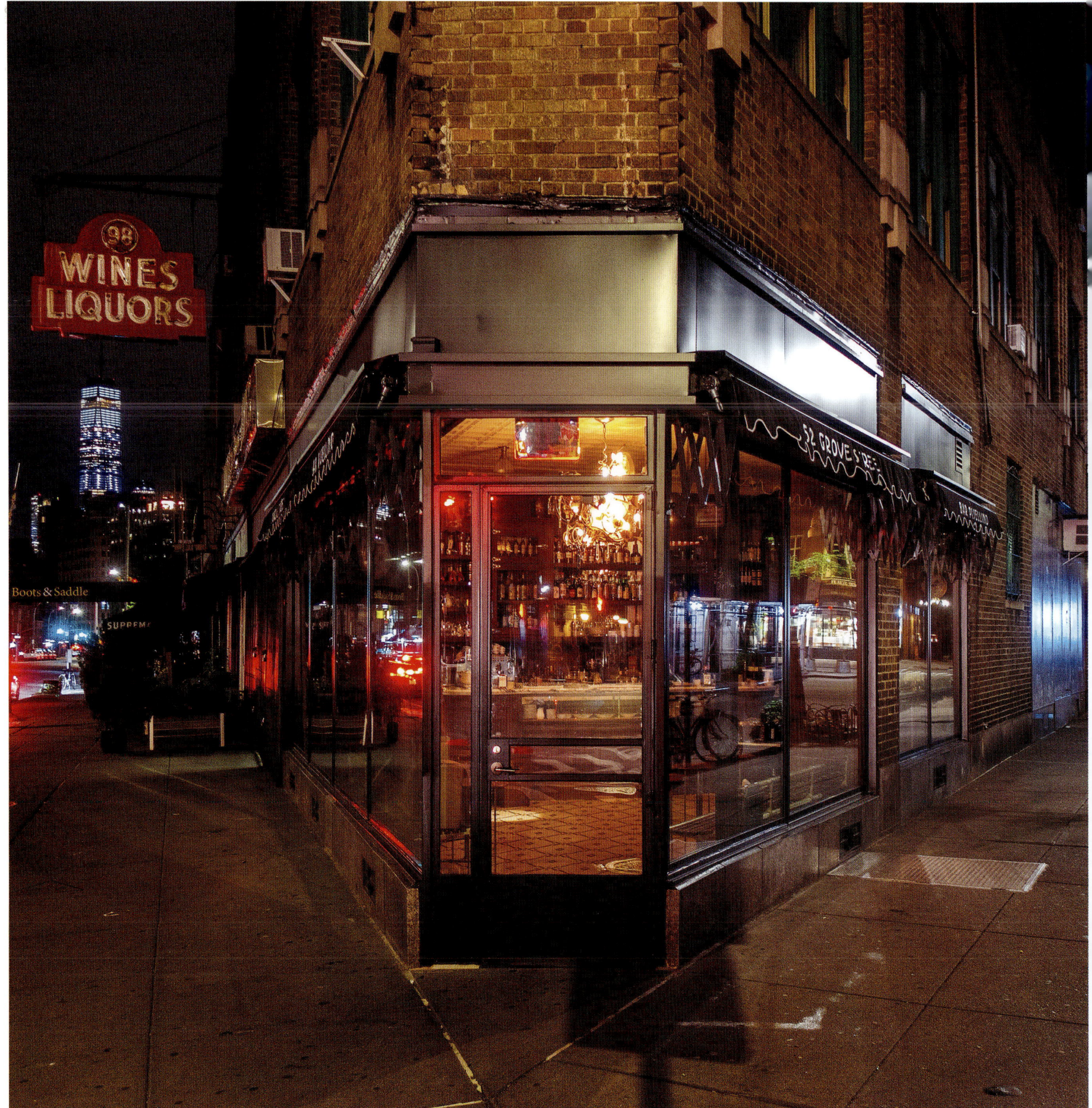

Bar Pisellino

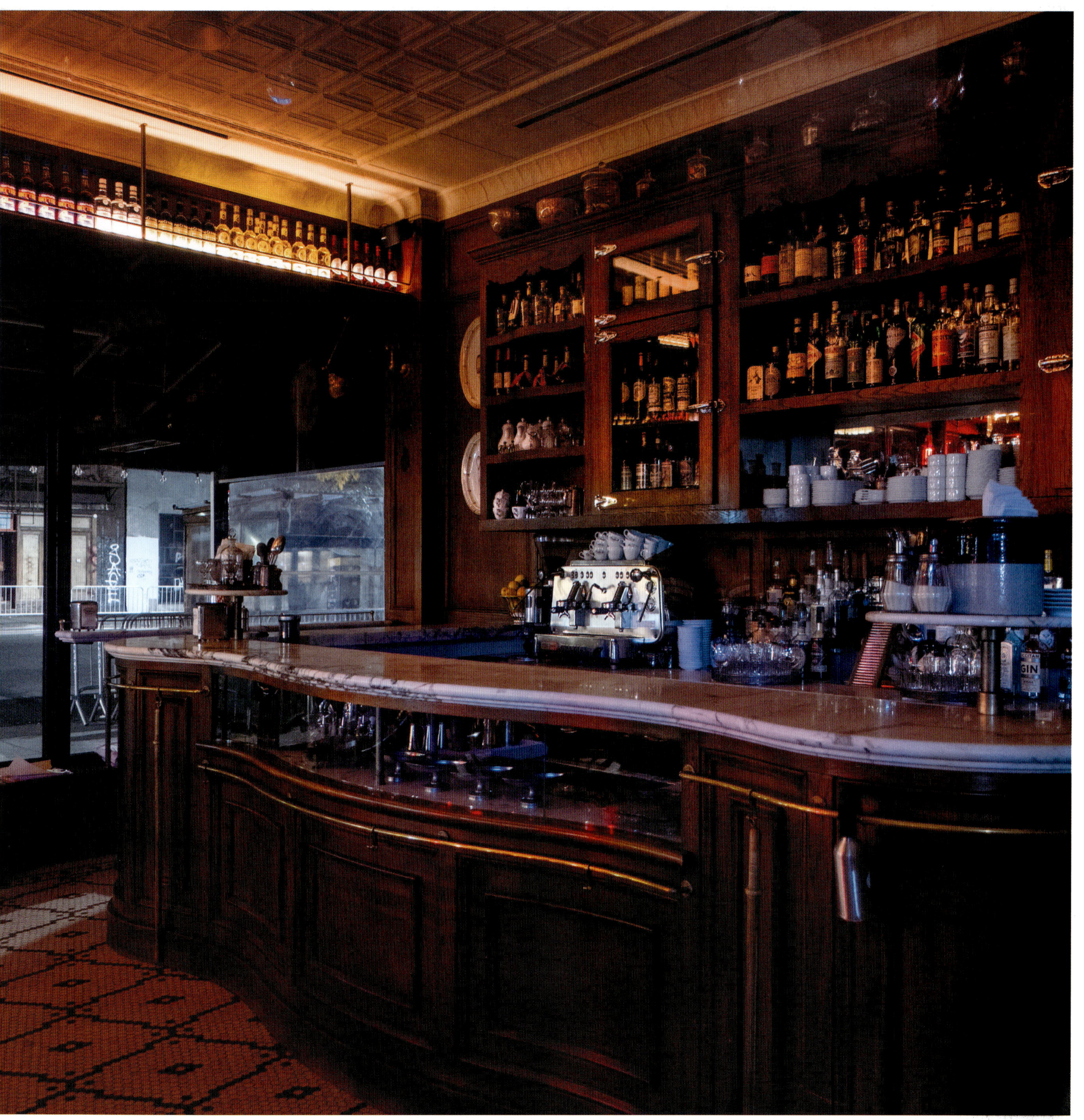

Bar Pisellino

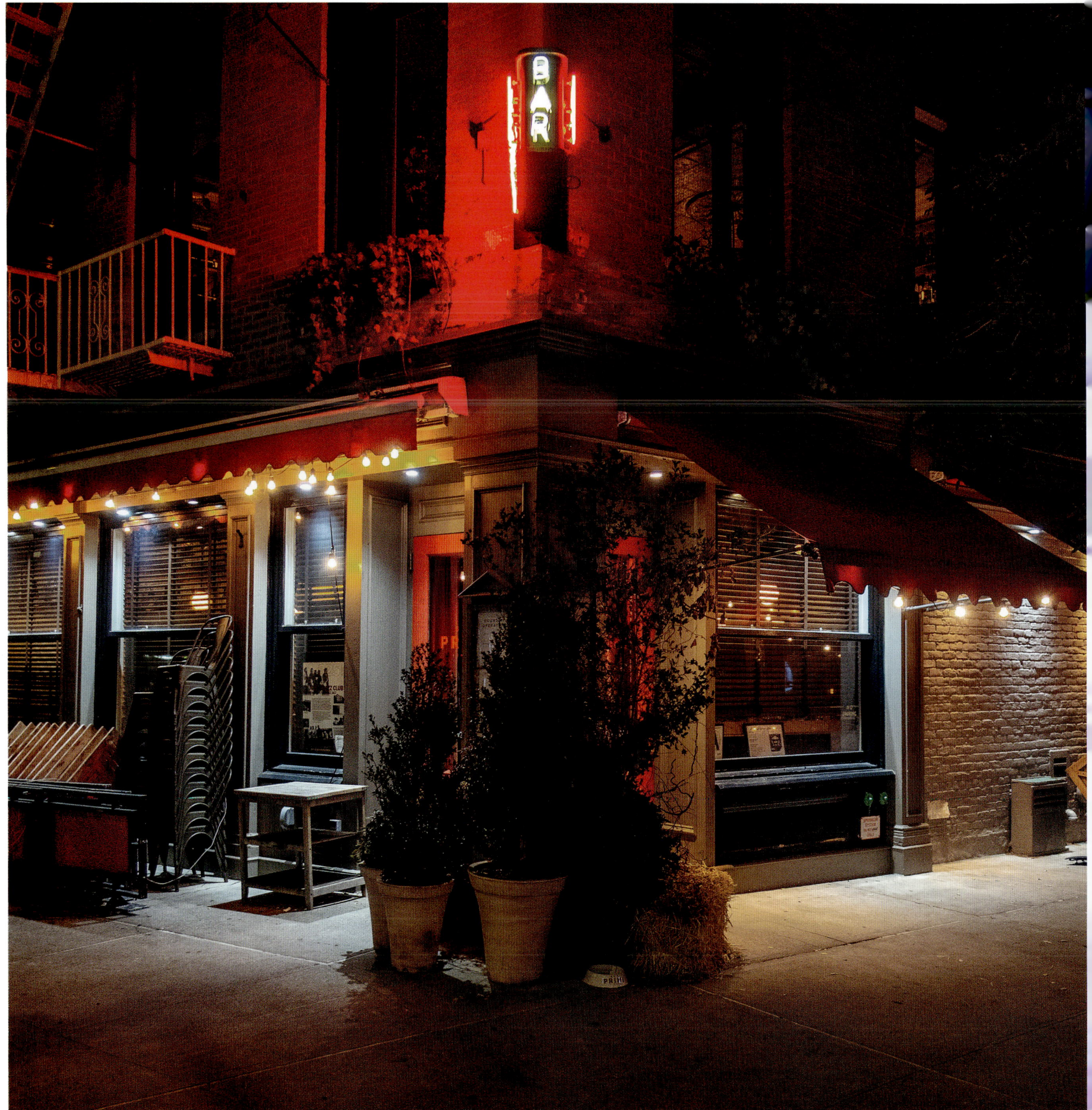

Bar Primi

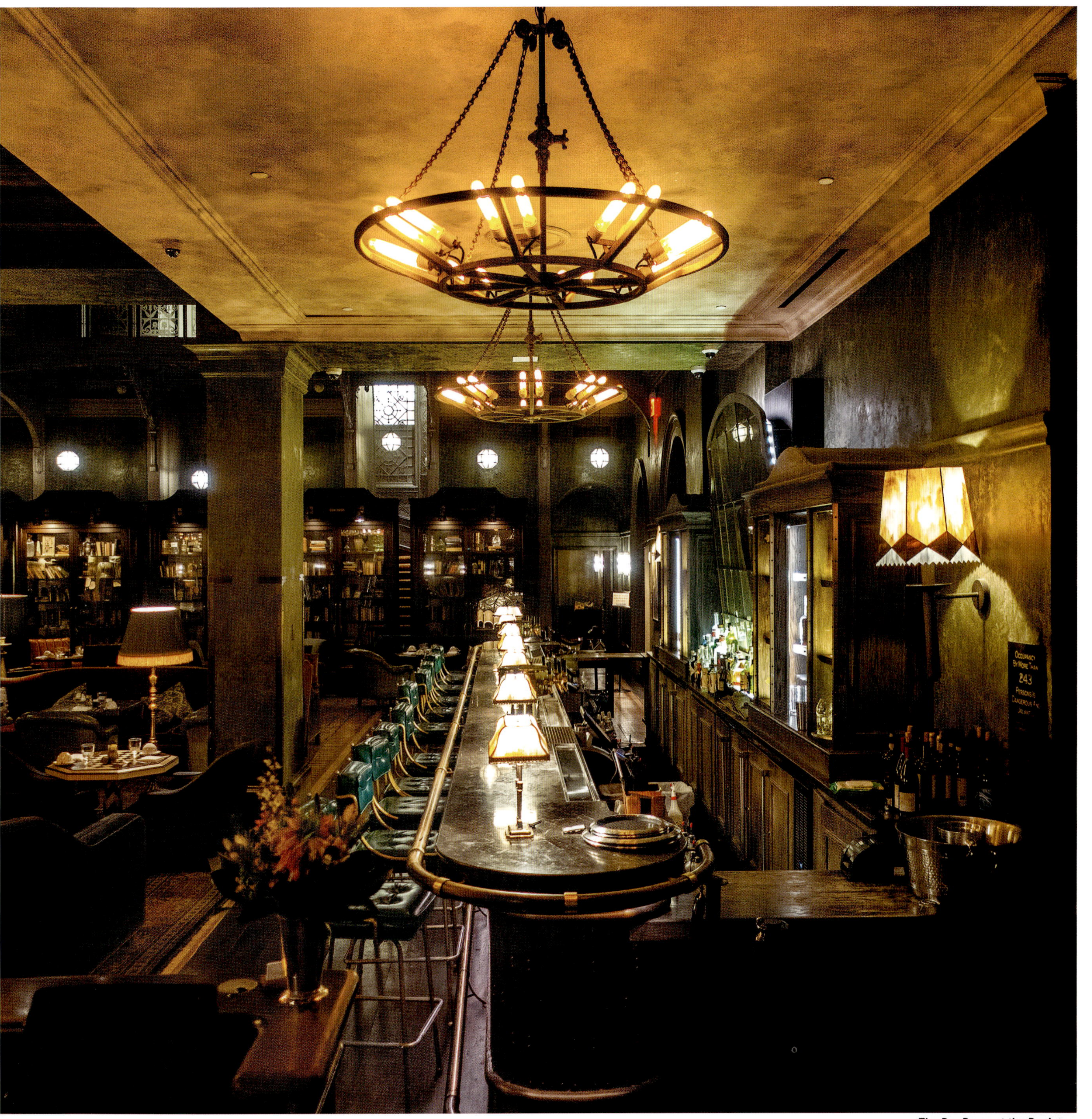

The **Bar Room** at the Beekman

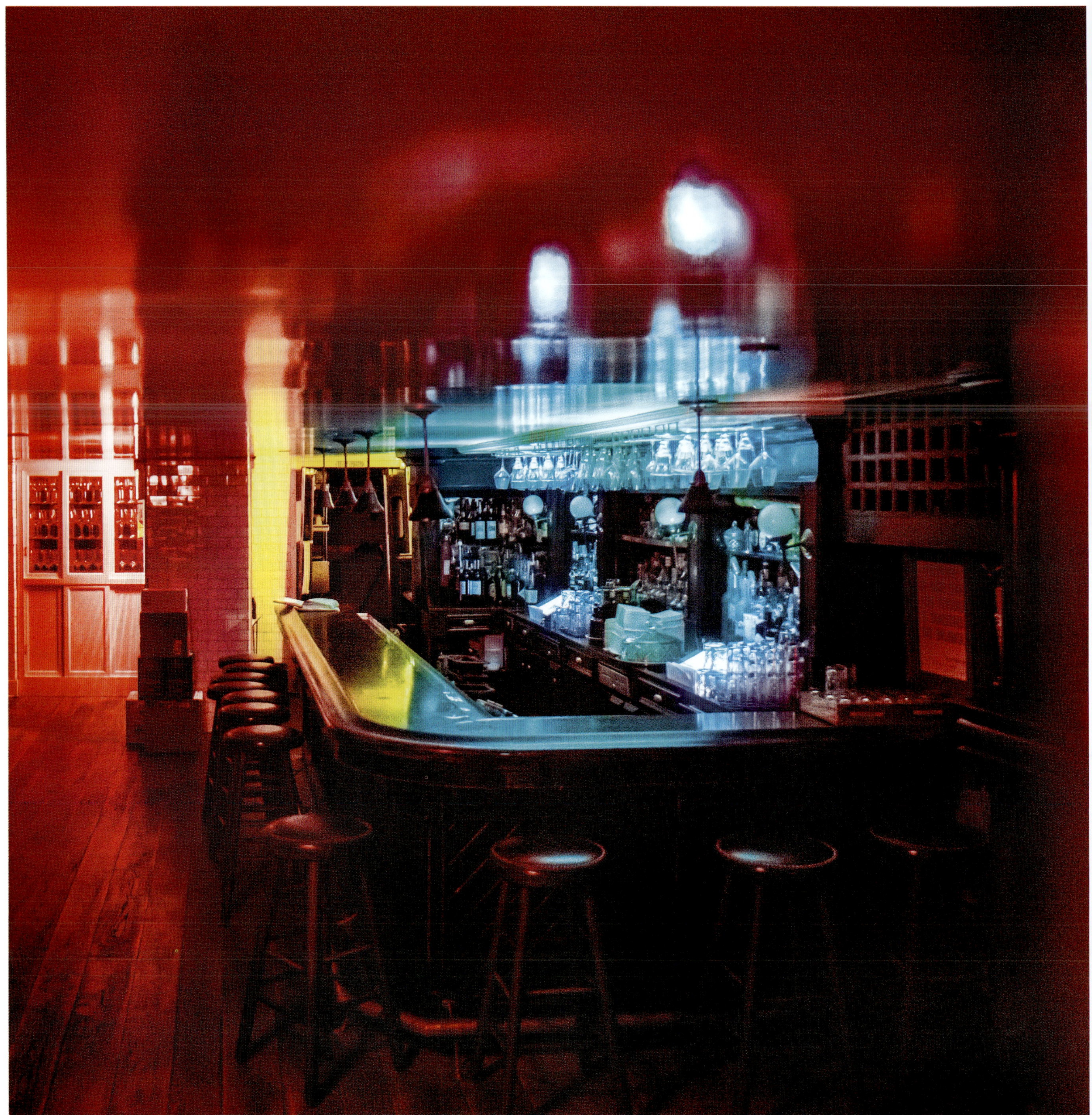

Beatrice Inn

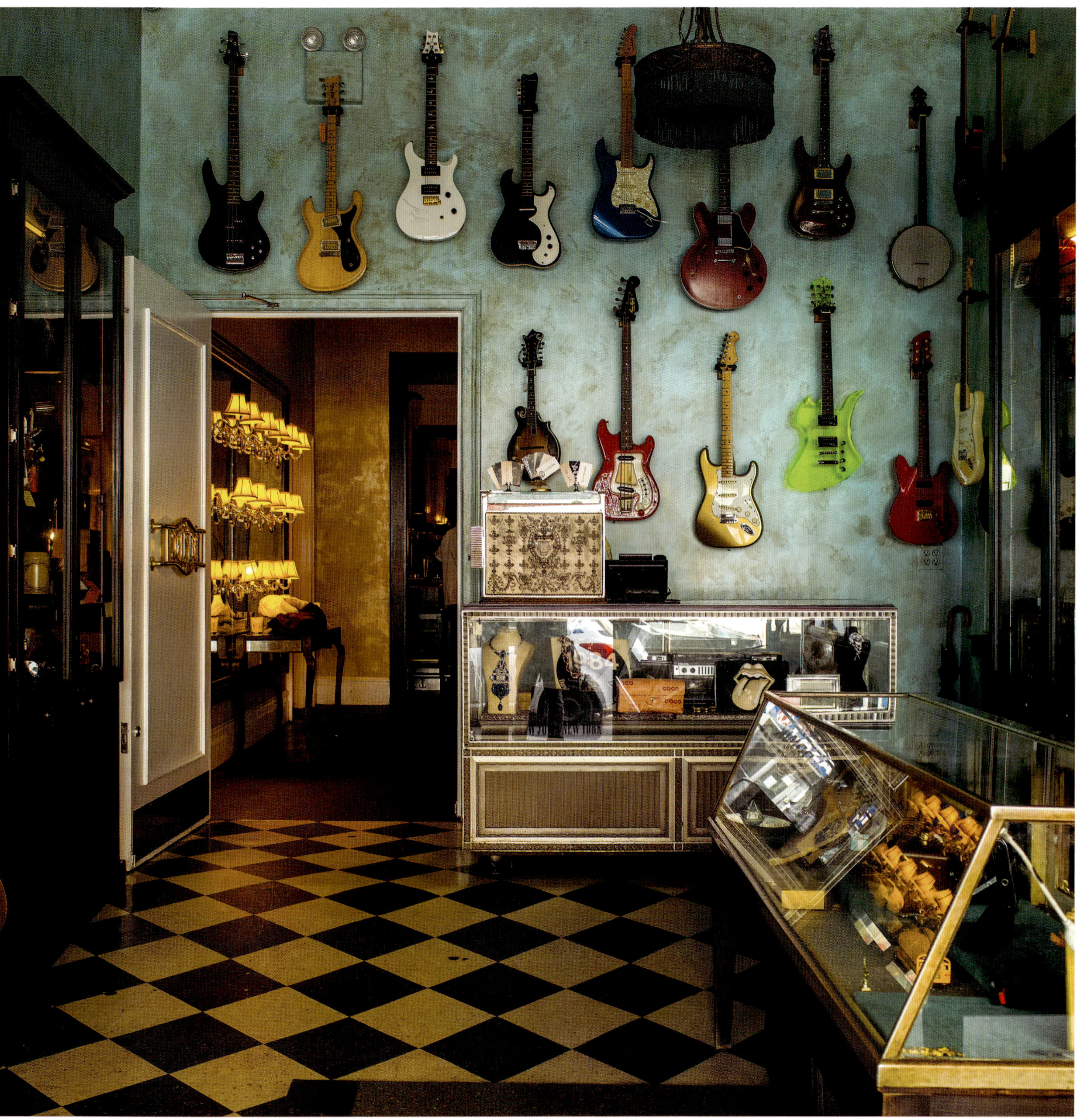

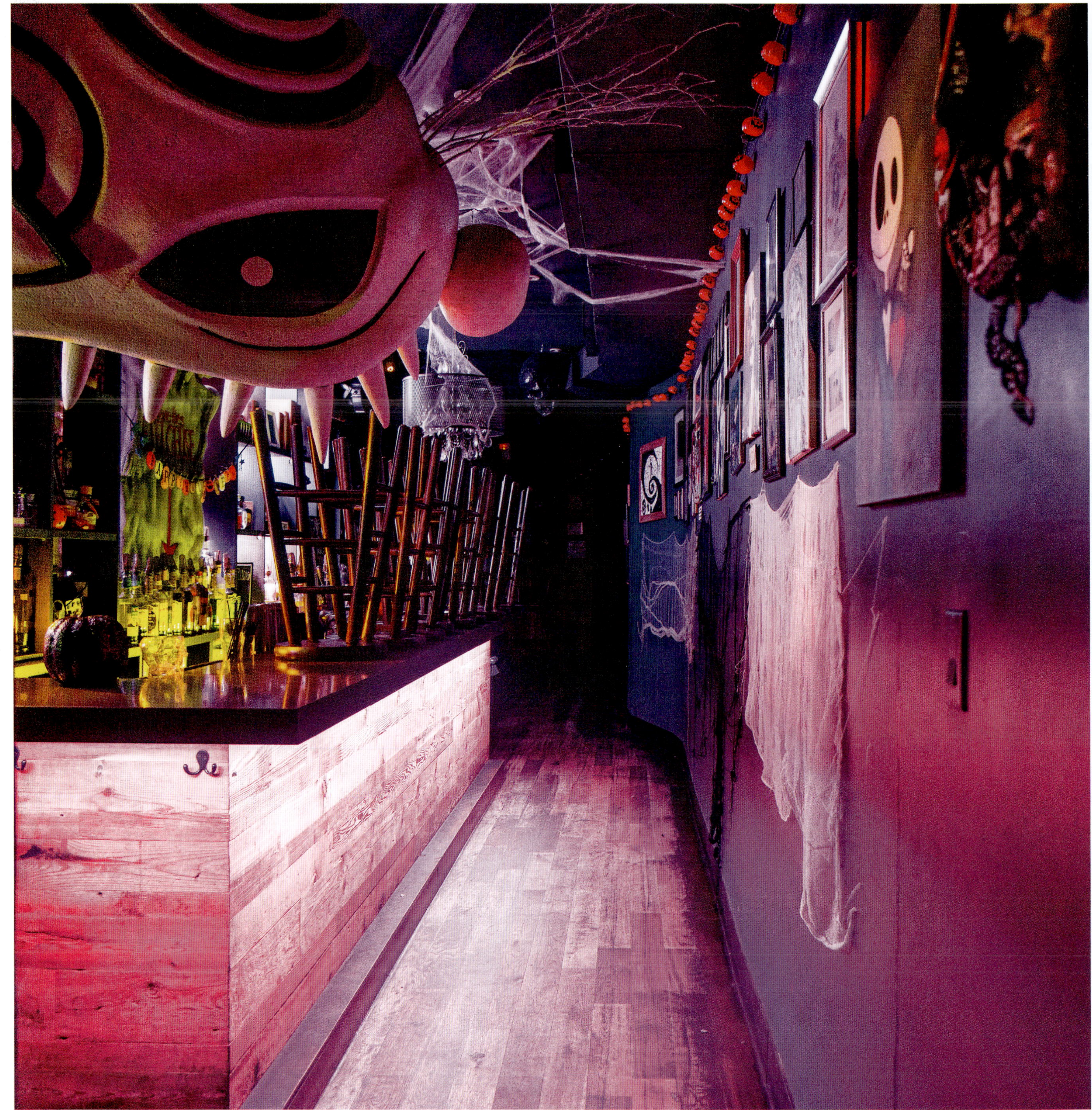

Beetle House

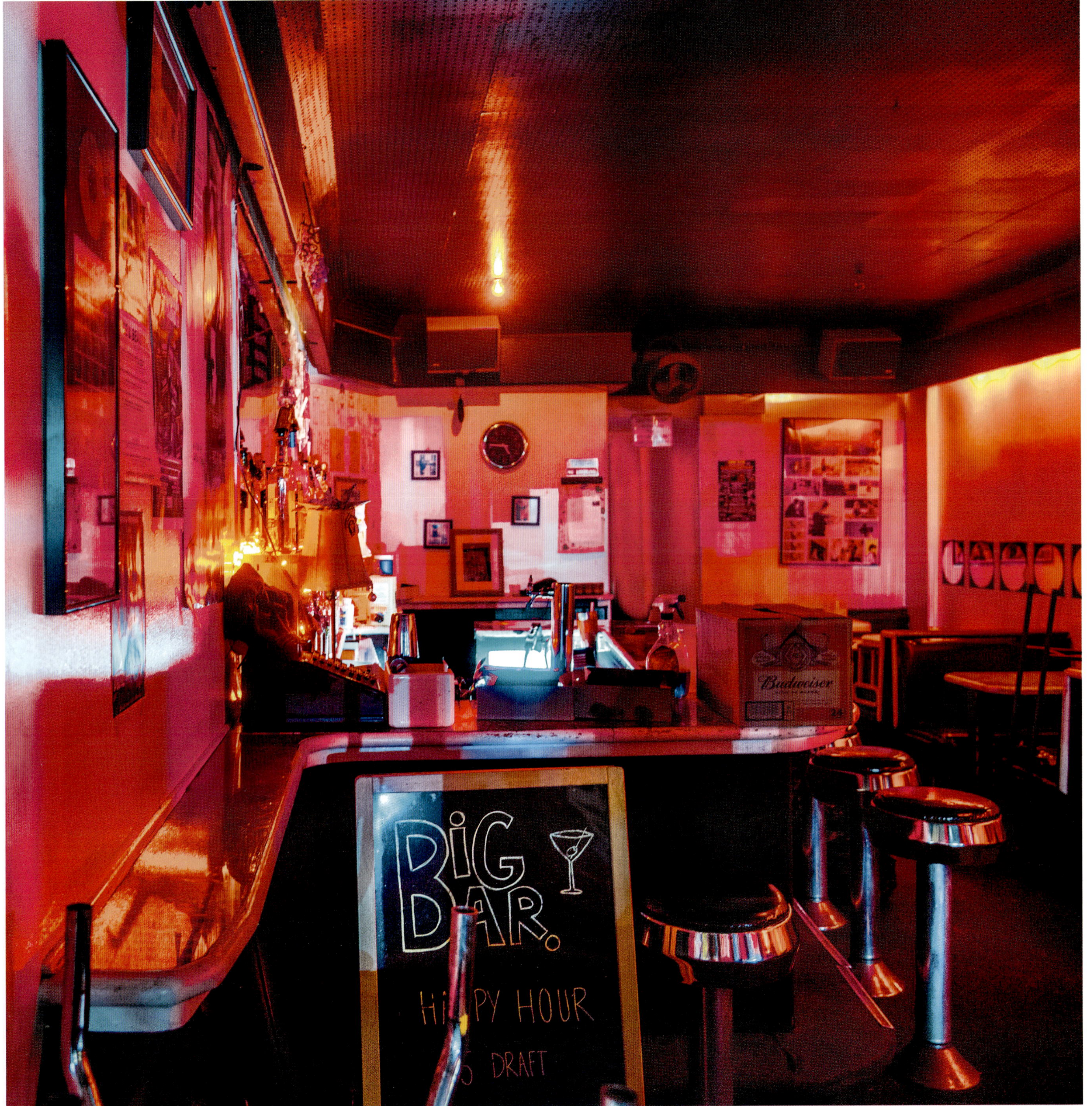

Big Bar

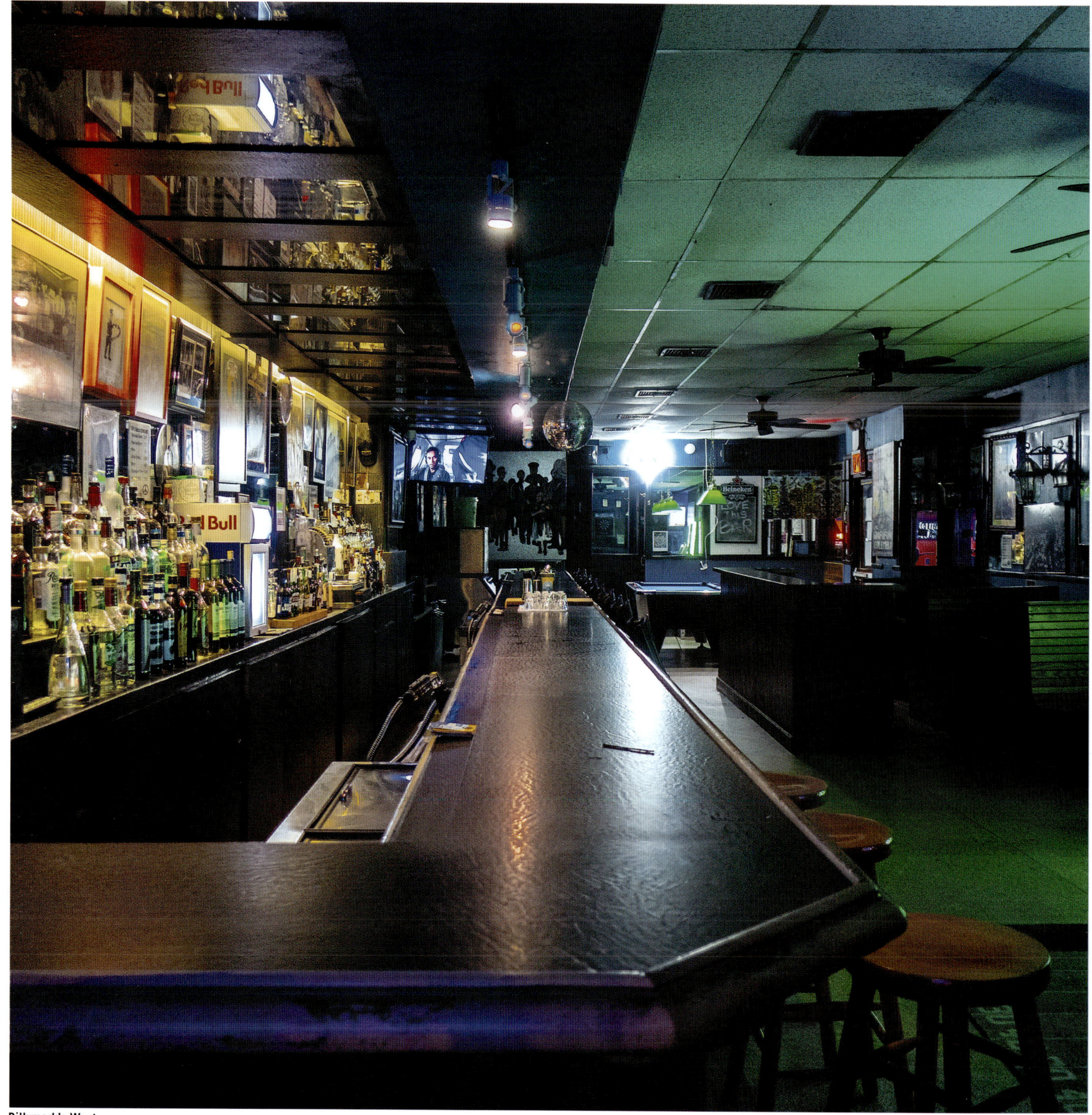

Billymark's West

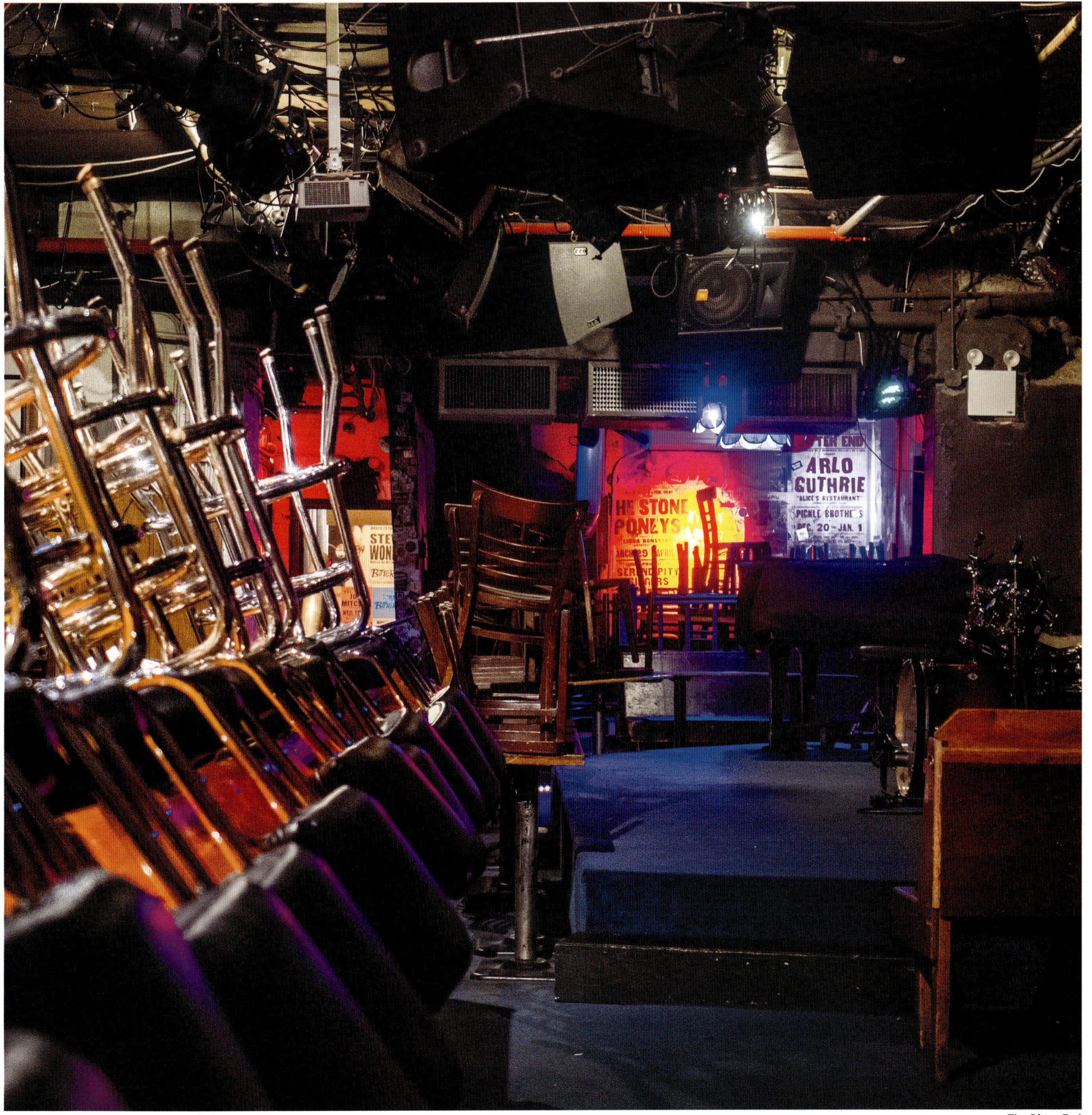

HE STONE
PONEYS
LINDA RONSTADT
ARLO
GUTHRIE
"ALICE'S RESTAURANT"
PICKLE BROTHERS
DEC. 20 — JAN. 1
STE
WOND

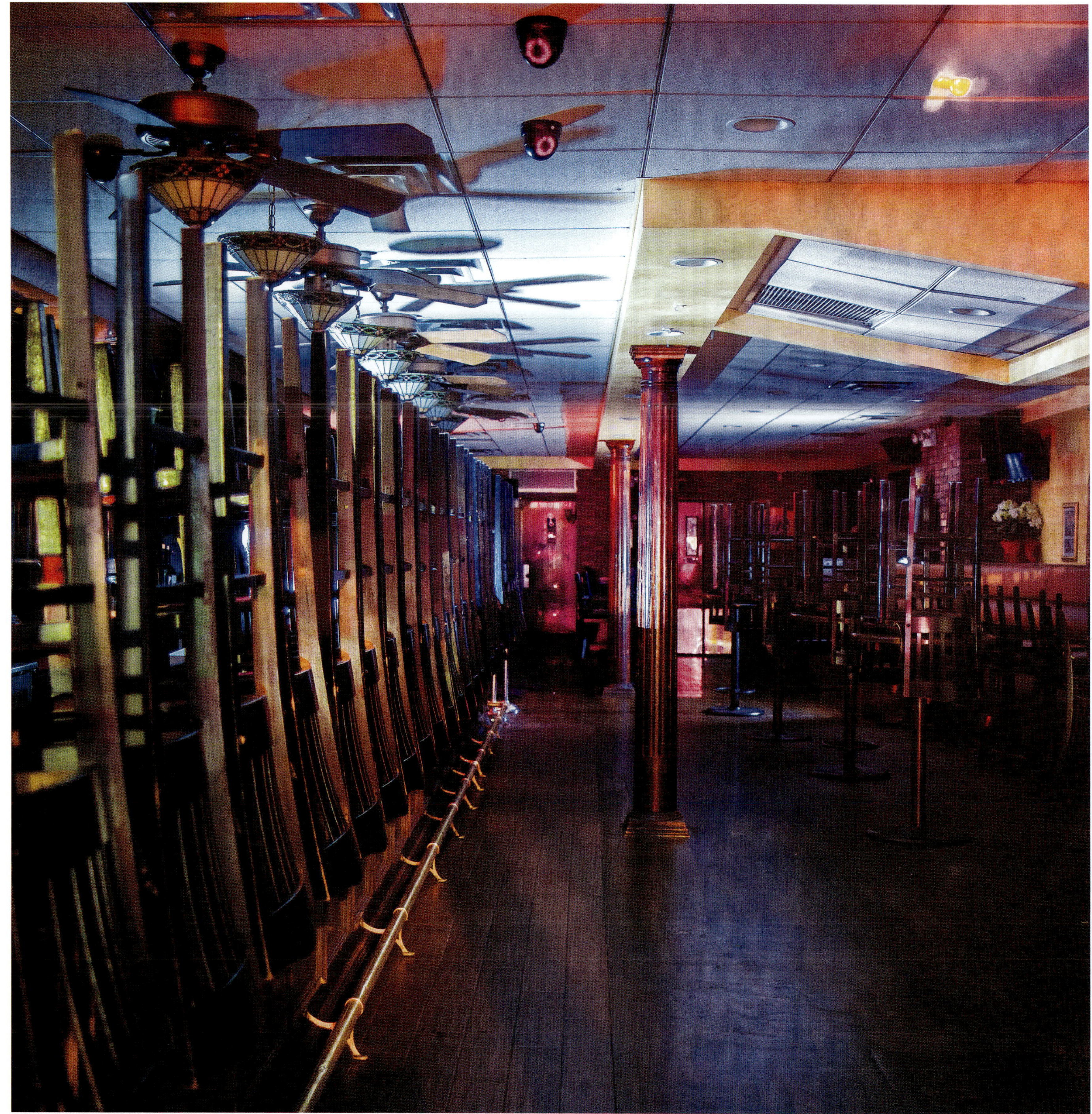

Blarney Stone

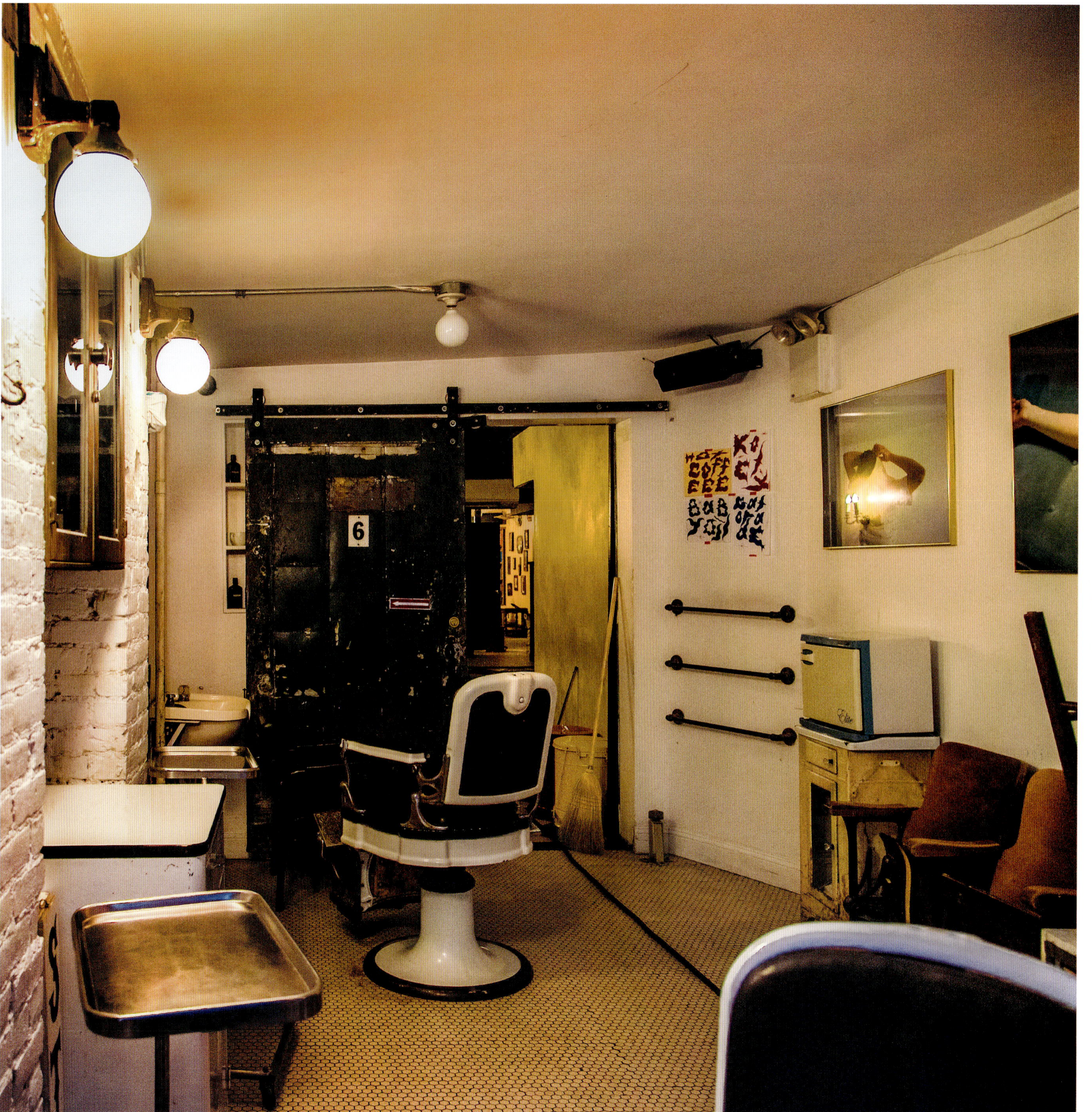

Blind Barber

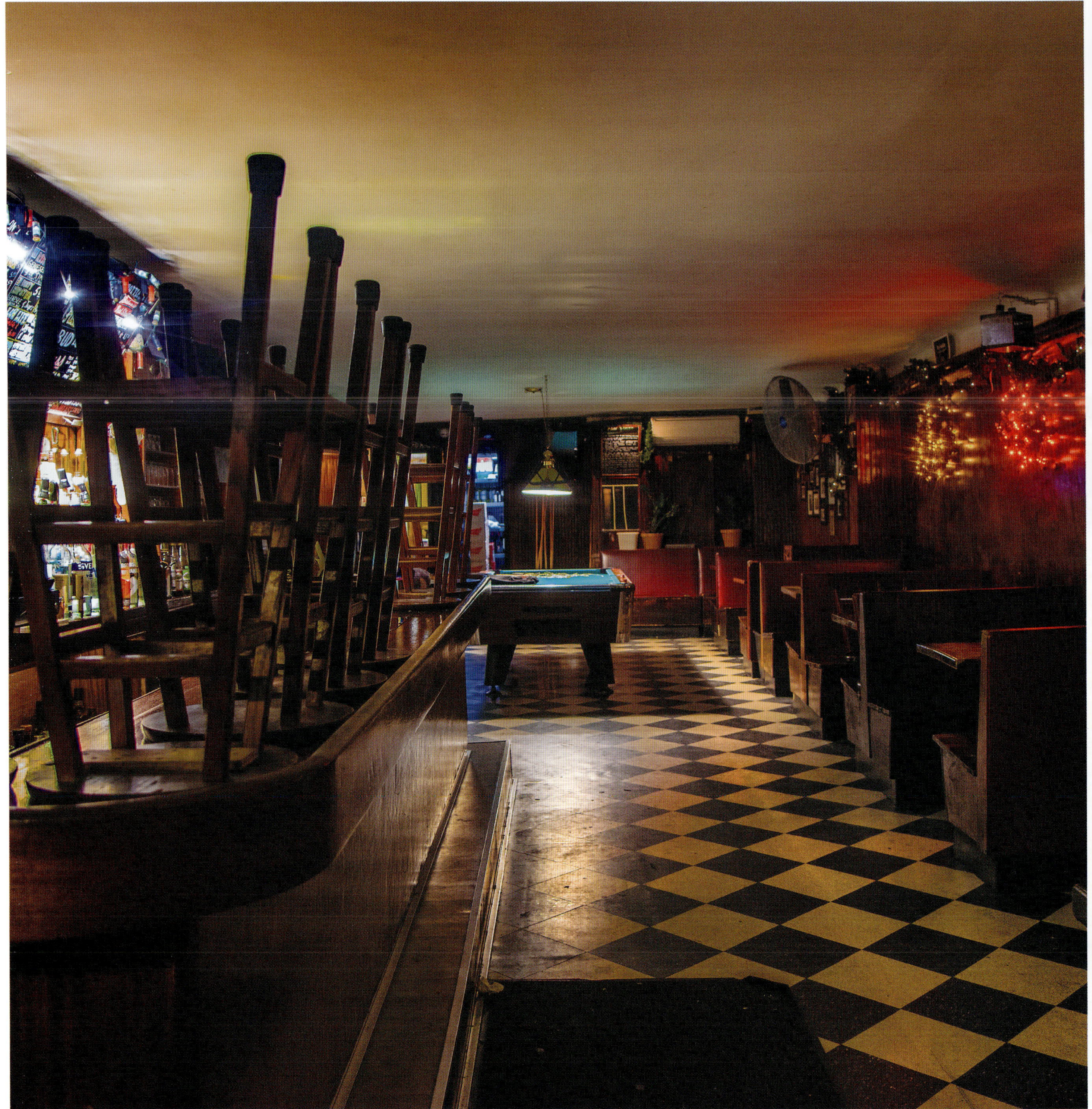

Blue and Gold

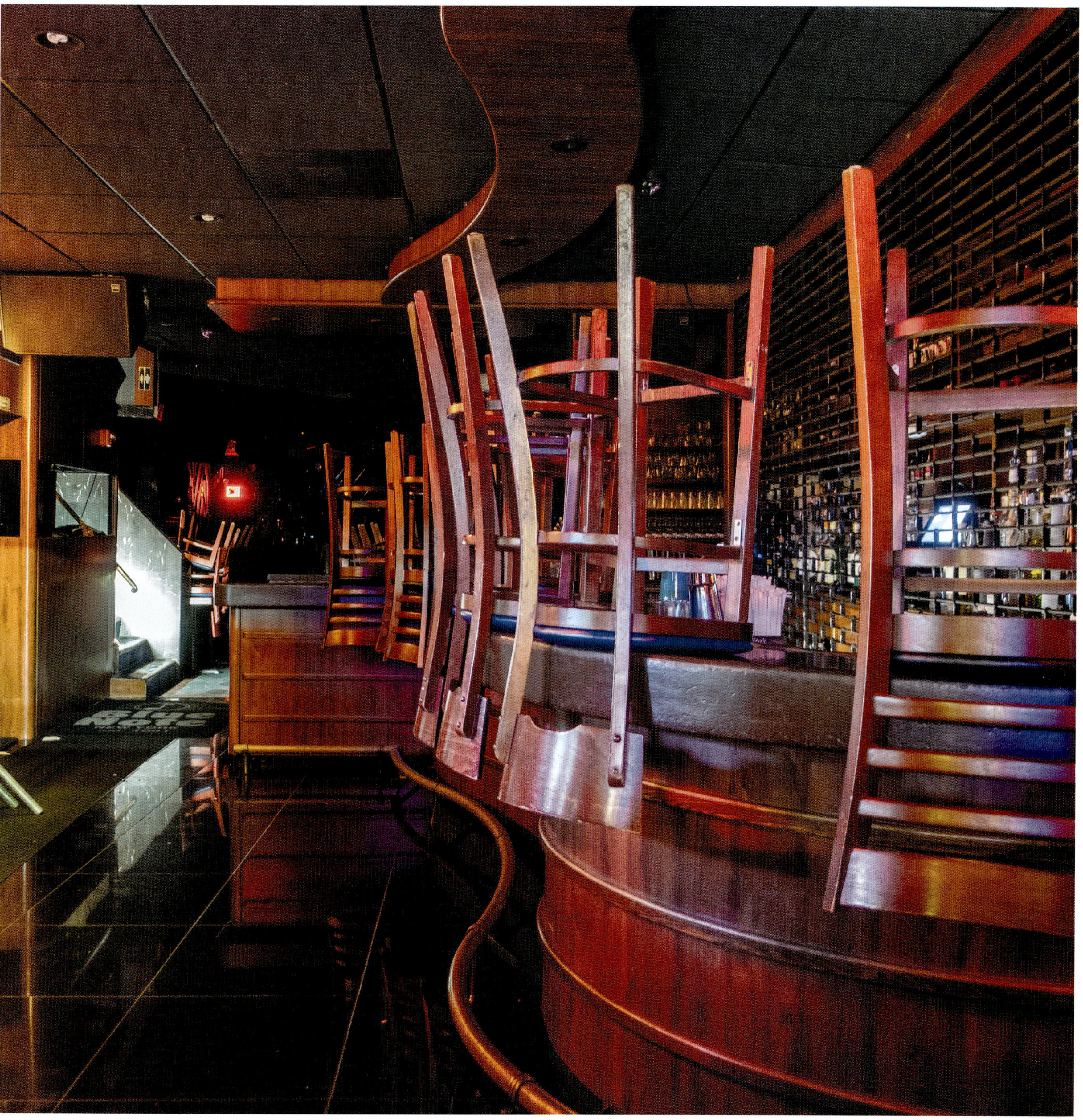

Blue Note

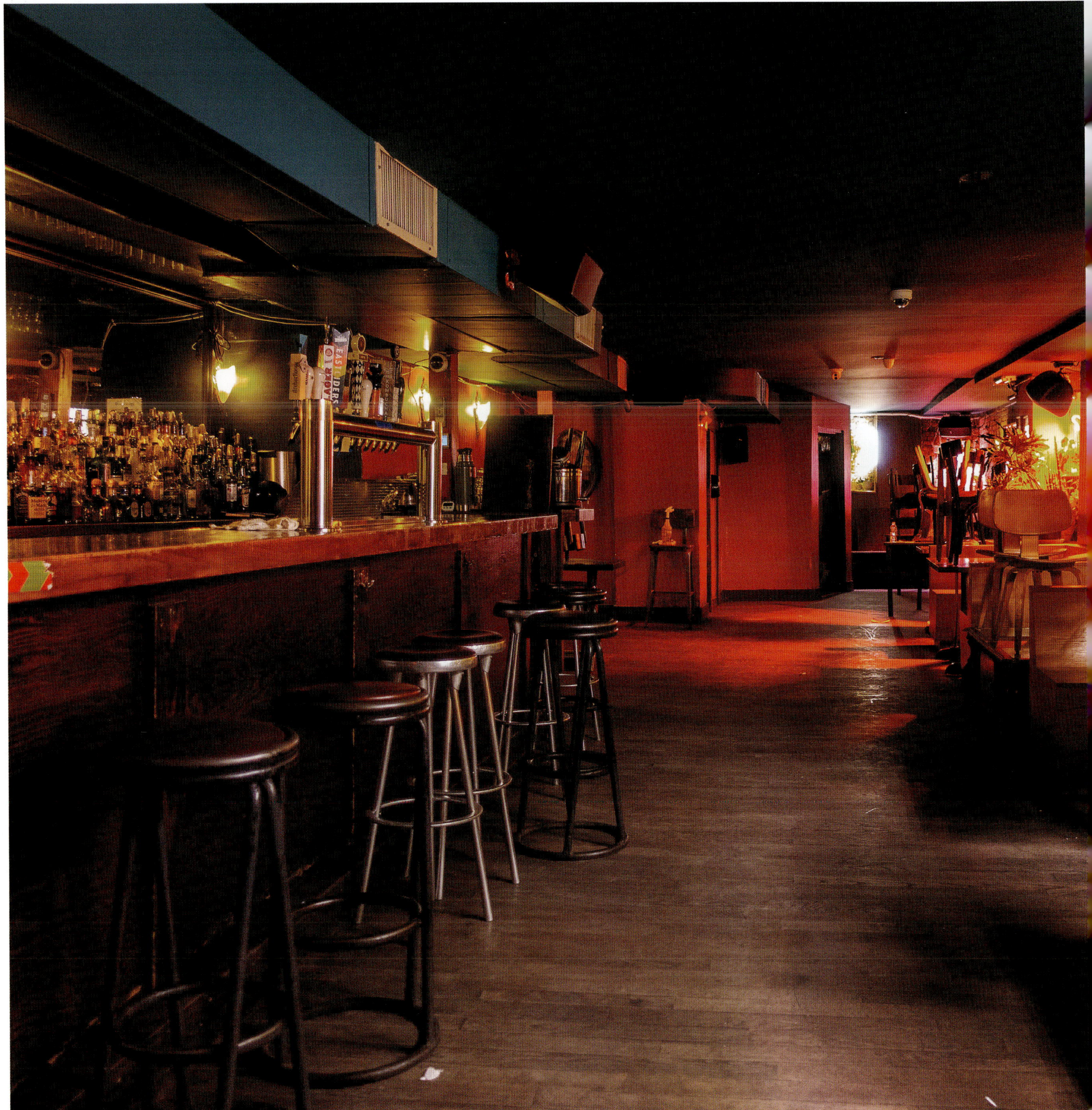

Botanica

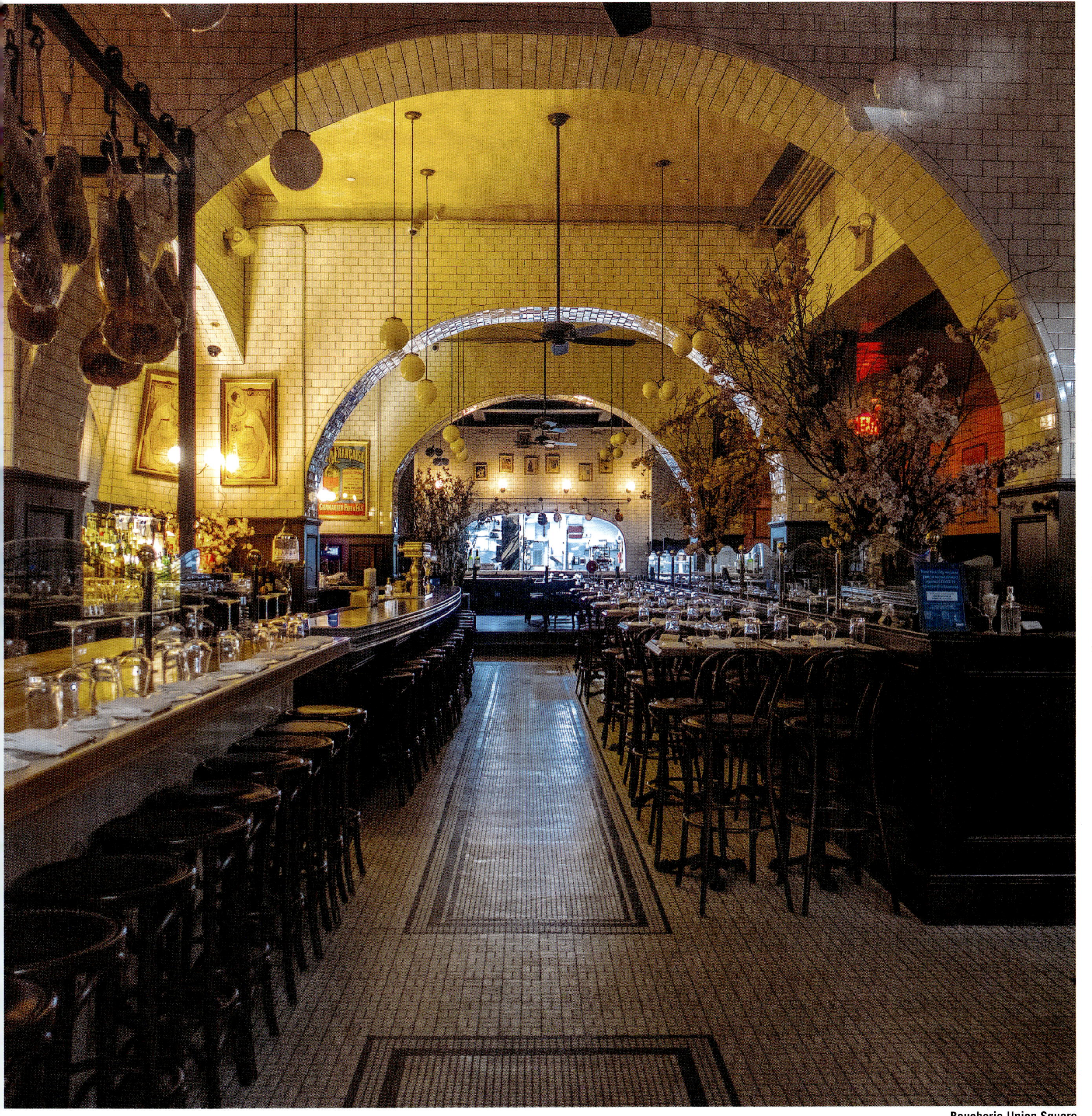

Boucherie Union Square

SOUTH STREET SEAPORT HISTORIC DISTRICT
Water St
Dover St
WAY
ONE WAY
Bridge Cafe

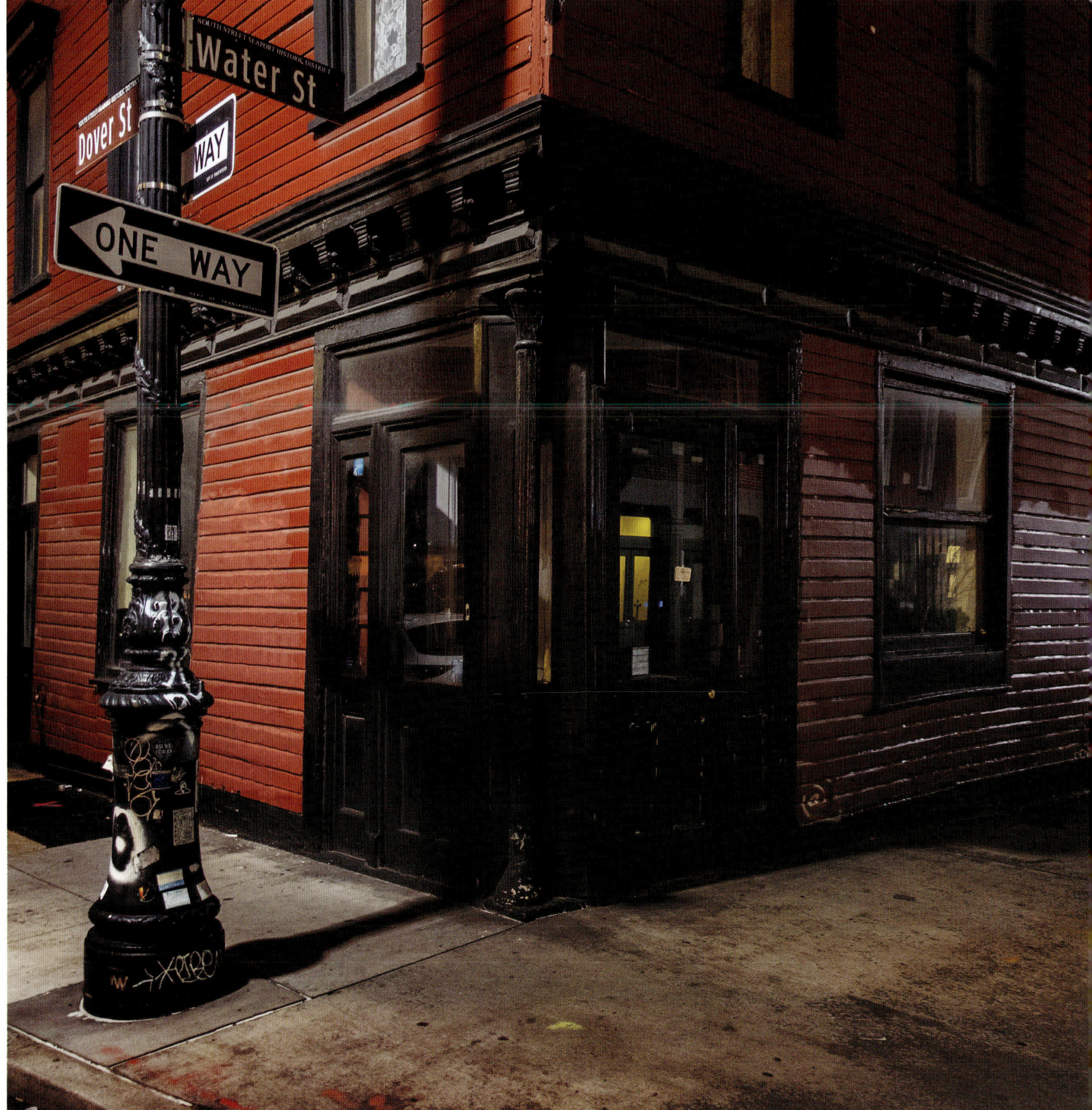

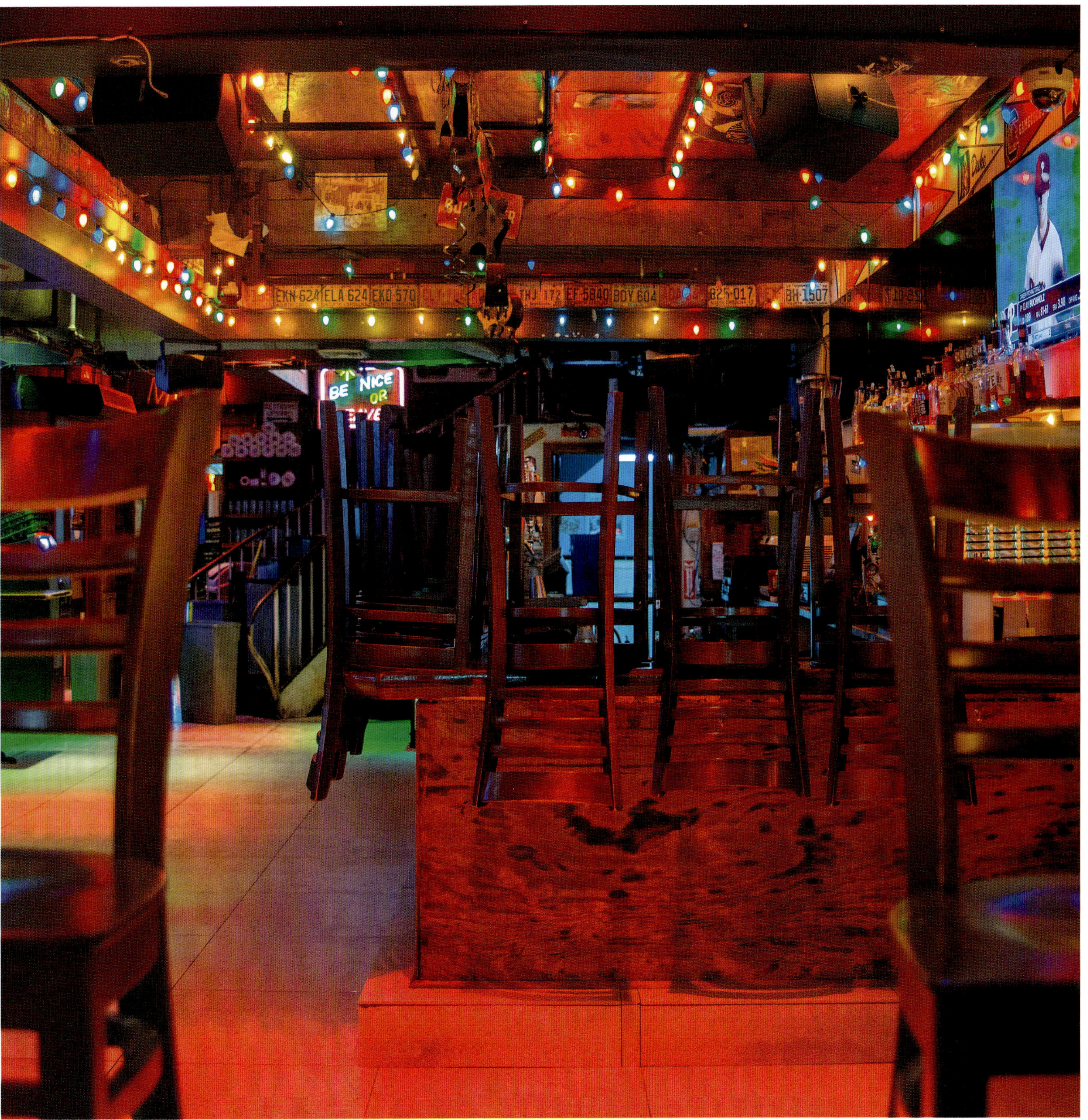

Brother Jimmy's

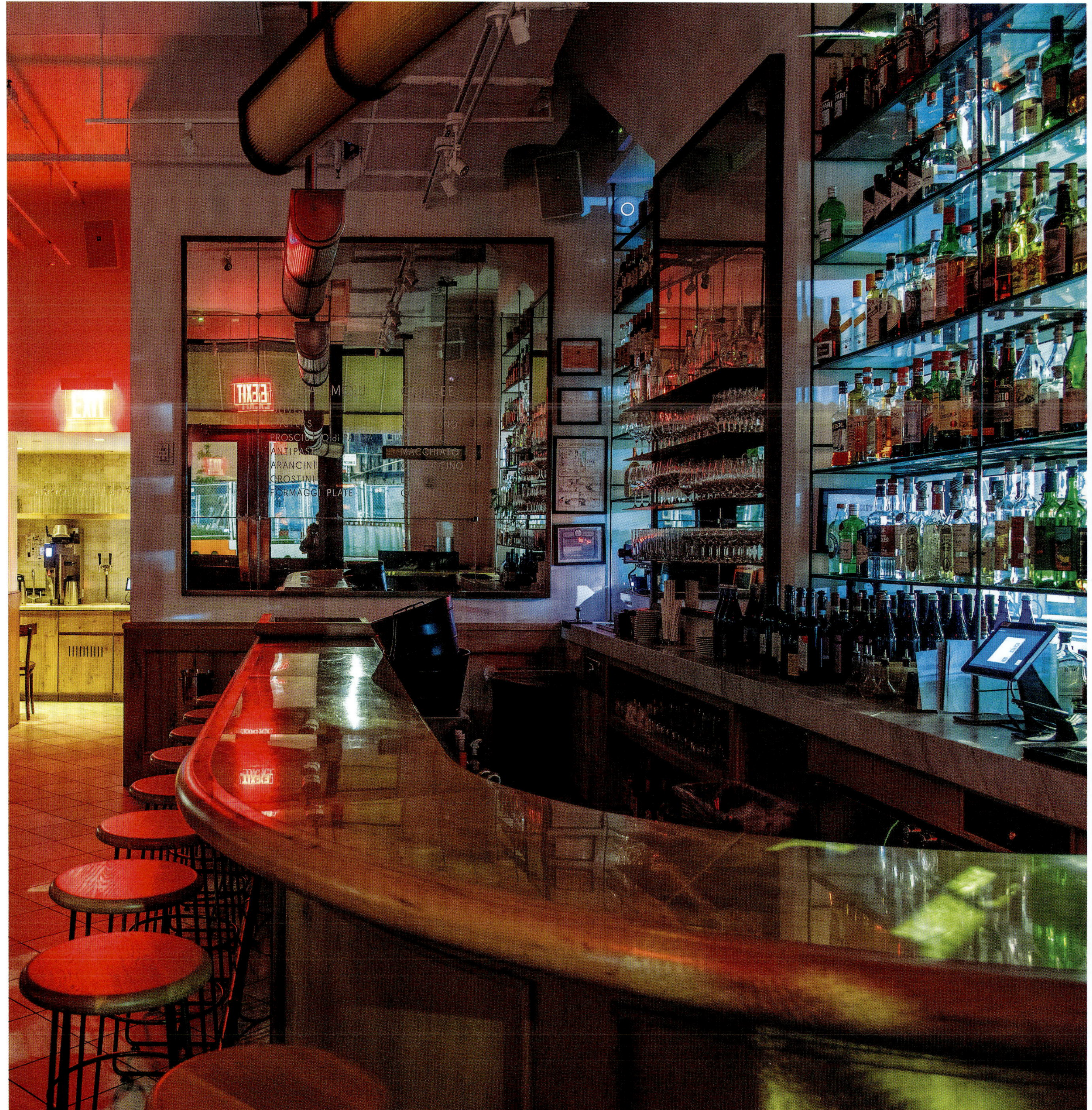

Café Altro Paradiso

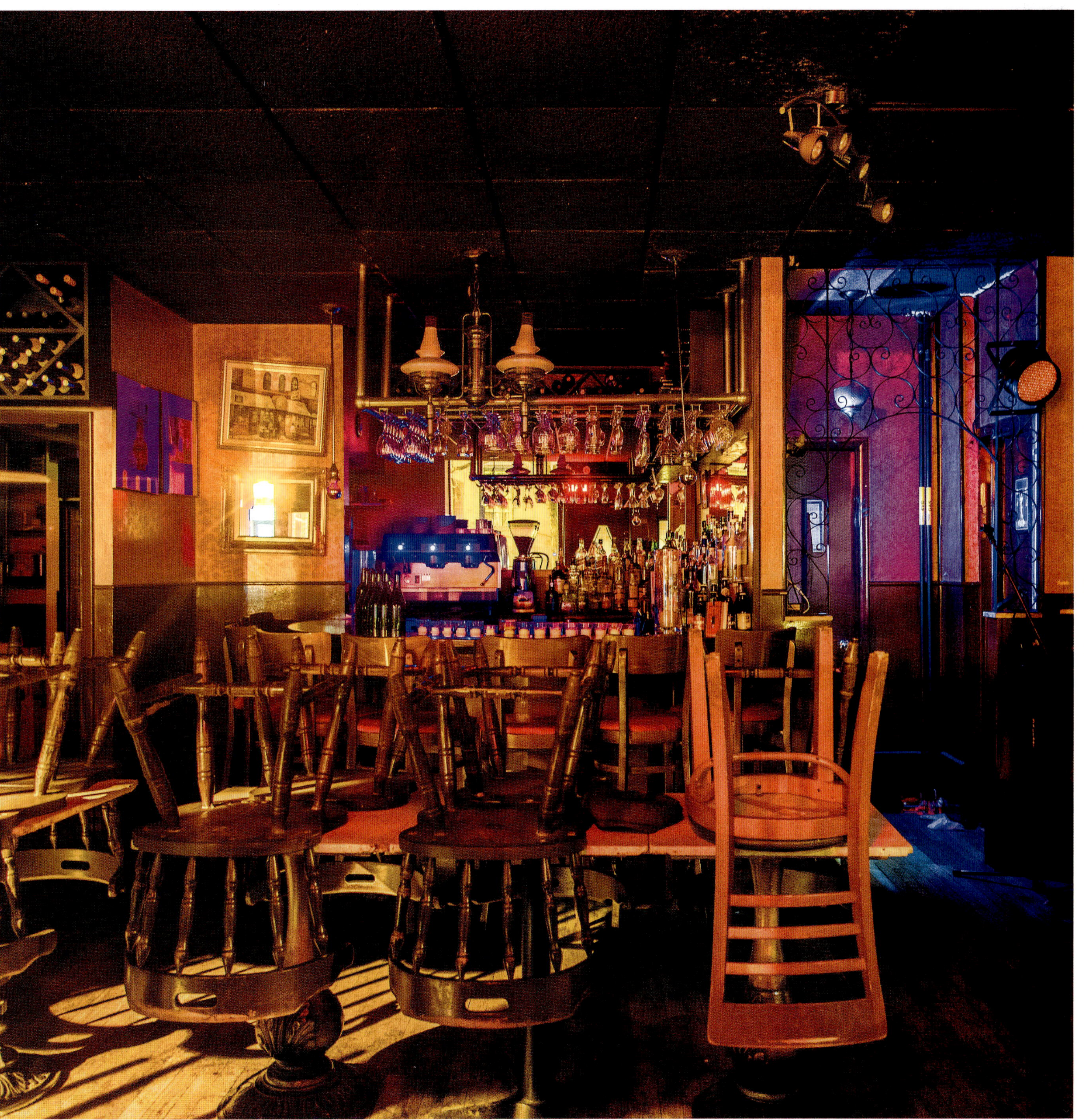

Caffè Vivaldi

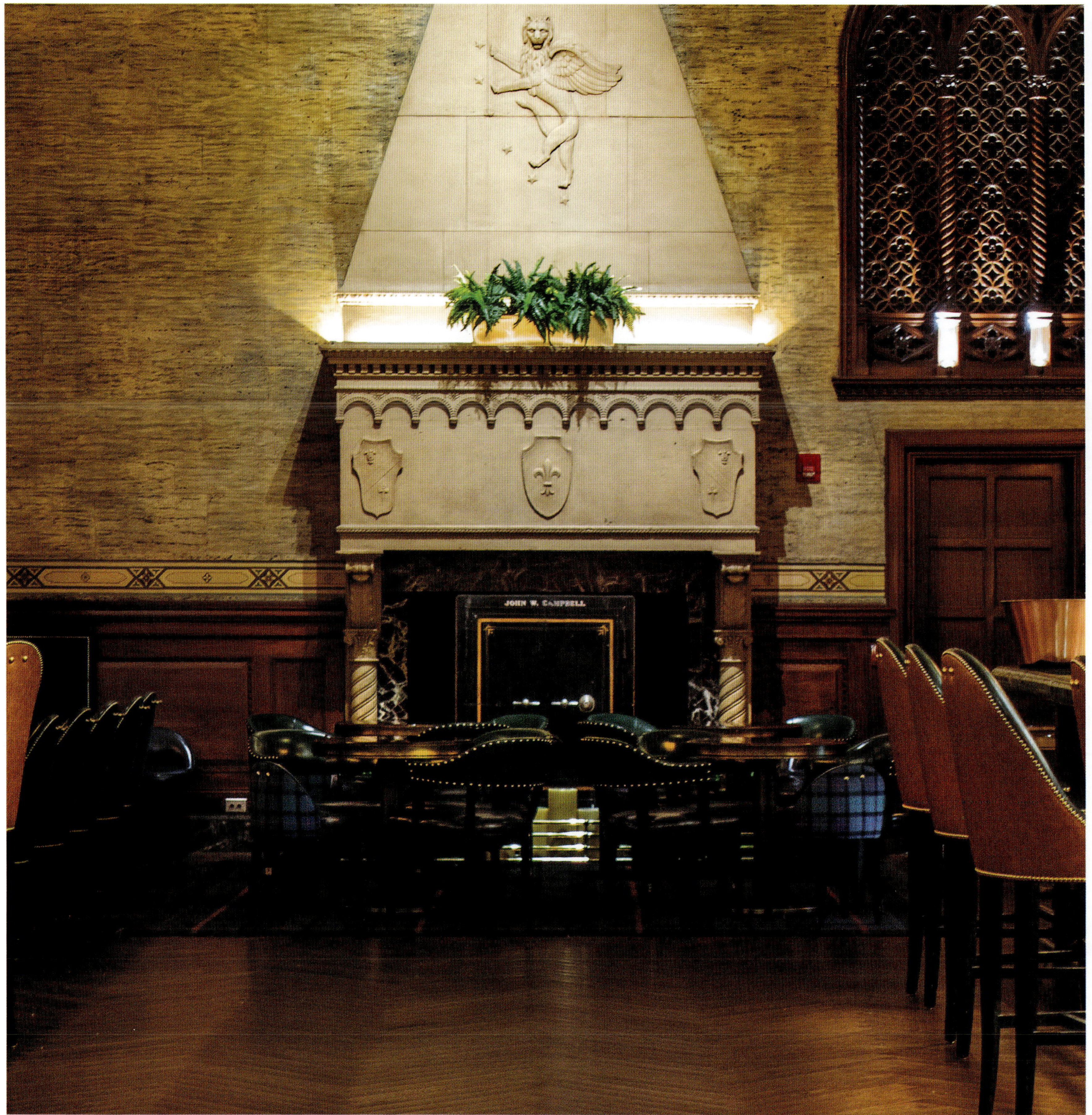

The Campbell

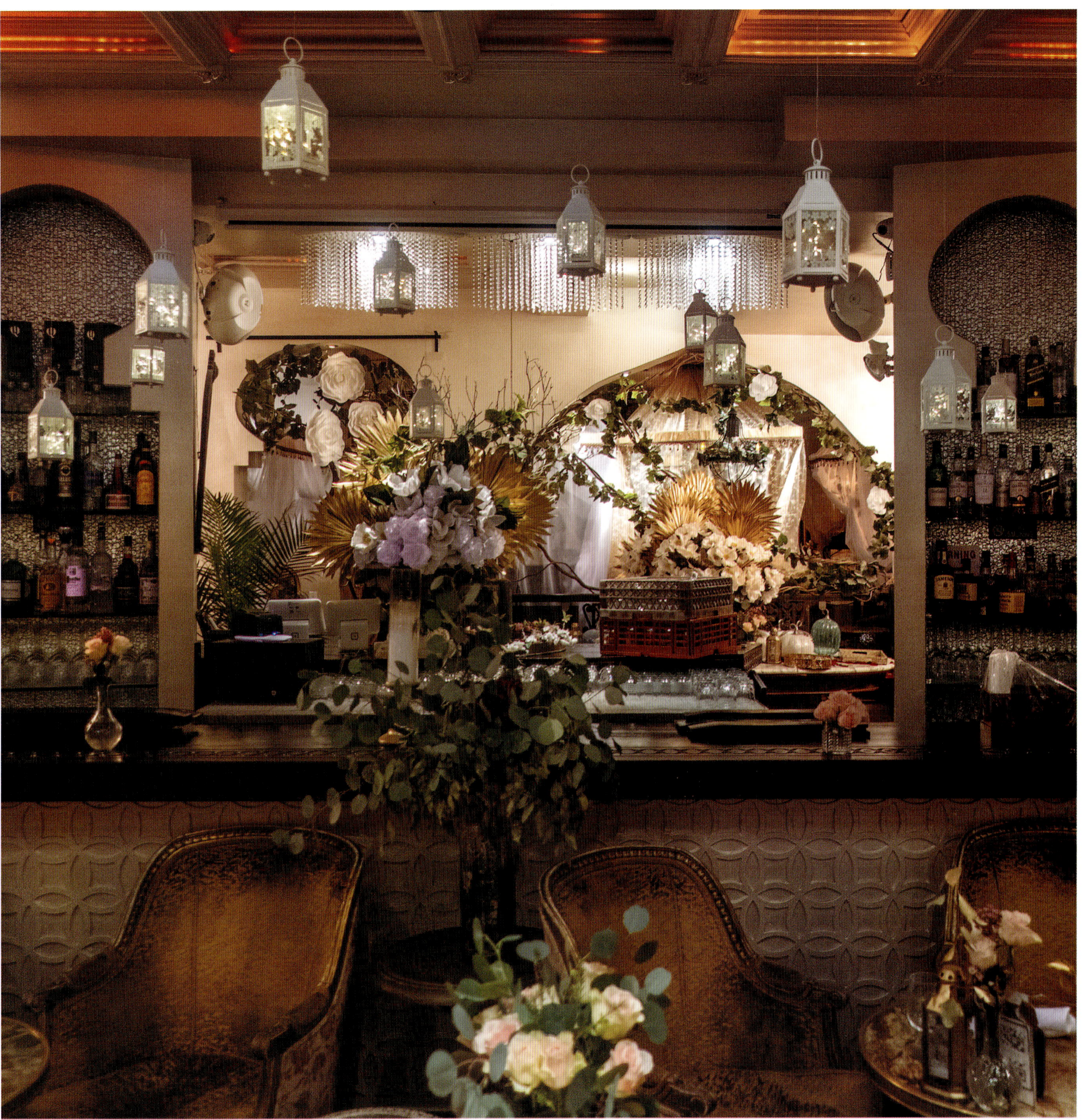

Casa La Femme

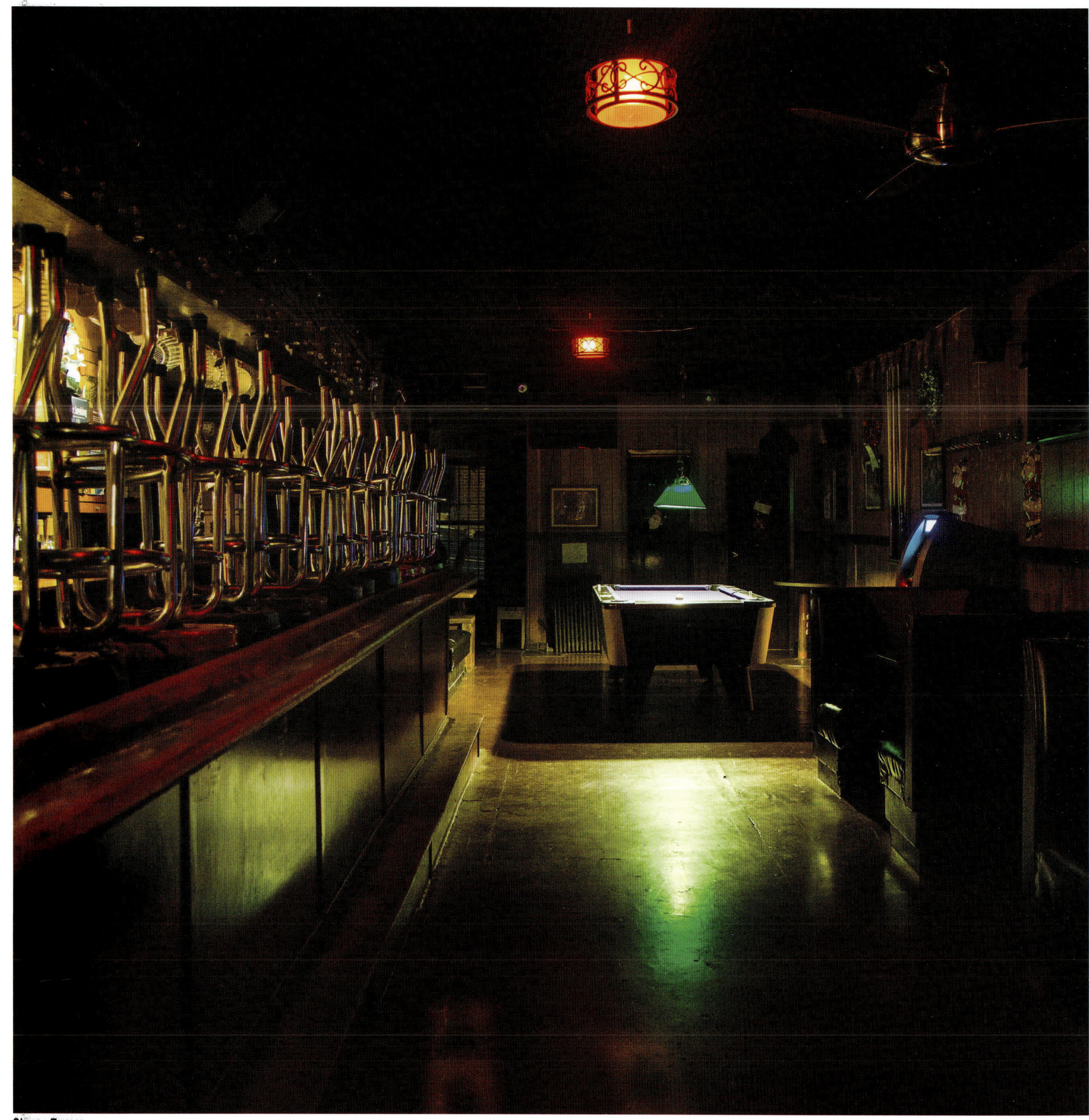

Cherry Tavern

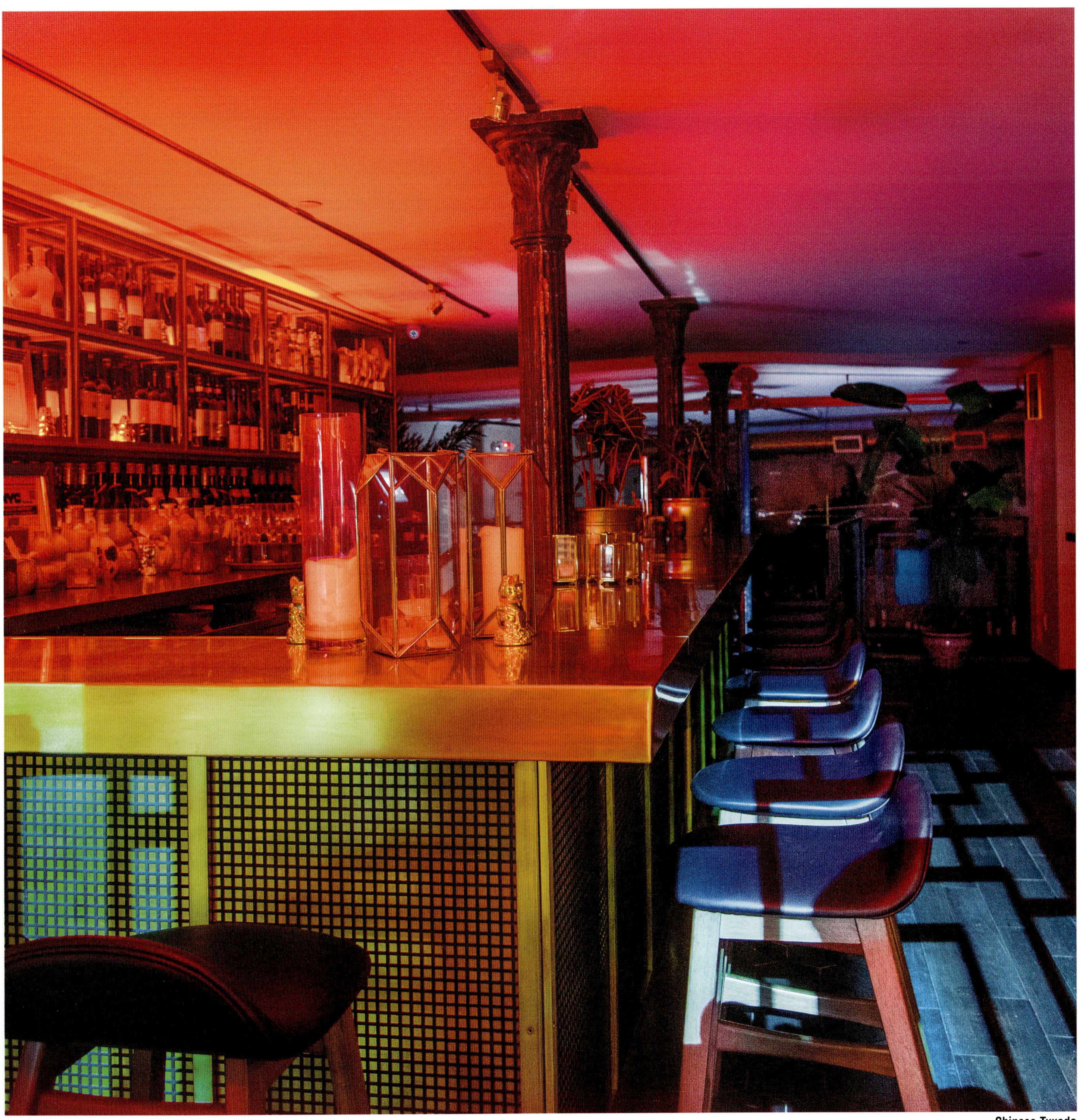

Chinese Tuxedo

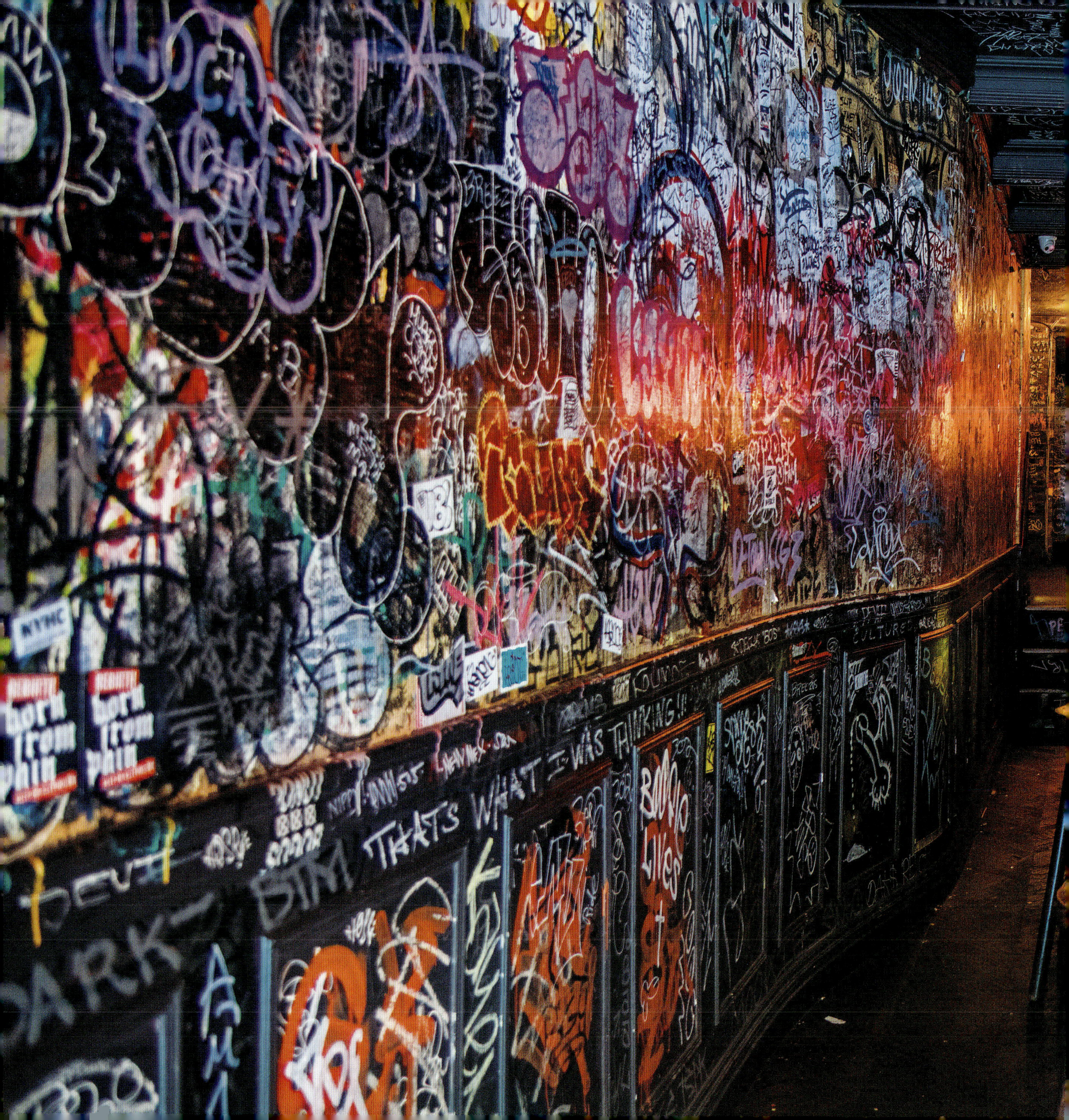

CLOCKWORK
DRUNK OF
THE DAY...
VEGAN
DIET
ROCK
STAR
Bathroom
for
Customers
Only
All Others $5

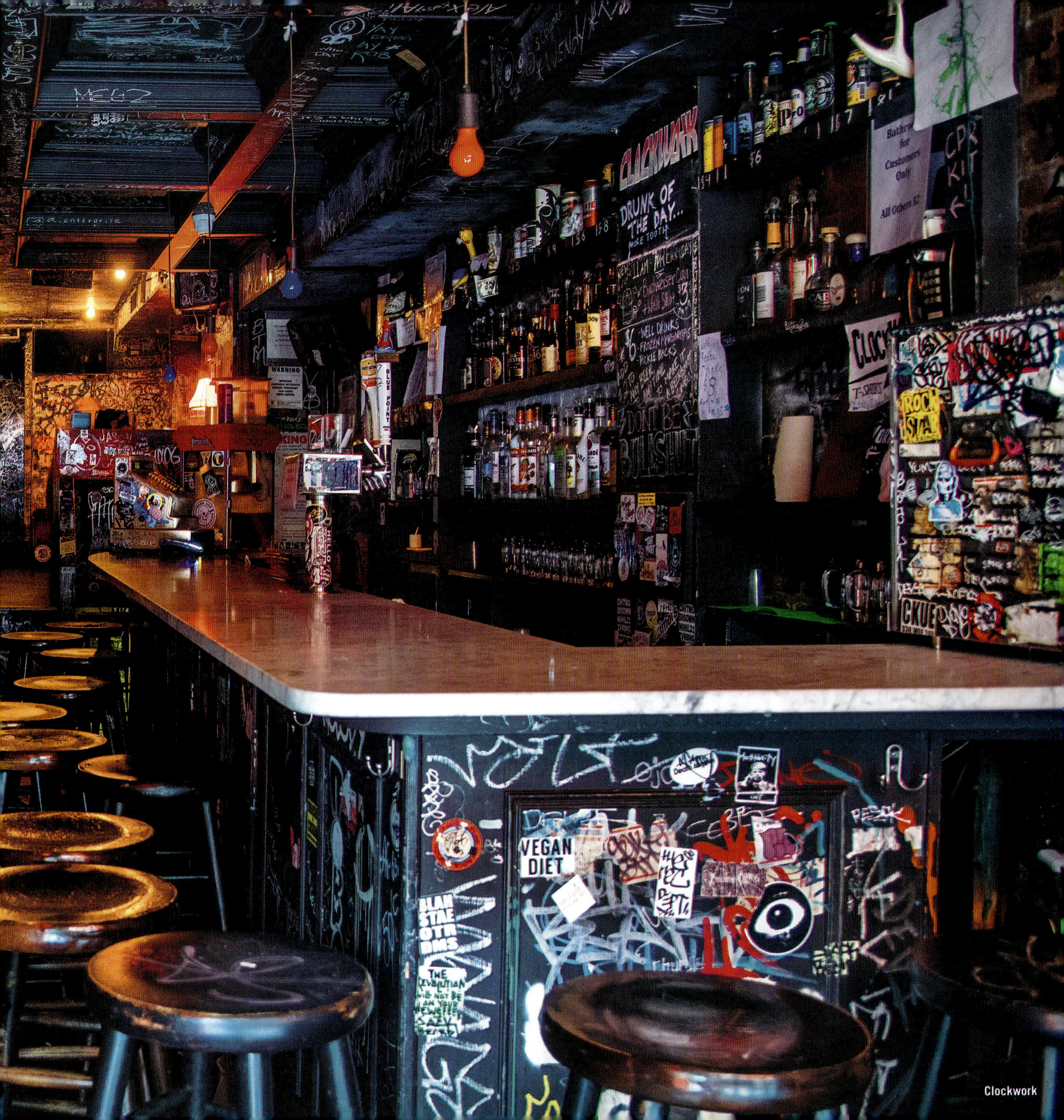

Clockwork

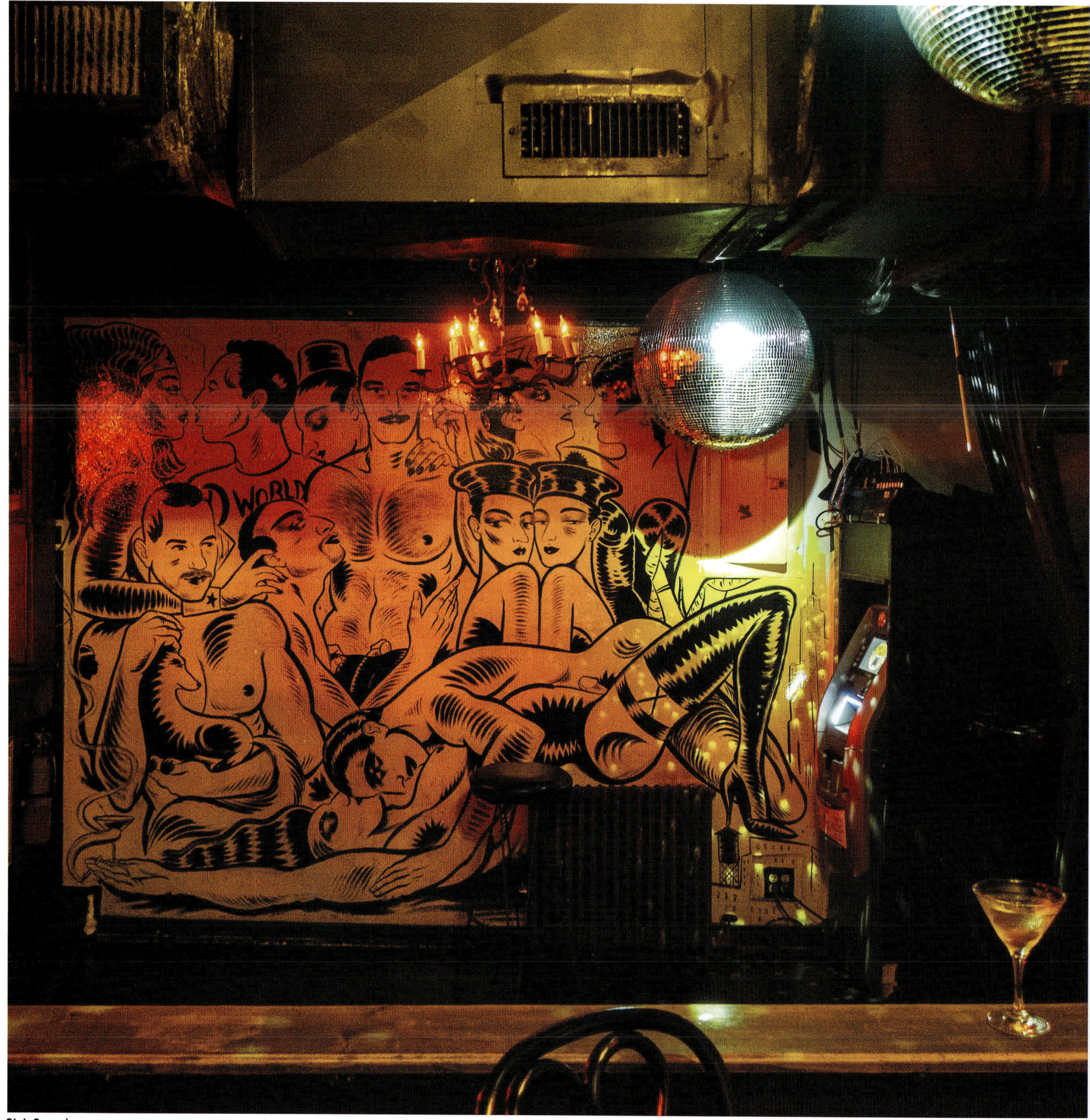

Club Cumming

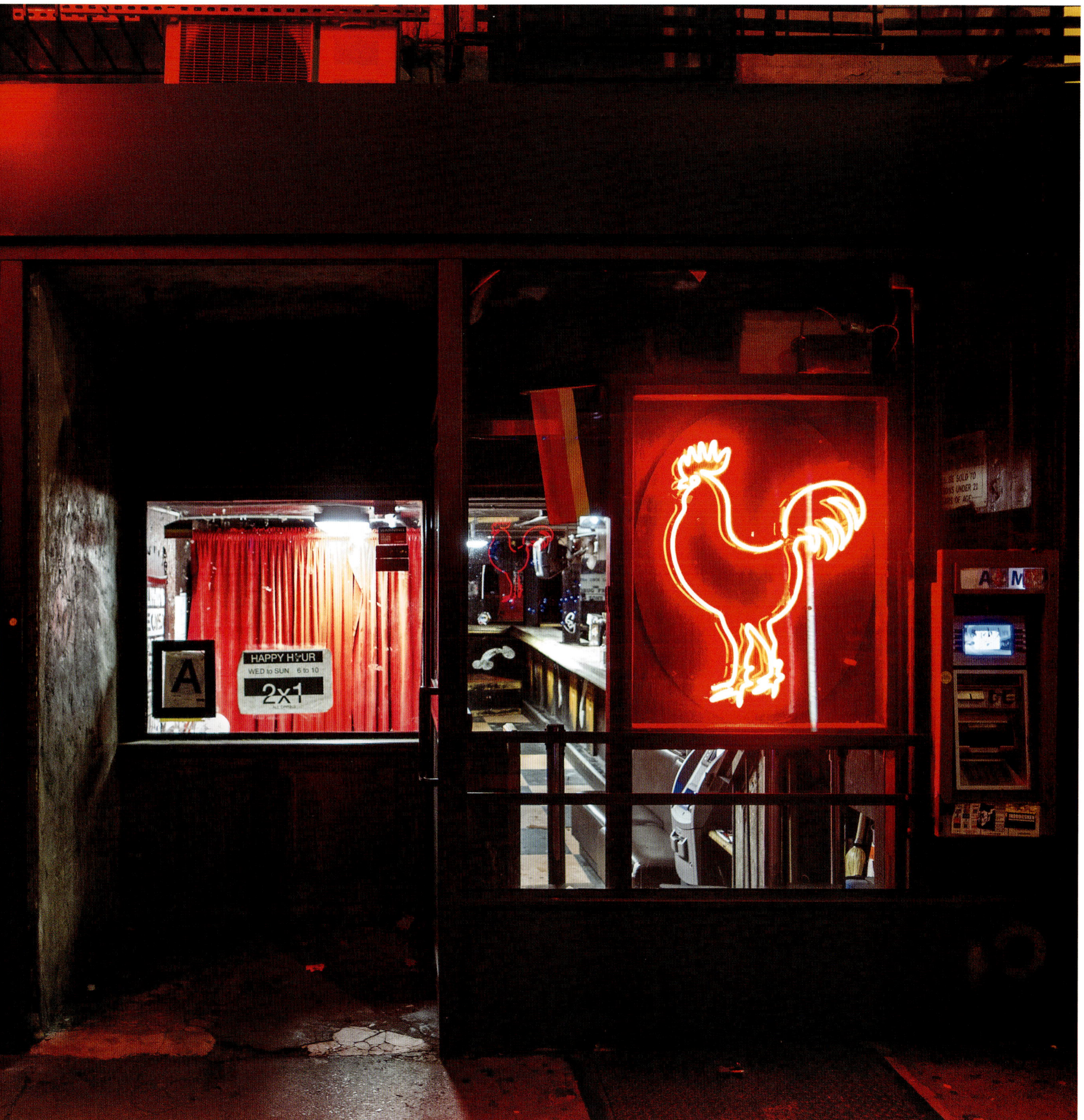
HAPPY HOUR
WED to SUN 6 to 10
2x1

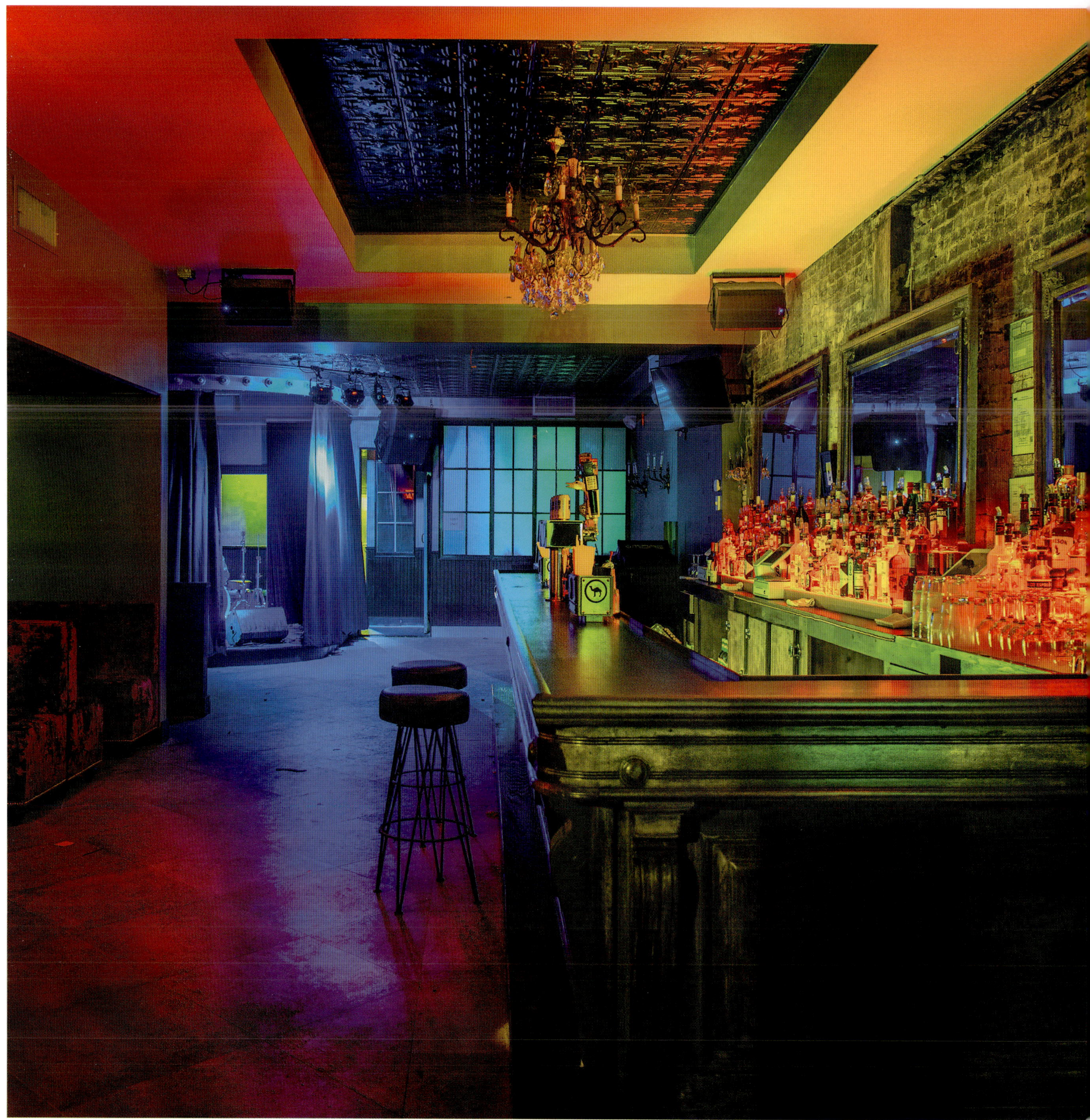

Coney Island Baby

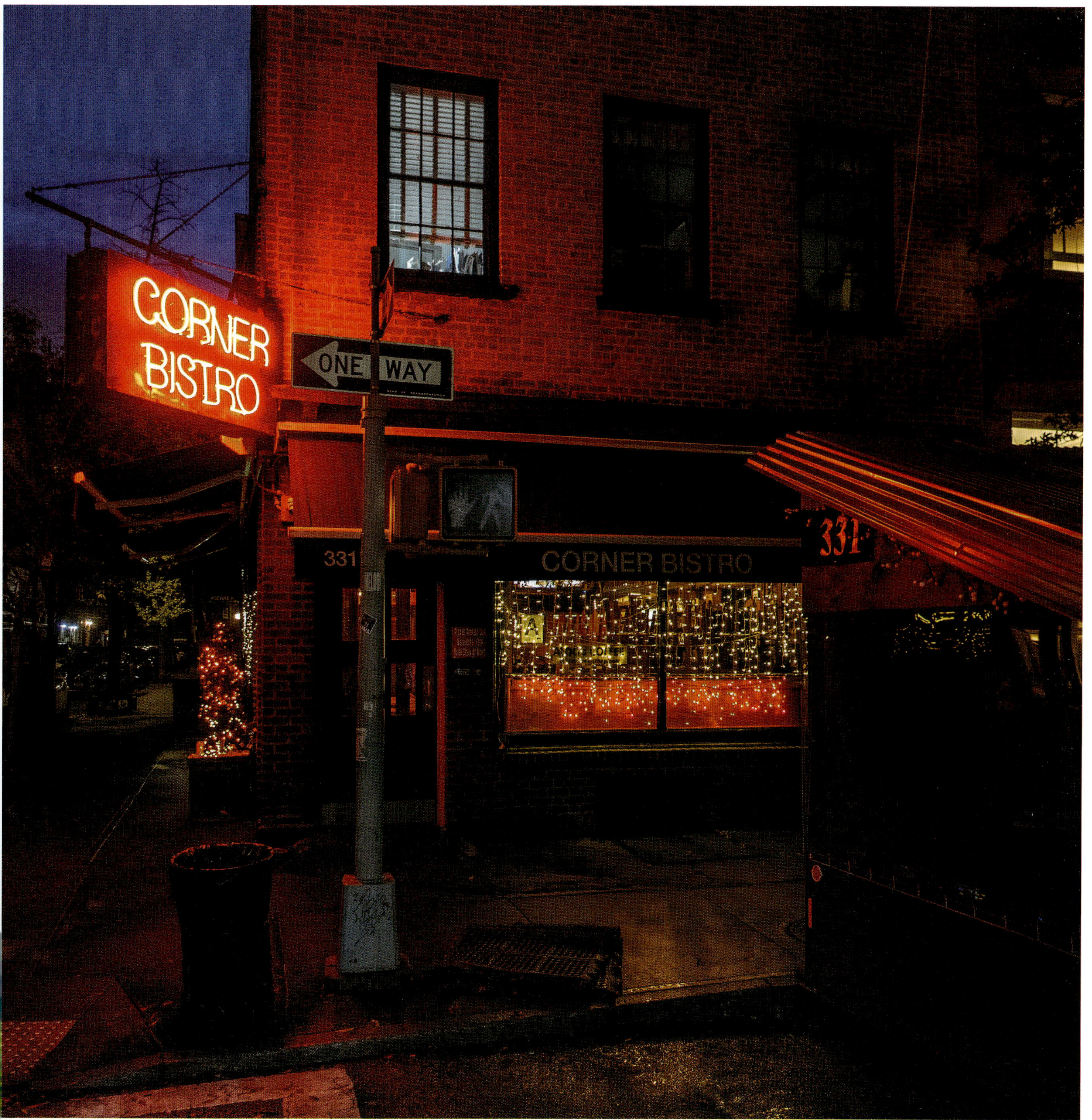

Corner Bistro

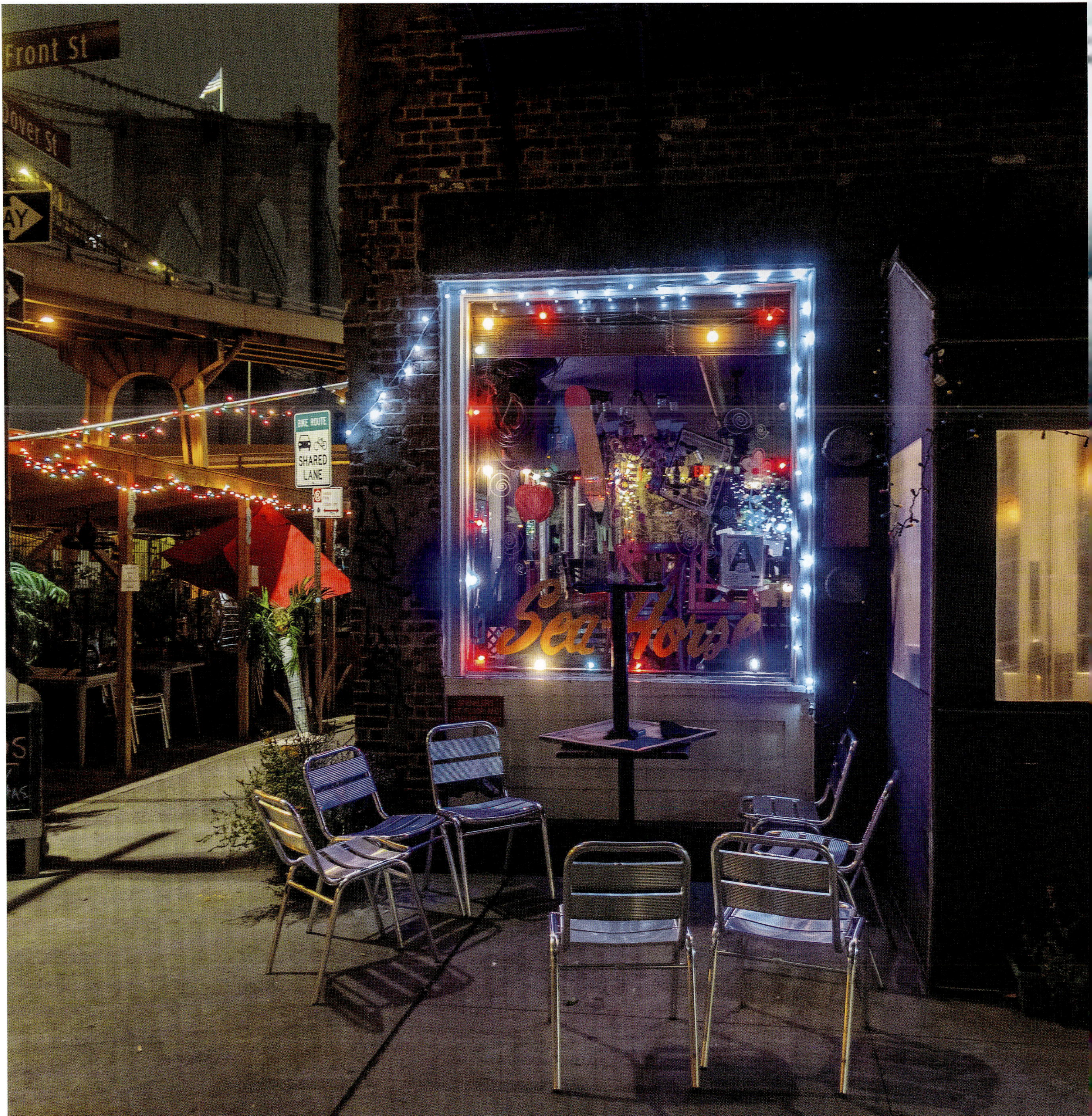

Cowgirl SeaHorse

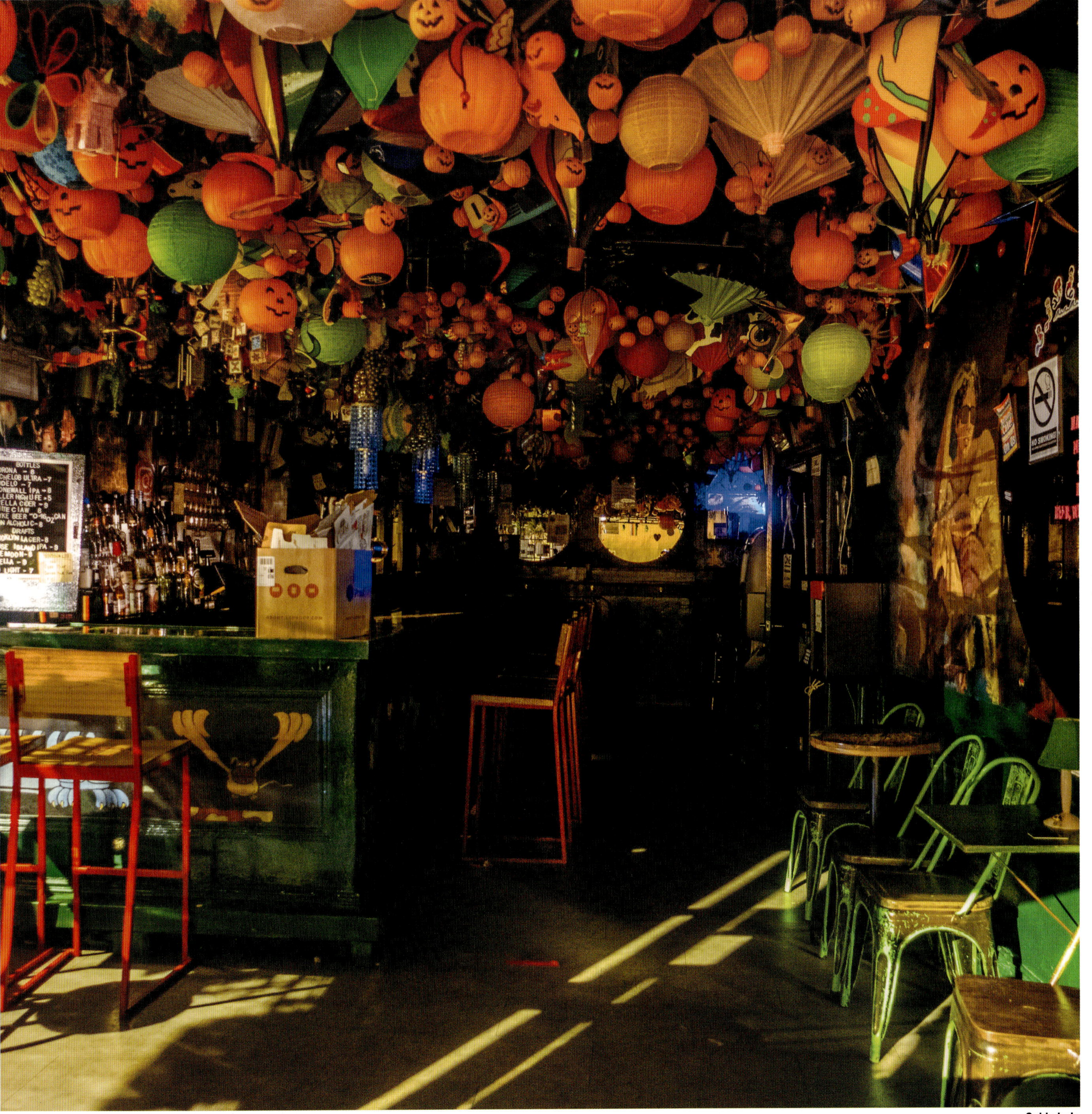

Cubbyhole

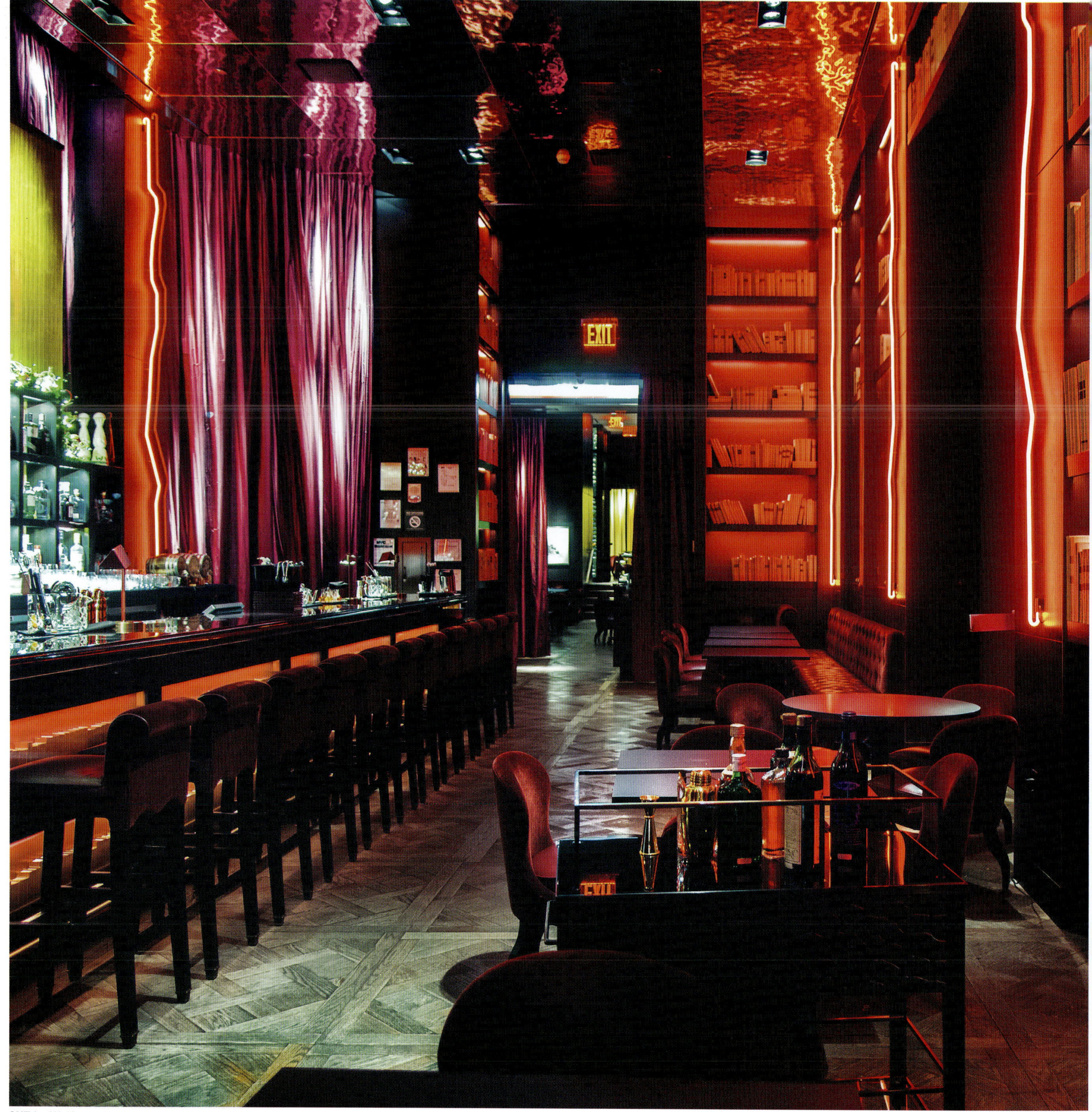

CUT by Wolfgang Puck

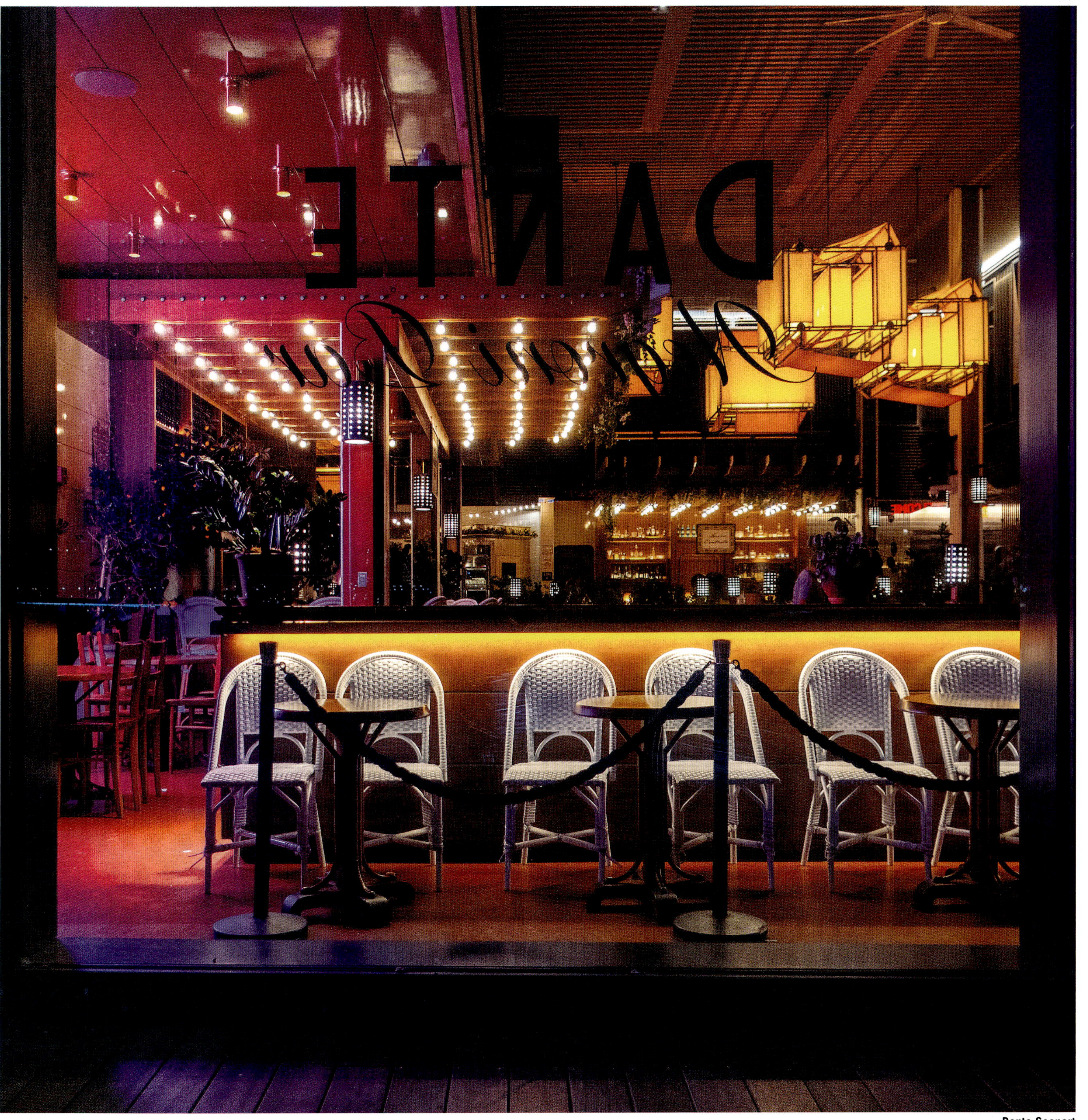

Dante Seaport

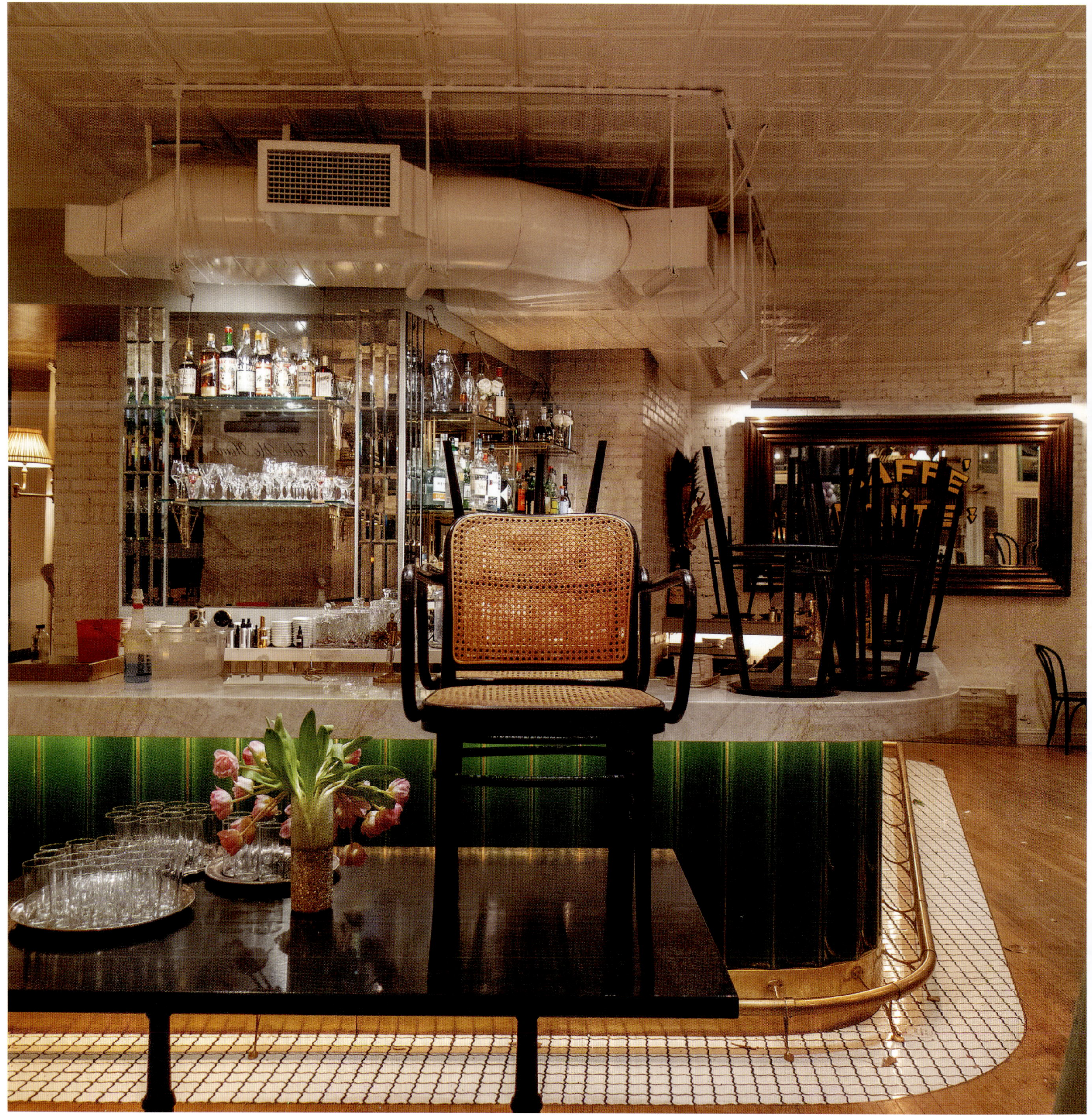

Dante West Village

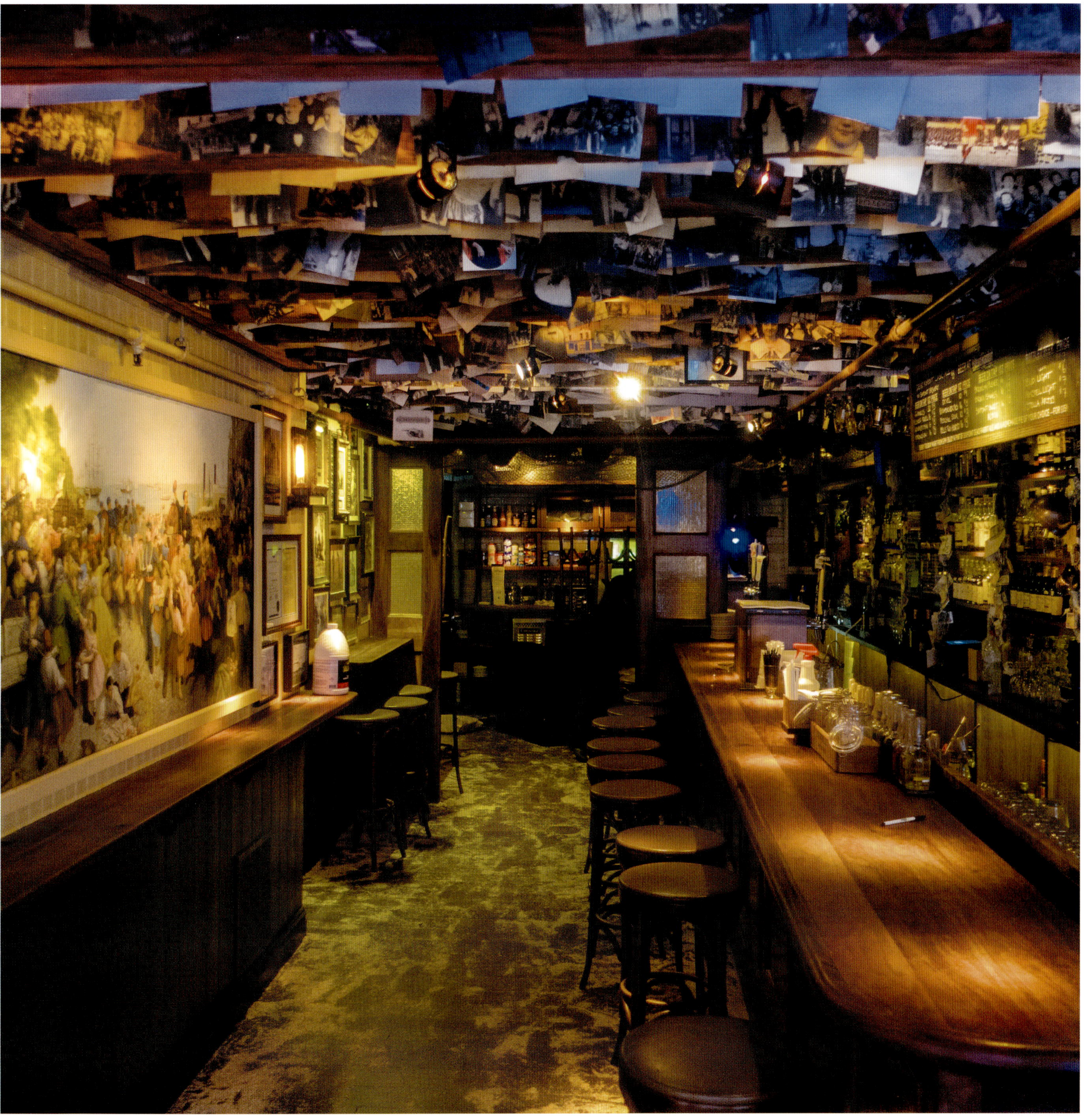

The Dead Rabbit

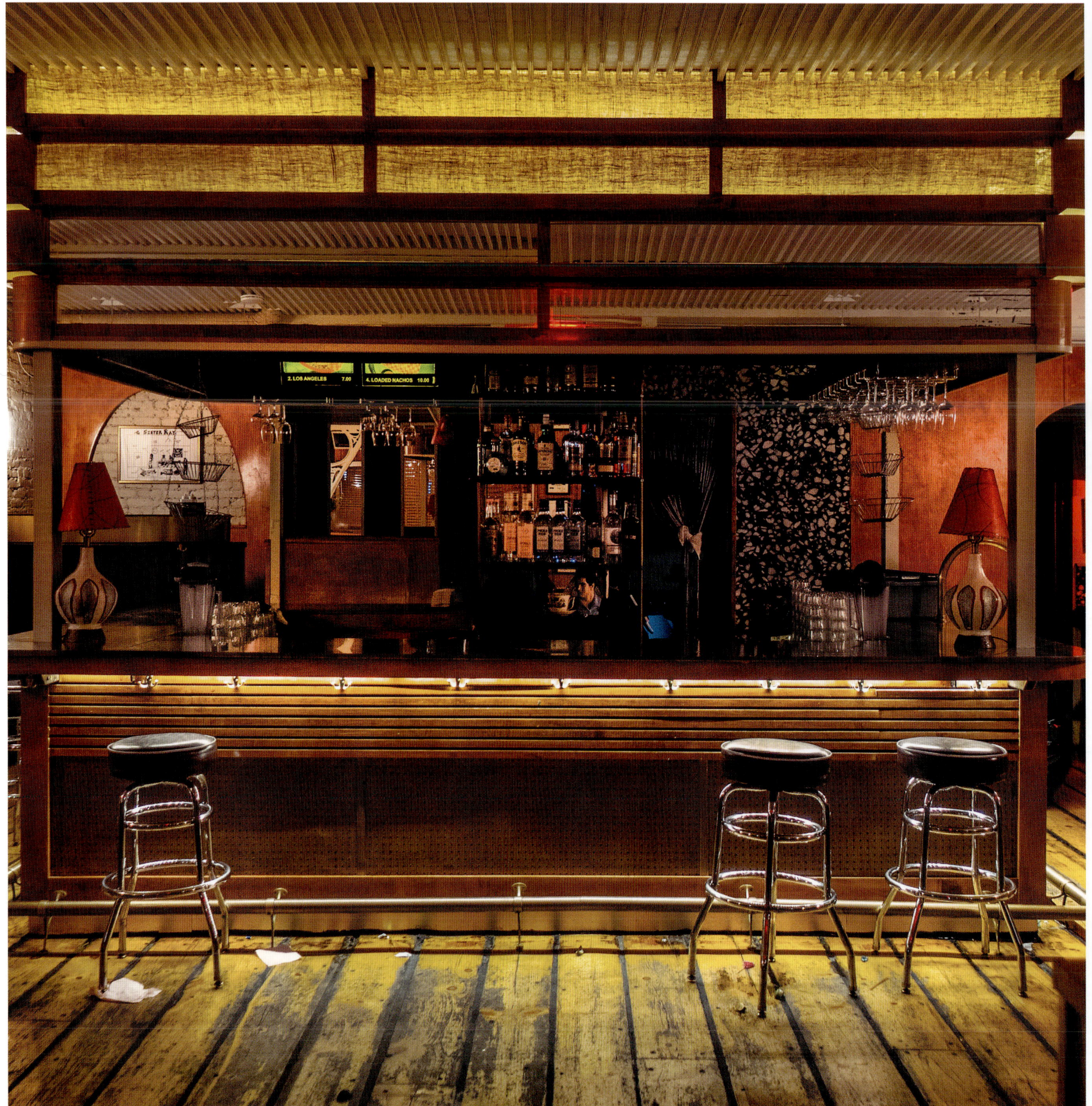

Ding-A-Ling

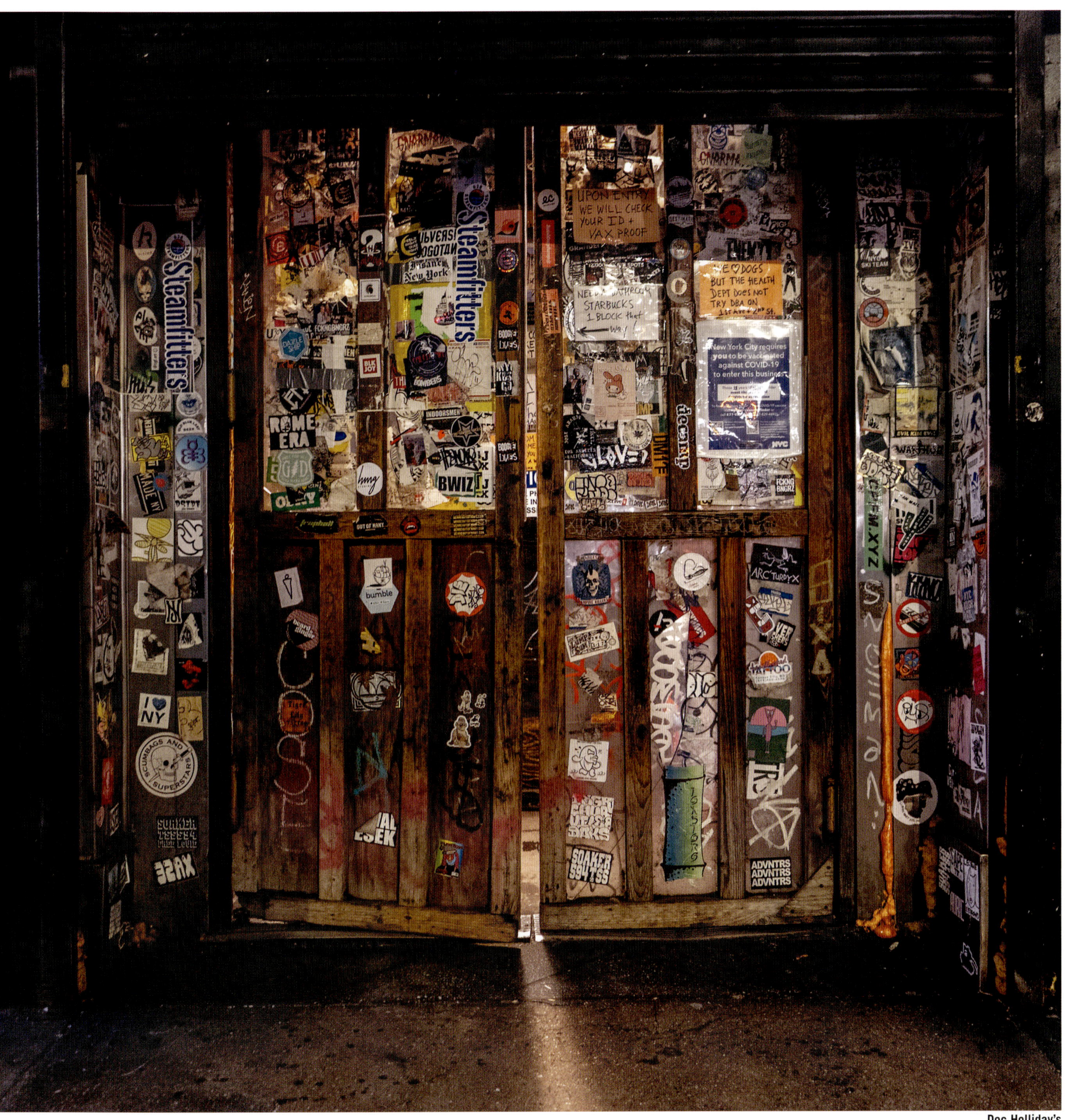

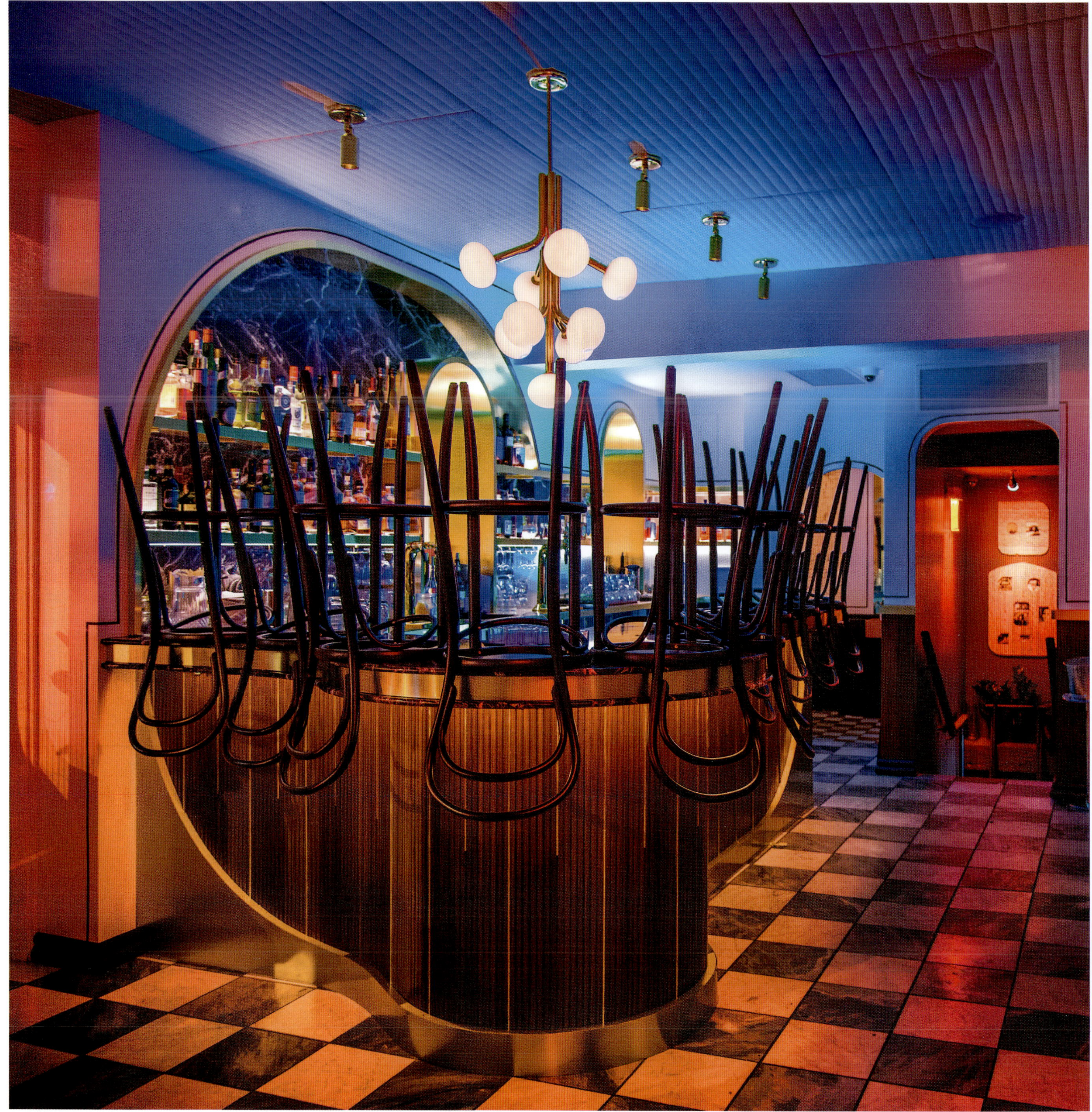

Don Angie

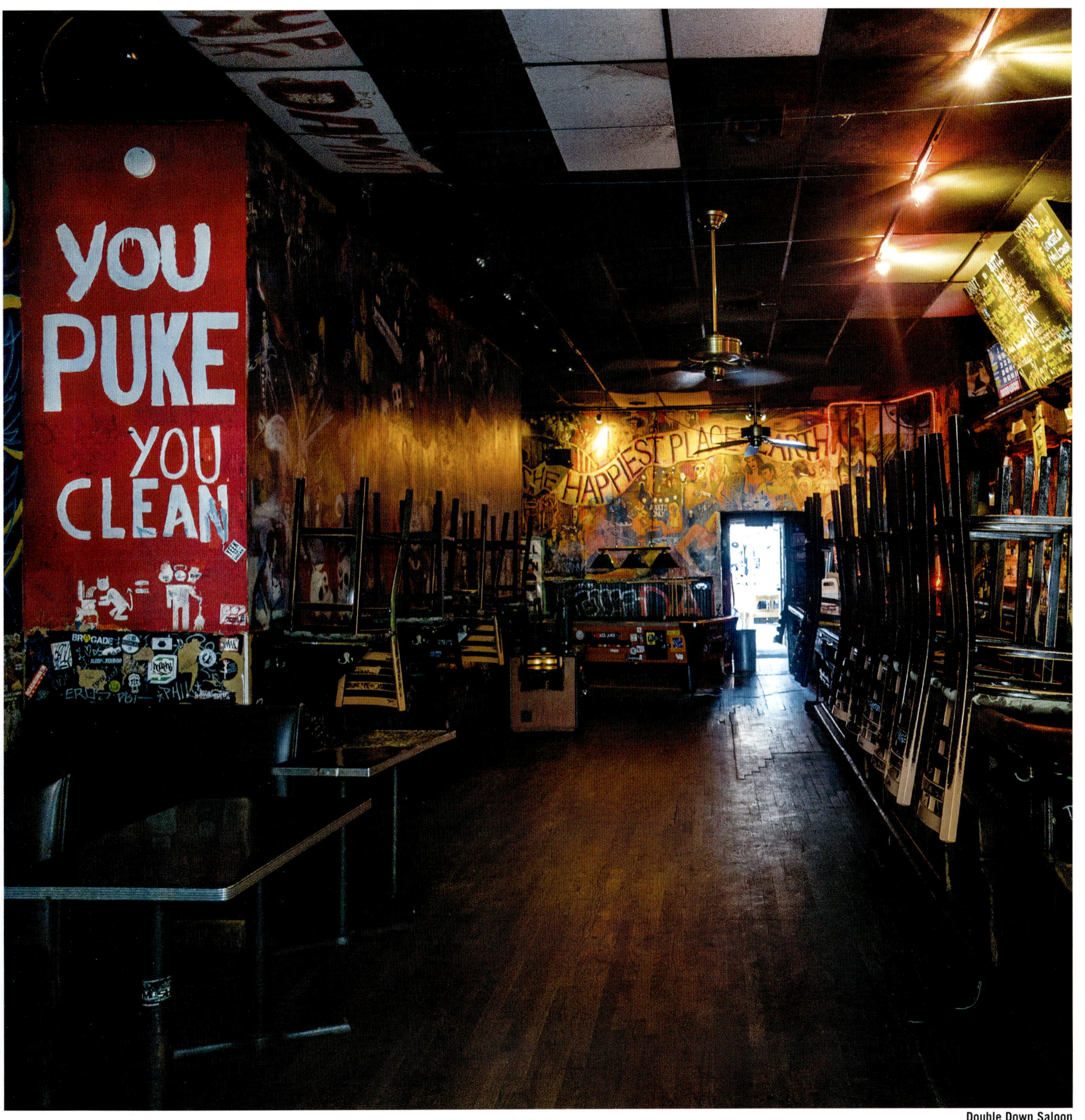

Double Down Saloon

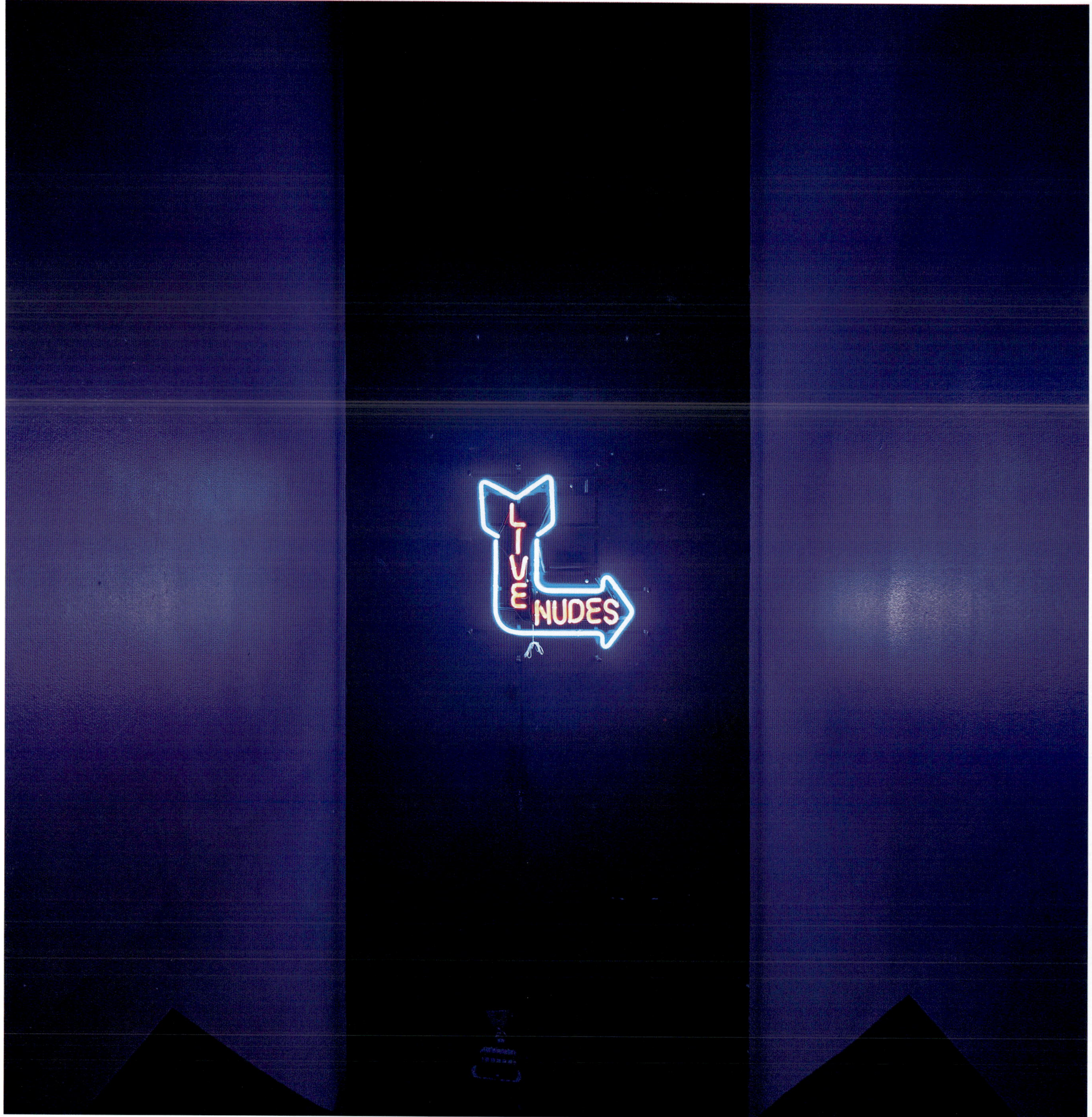

Downtime

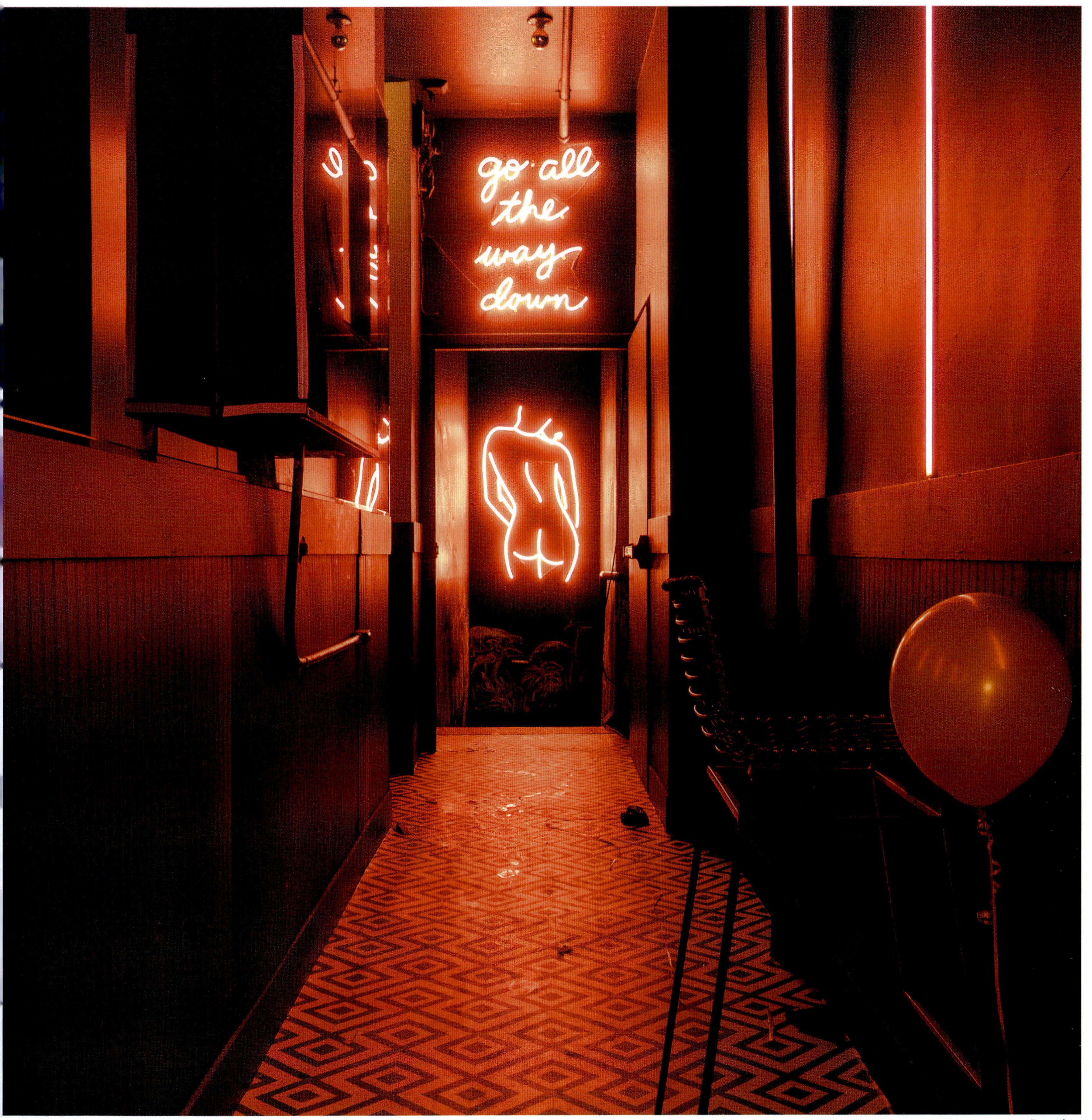
go all
the
way
down

BAR
RESTAURANT
WINNIE
BAR & RESTAURANT
クラーク博士
北海道スタイル
レストラン＆バー

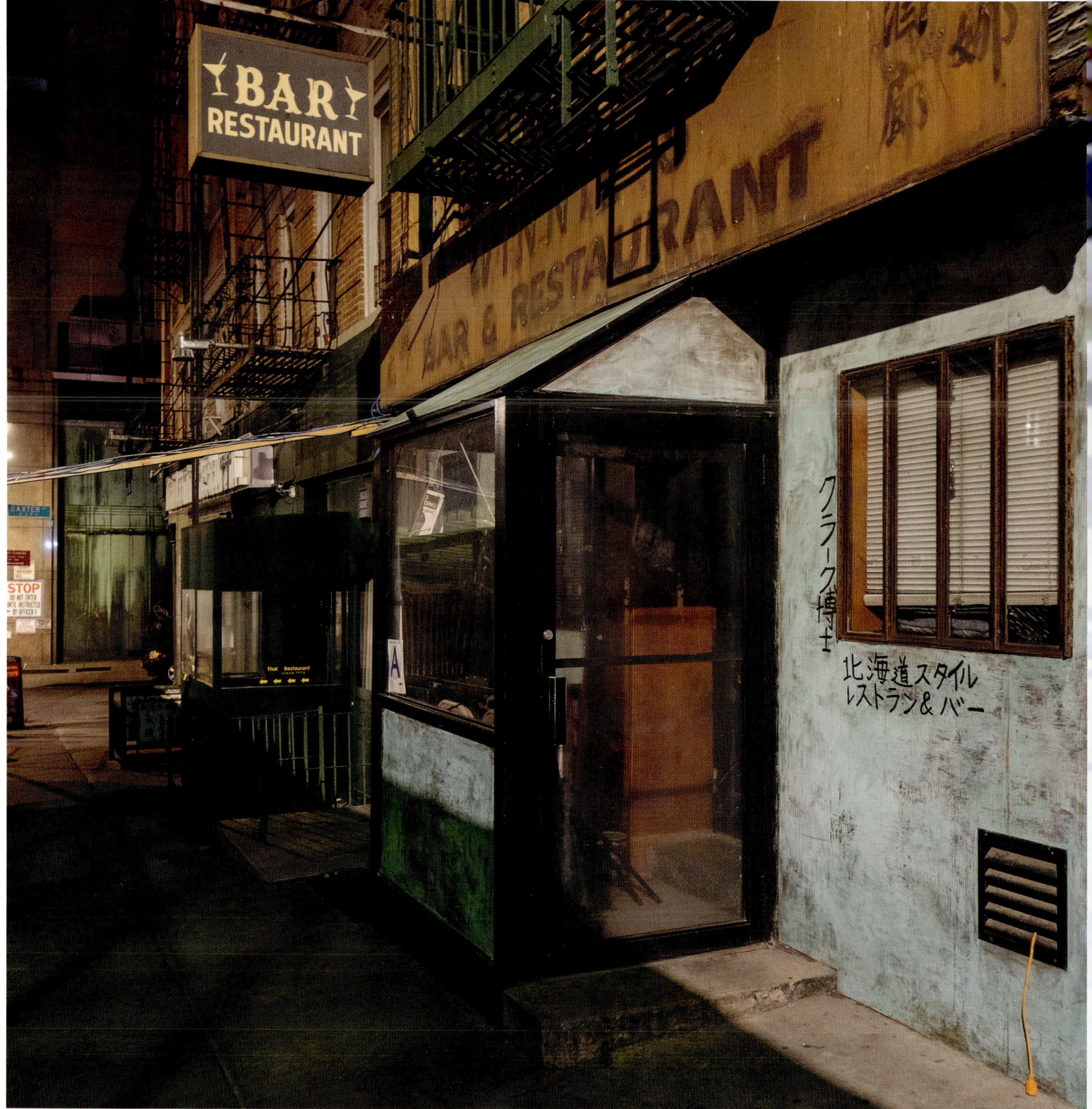

Dr. Clark

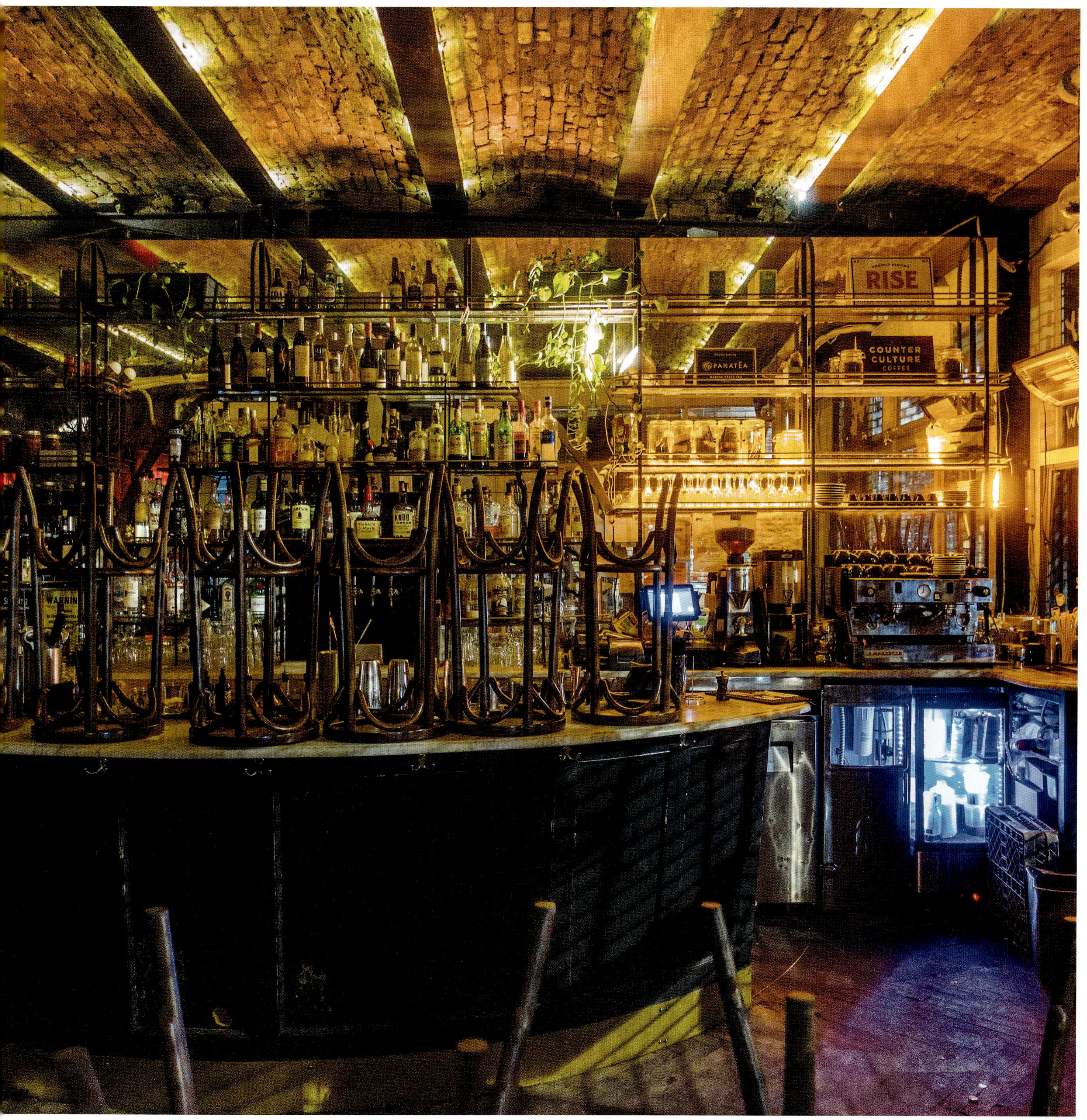

Dudley's

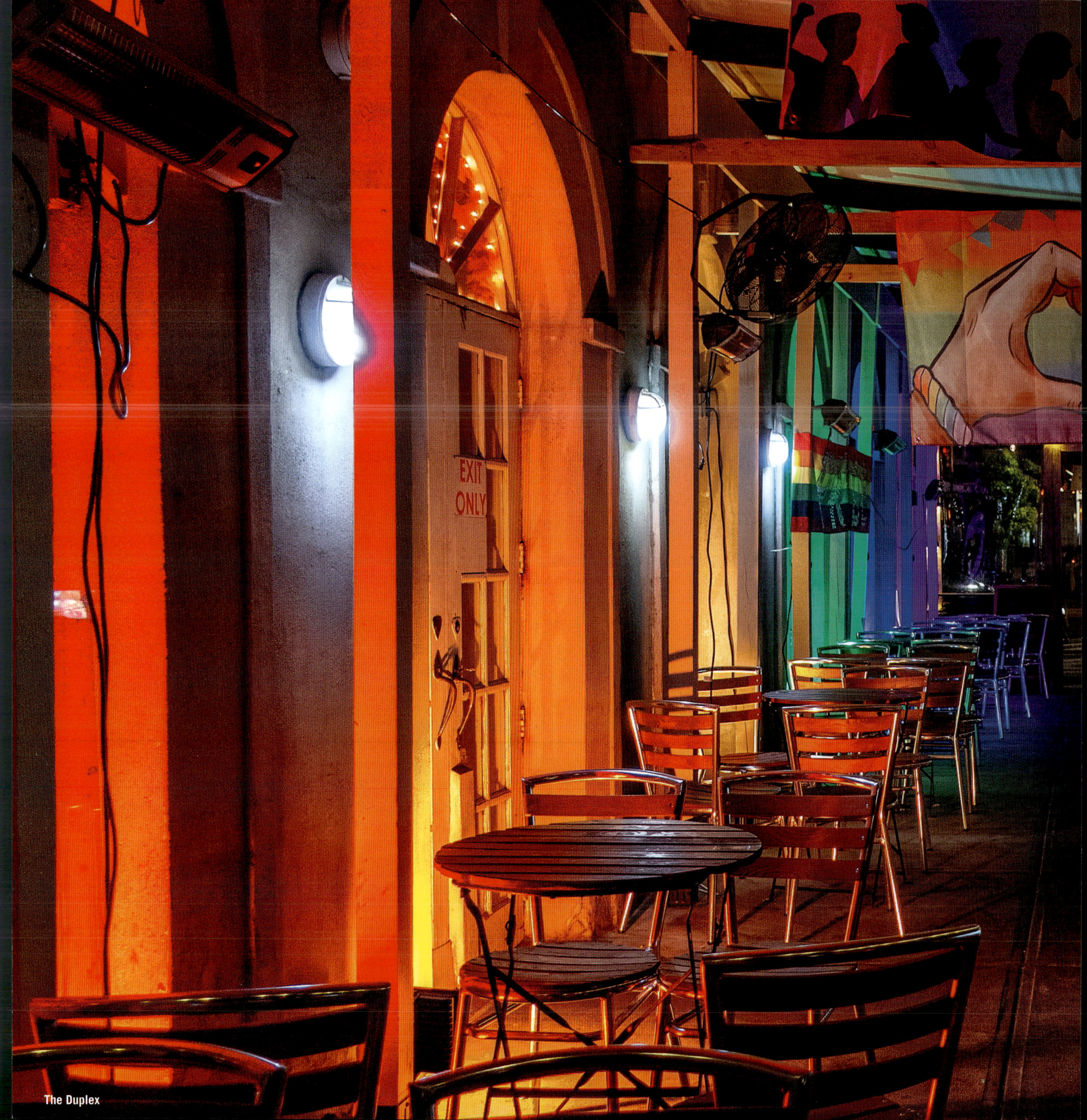

The Duplex

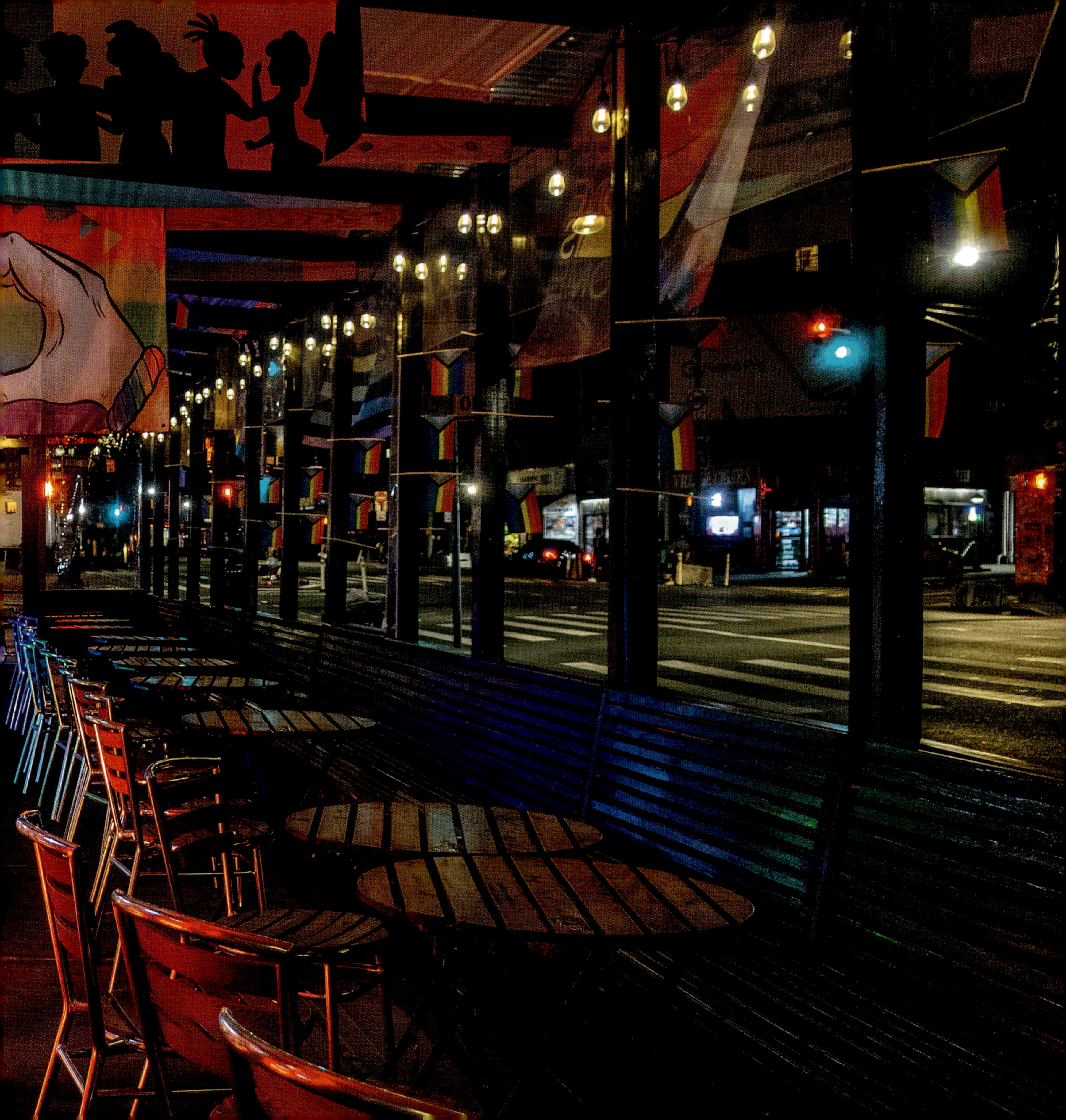

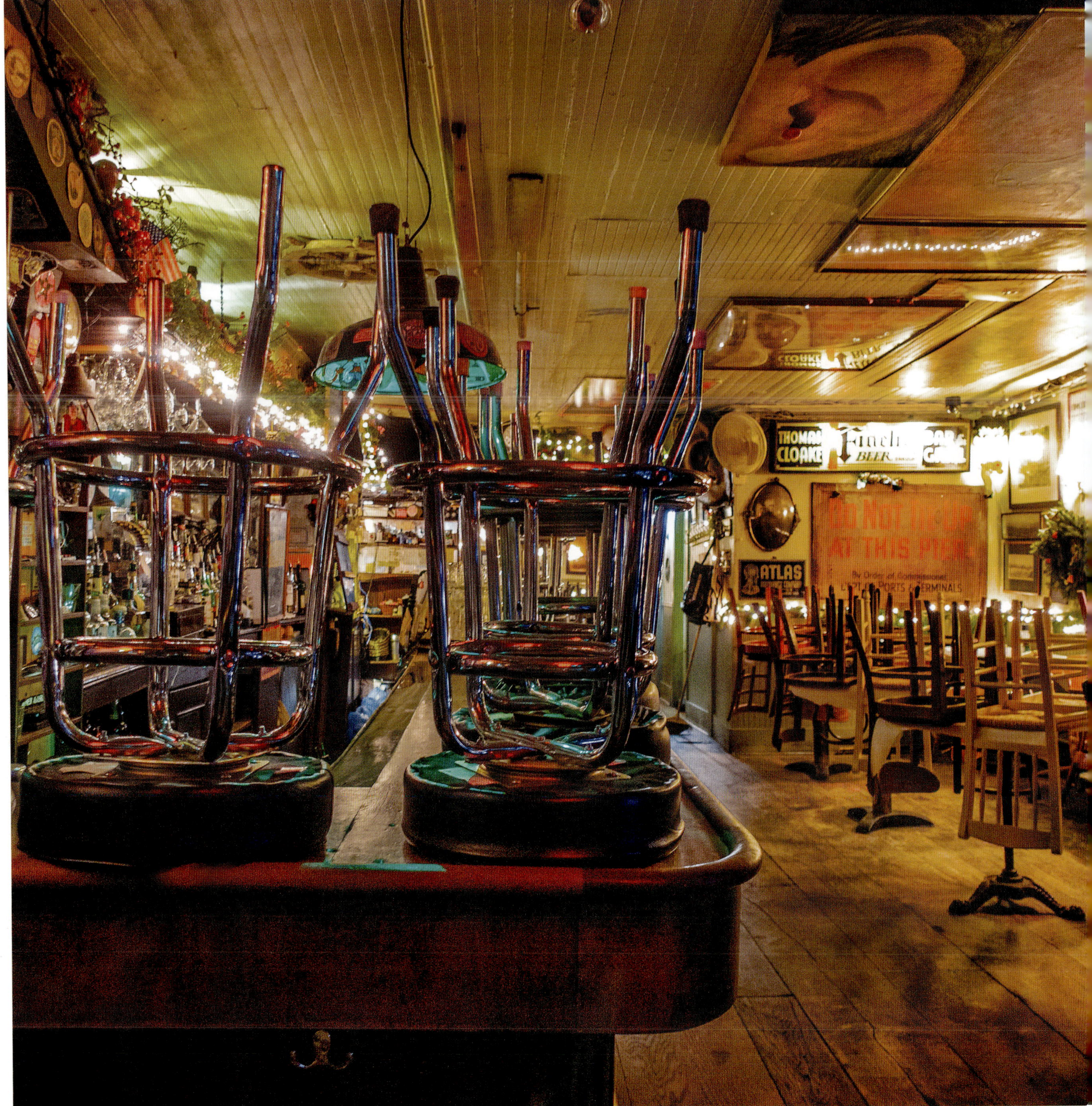

Ear Inn

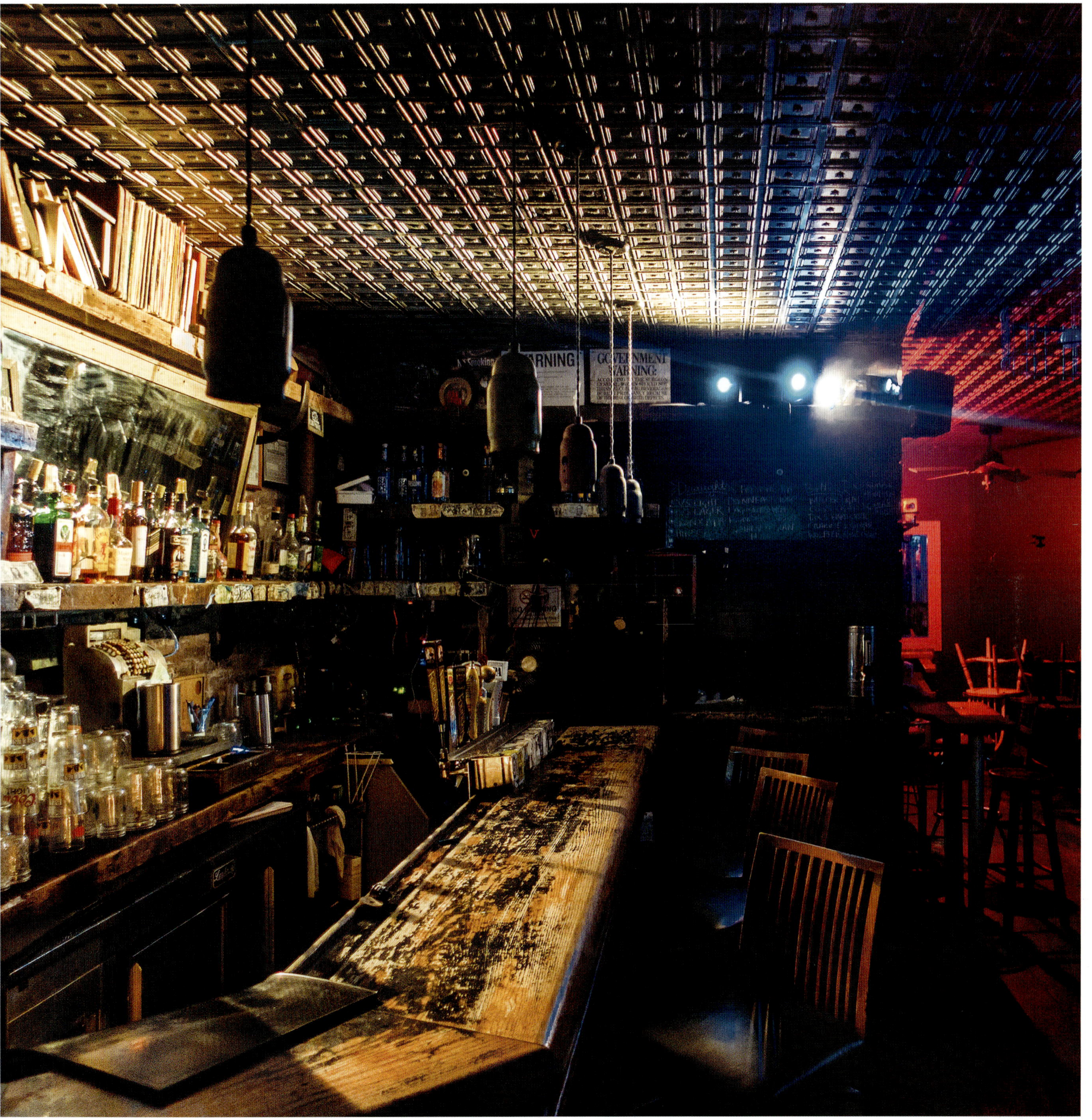

East Village Social

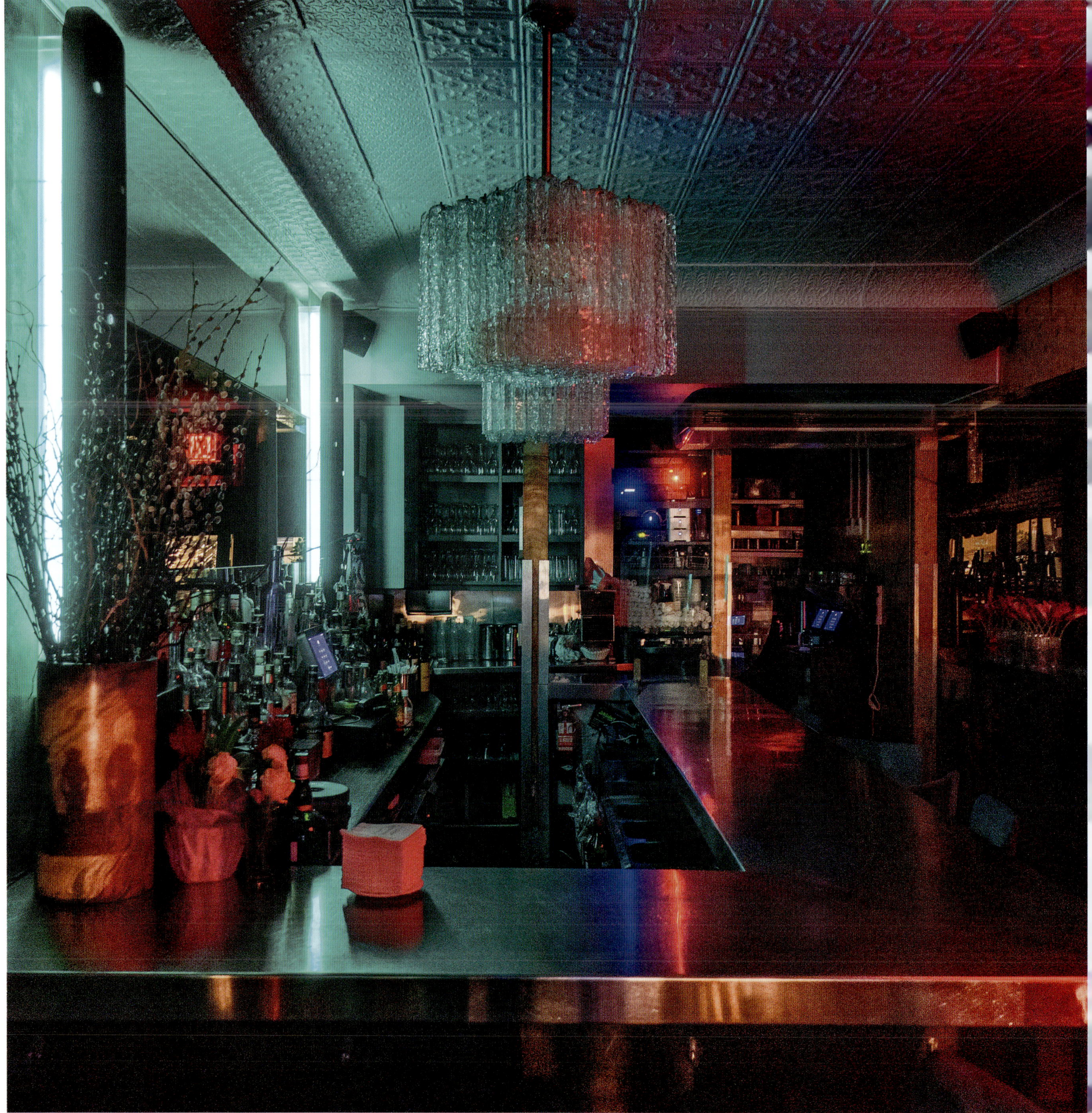

Extra Virgin

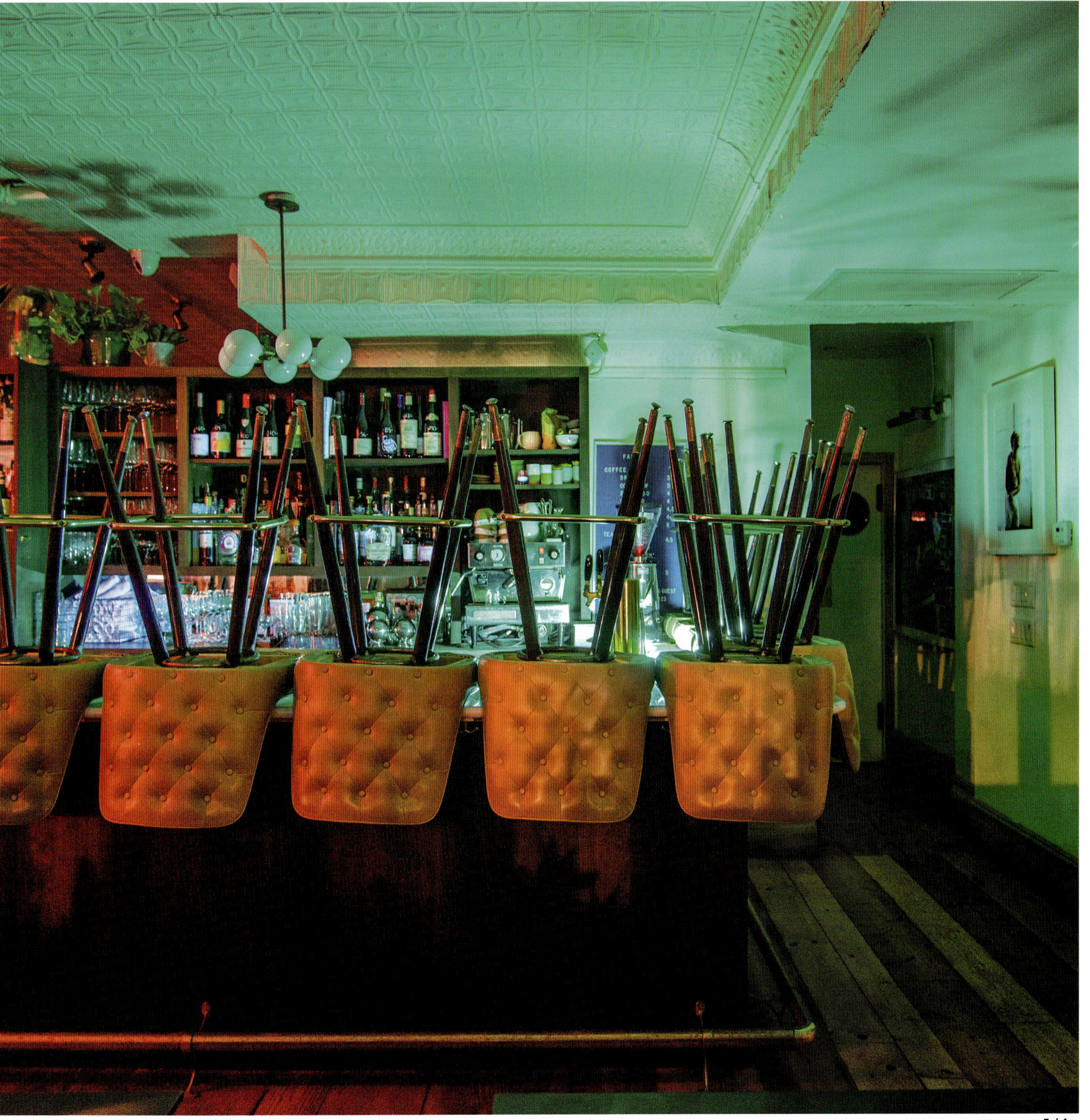

Fairfax

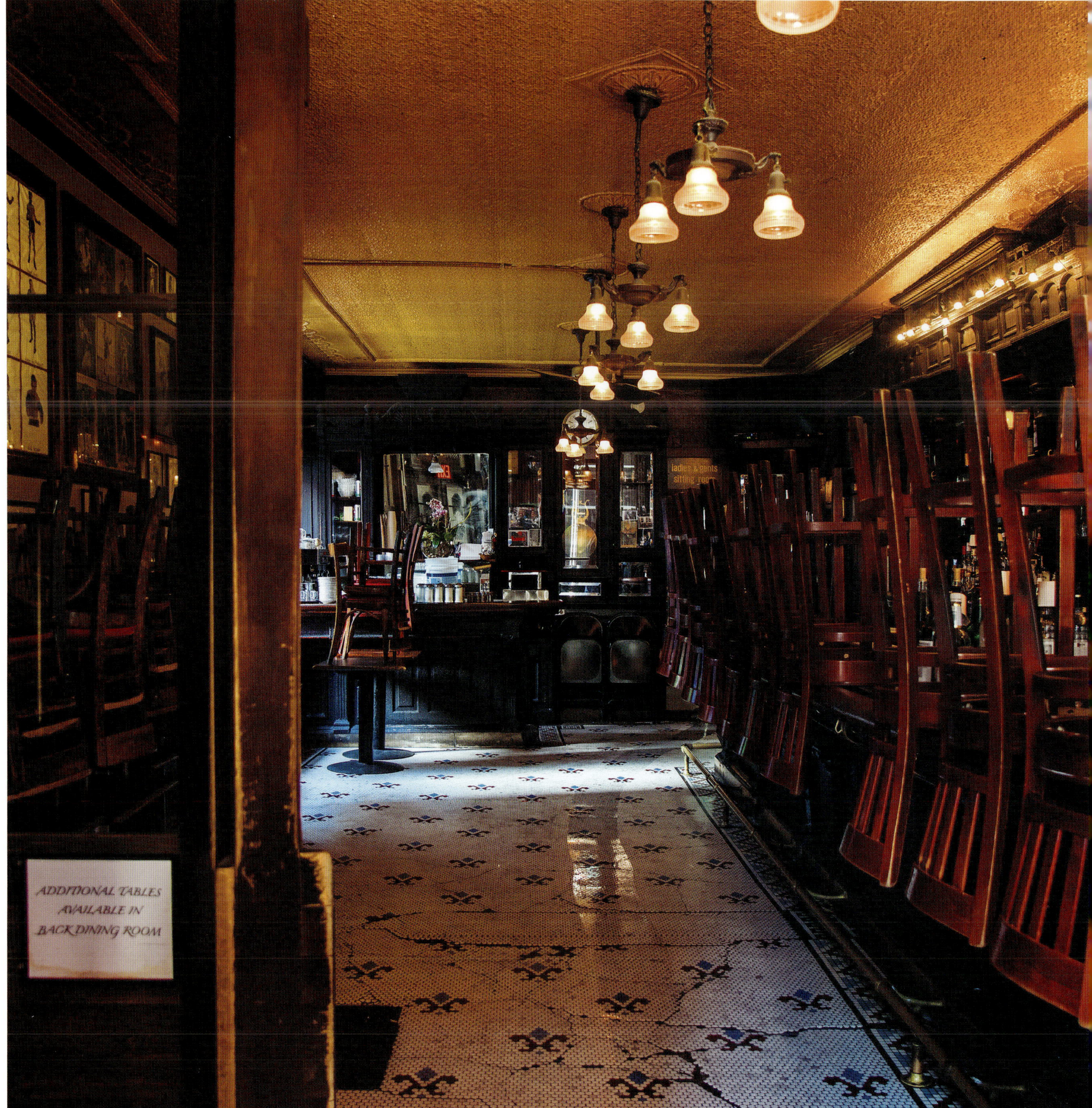

Fanelli Cafe

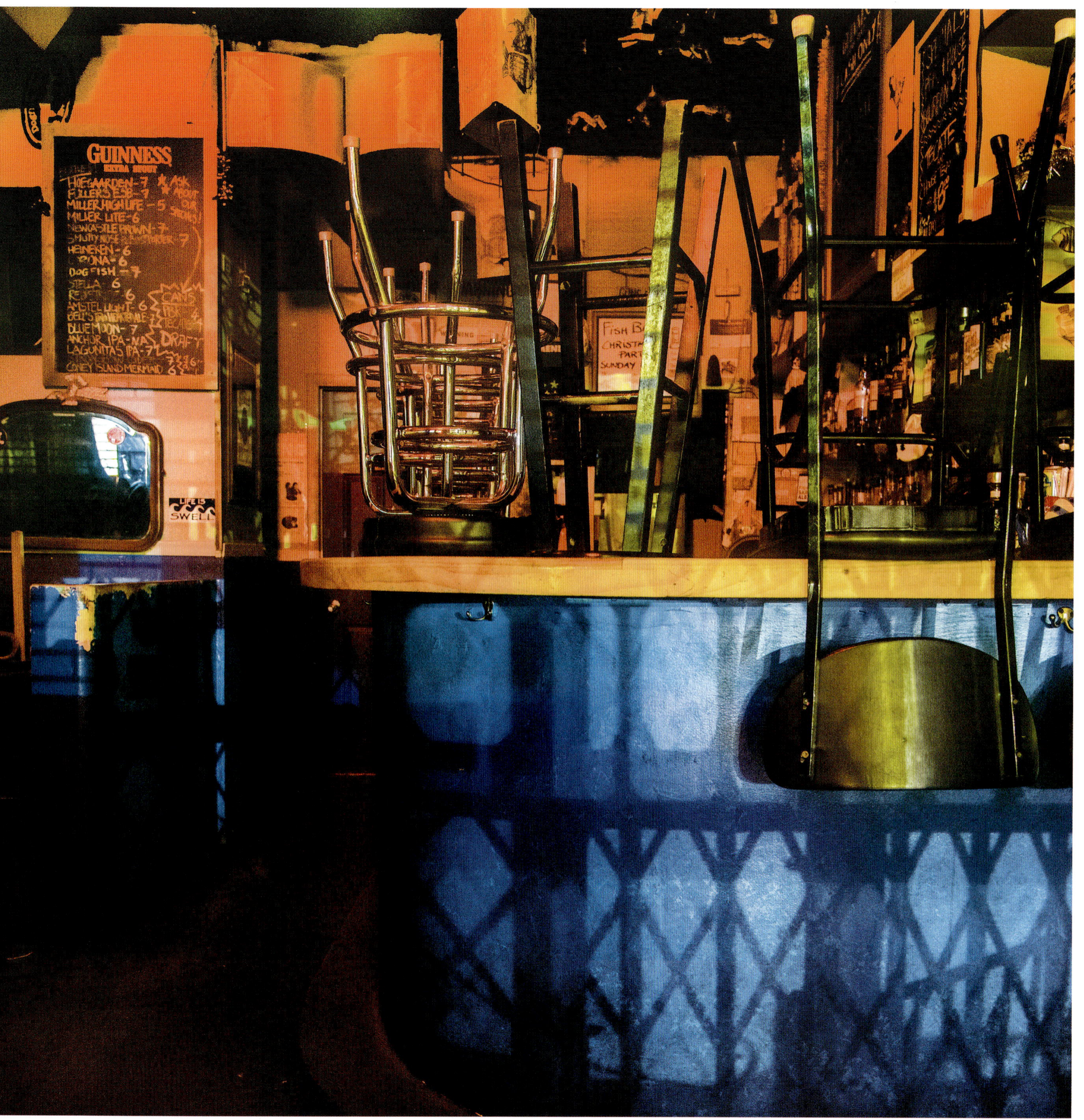

Fish Bar

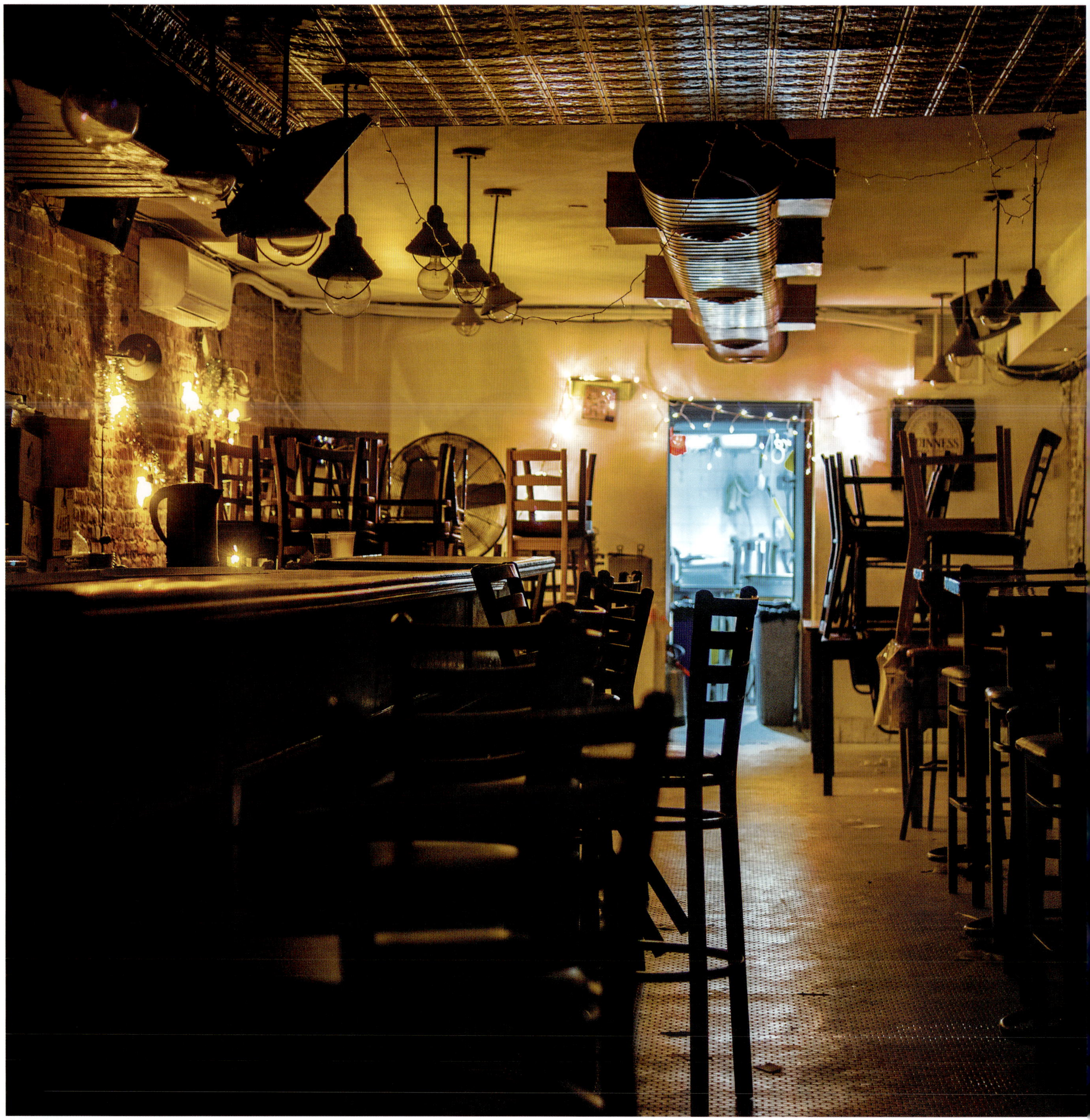

Fishmarket

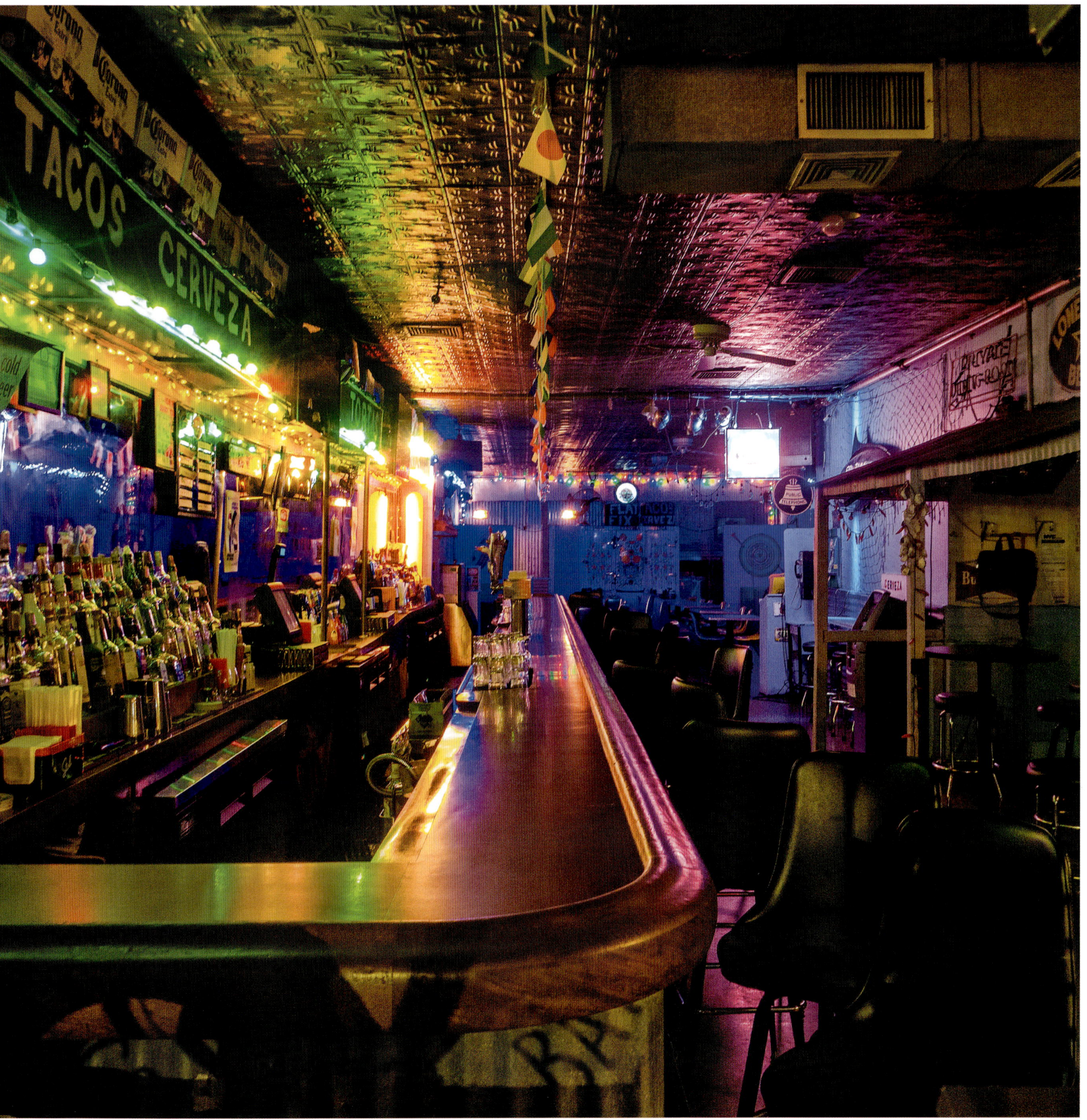

TACOS
CERVEZA
Corona

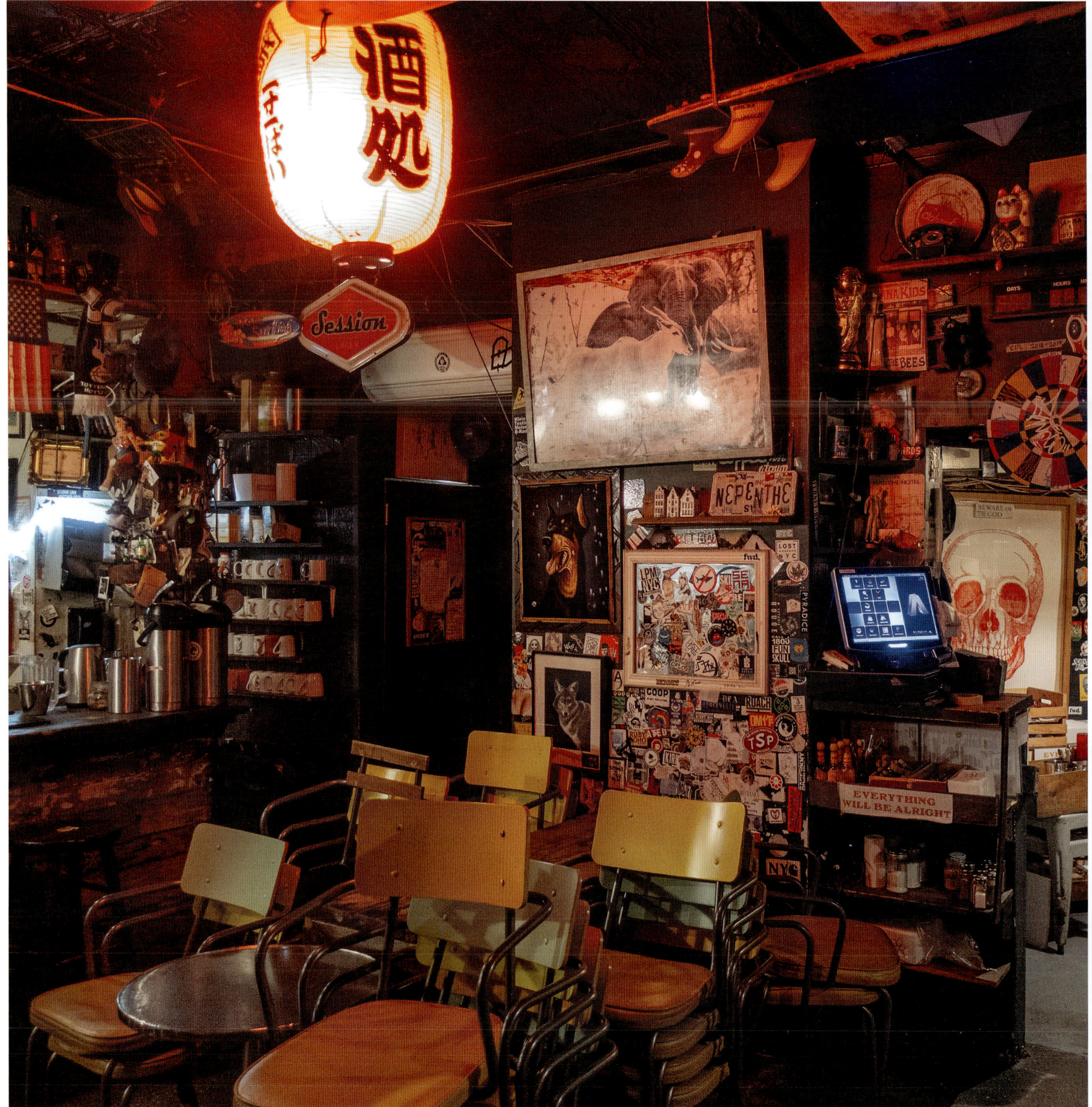

FMN General Store

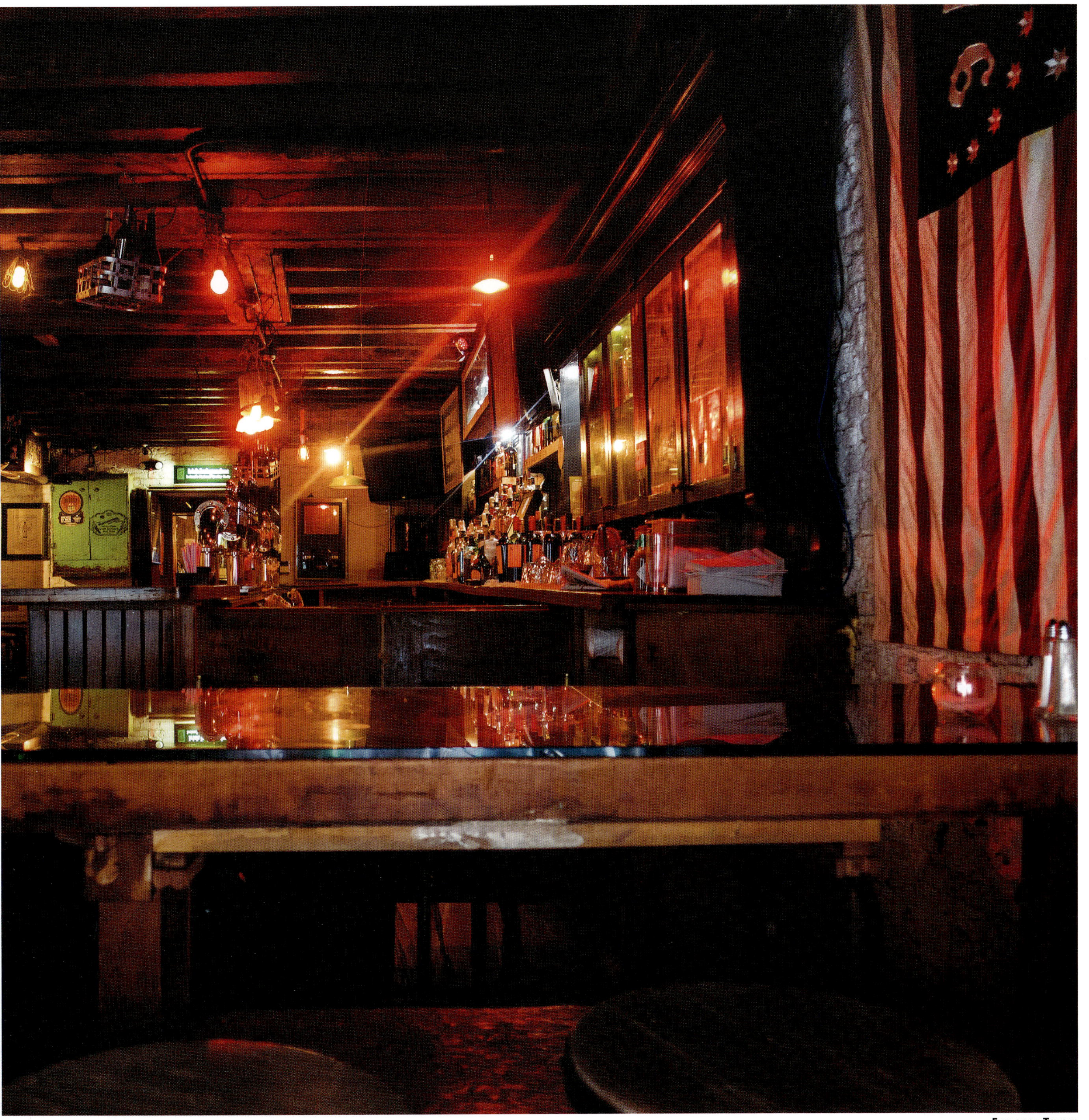

Fraunces Tavern

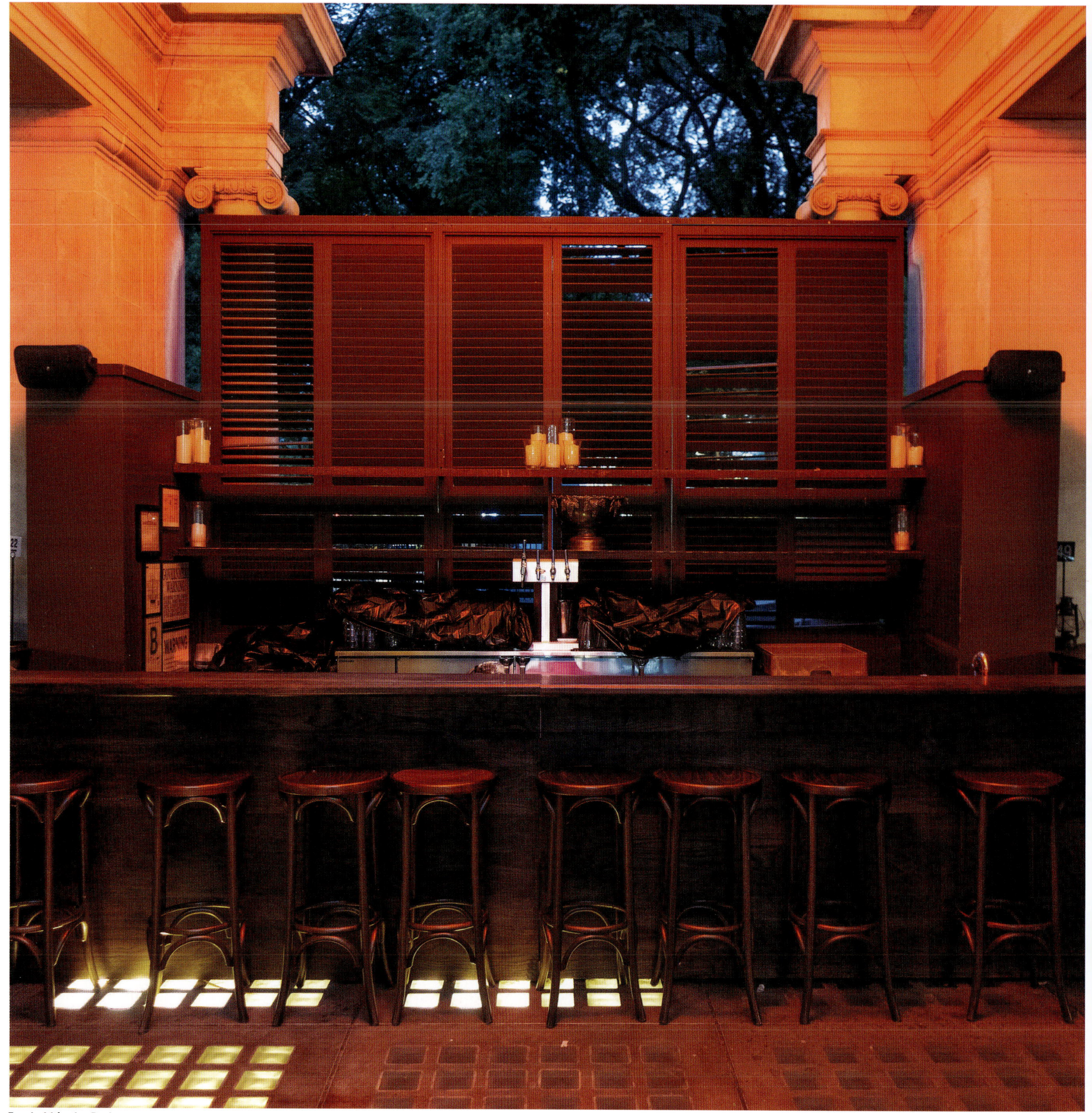

Freehold in the Park

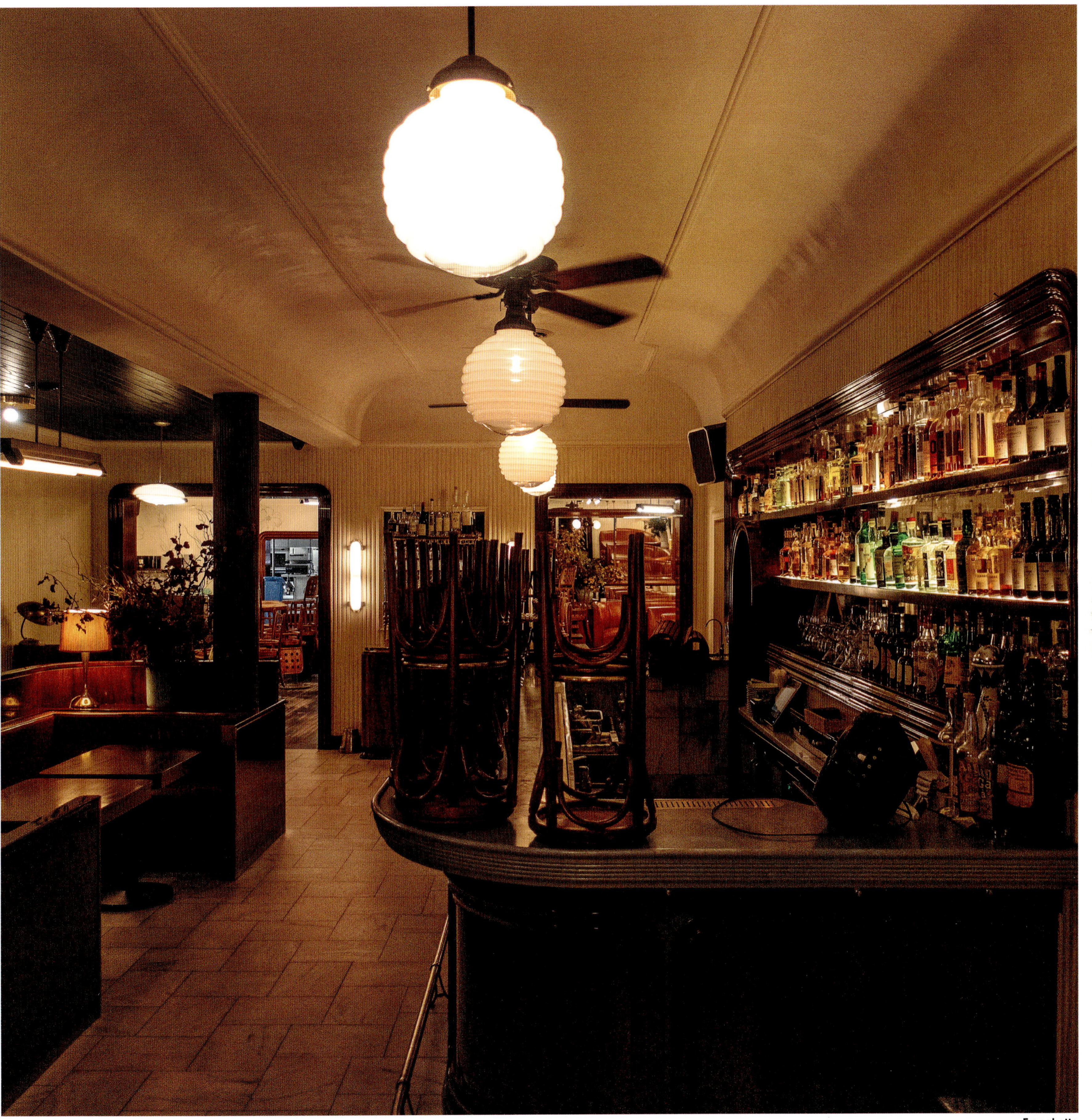

Frenchette

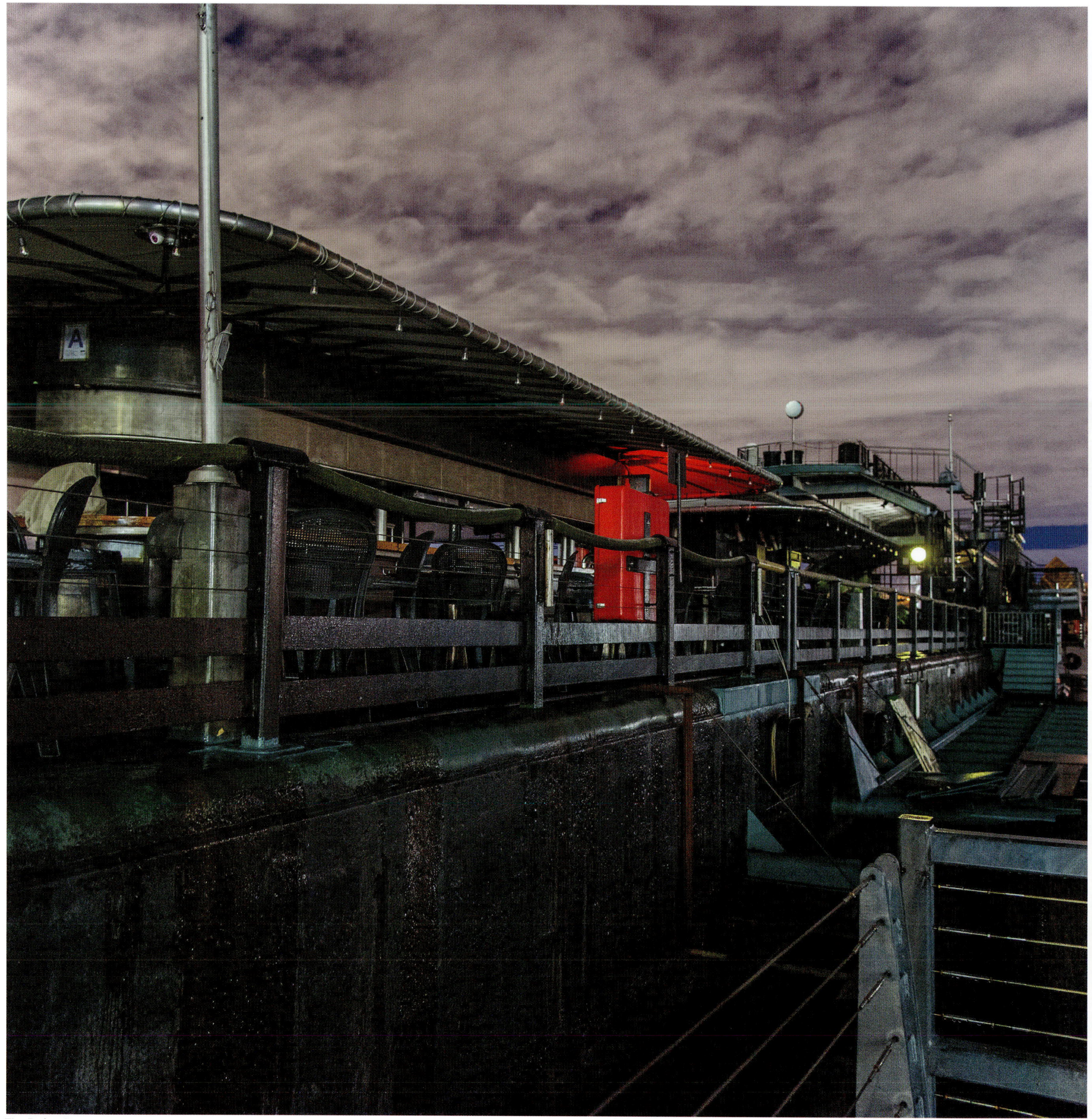

The Frying Pan

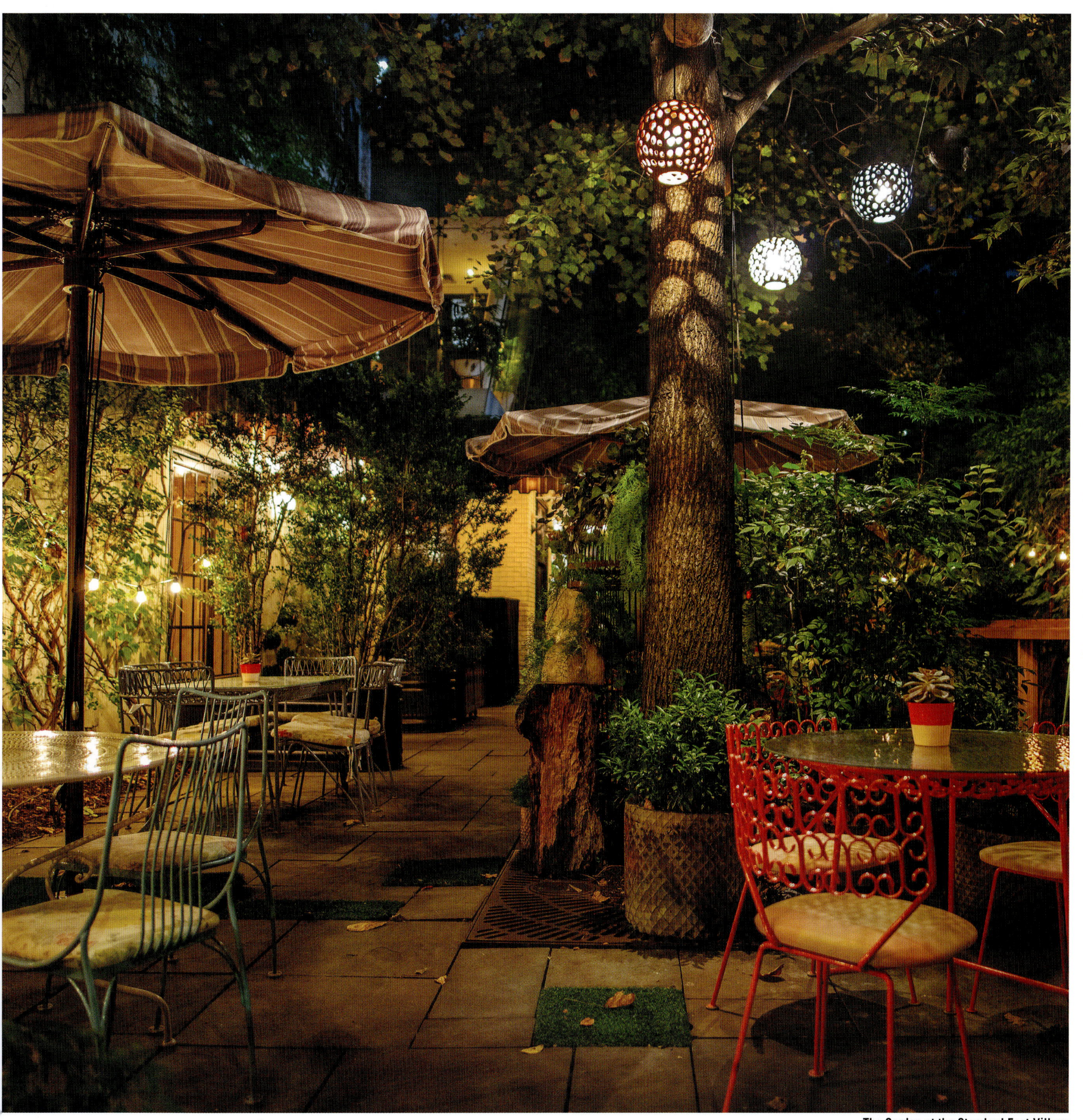

The Garden at the Standard East Village

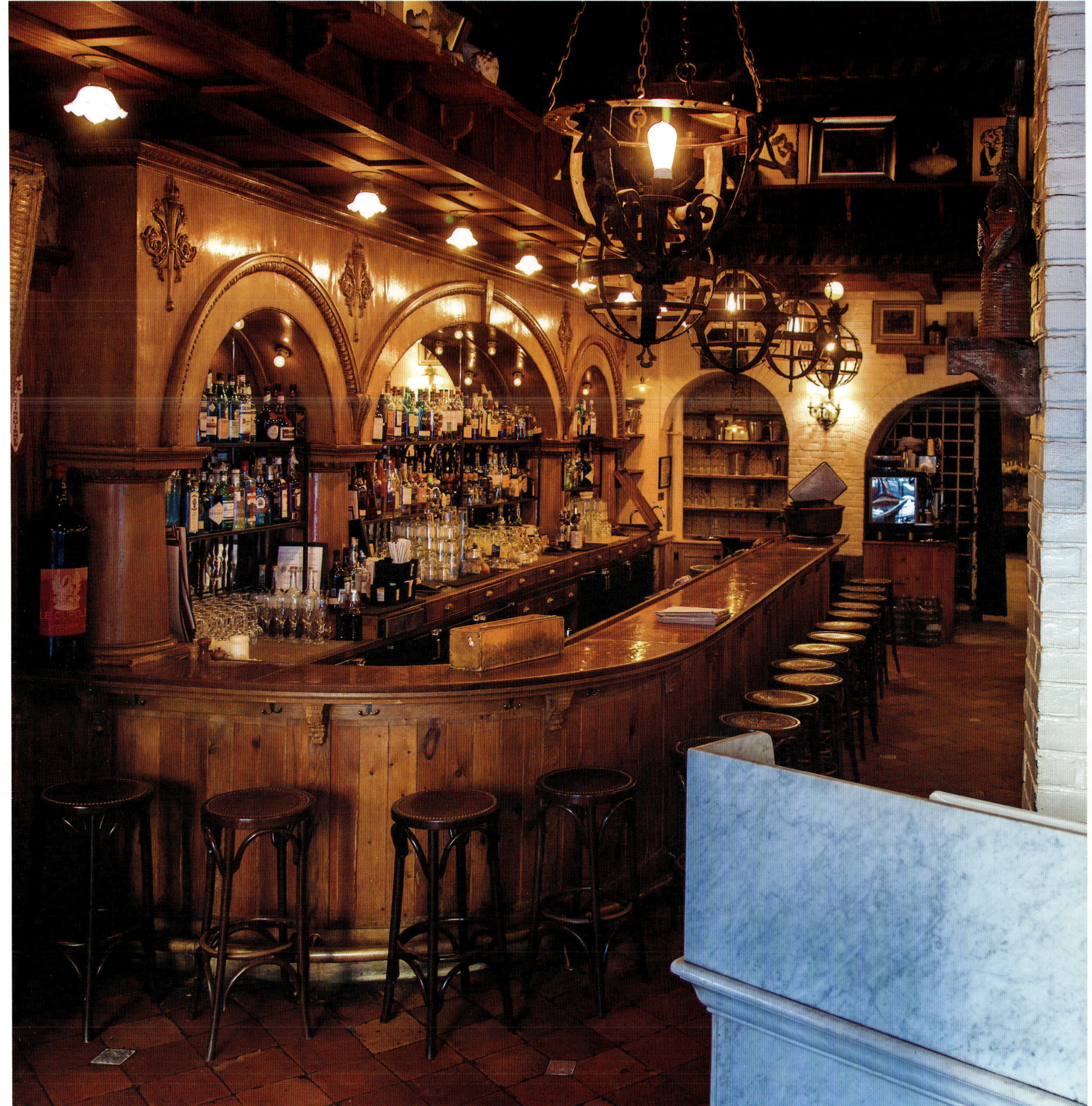

Gemma

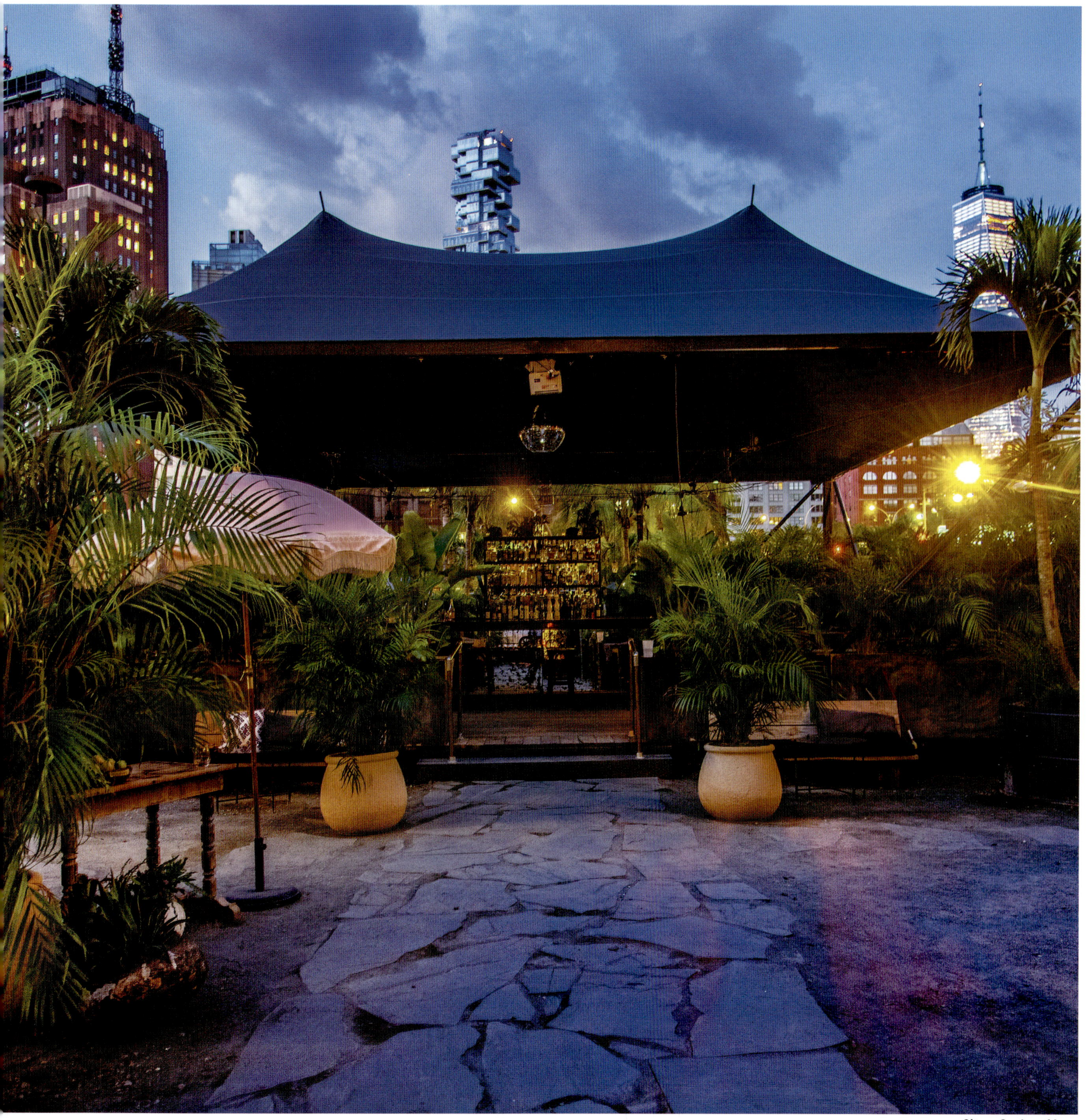

Gitano Garden of Love

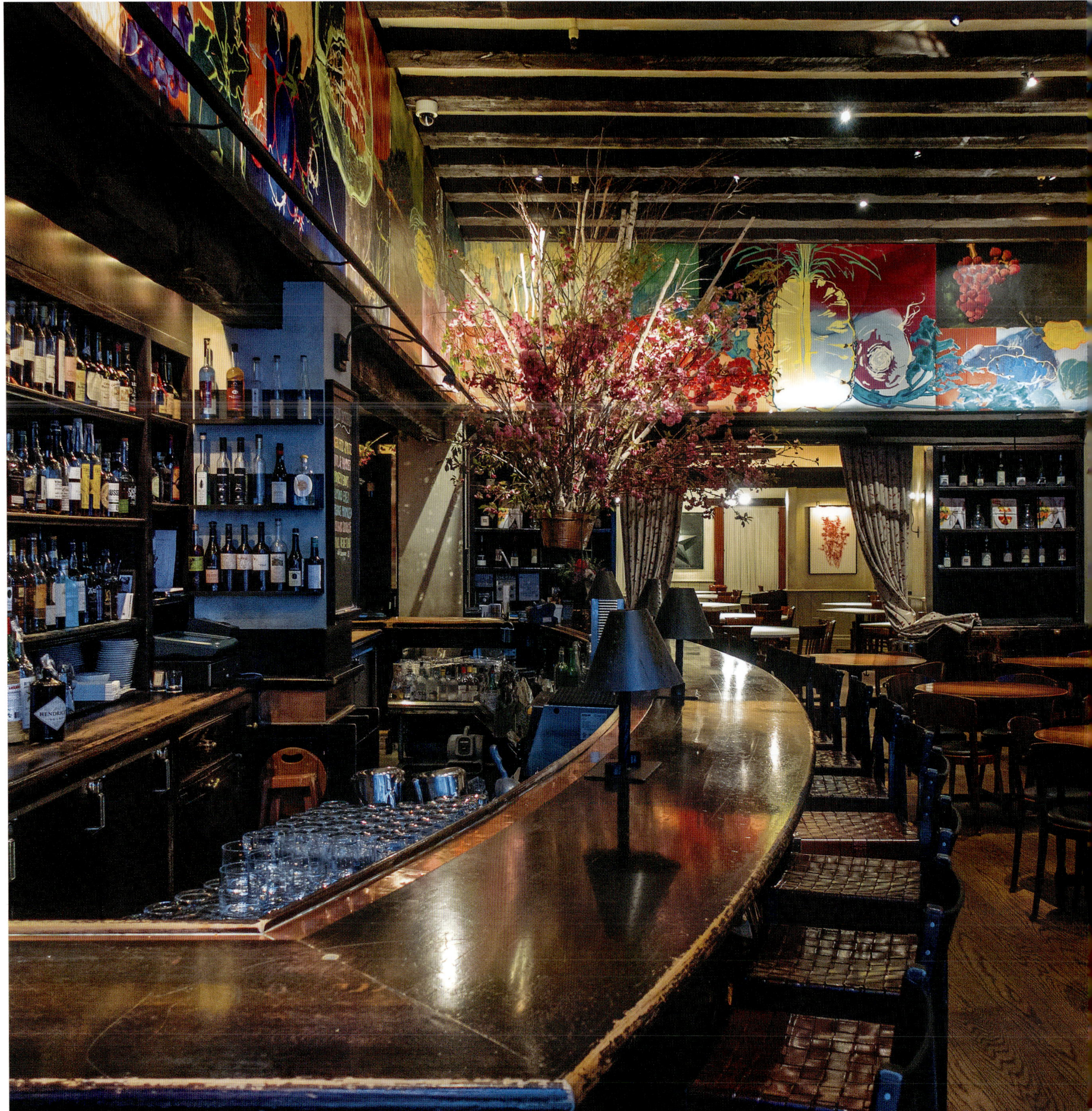

Gramercy Tavern

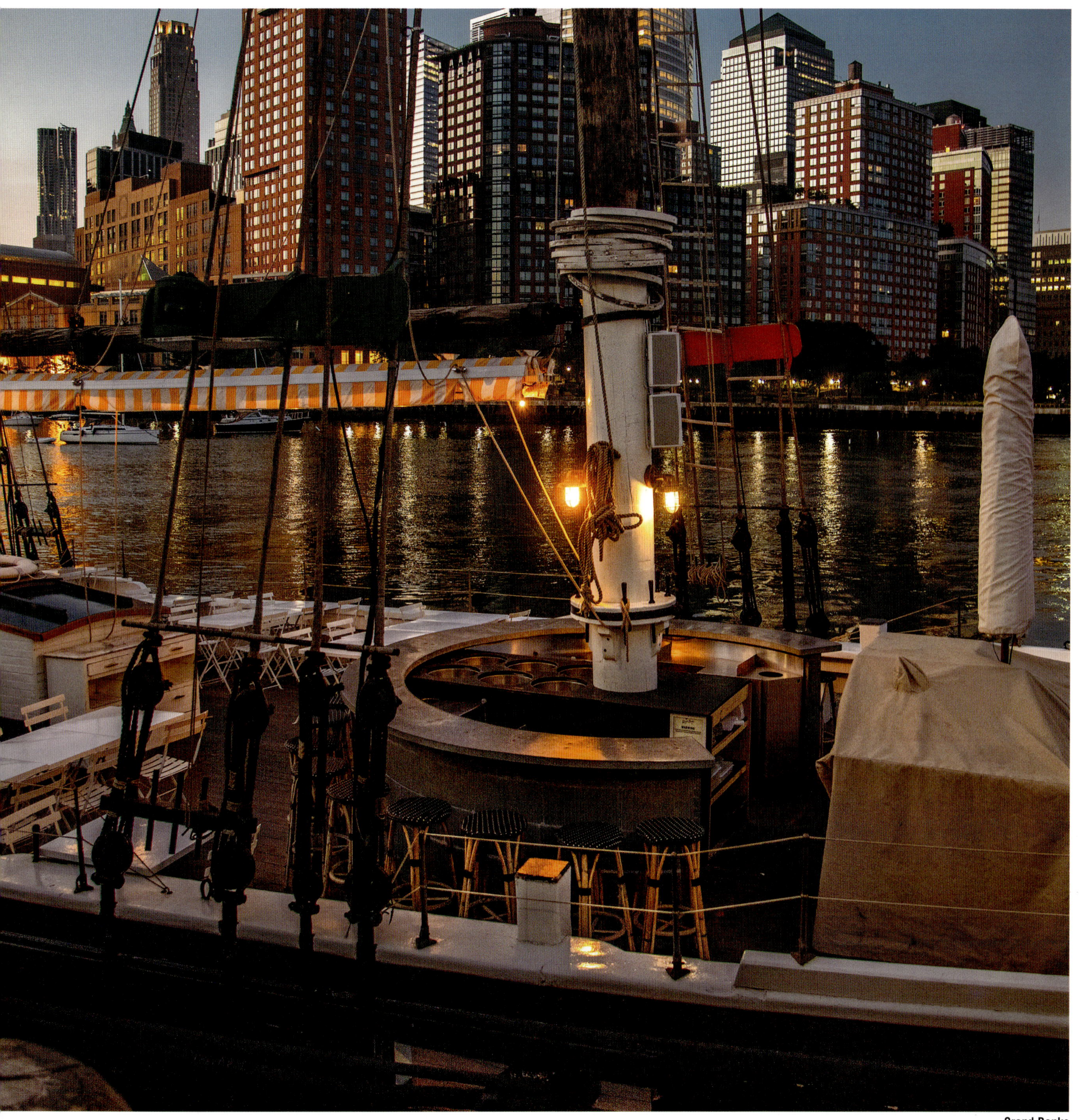

Grand Banks

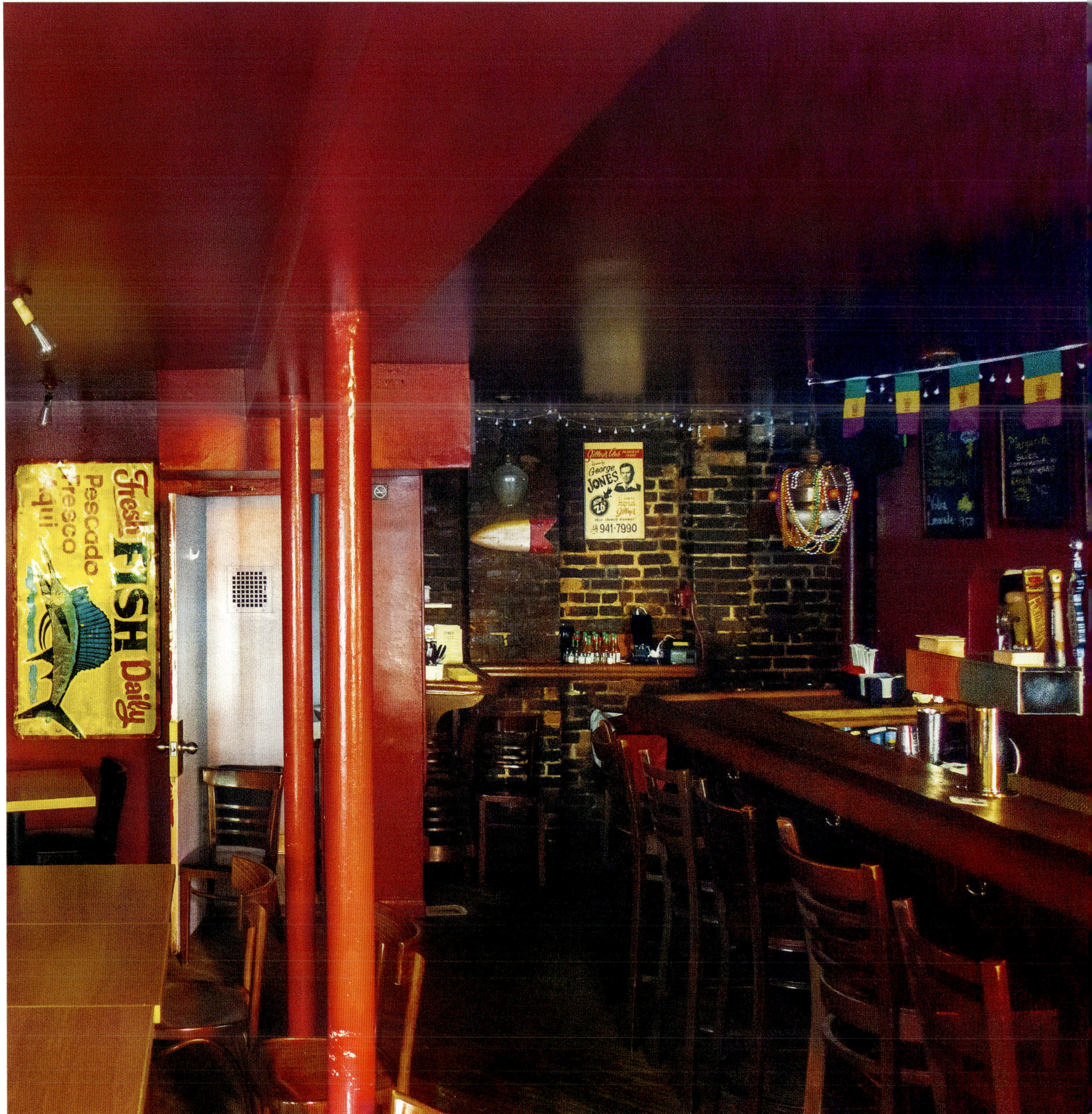

Great Jones Cafe

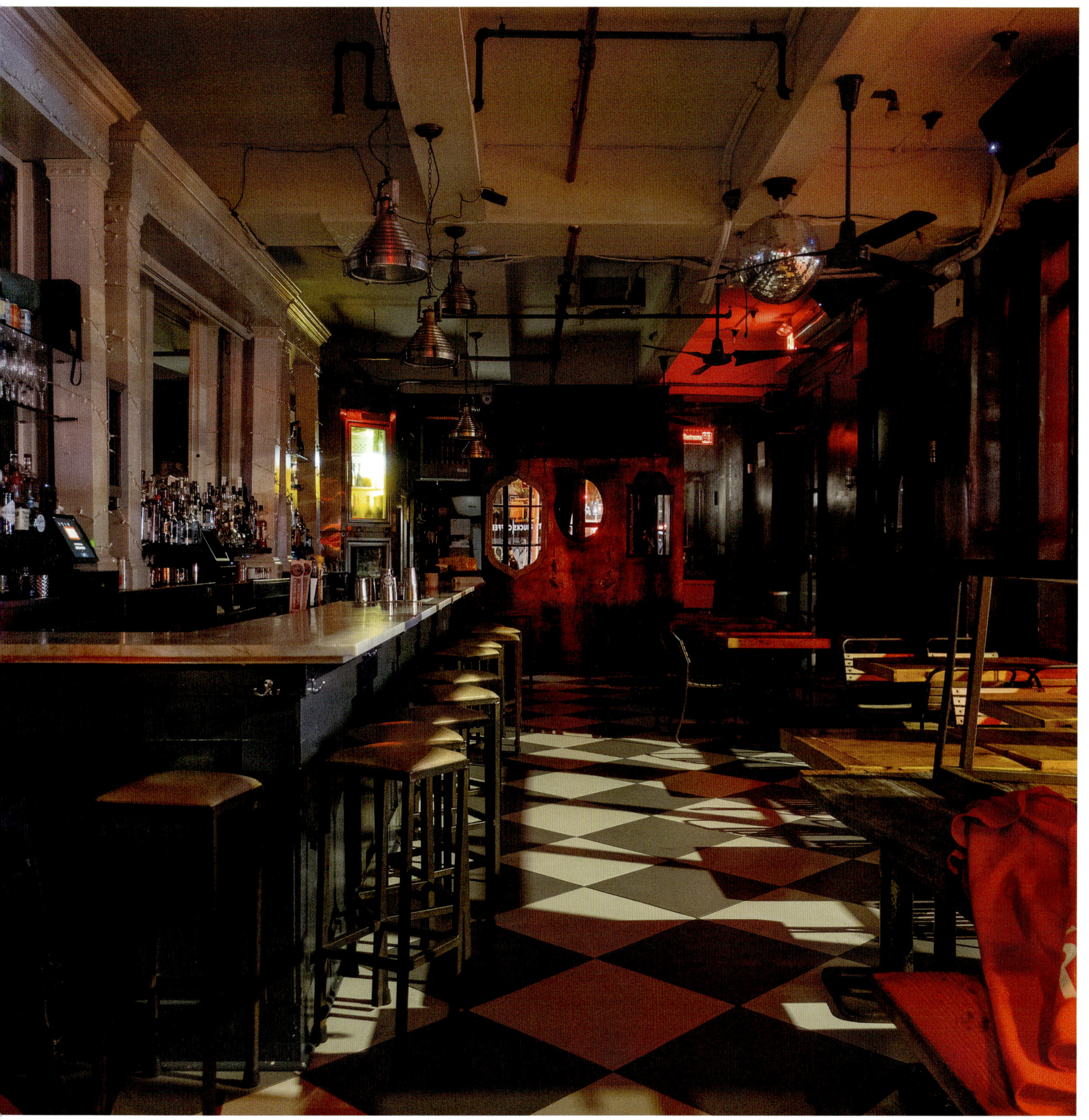

Grey Lady

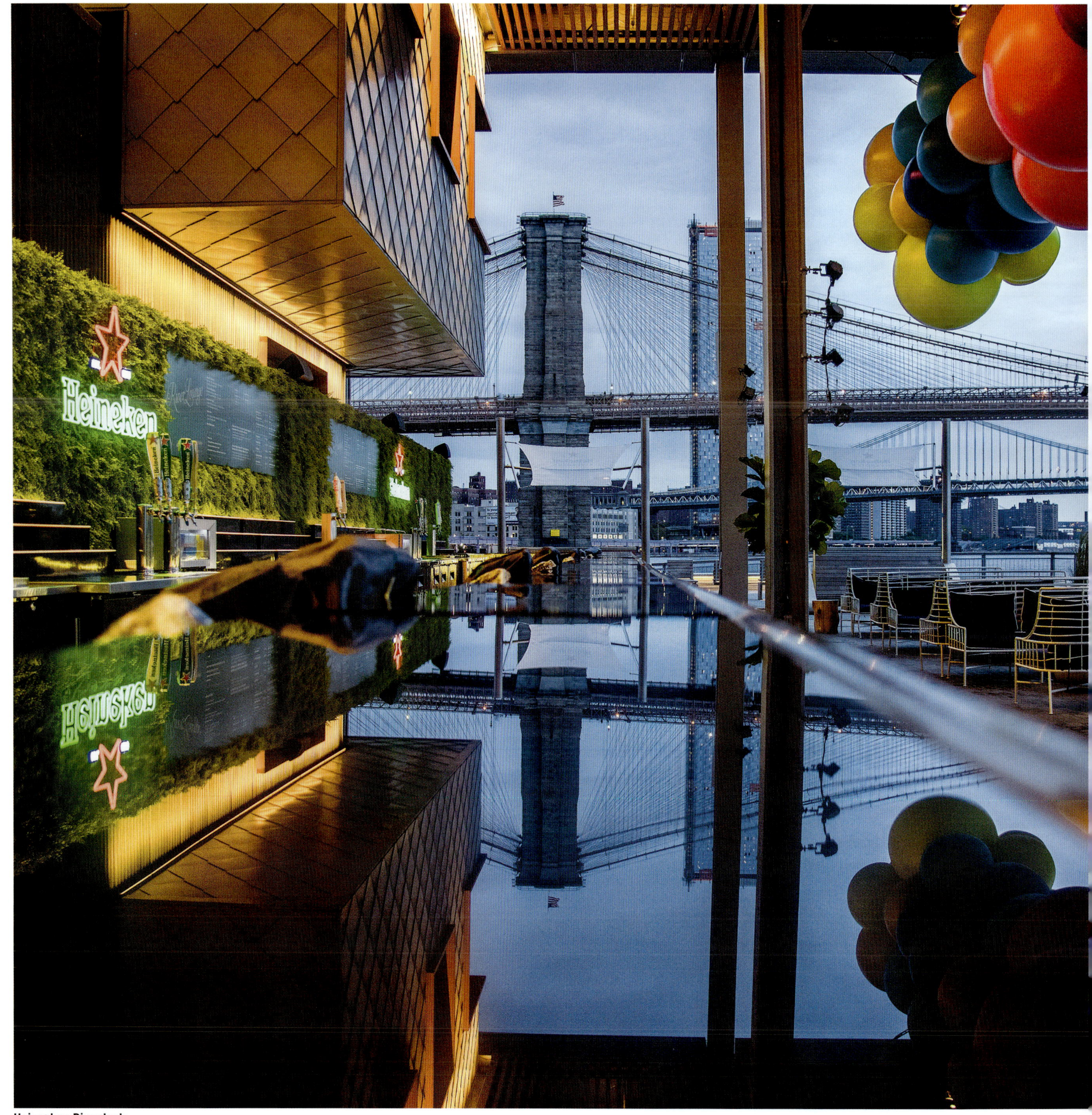

Heinecken Riverdeck

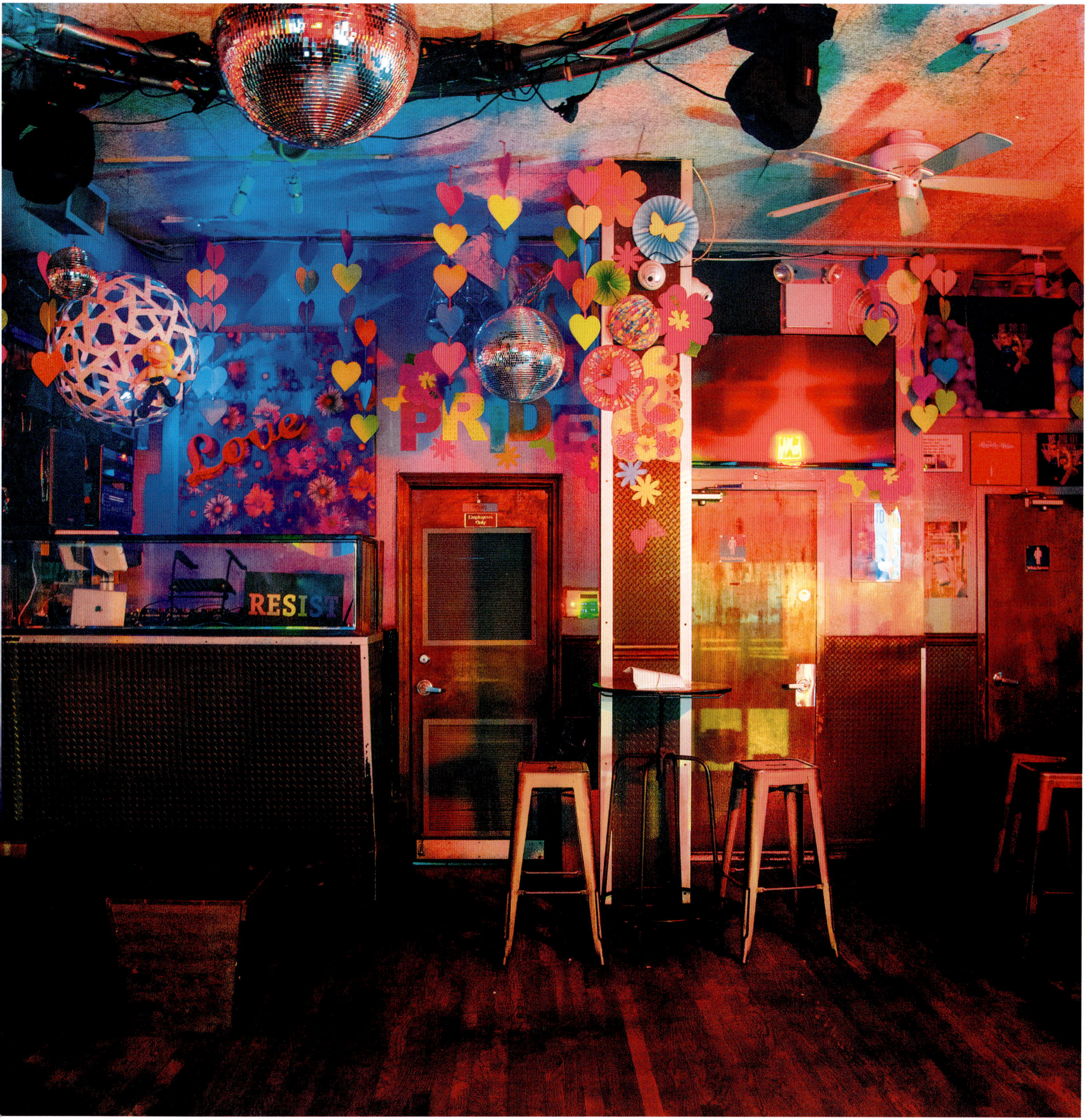

Henrietta Hudson

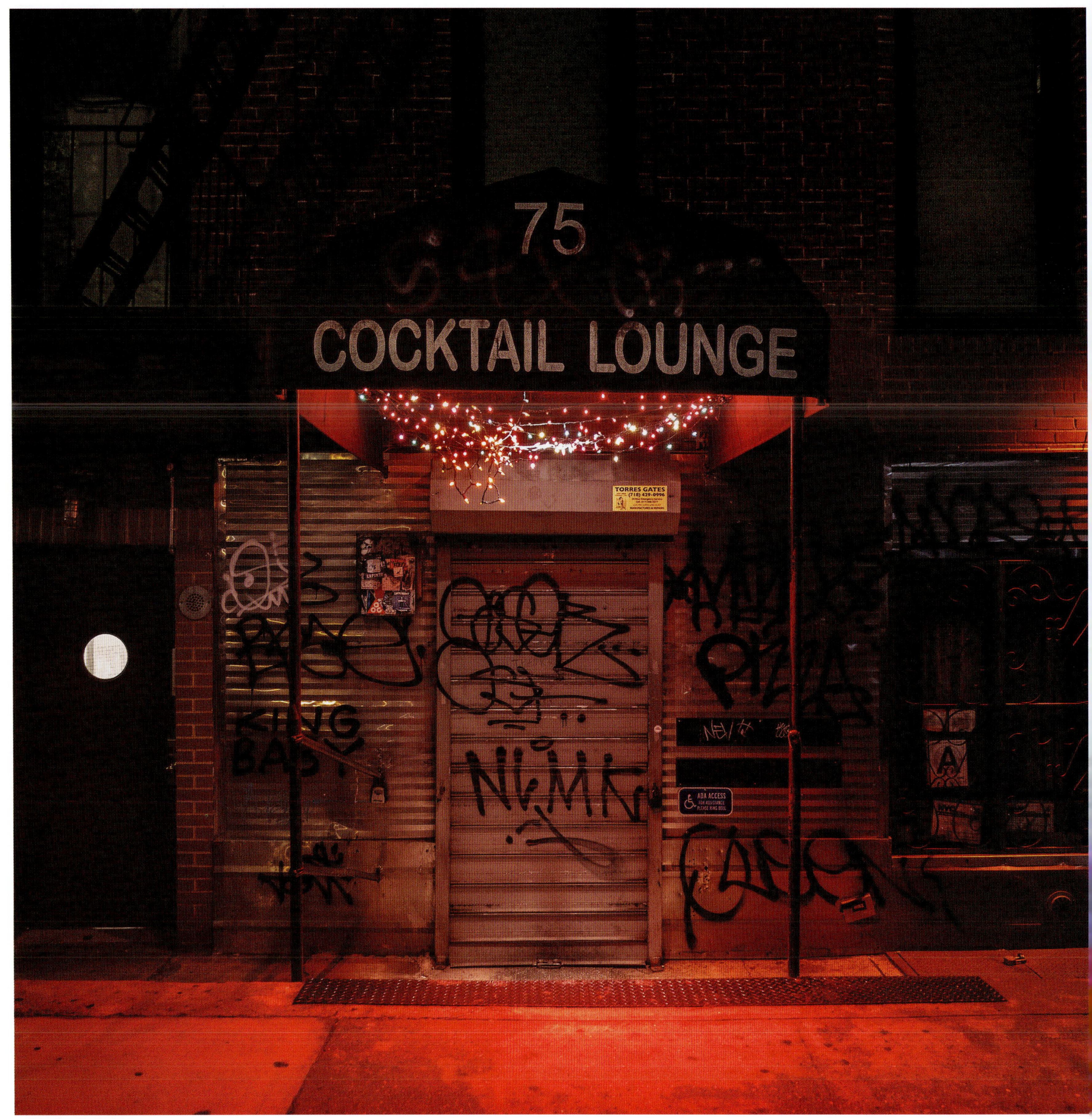

Holiday Cocktail Lounge

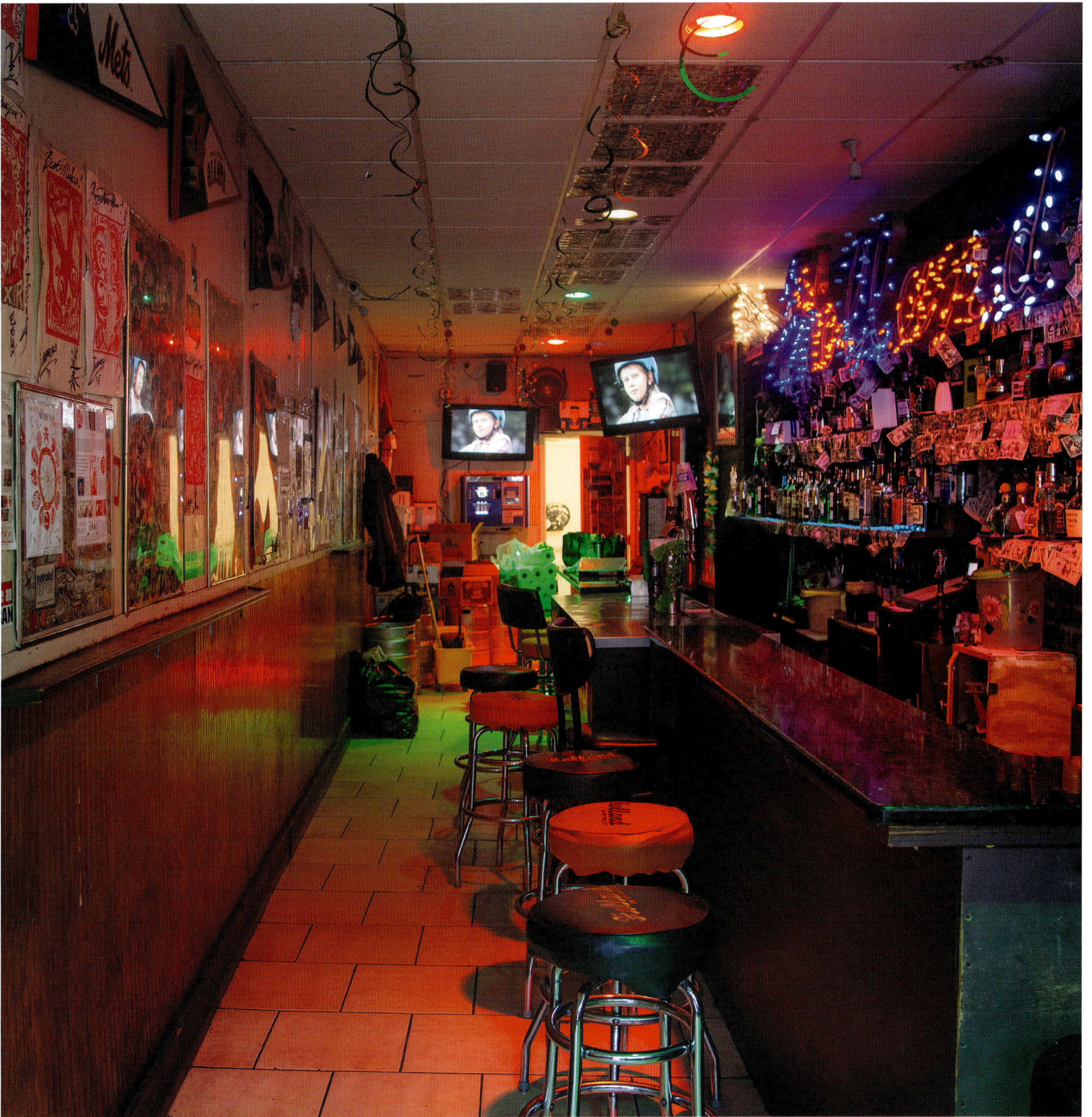

Holland Bar

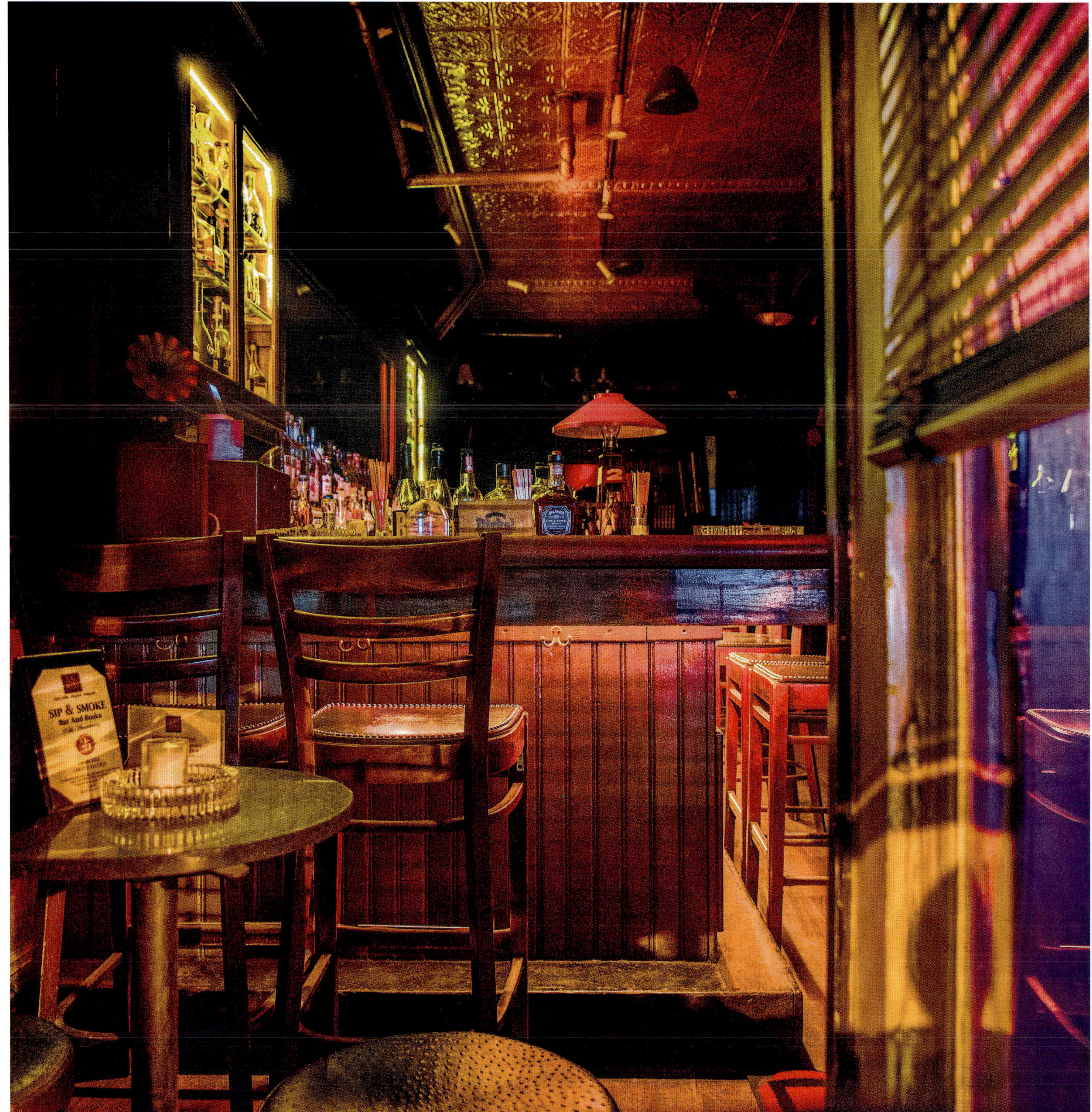

Hudson Bar and Books

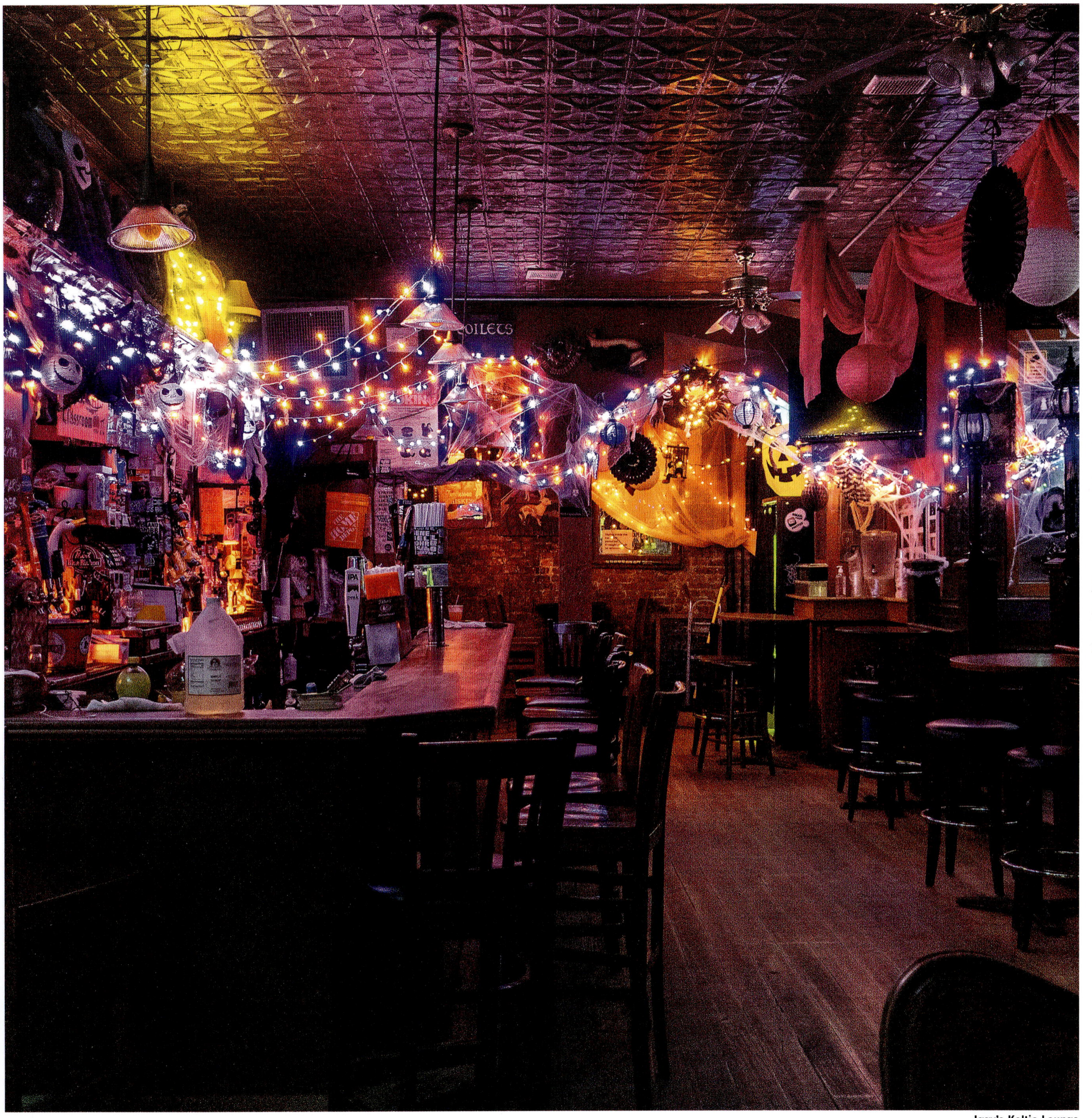

Iggy's Keltic Lounge

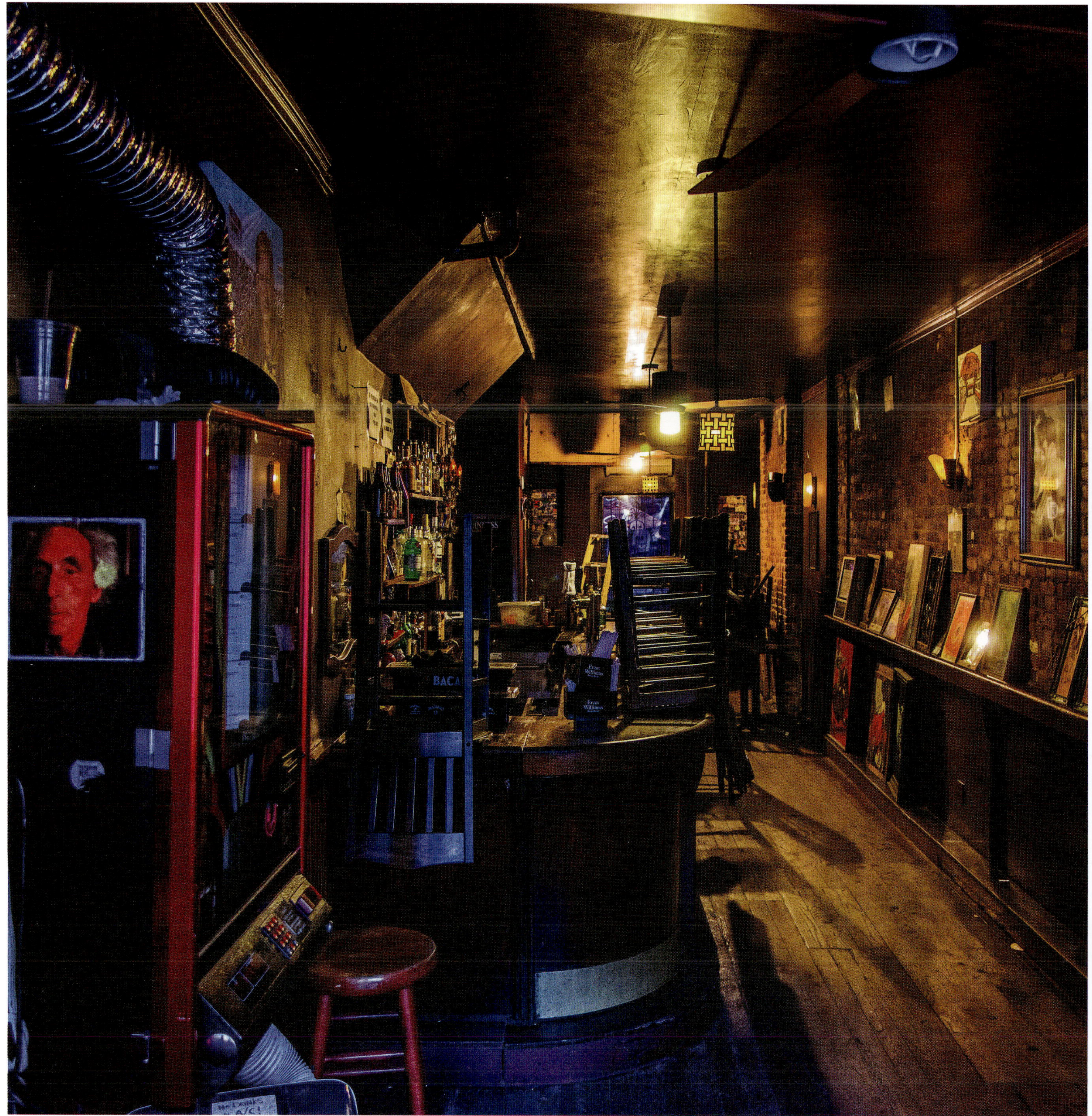

International Bar

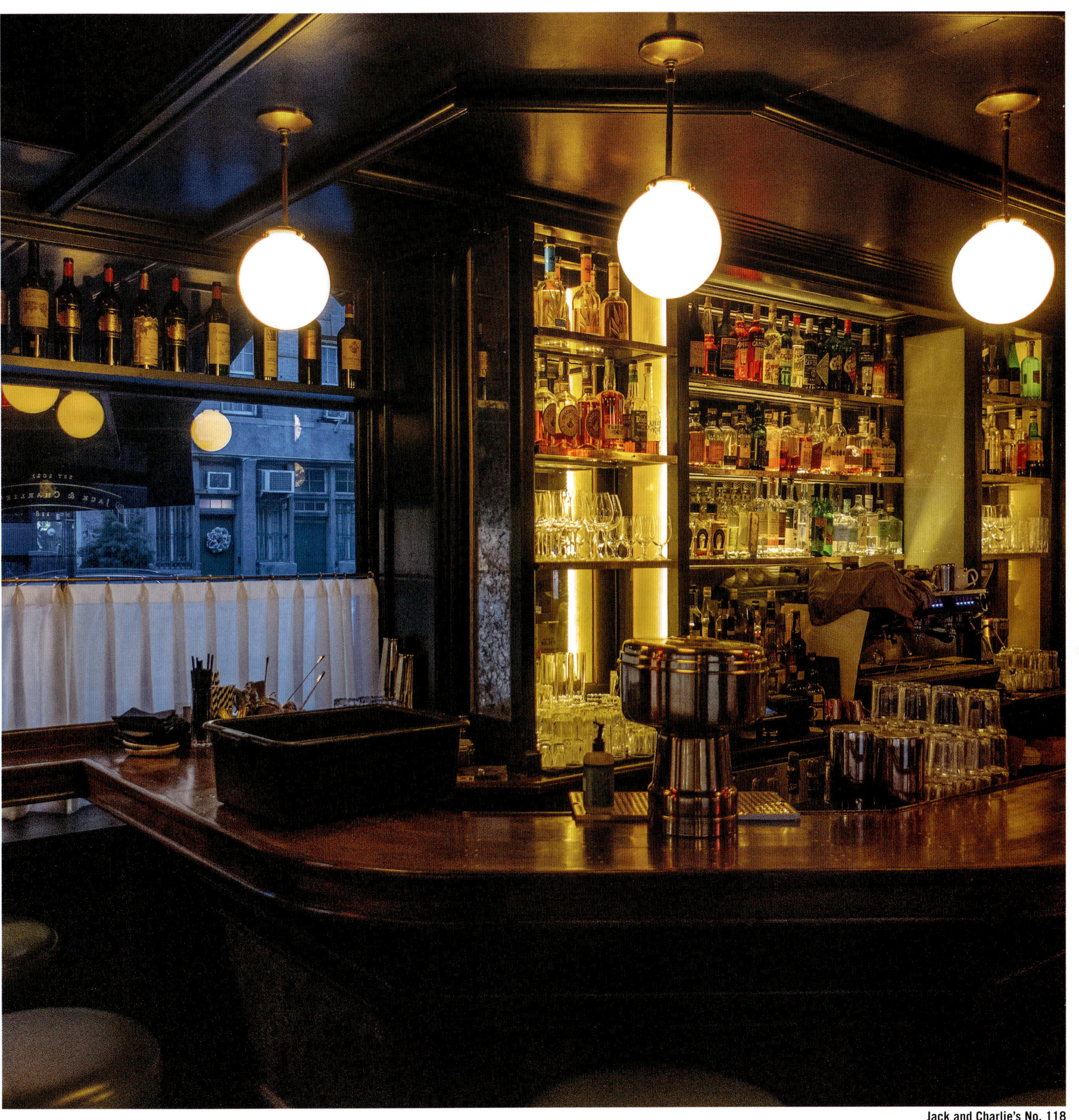

Jack and Charlie's No. 118

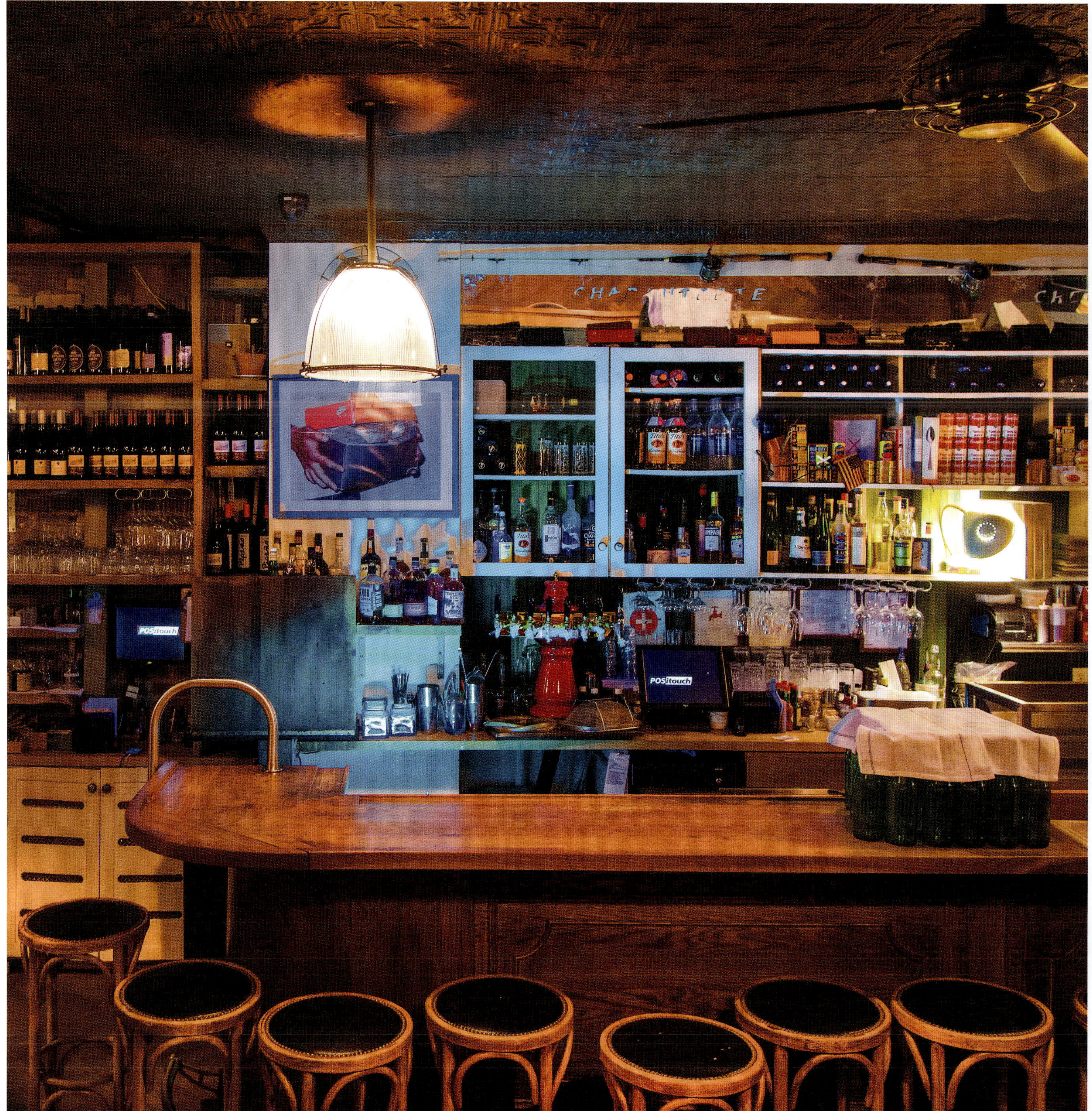

Jeffrey's Grocery

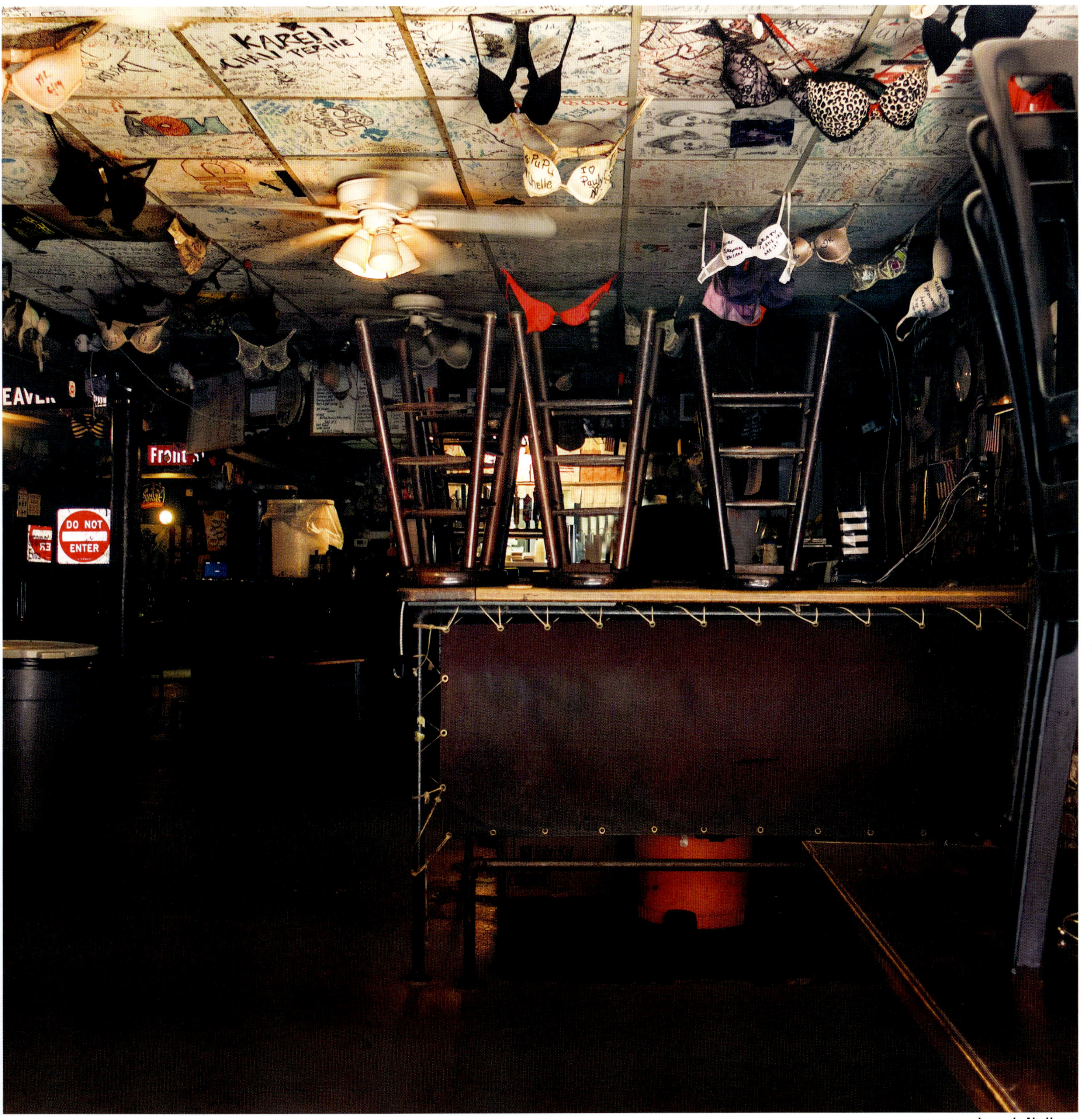

Jeremy's Ale House

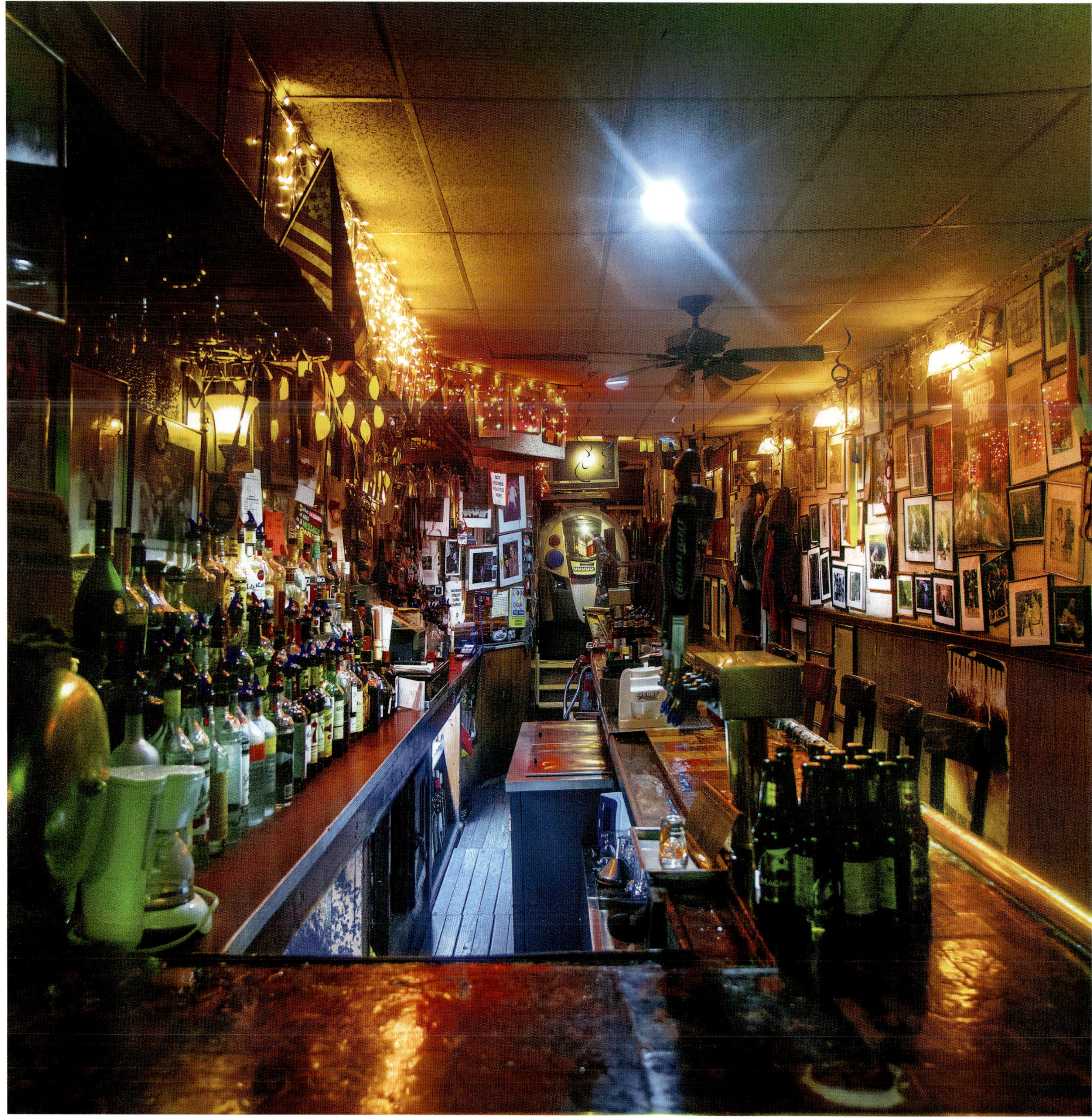

Jimmy's Corner

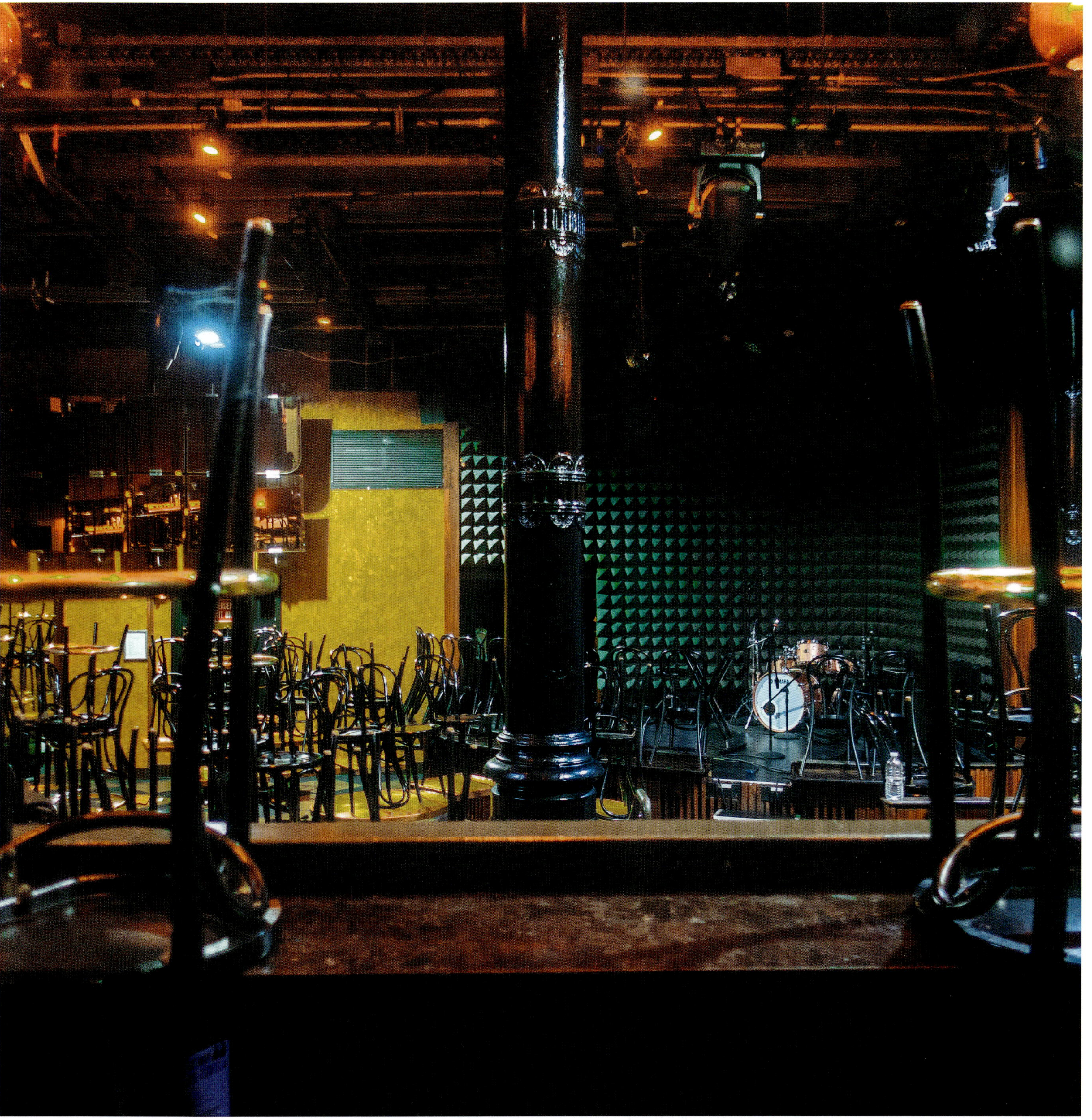

Joe's Pub

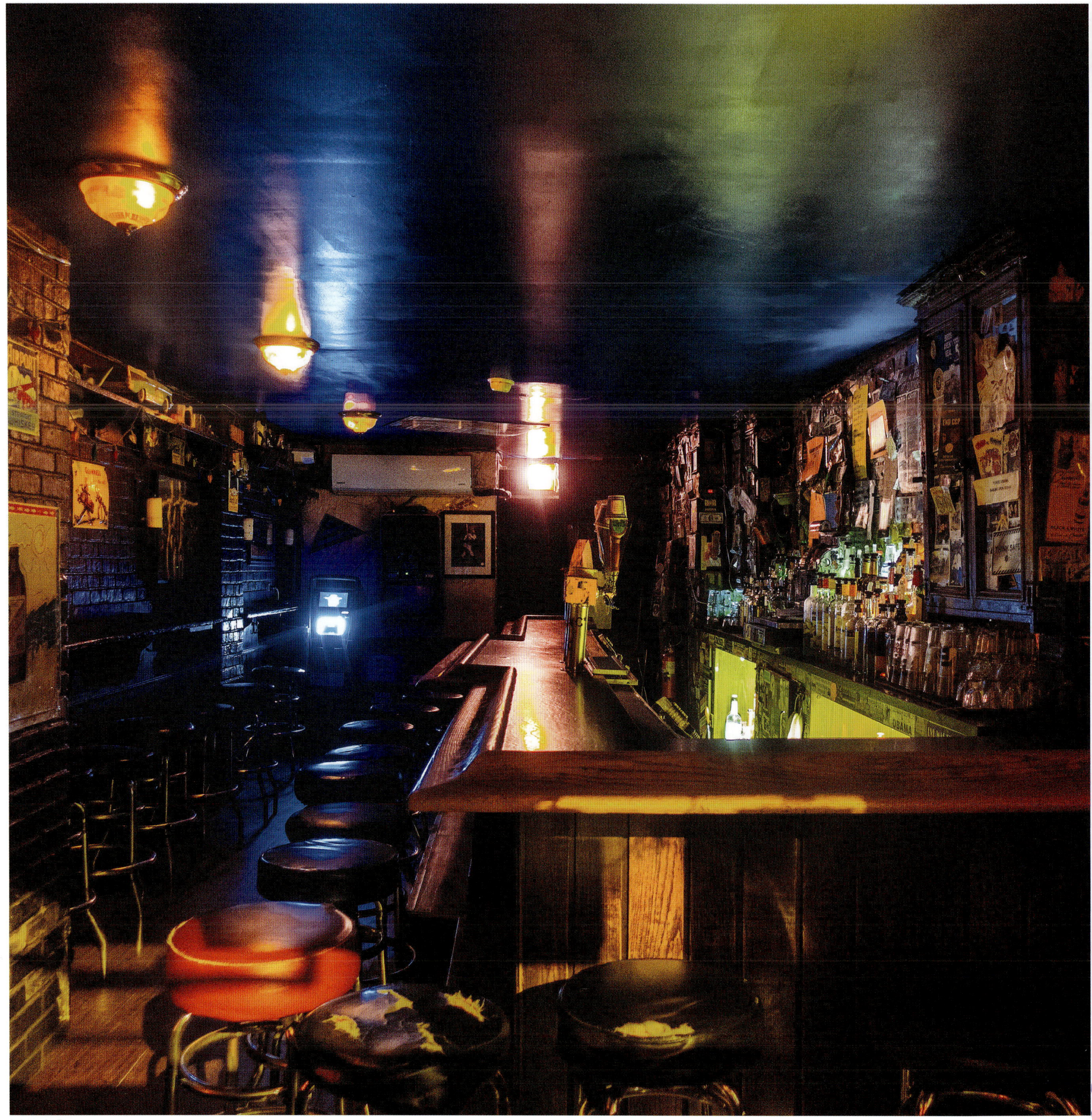

Johnny's Bar

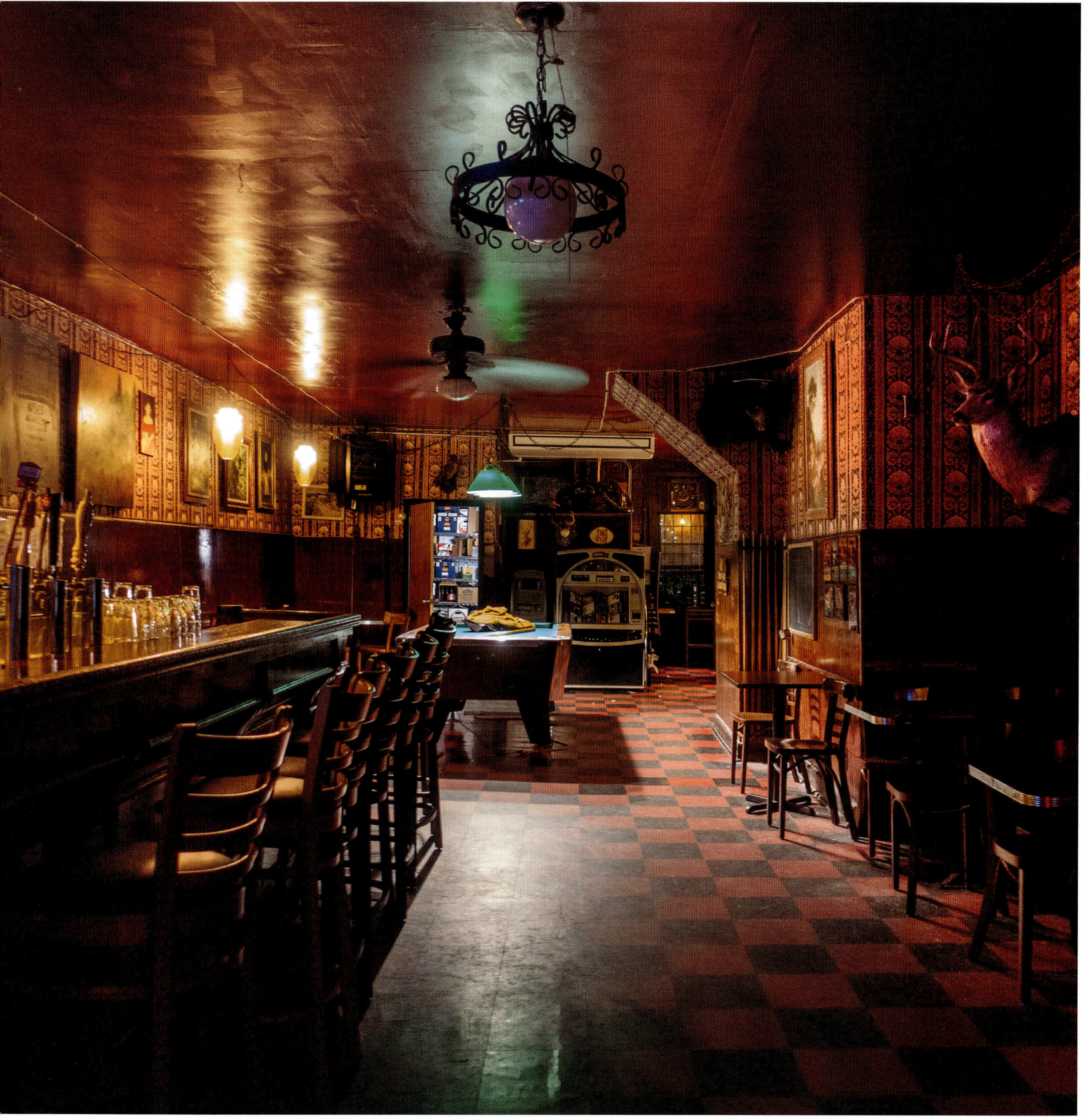

Josie's

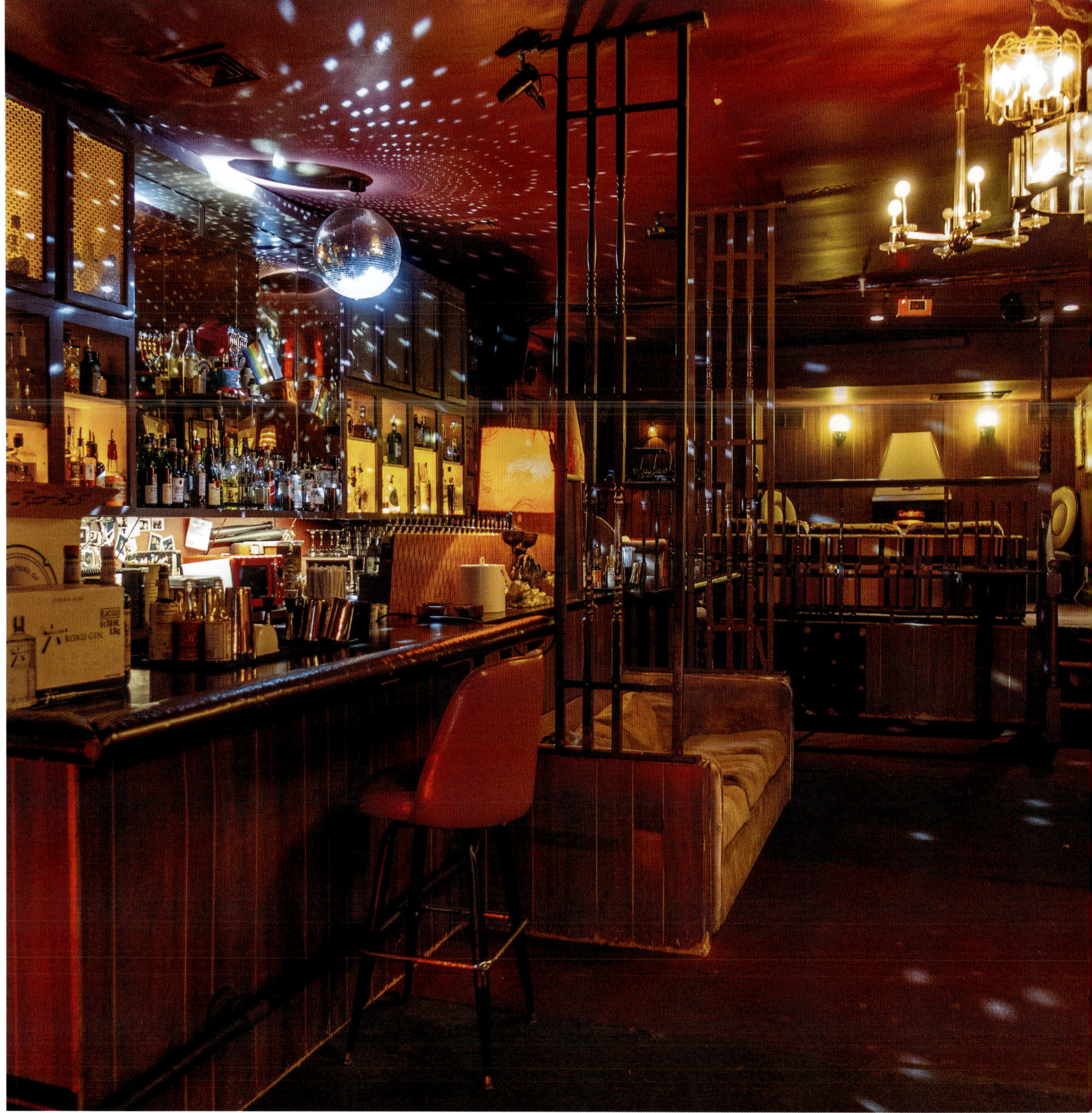

Joyface

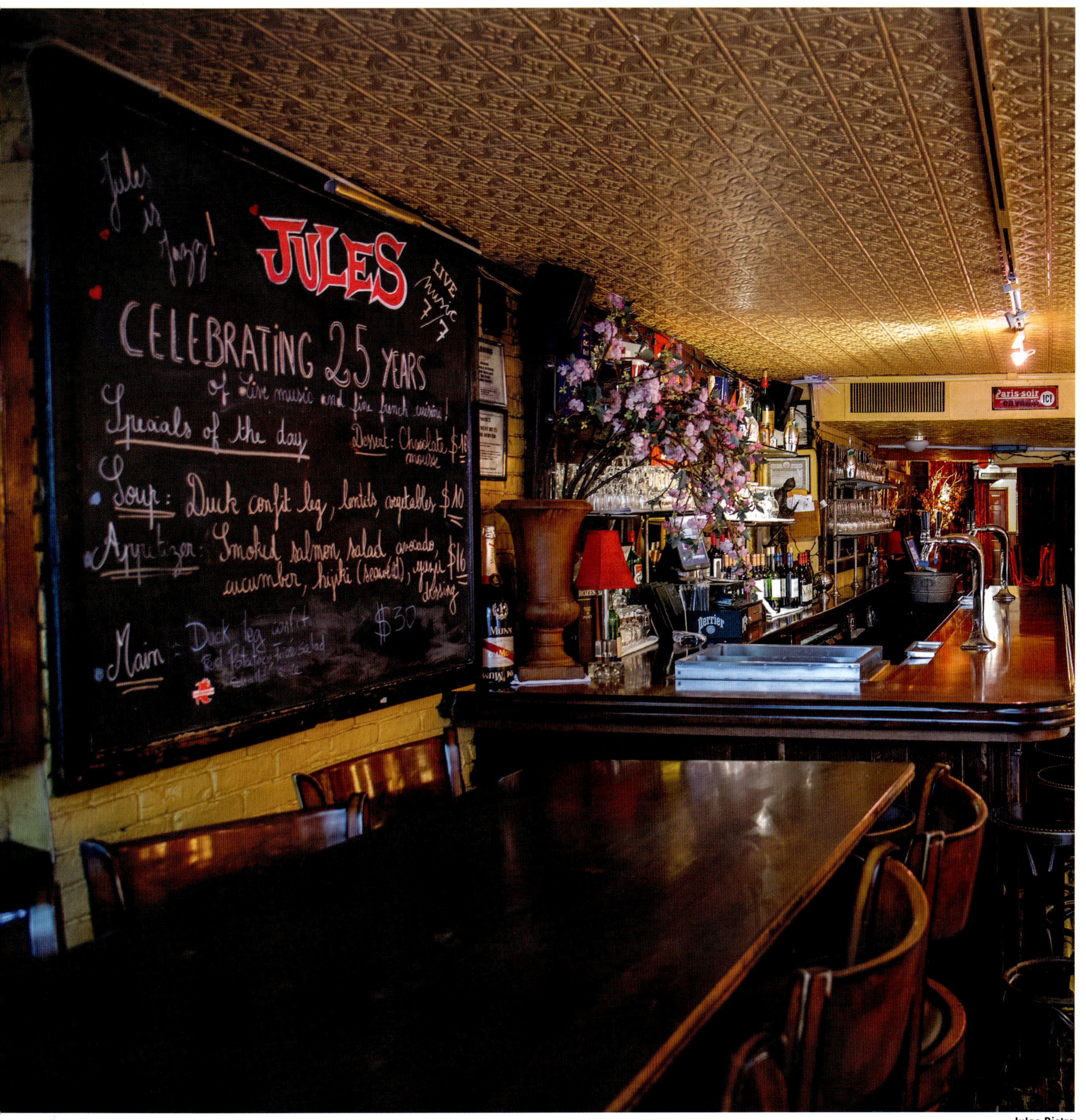

Jules Bistro

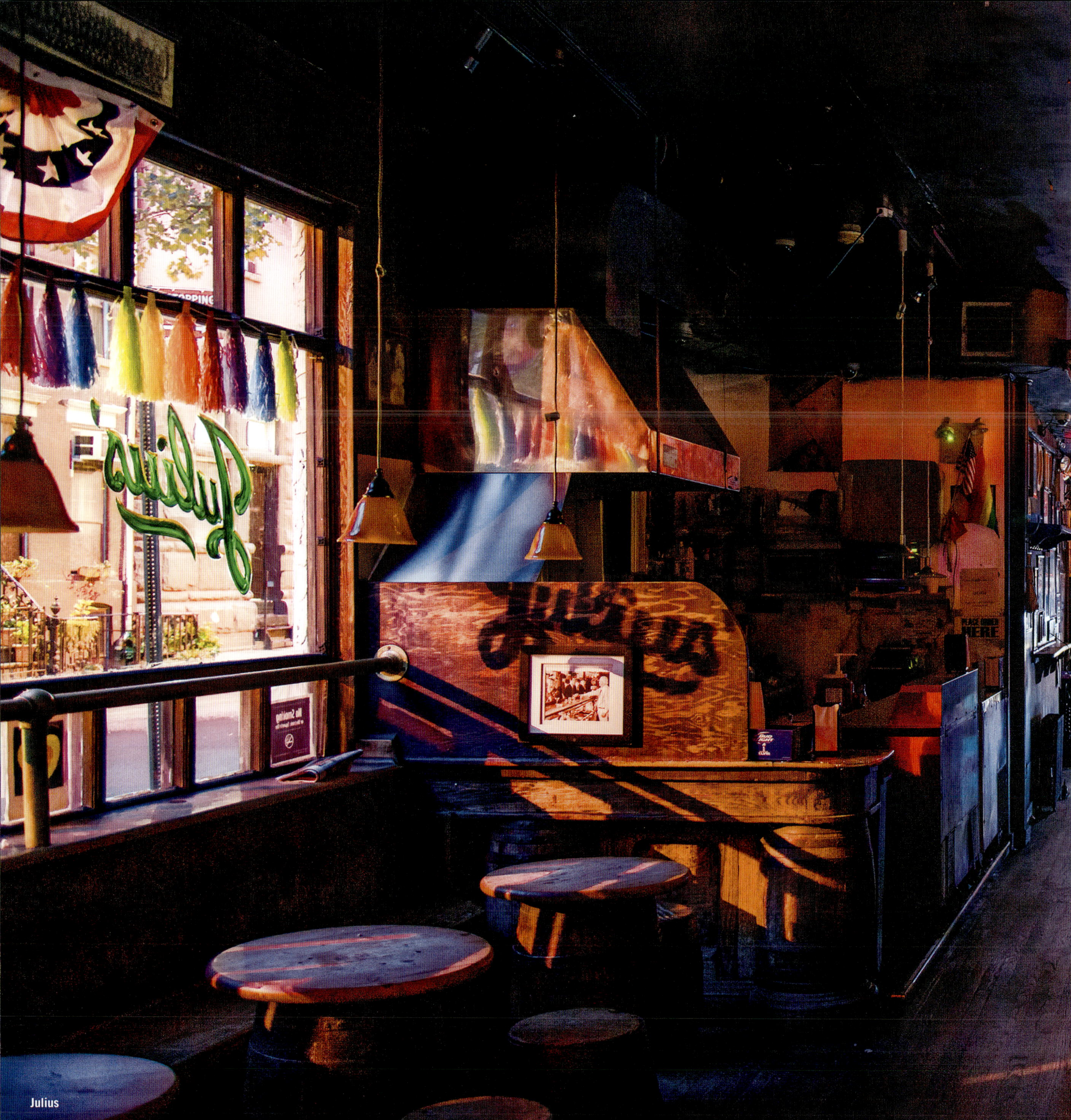

Julius

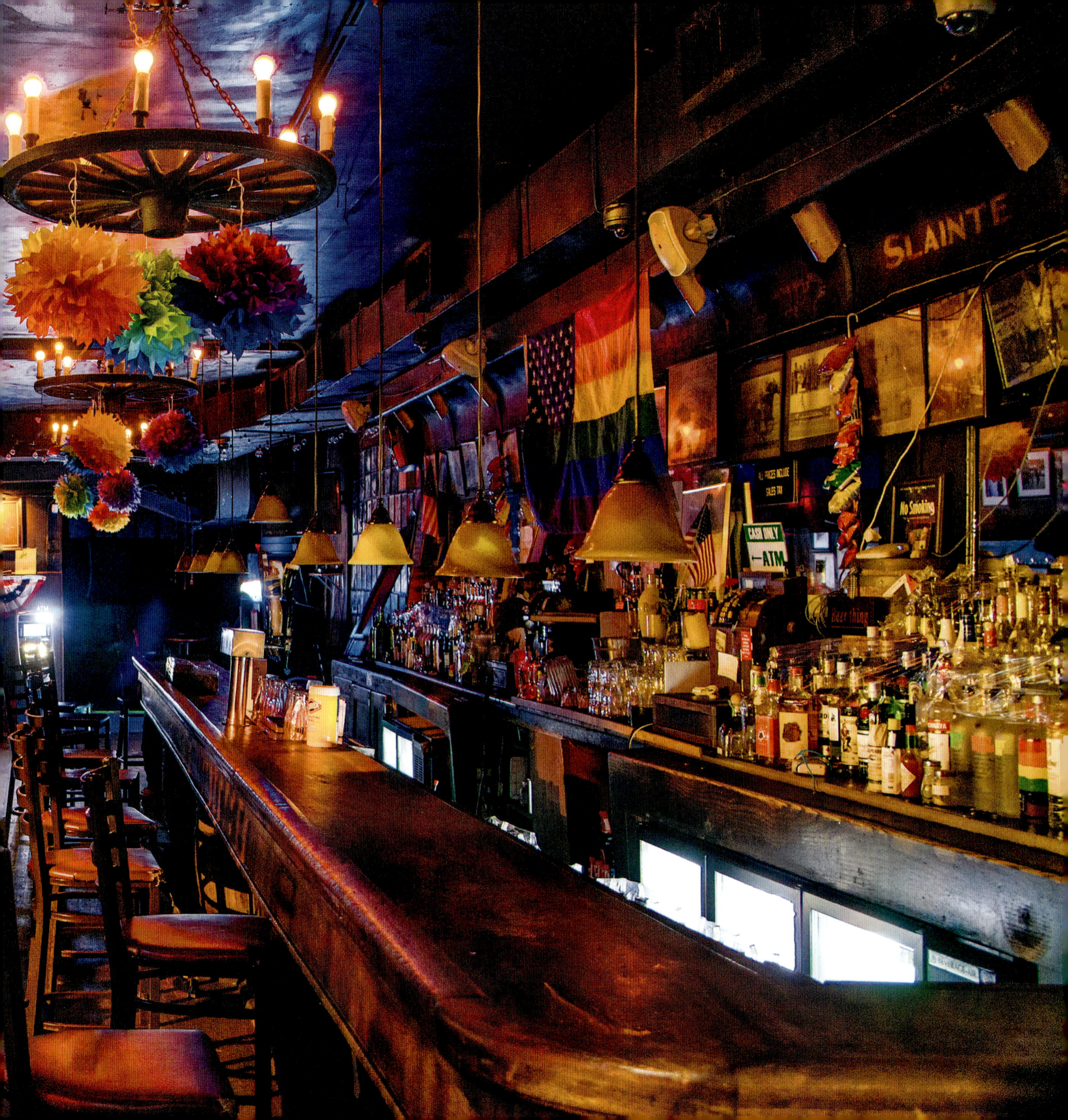

SLAINTE
No Smoking
ALL PRICES INCLUDE SALES TAX
CASH ONLY
ATM
Beer Thing

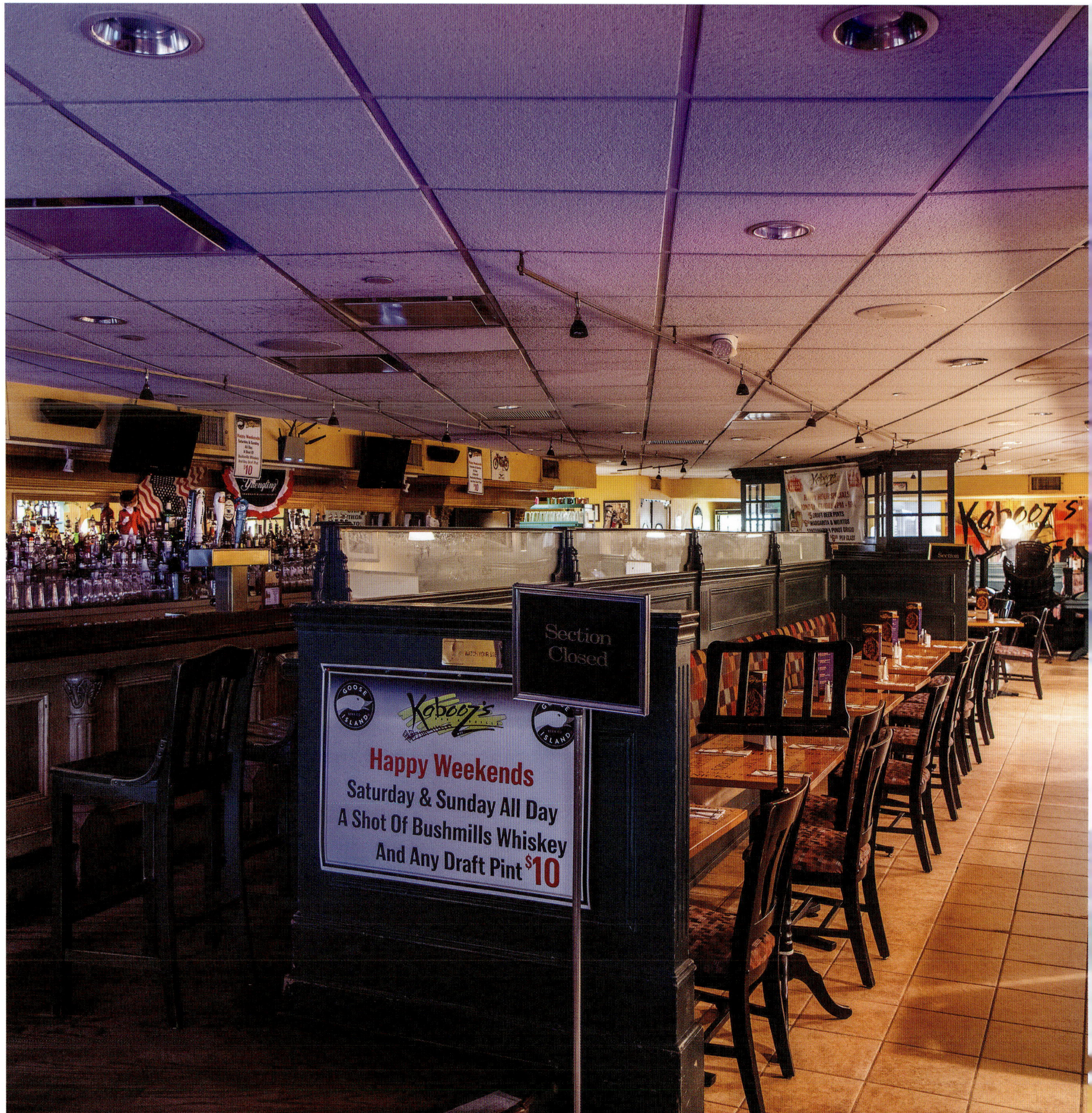

Kabooz's Bar and Grill

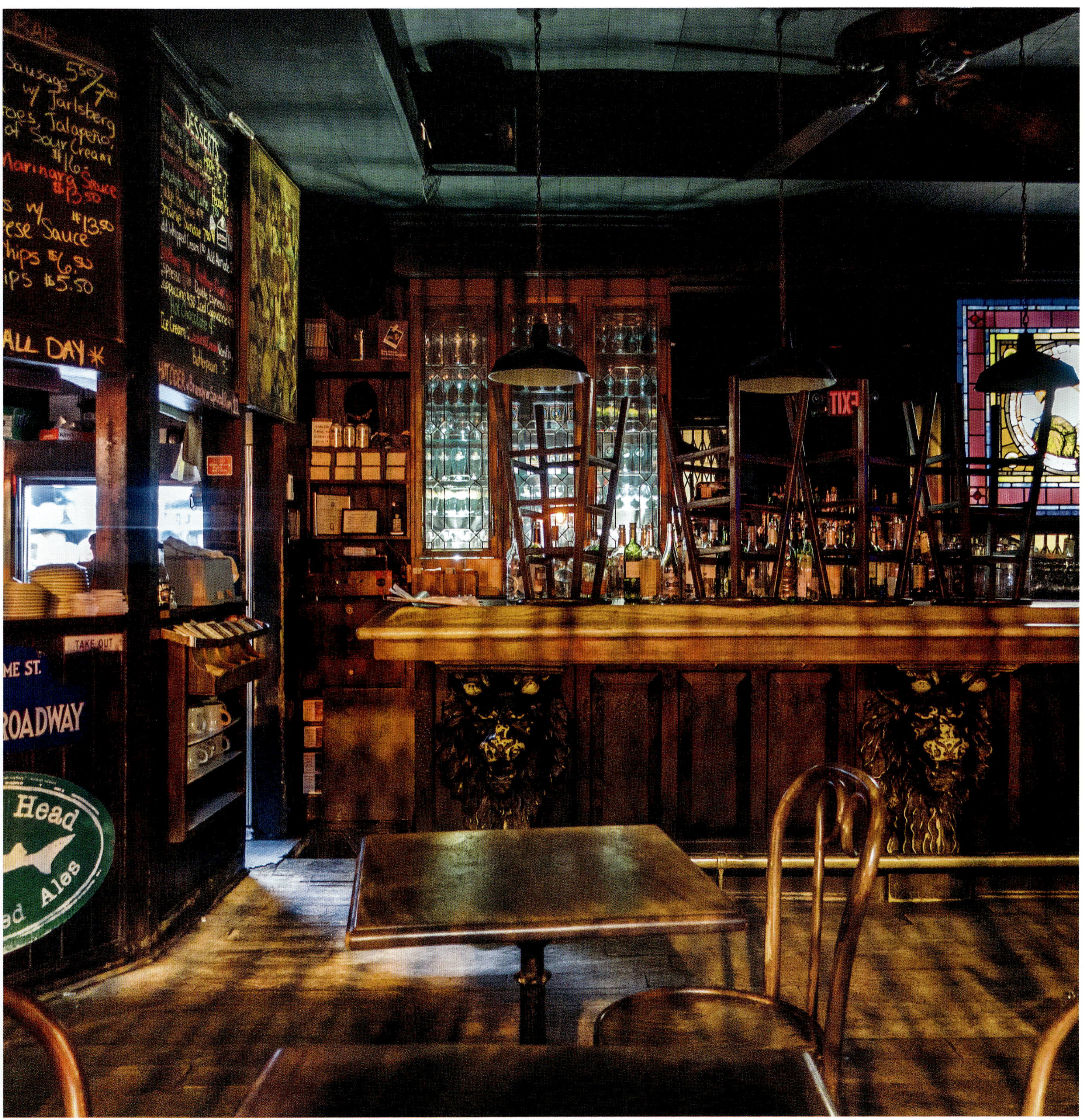

Kenn's Broome Street Bar

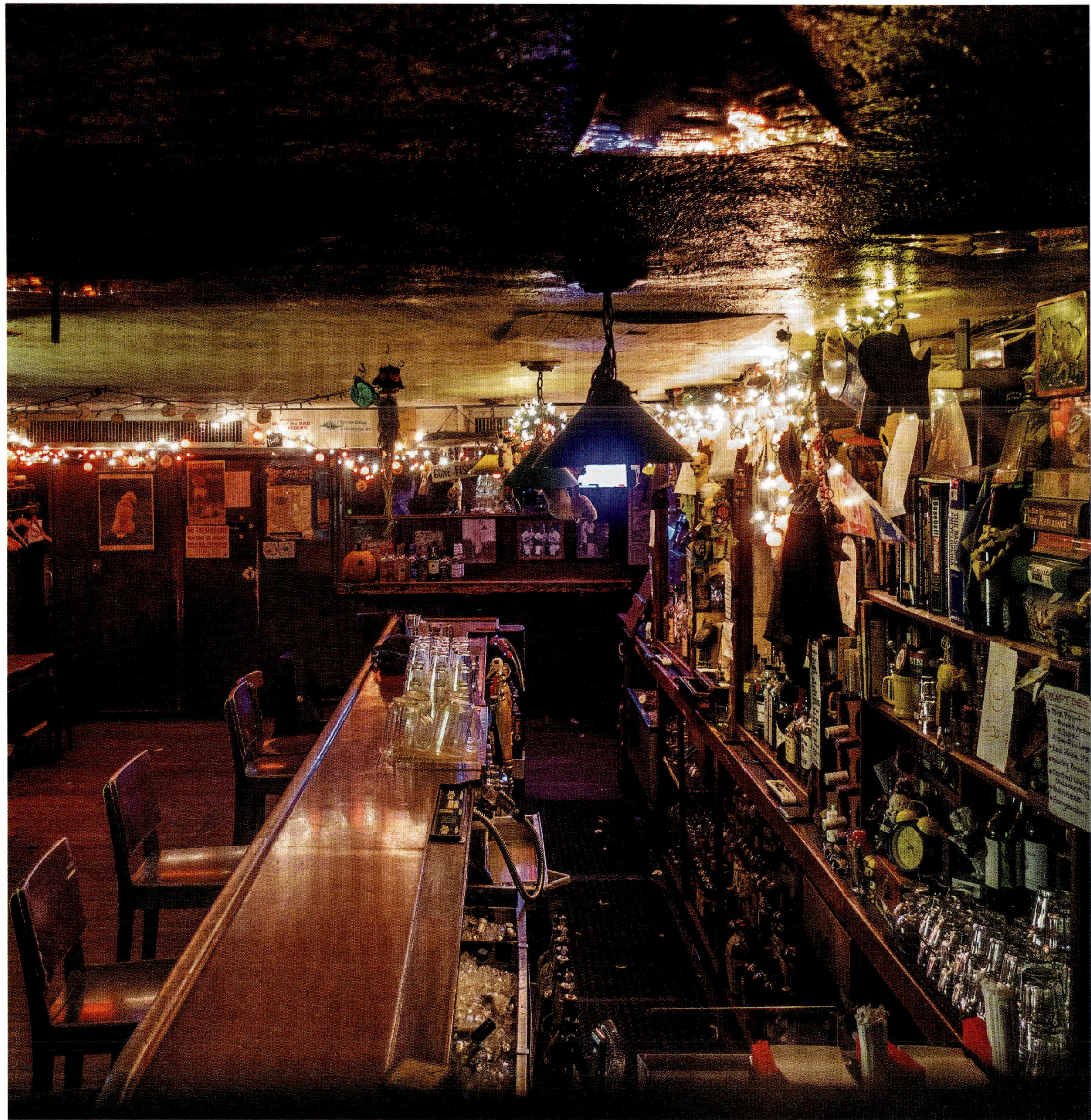

Kettle of Fish

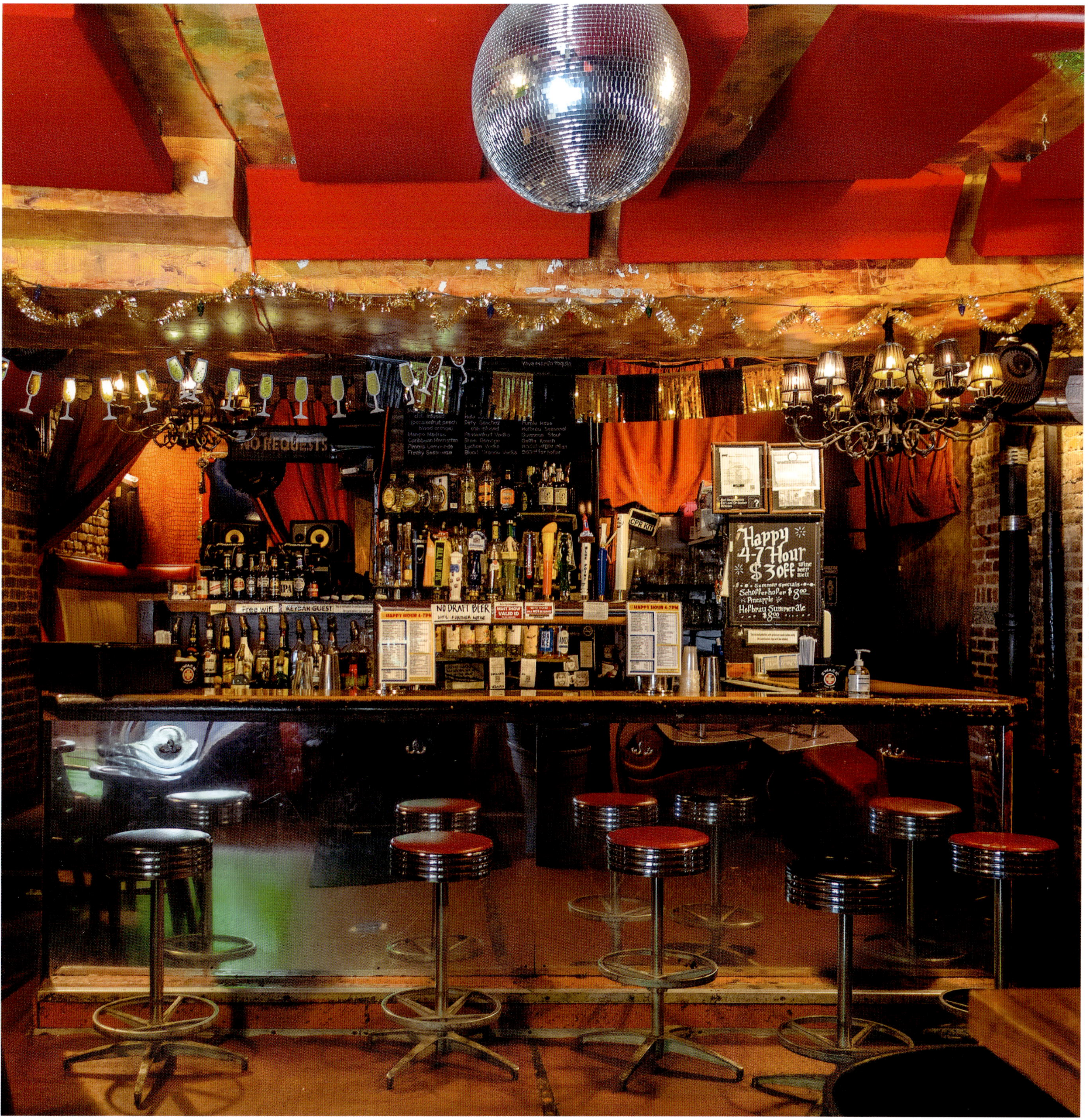

Key Bar

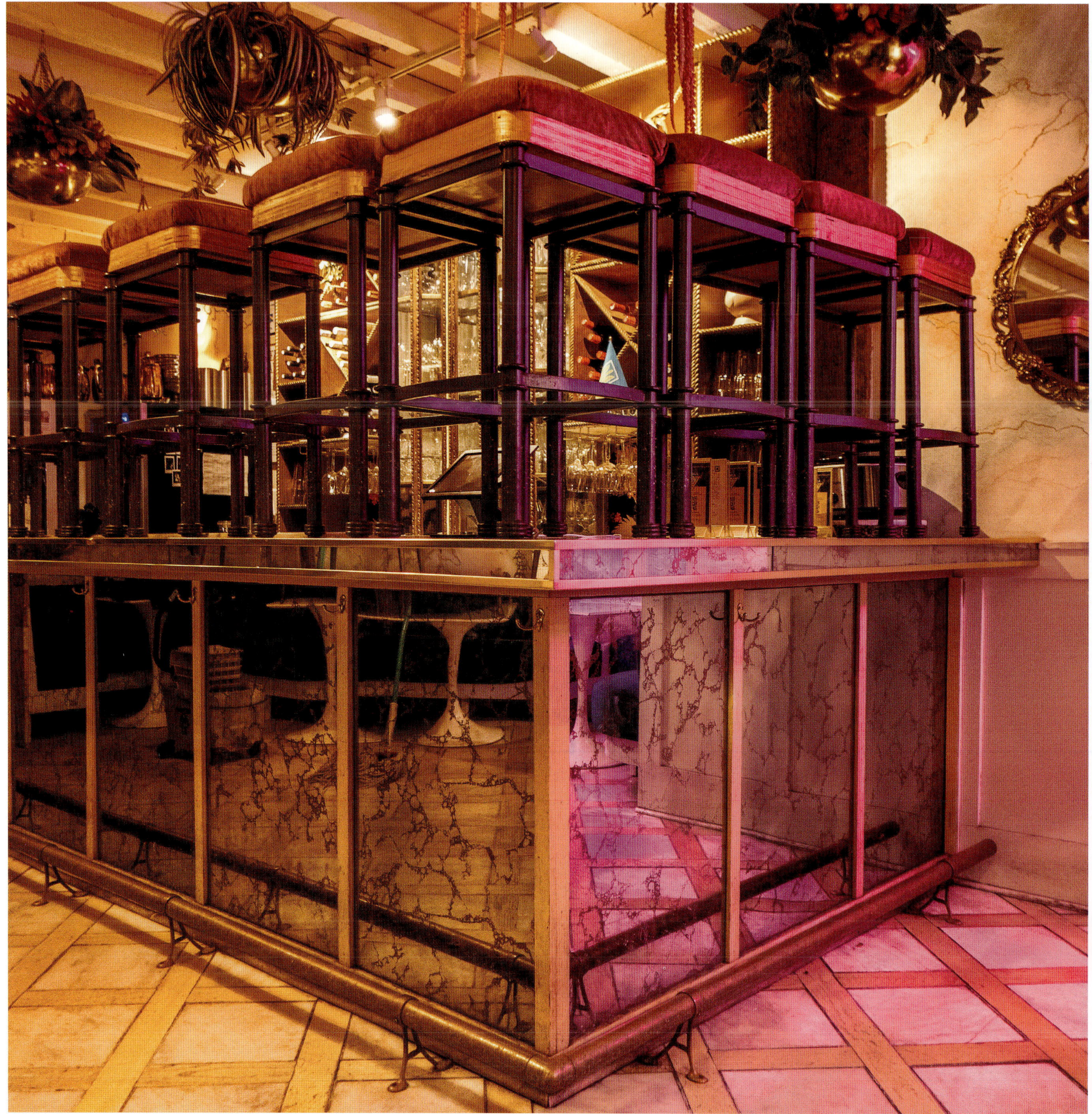

Ladybird

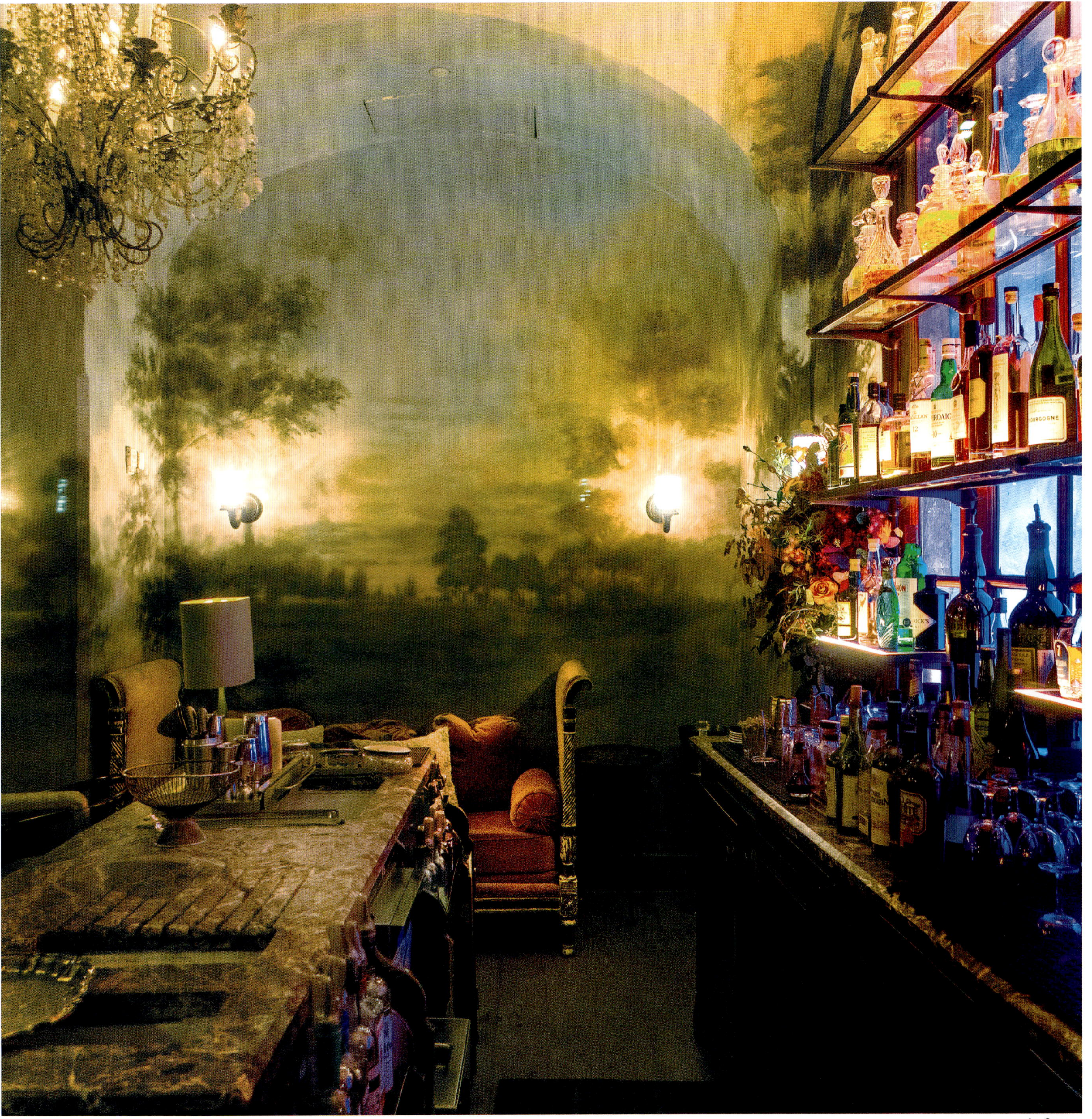

Le Coucou

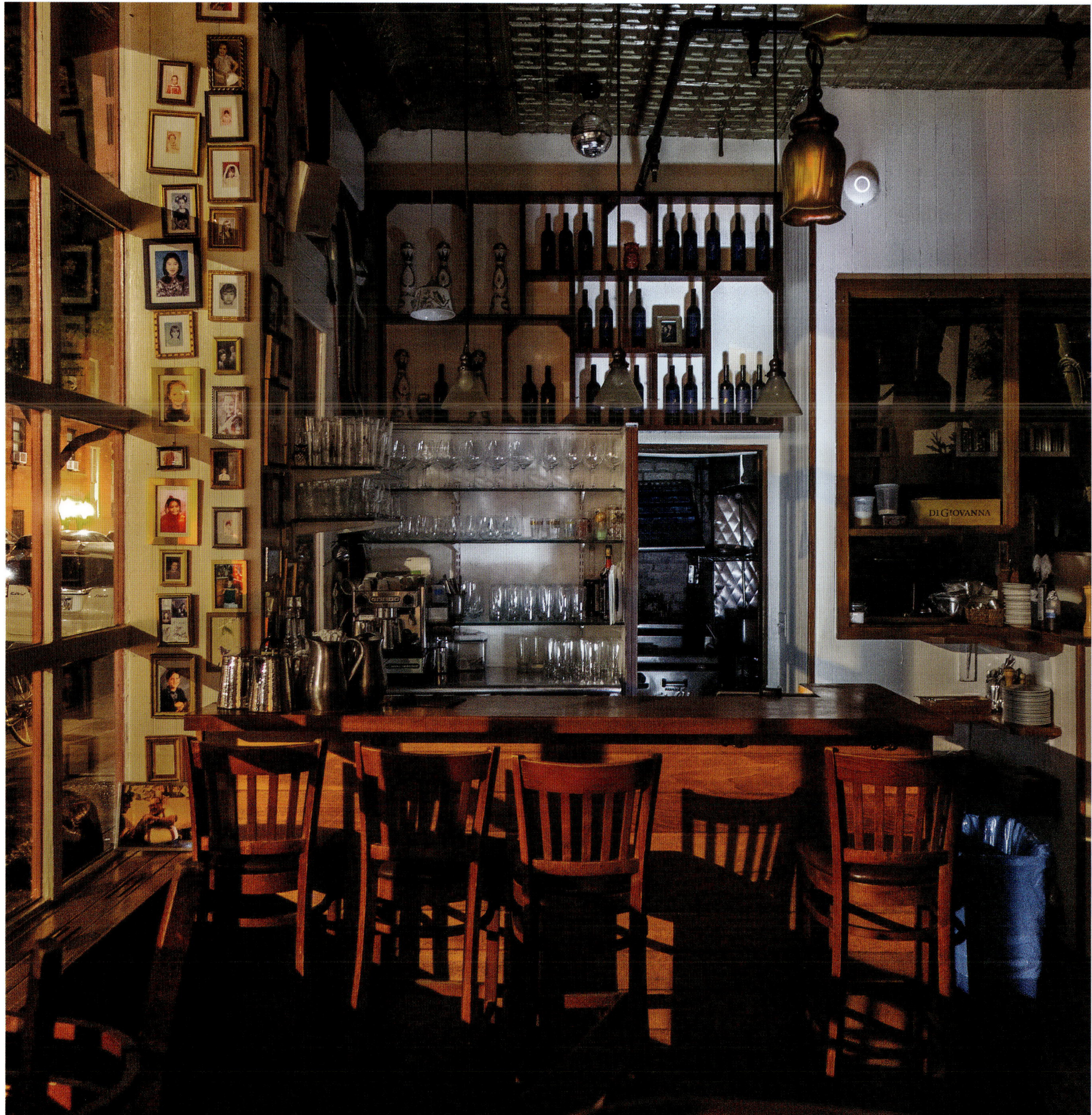

Little Owl

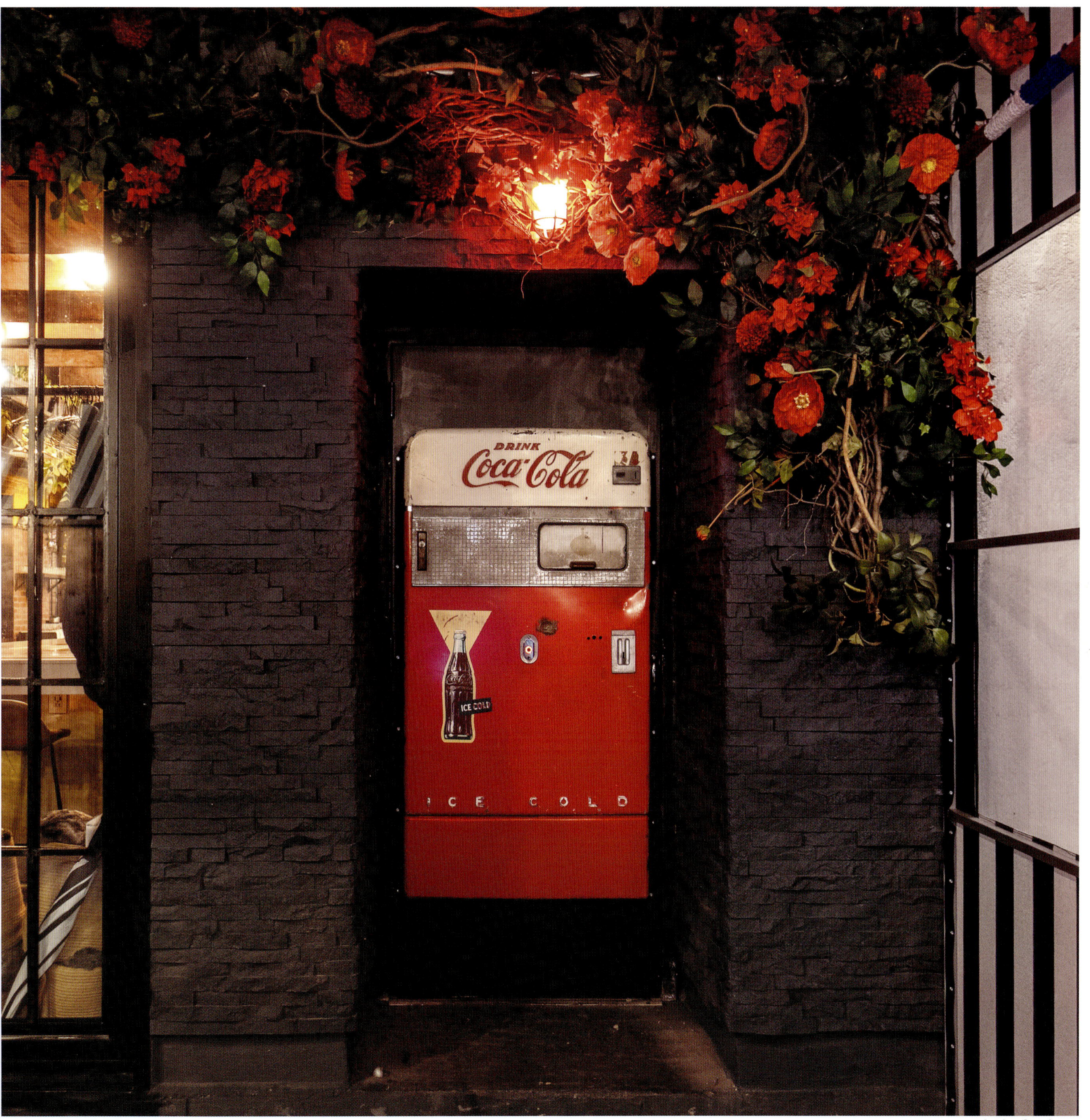

Loulou Speakeasy

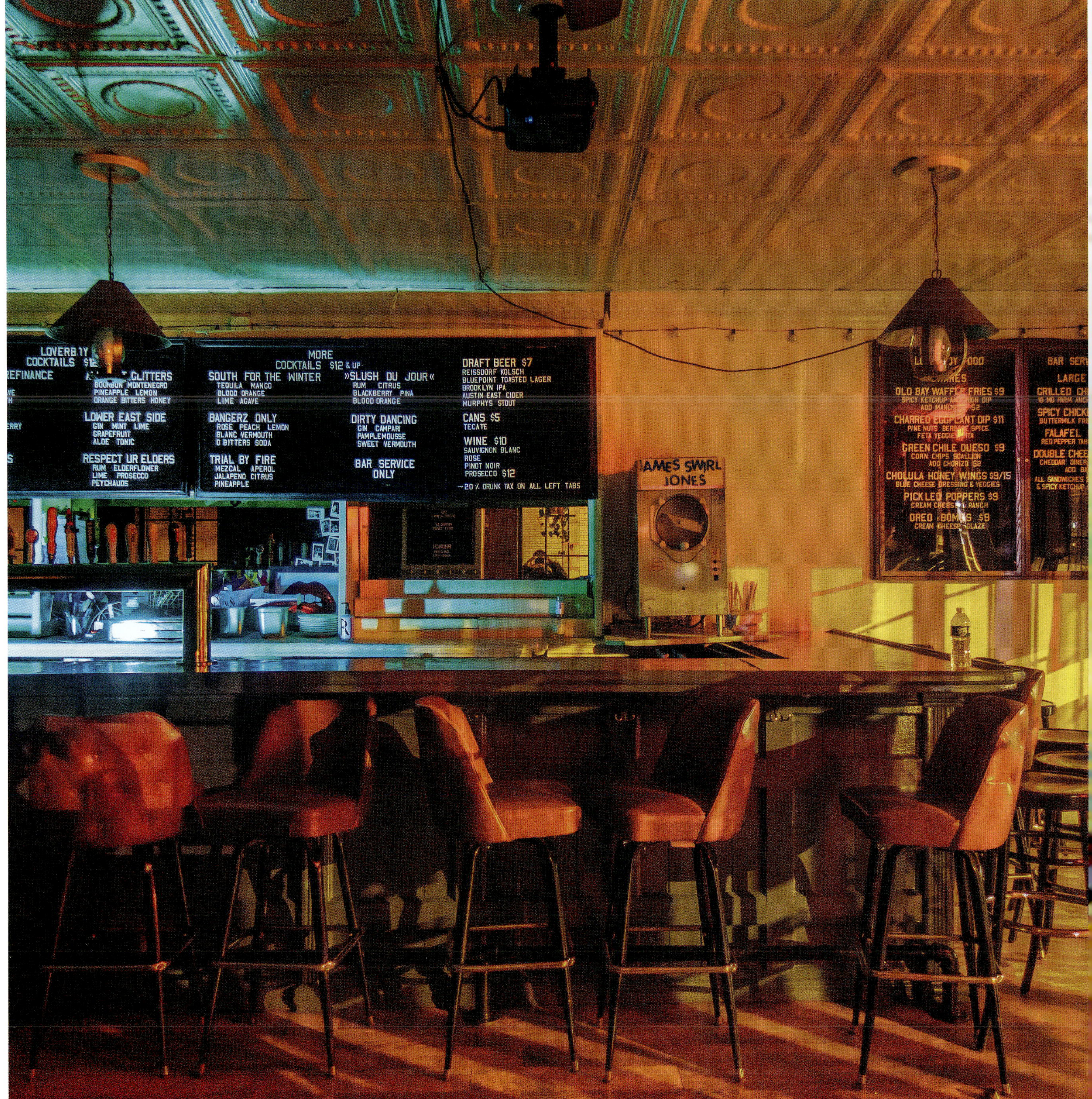

LOVERBOY
COCKTAILS $12
REFINANCE
ALL THAT GLITTERS
BOURBON MONTENEGRO
PINEAPPLE LEMON
ORANGE BITTERS HONEY
LOWER EAST SIDE
GIN MINT LIME
GRAPEFRUIT
ALOE TONIC
RESPECT UR ELDERS
RUM ELDERFLOWER
LIME PROSECCO
PEYCHAUDS
MORE
COCKTAILS $12 & UP
SOUTH FOR THE WINTER
TEQUILA MANGO
BLOOD ORANGE
LIME AGAVE
BANGERZ ONLY
ROSE PEACH LEMON
BLANC VERMOUTH
O BITTERS SODA
TRIAL BY FIRE
MEZCAL APEROL
JALAPENO CITRUS
PINEAPPLE
»SLUSH DU JOUR«
RUM CITRUS
BLACKBERRY PINA
BLOOD ORANGE
DIRTY DANCING
GIN CAMPARI
PAMPLEMOUSSE
SWEET VERMOUTH
BAR SERVICE
ONLY
DRAFT BEER $7
REISSDORF KOLSCH
BLUEPOINT TOASTED LAGER
BROOKLYN IPA
AUSTIN EAST CIDER
MURPHYS STOUT
CANS $5
TECATE
WINE $10
SAUVIGNON BLANC
ROSE
PINOT NOIR
PROSECCO $12
→ 20 % DRUNK TAX ON ALL LEFT TABS
LOVERBOY FOOD
SHARES
OLD BAY WAFFLE FRIES $9
SPICY KETCHUP SCALLION DIP
ADD MANCHEGO $2
CHARRED EGGPLANT DIP $11
PINE NUTS BERBERE SPICE
FETA VEGGIE PITA
GREEN CHILE QUESO $9
CORN CHIPS SCALLION
ADD CHORIZO $2
CHOLULA HONEY WINGS $9/15
BLUE CHEESE DRESSING & VEGGIES
PICKLED POPPERS $9
CREAM CHEESE RANCH
OREO BOMBS $9
CREAM CHEESE GLAZE
BAR SERVICE
LARGE
GRILLED CH
16 MO FARM ANCH
SPICY CHICKEN
BUTTERMILK FRI
FALAFEL
RED PEPPER TAHI
DOUBLE CHEE
CHEDDAR DINER
ADD BA
ALL SANDWICHES
& SPICY KETCHUP
JAMES SWIRL JONES

Loverboy

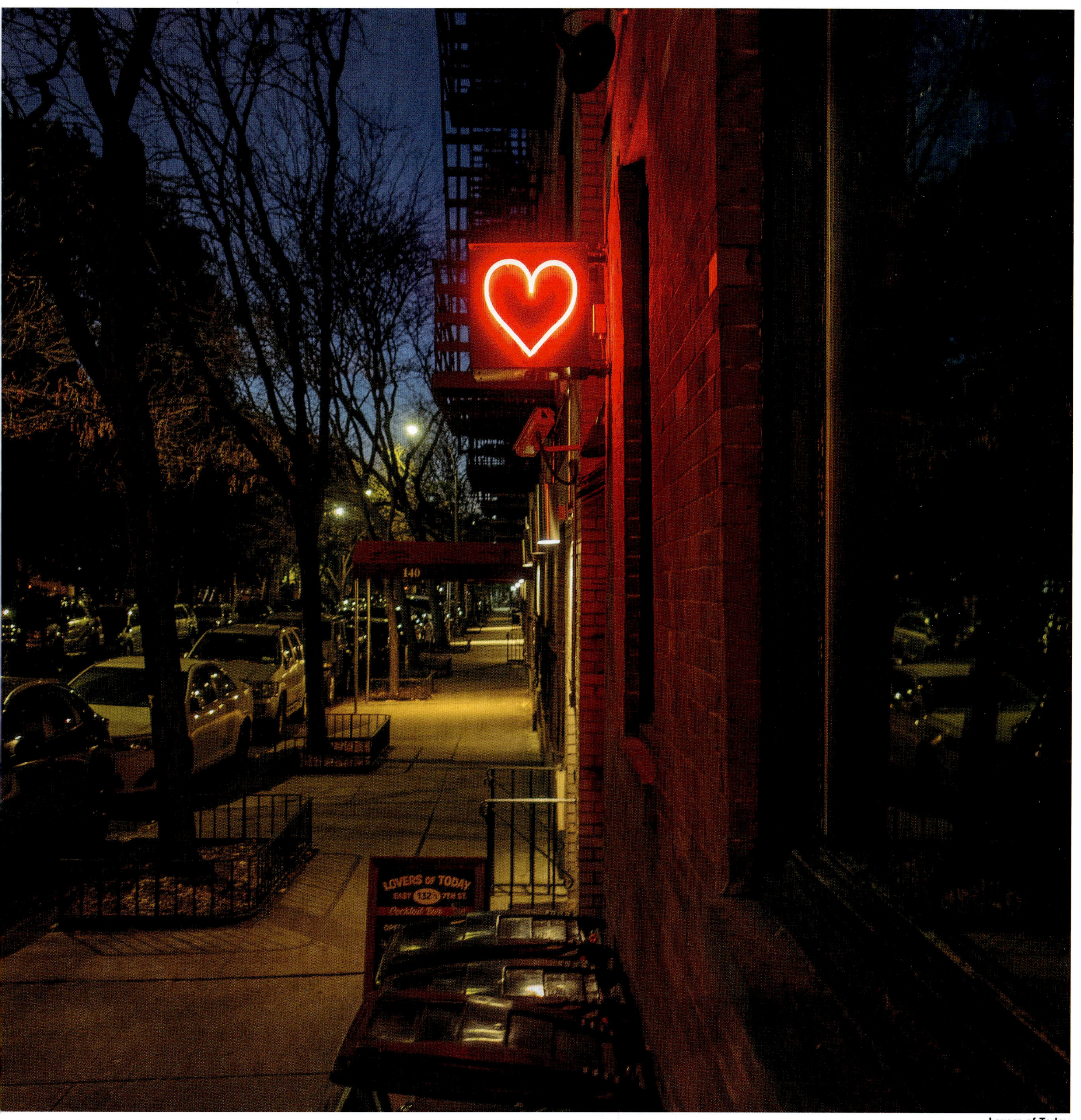

Lovers of Today

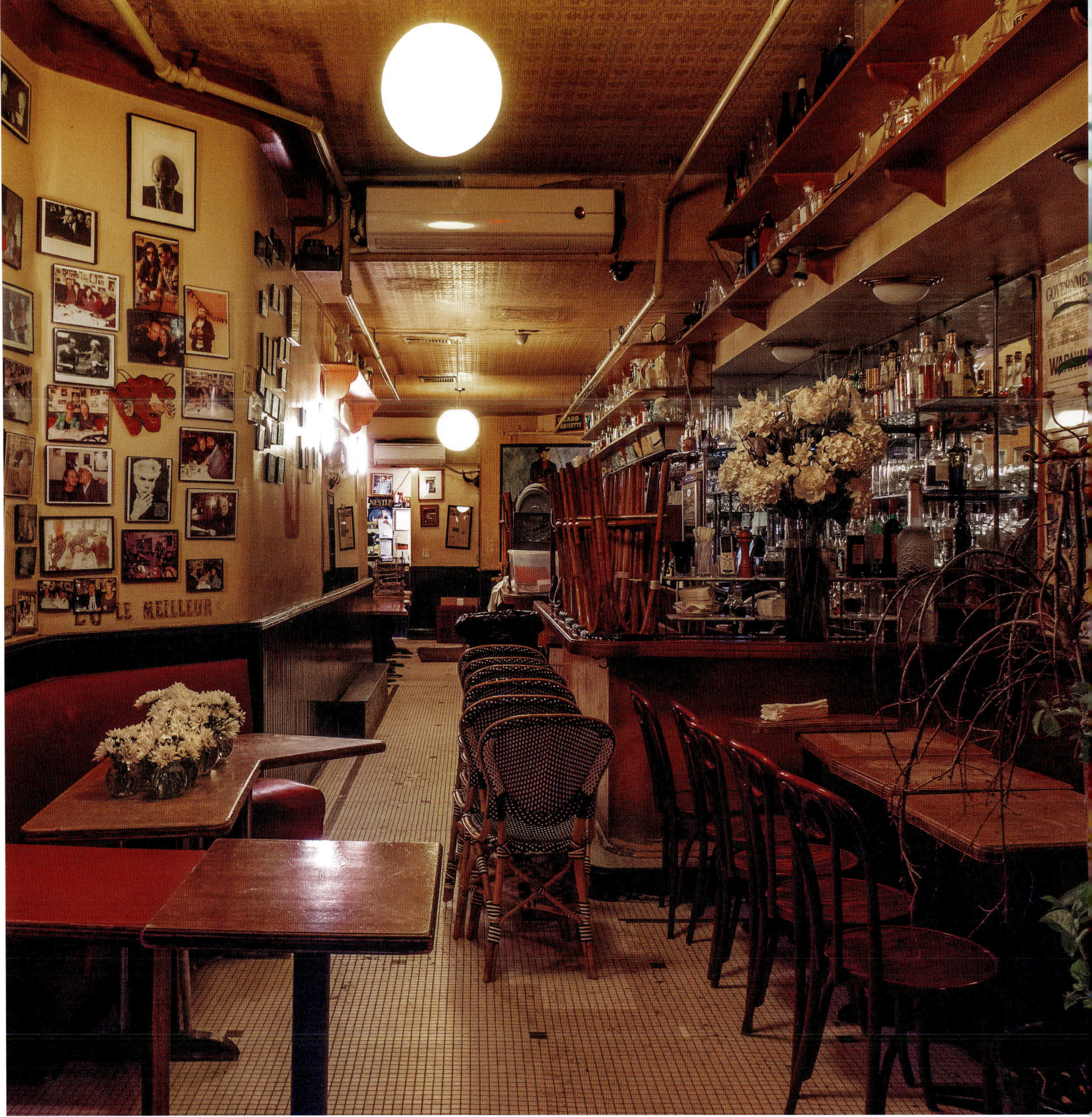

Lucien

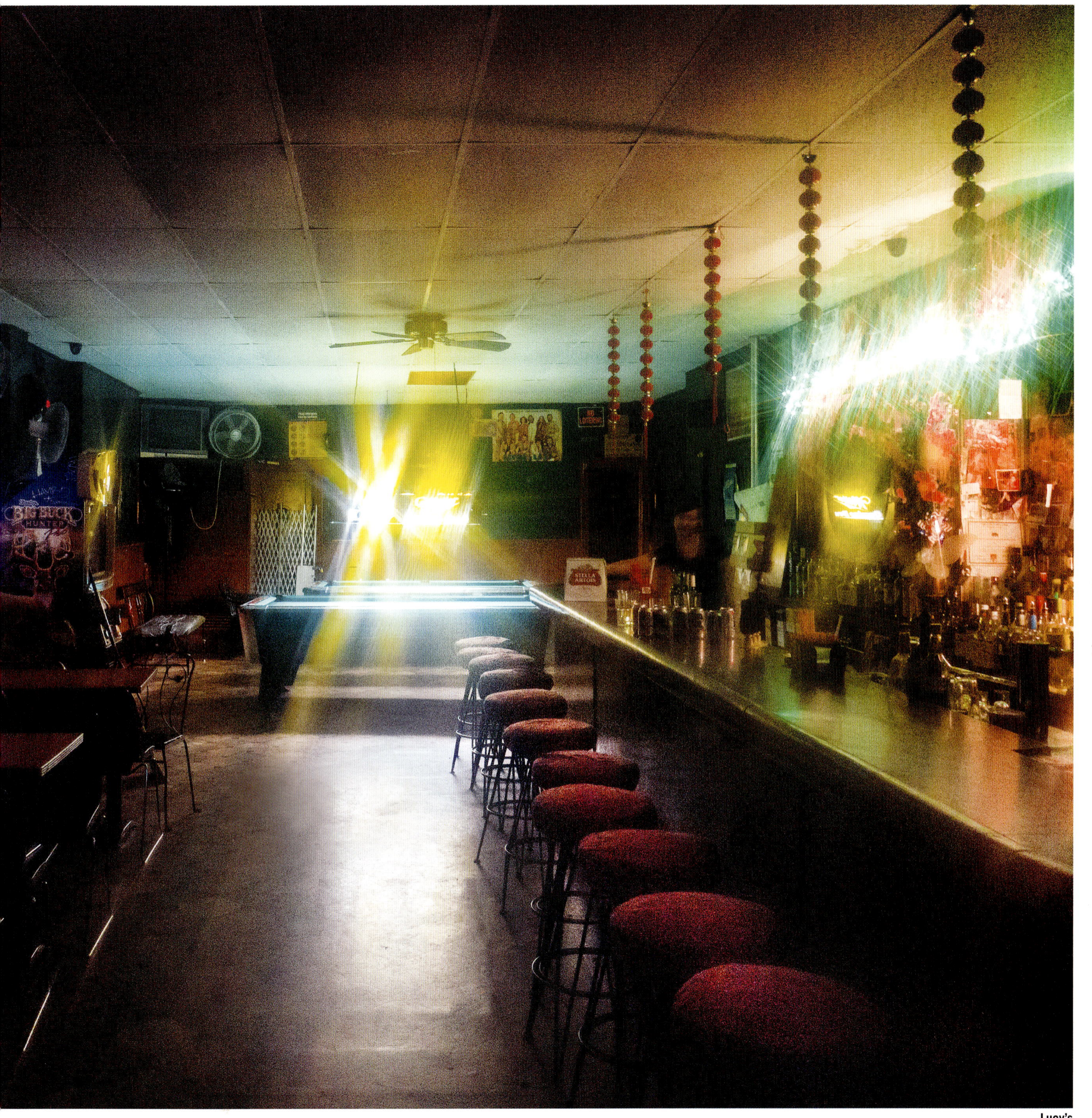

Lucy's

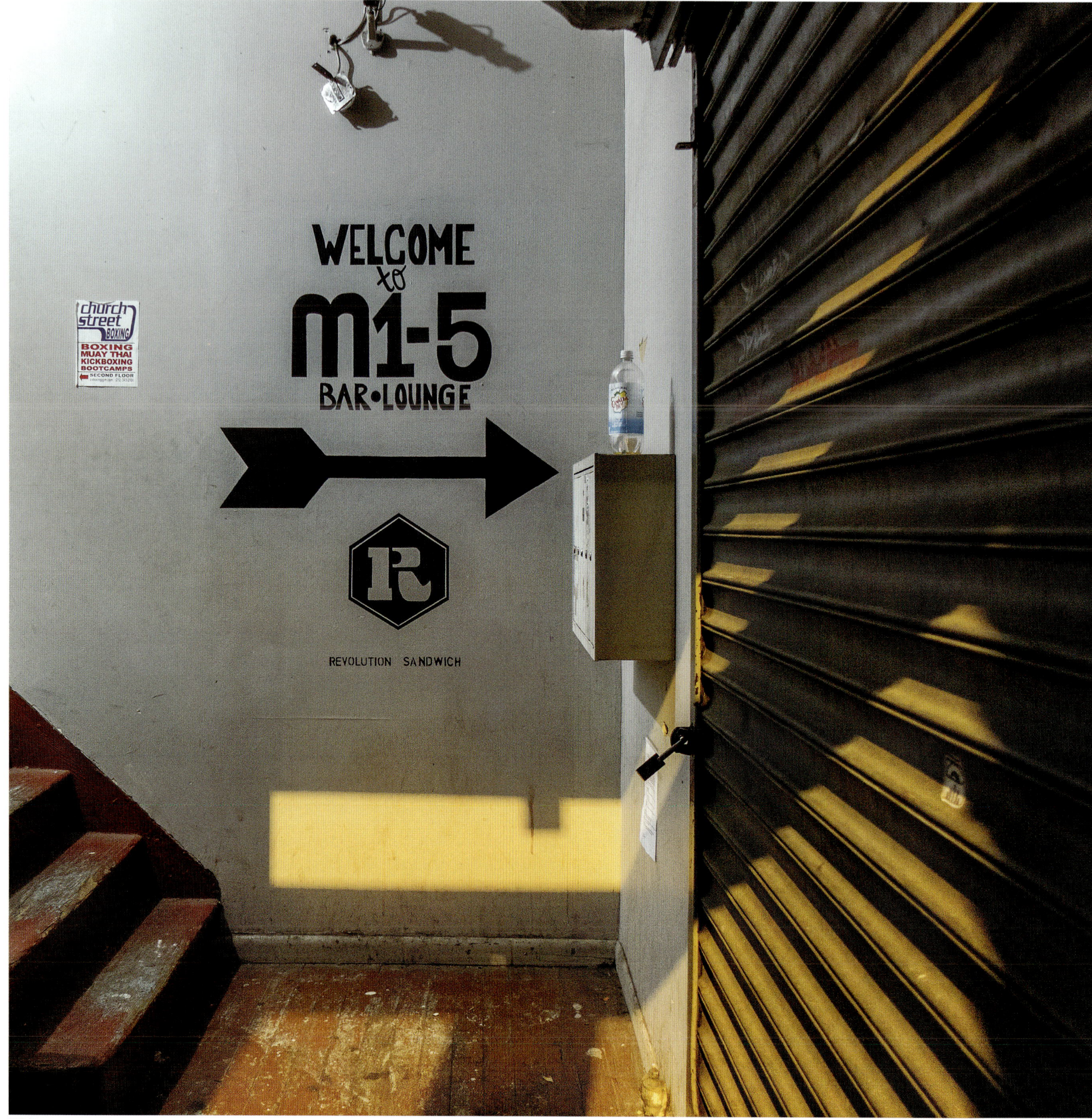

church street BOXING
BOXING
MUAY THAI
KICKBOXING
BOOTCAMPS
SECOND FLOOR
WELCOME to M1-5 BAR•LOUNGE
REVOLUTION SANDWICH

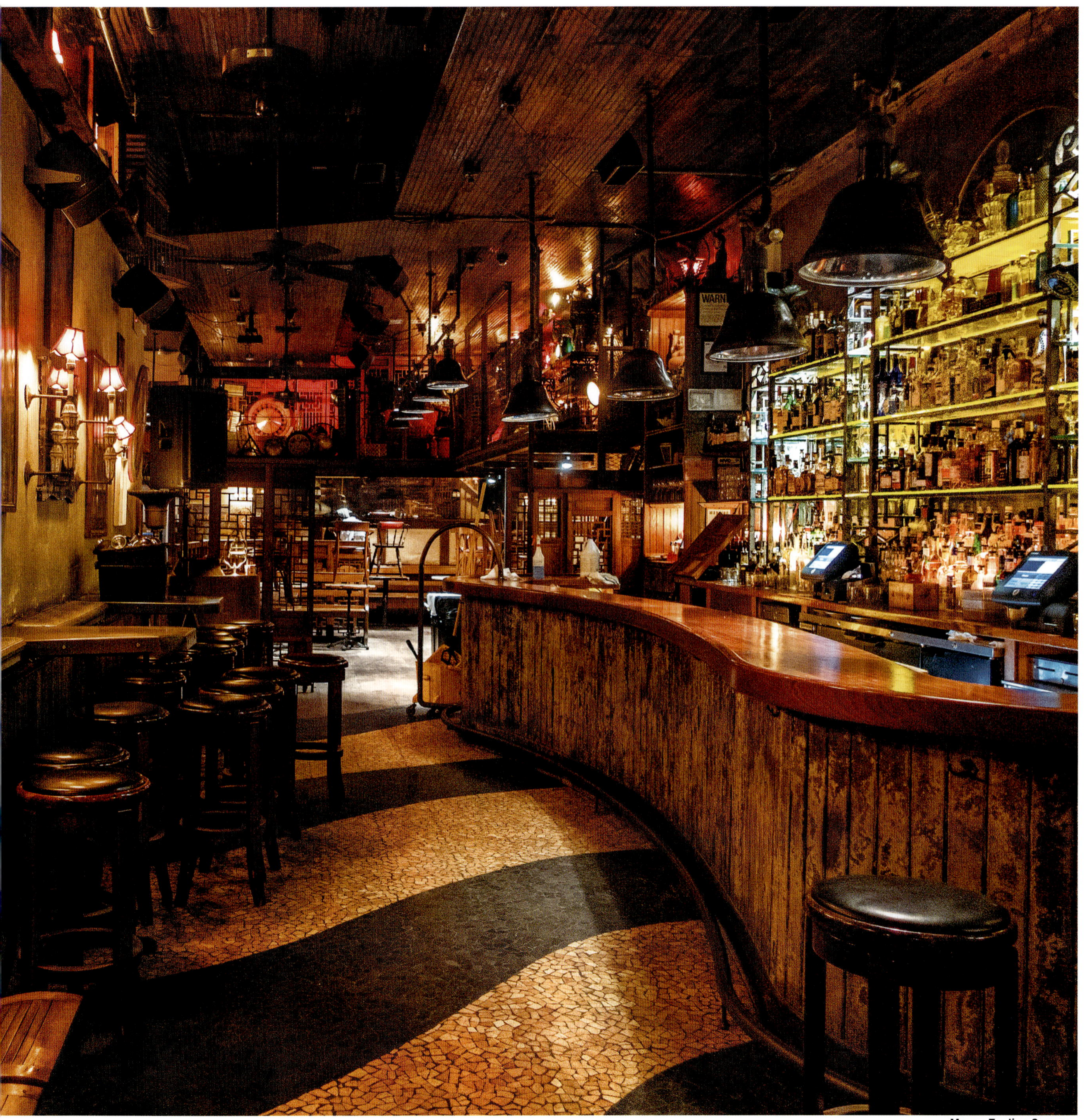

Macao Trading Company

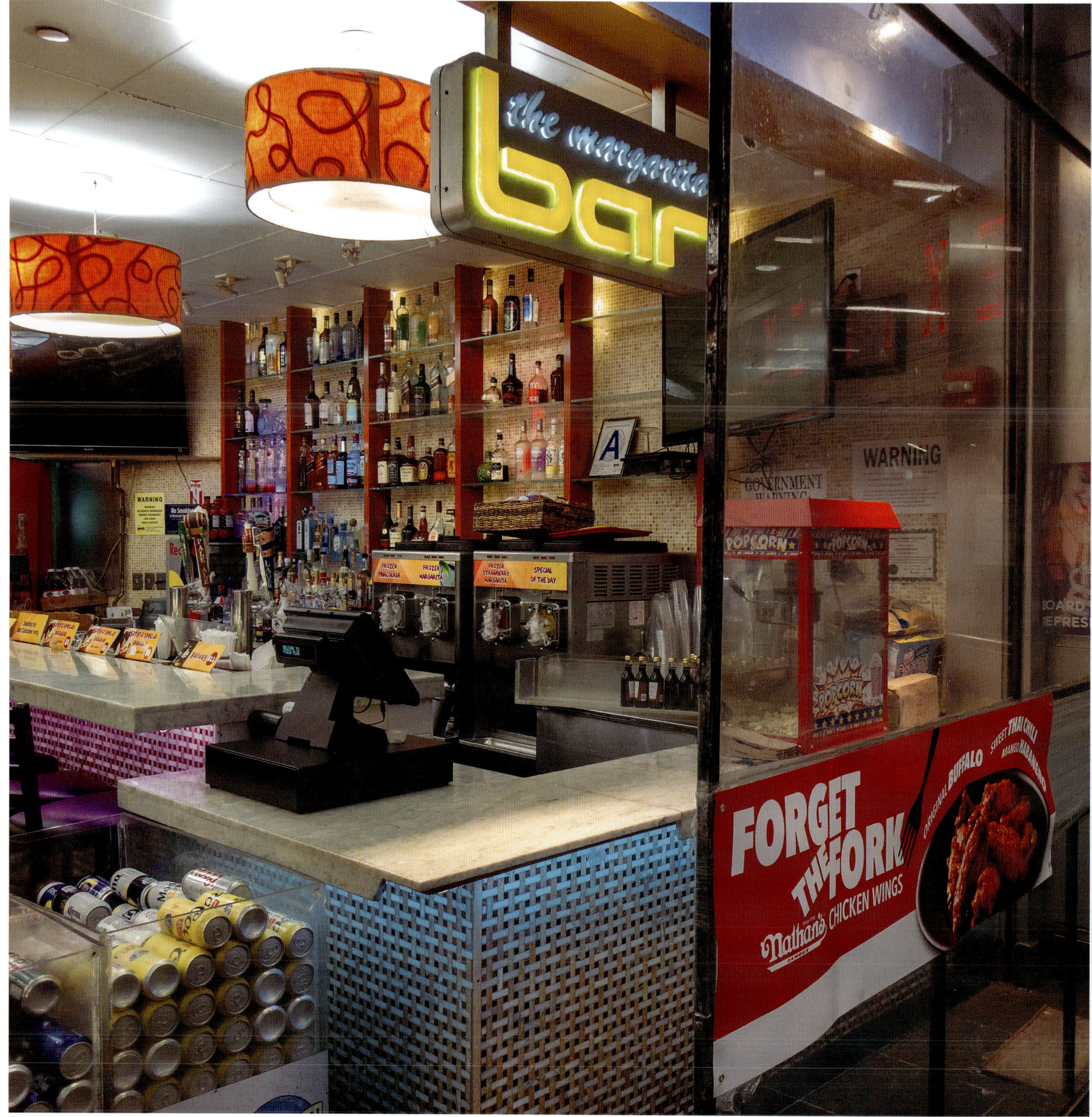

The Margarita Bar

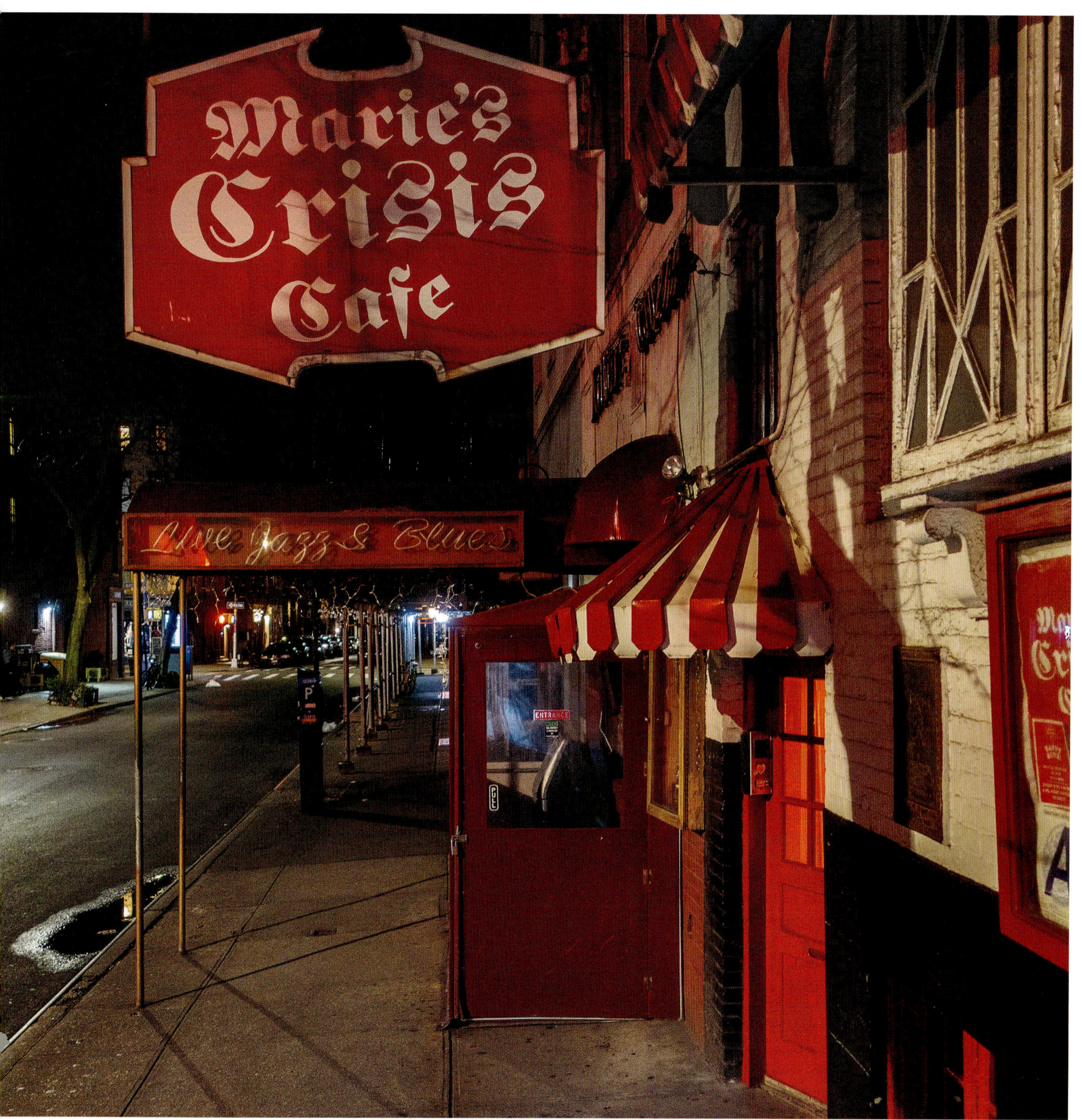

Marie's Crisis Cafe

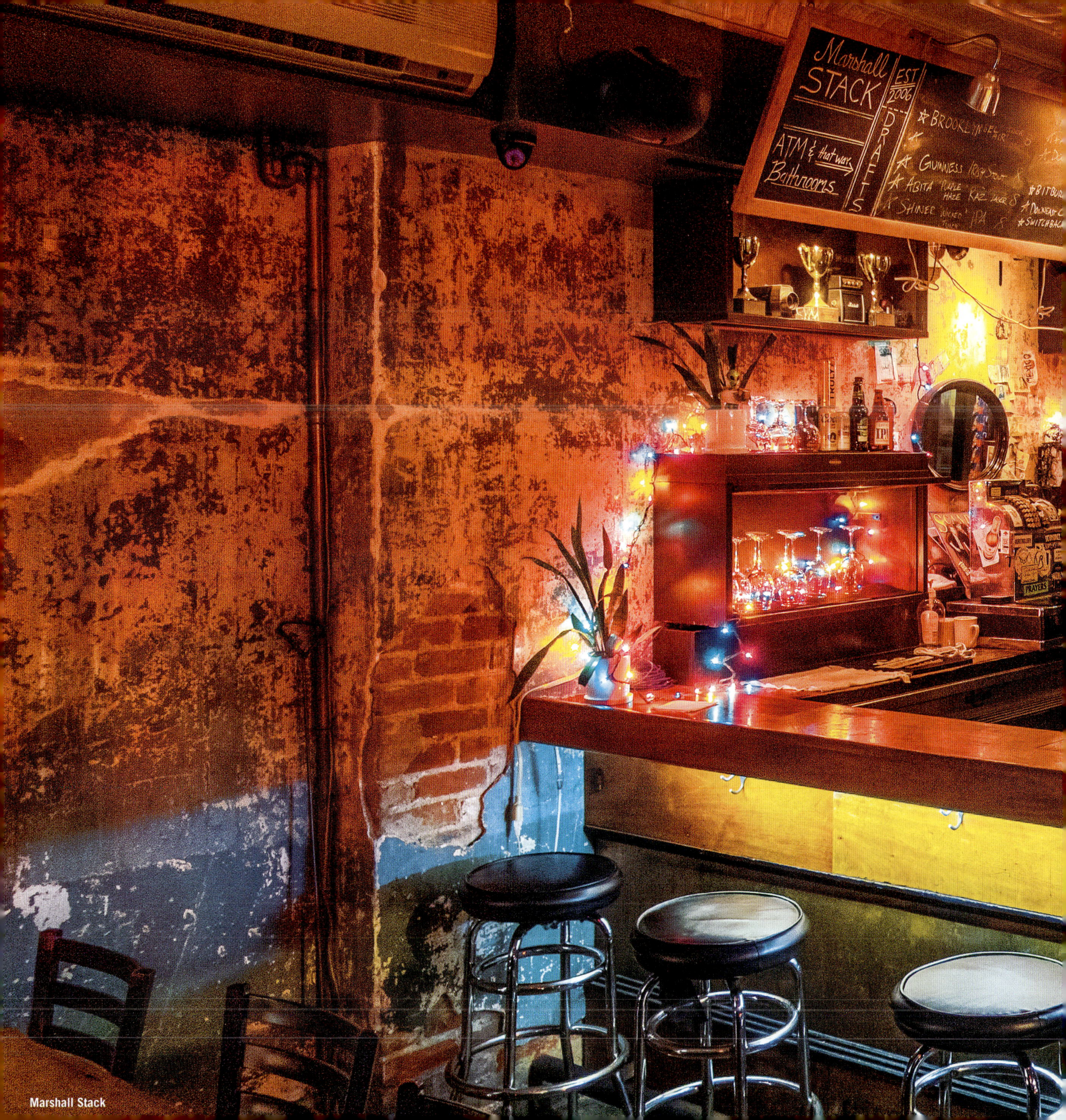

Marshall Stack

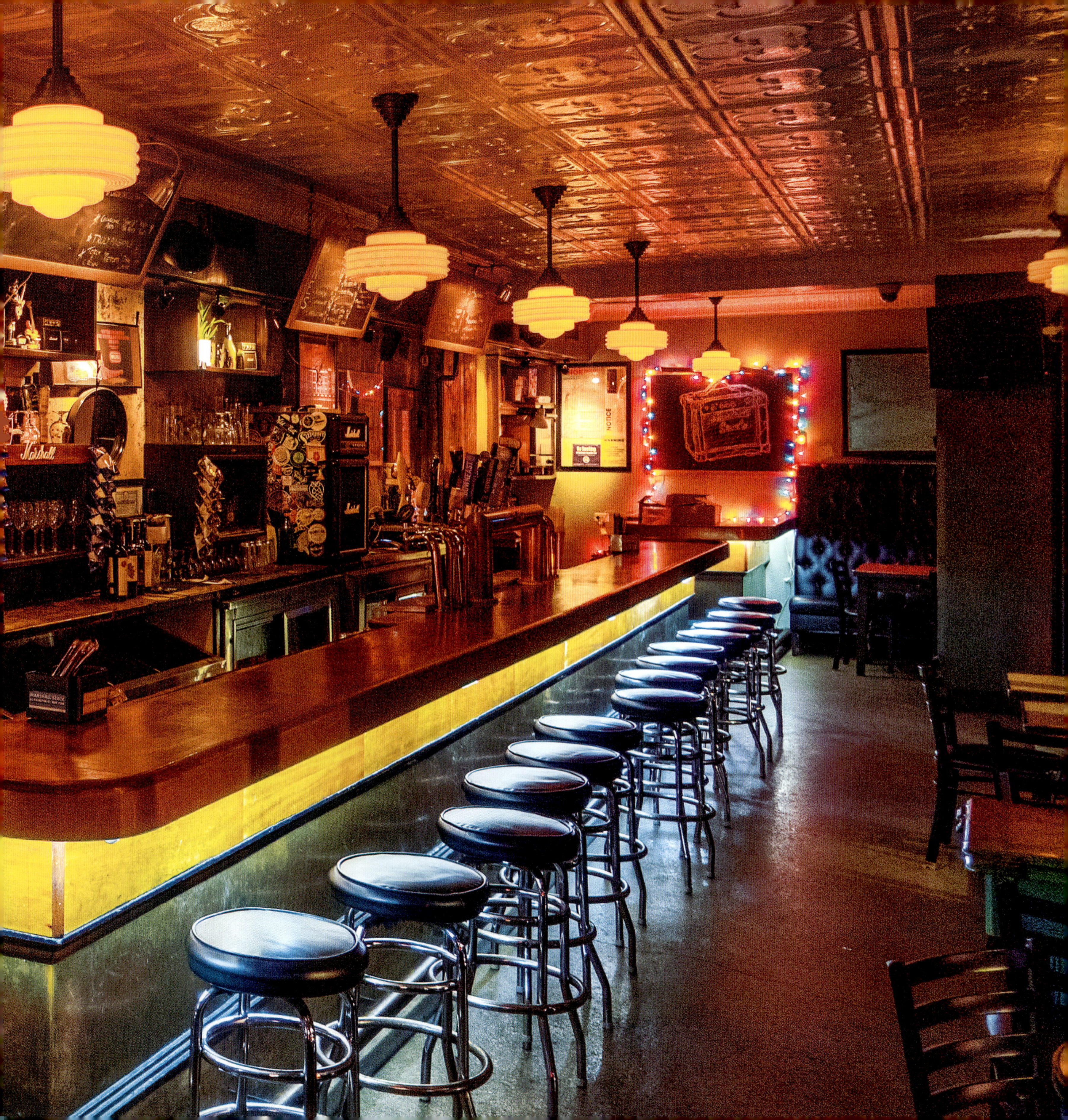

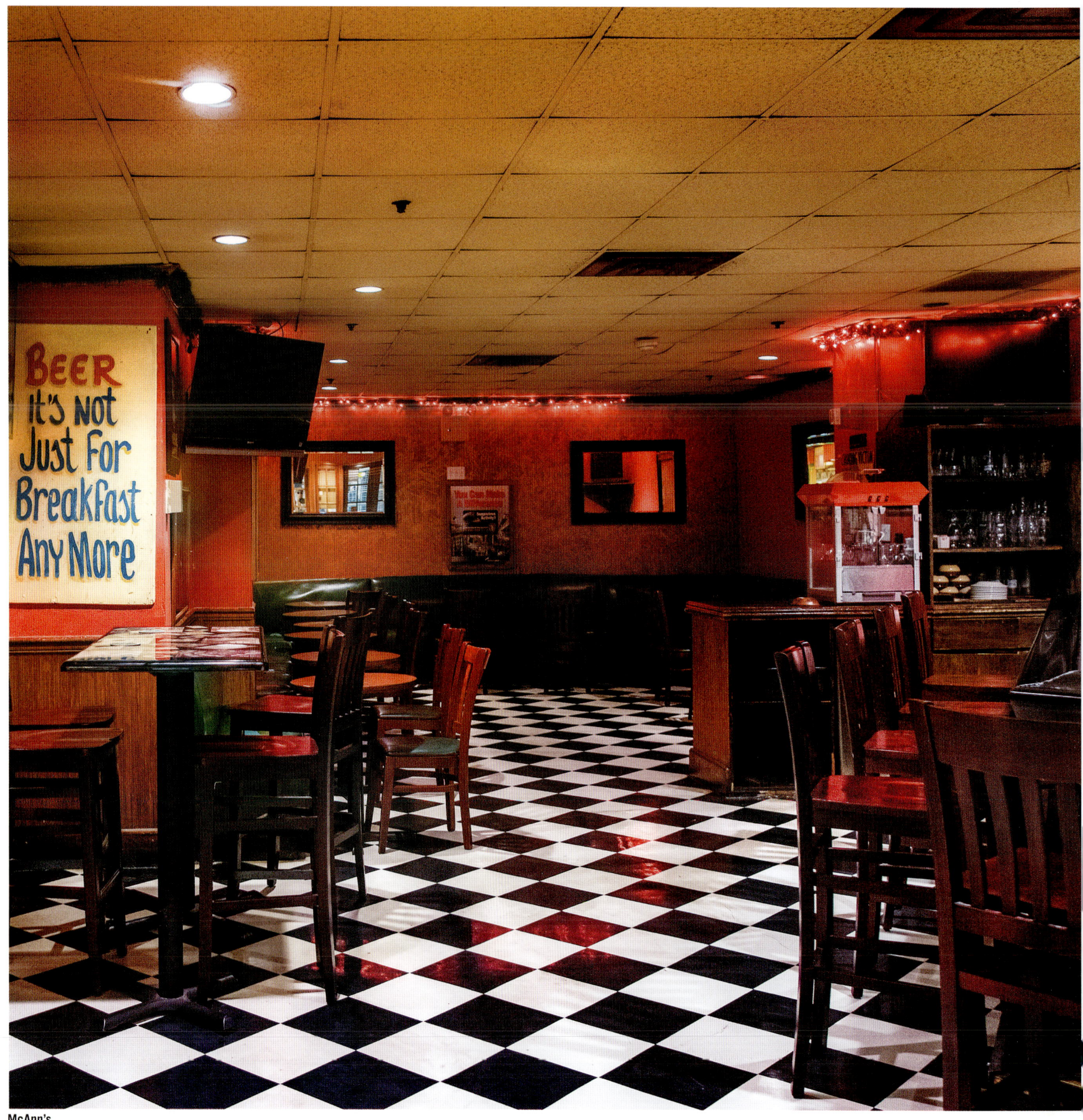

McAnn's

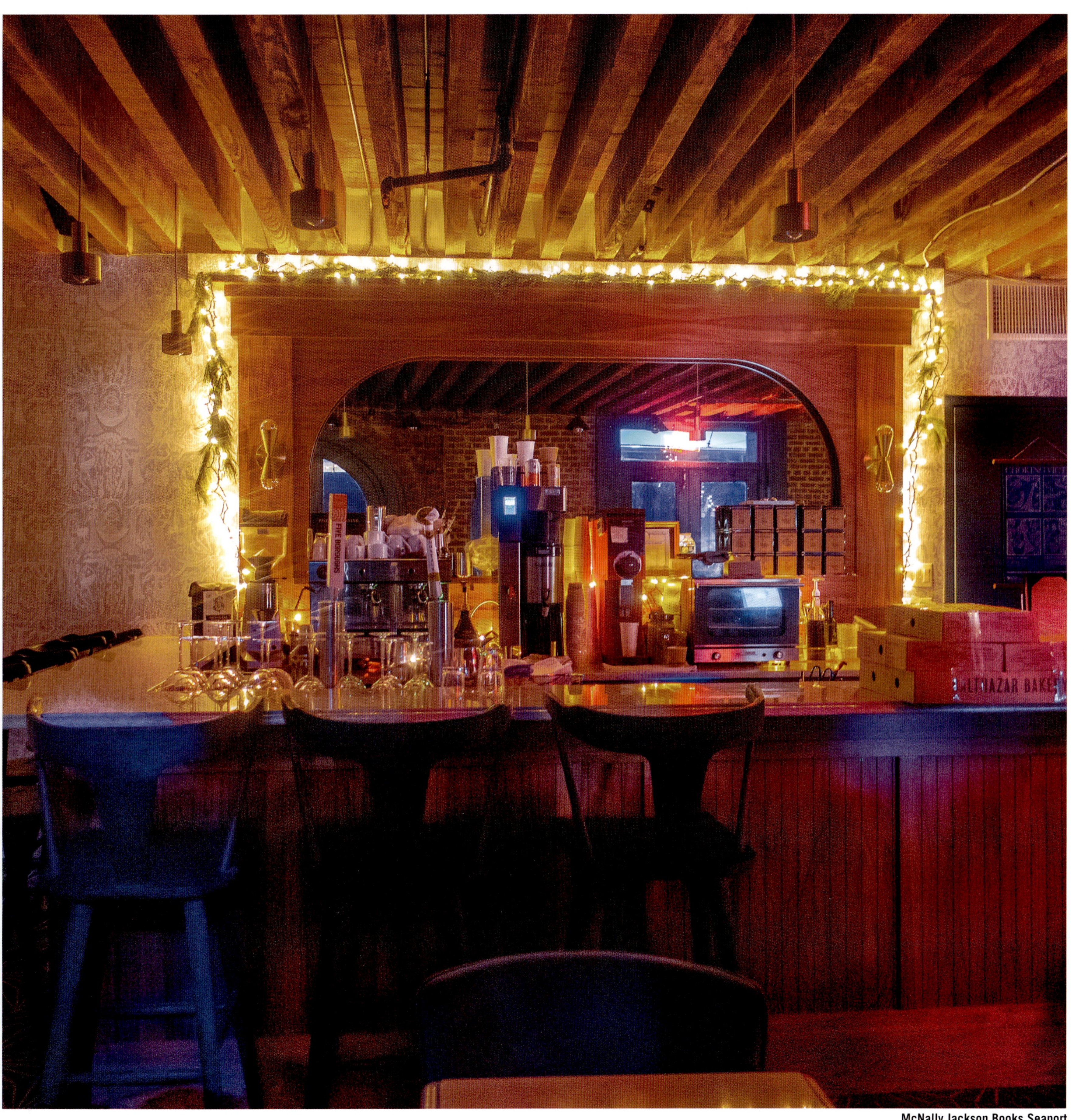

McNally Jackson Books Seaport

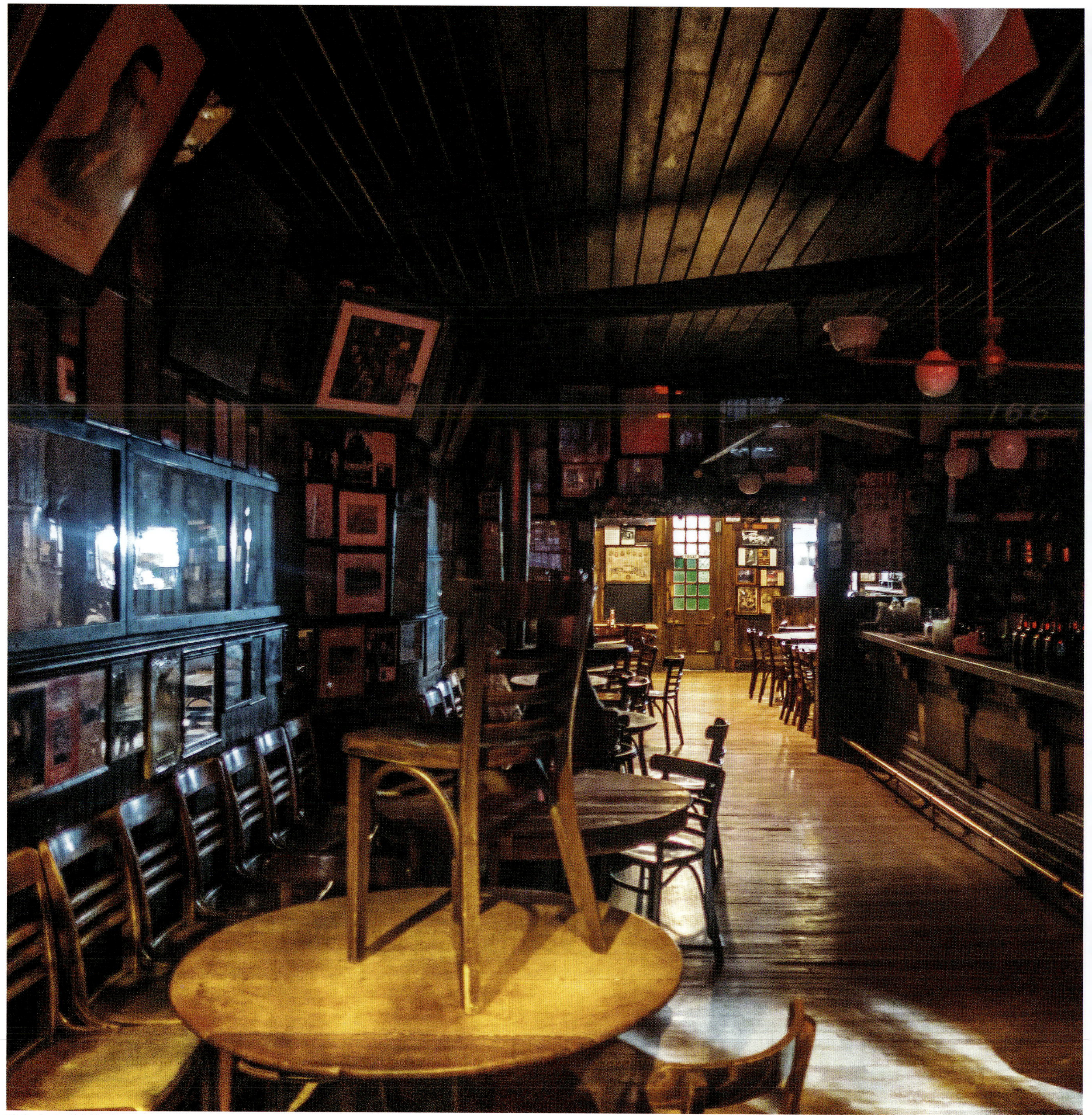

McSorley's Old Ale House

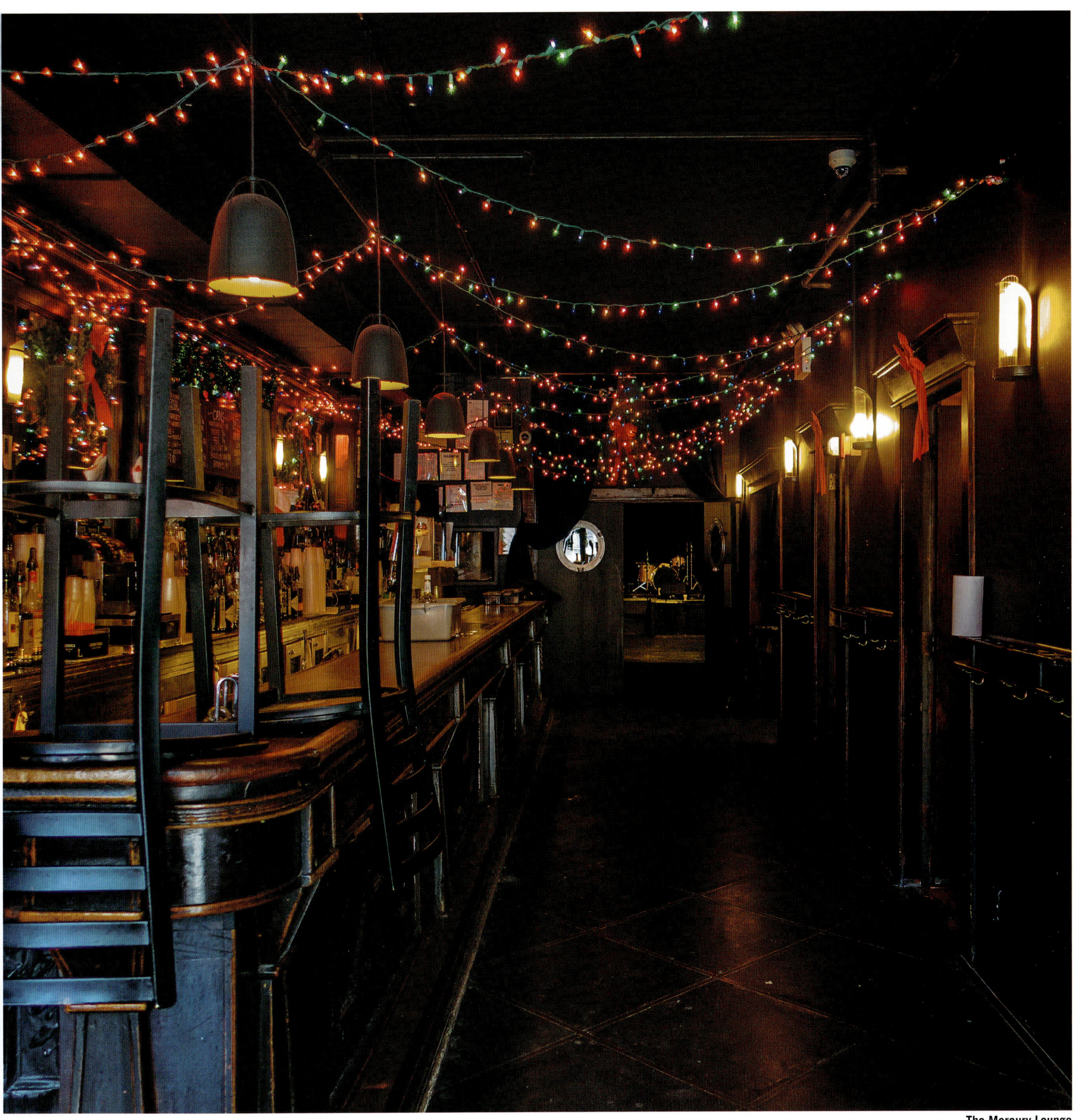

The Mercury Lounge

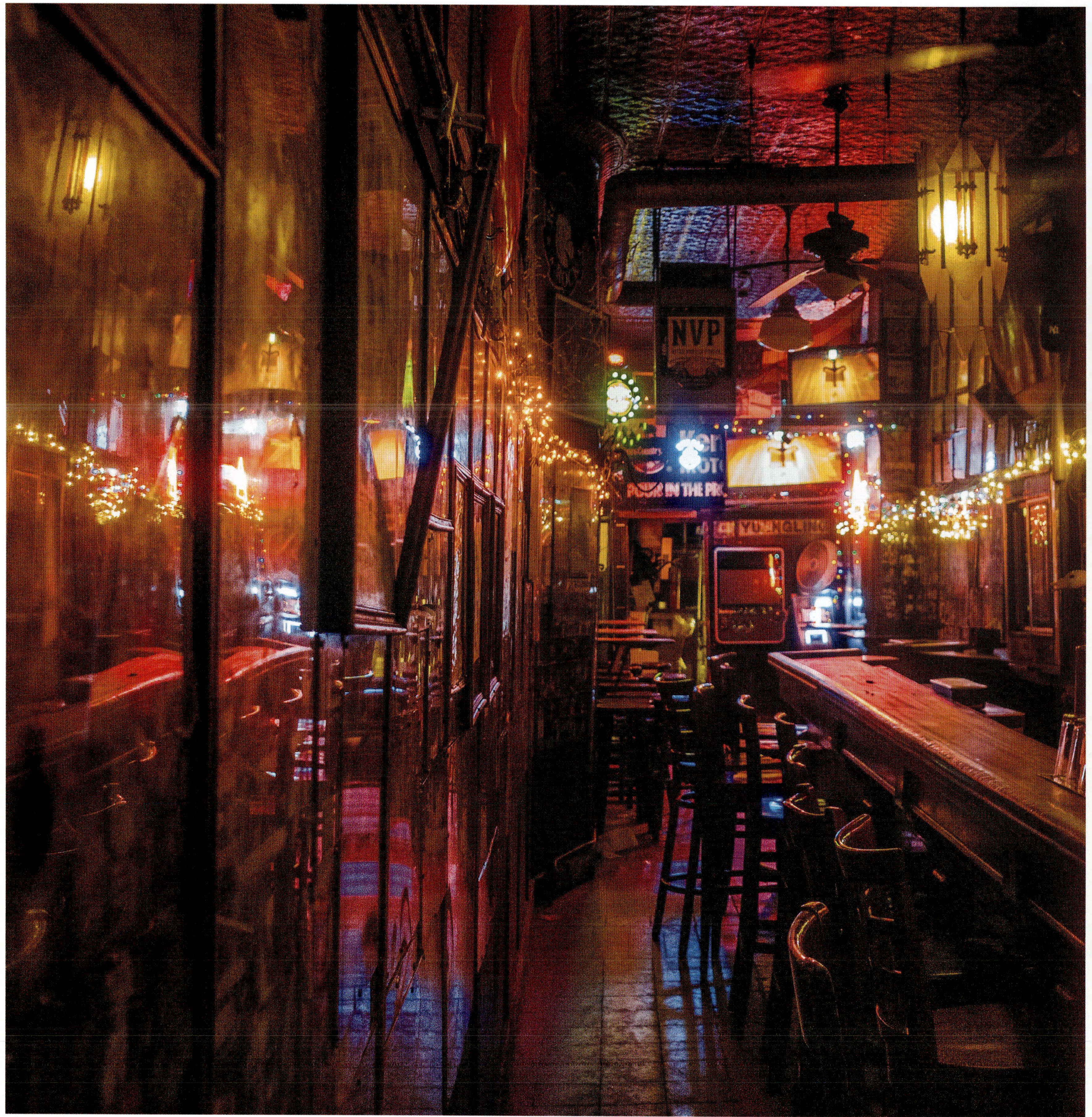

Milano's Bar

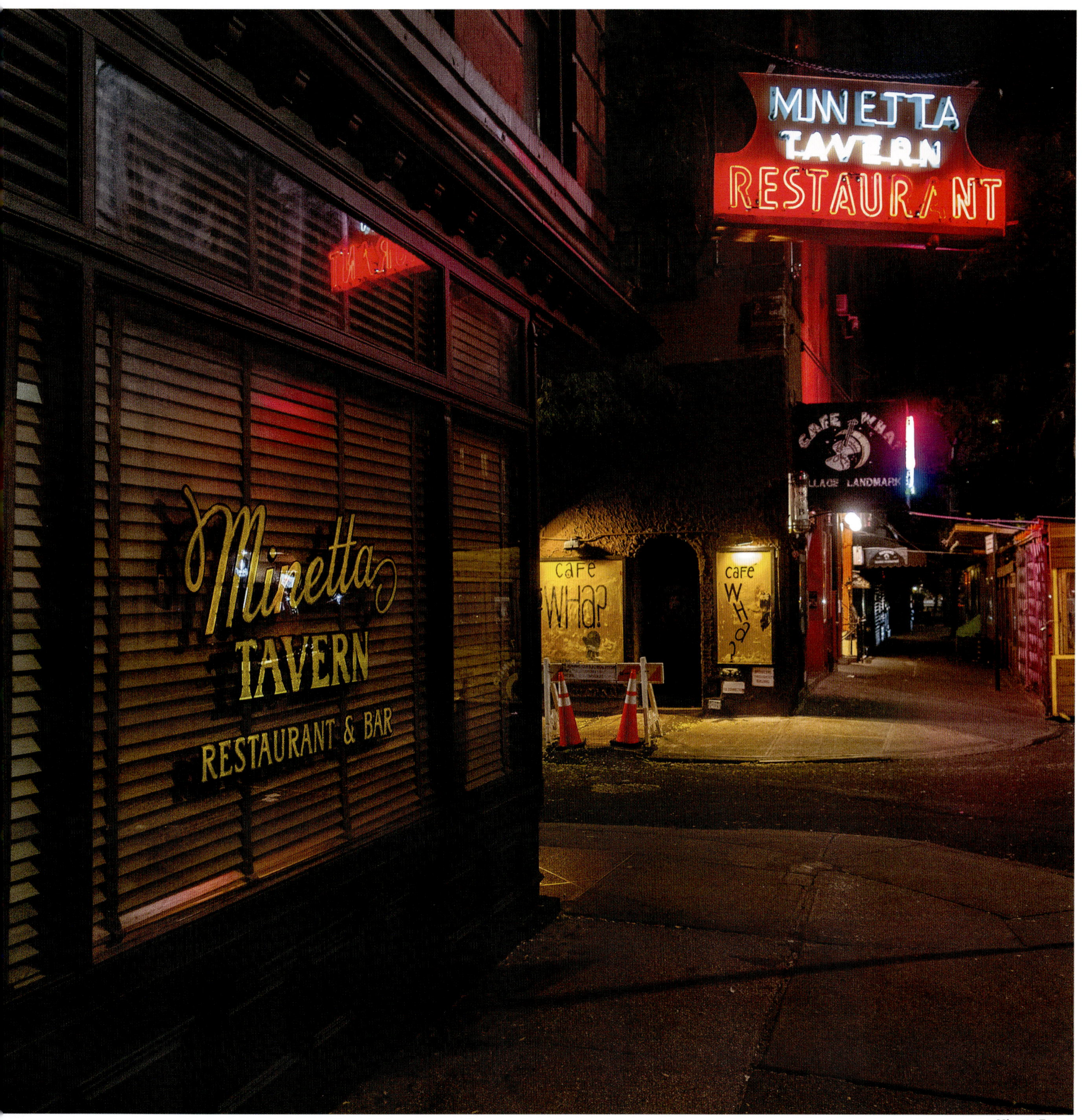

Minetta Tavern

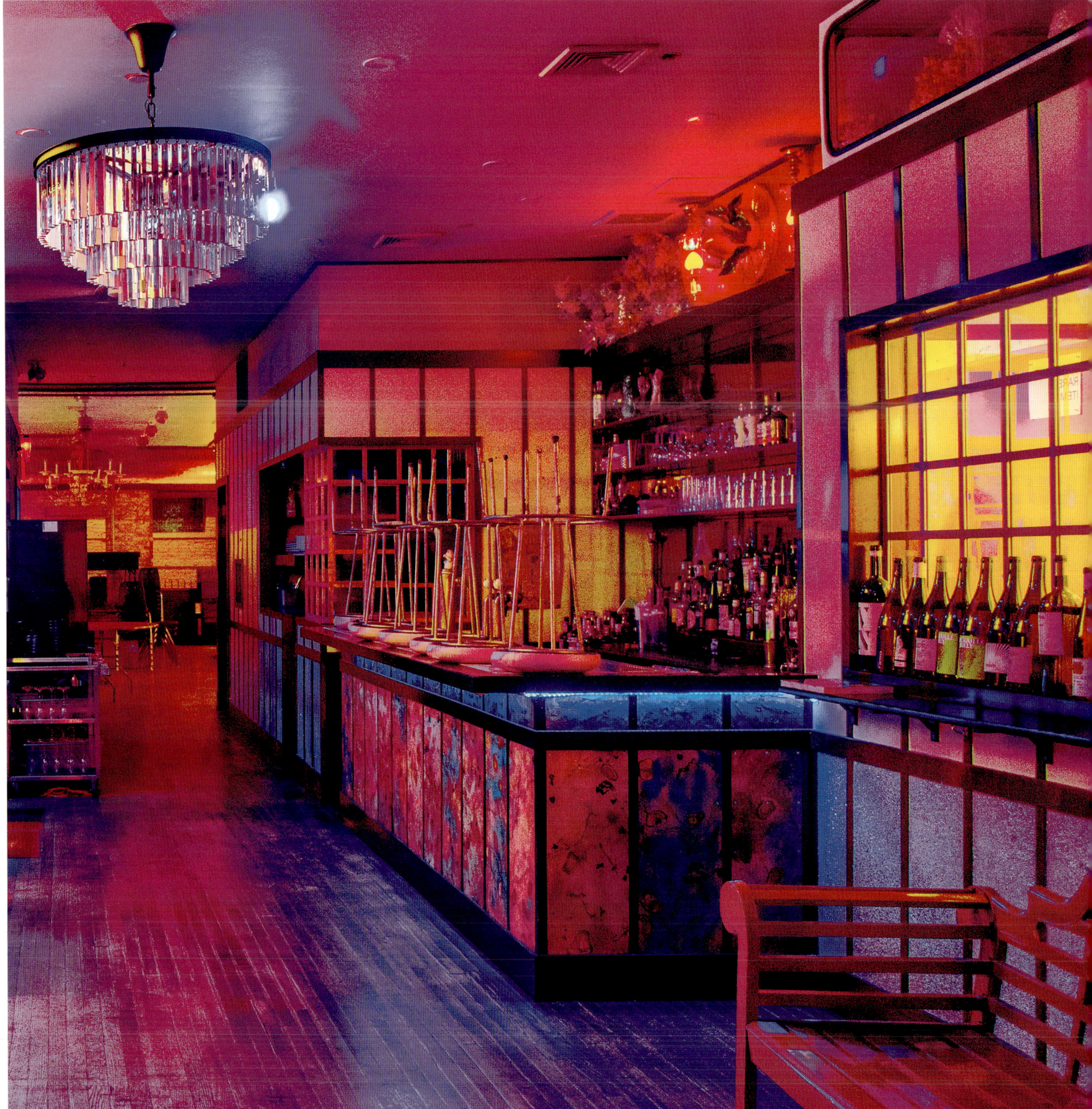

Mission Chinese

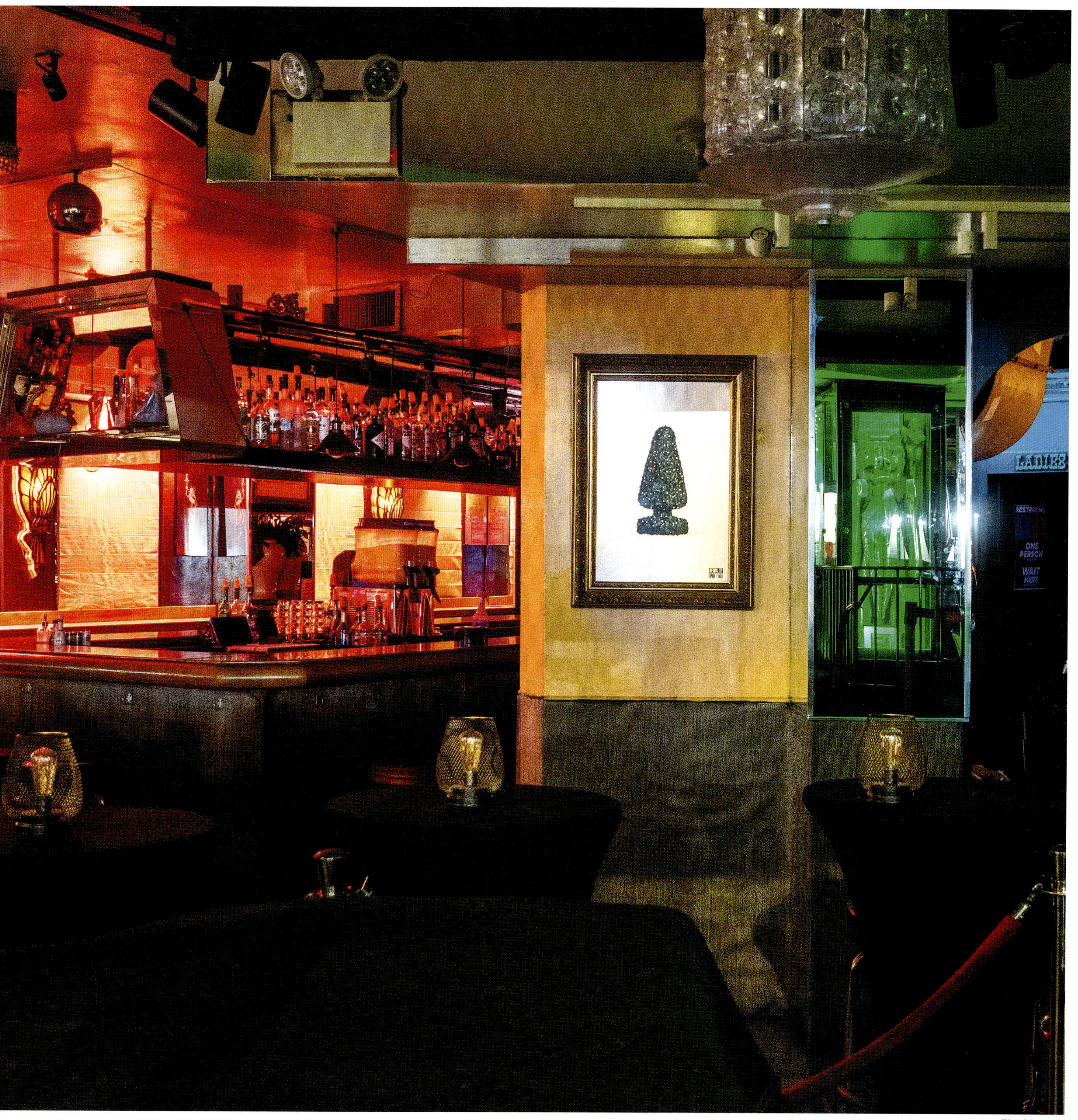

The Monster

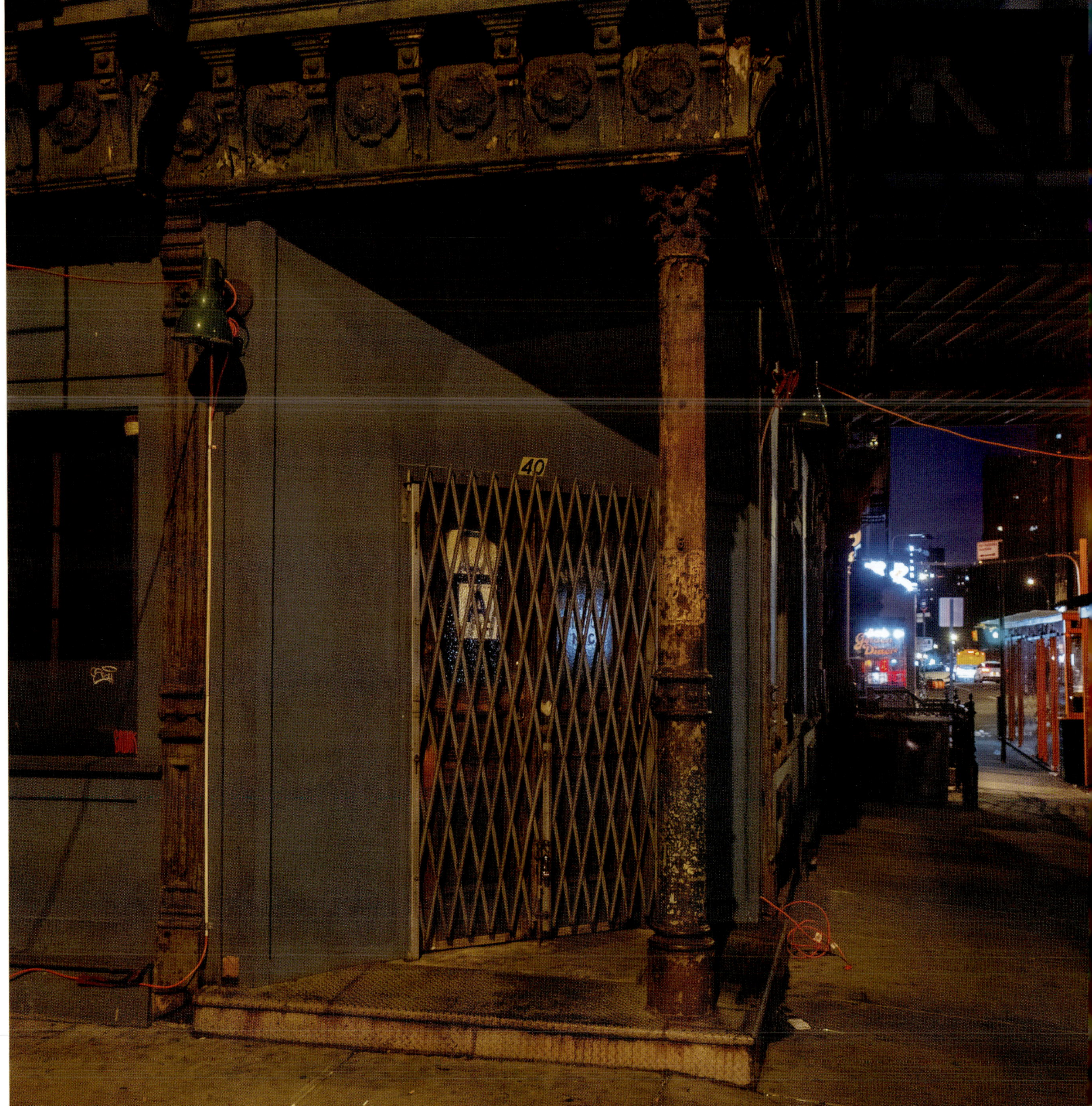

Mr. Fong's

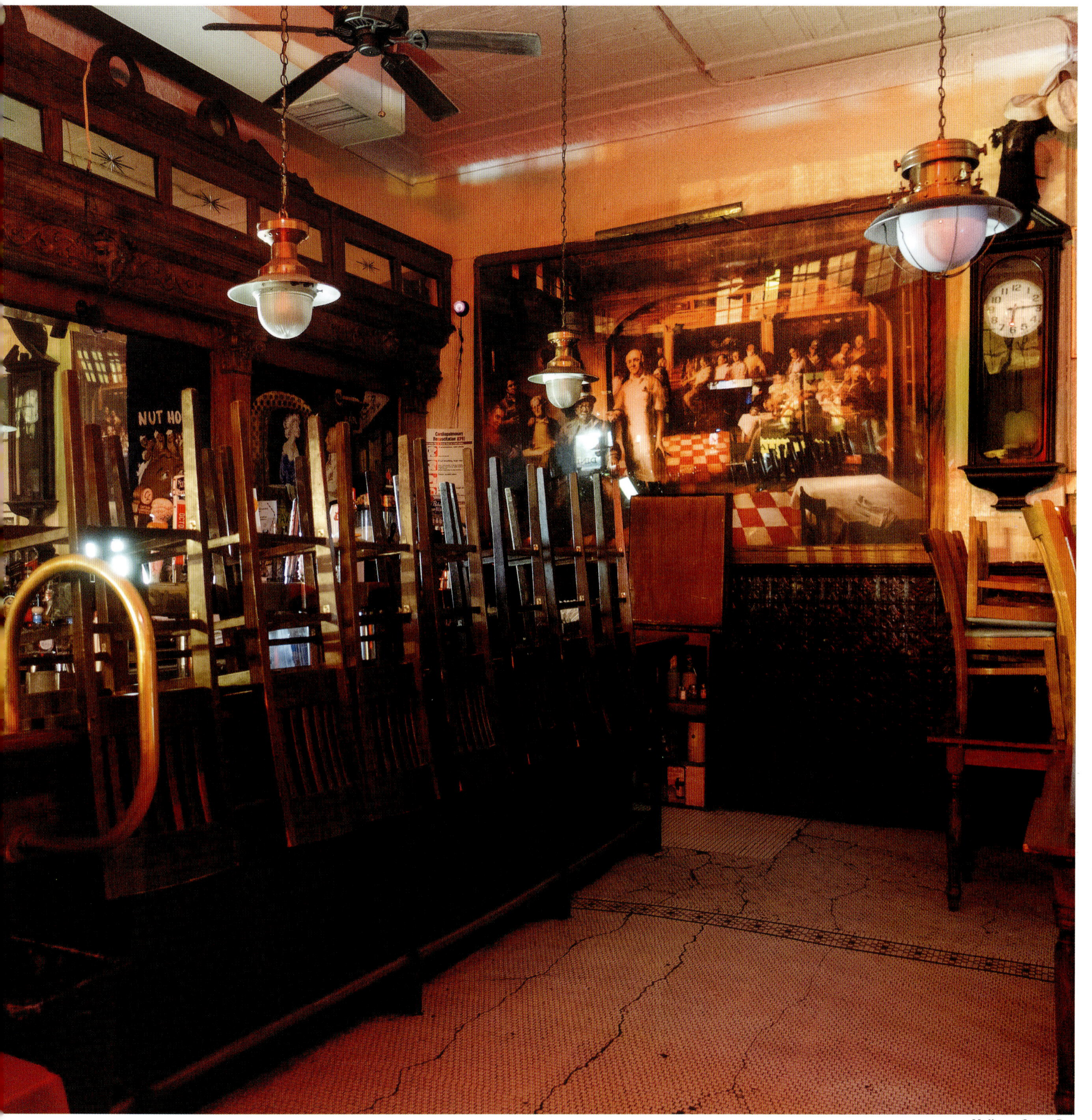

Mulberry Street Bar

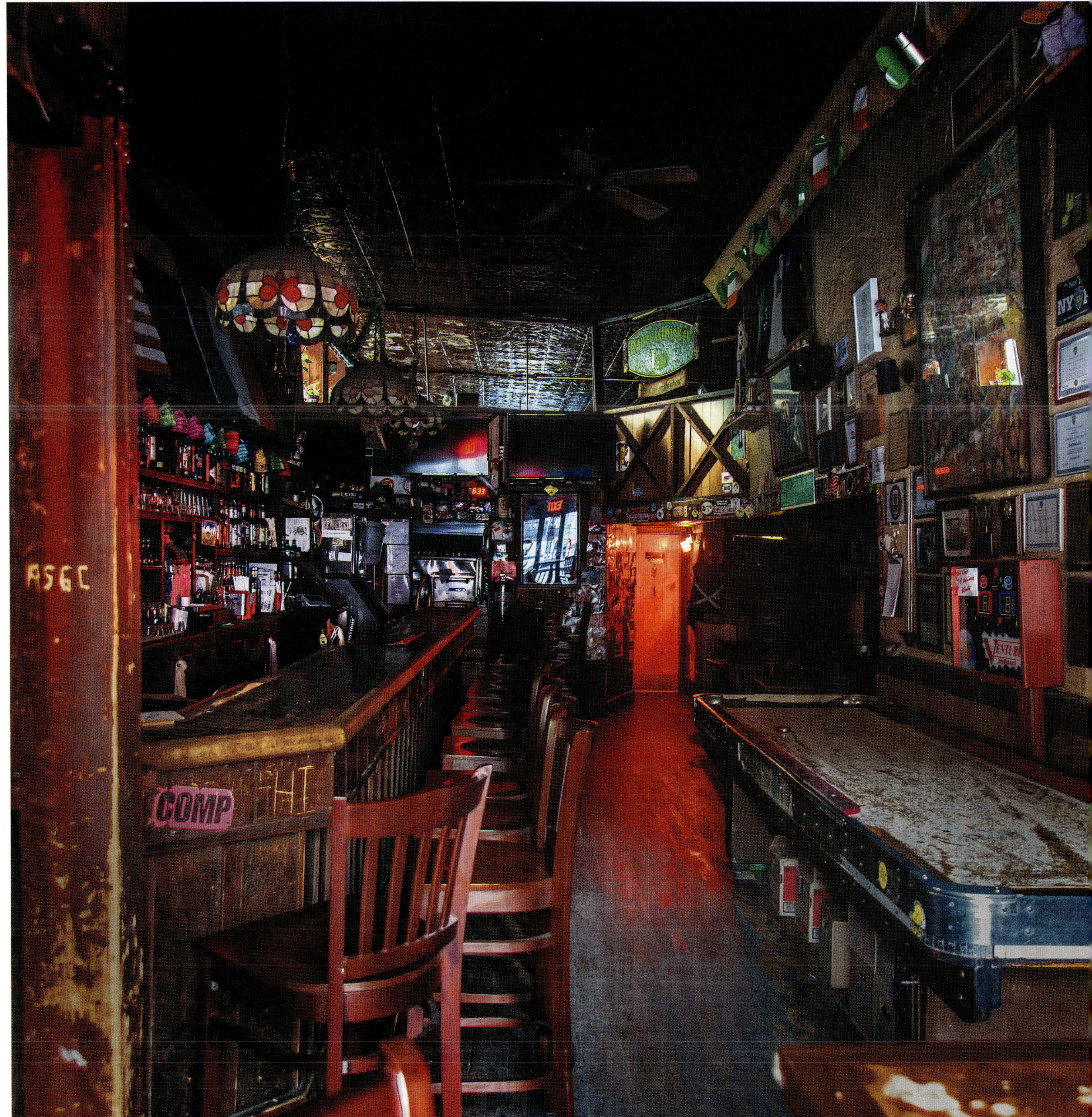

Nancy Whiskey Pub

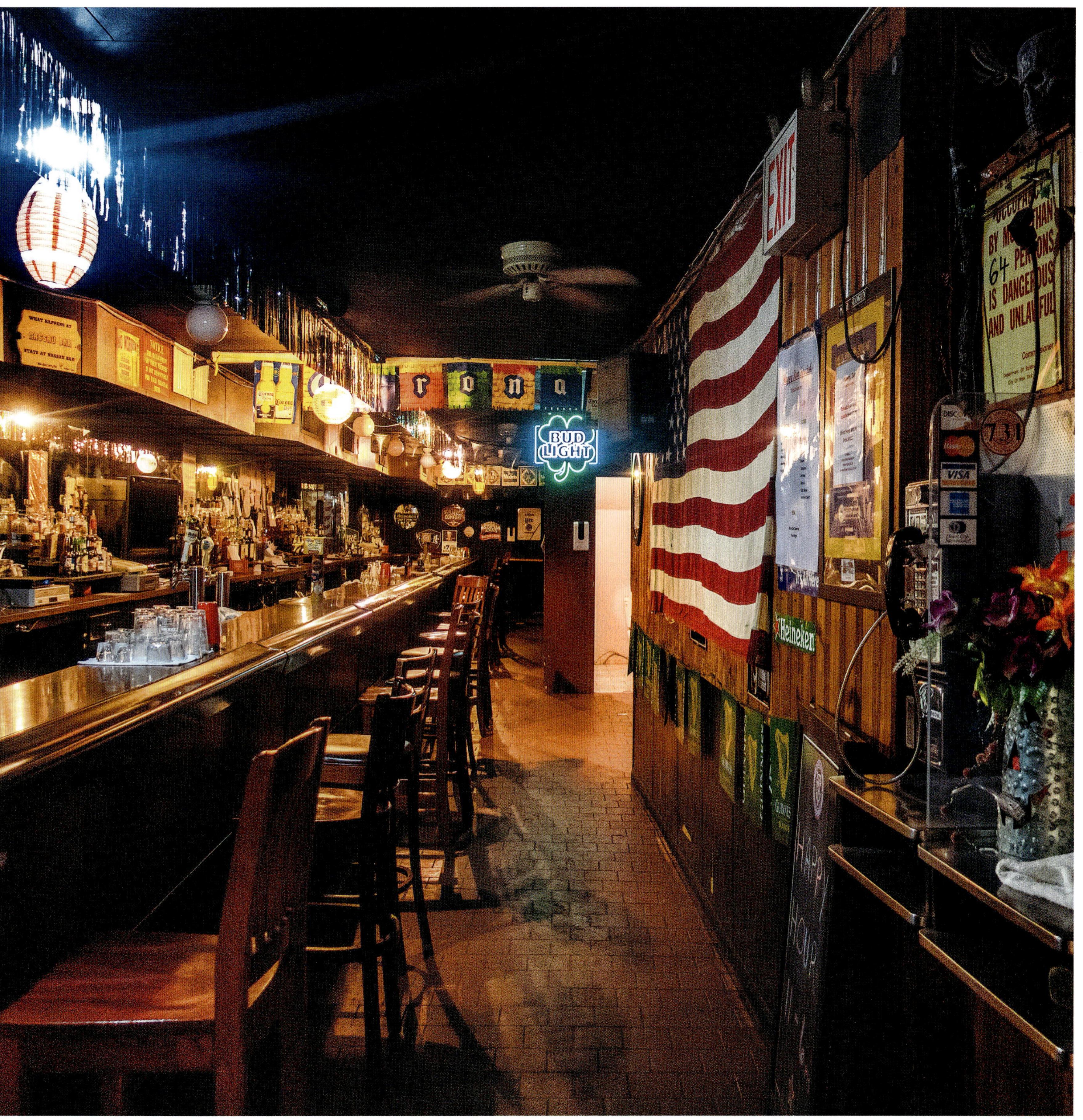

Nassau Bar

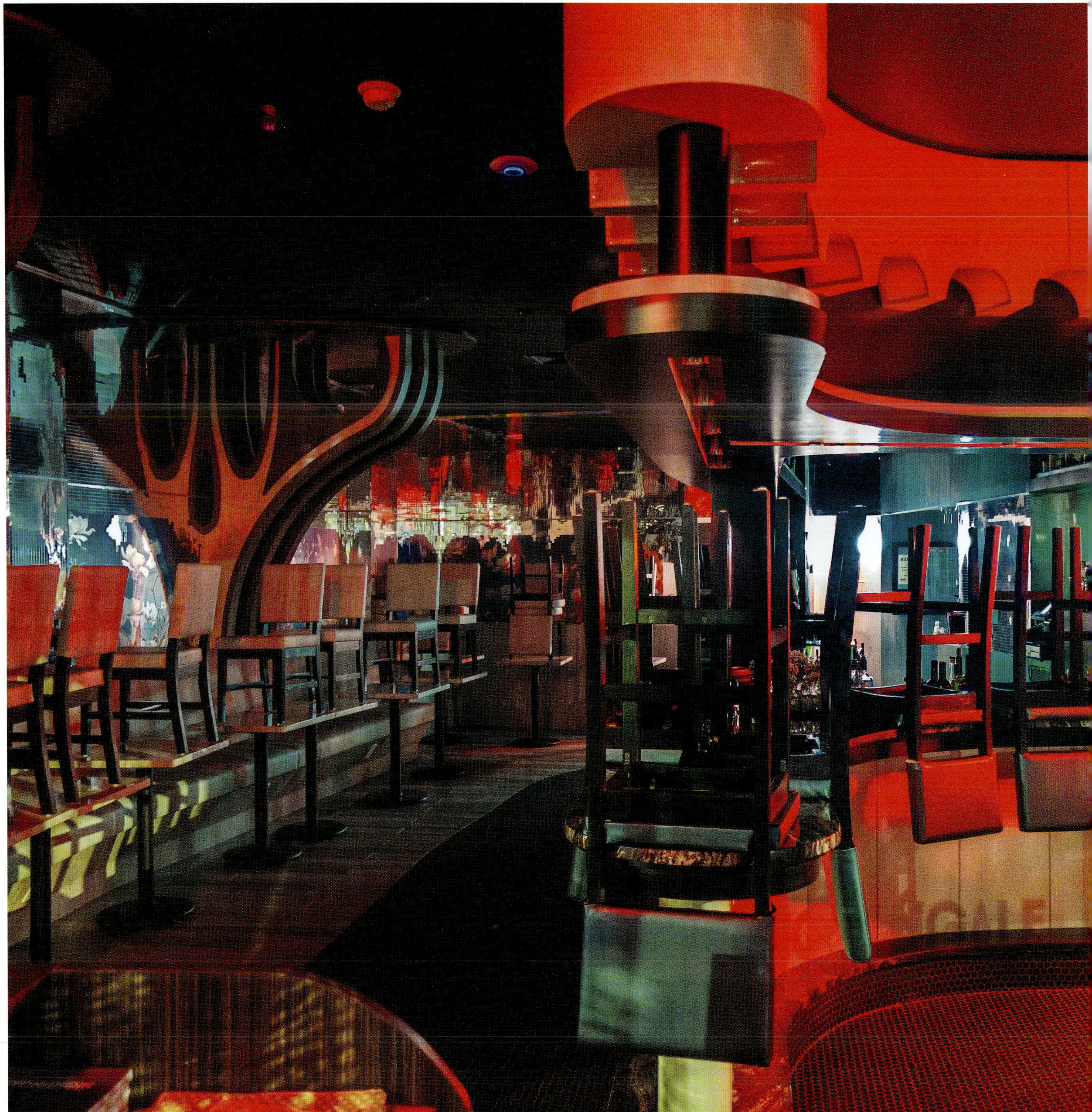

Nightingale

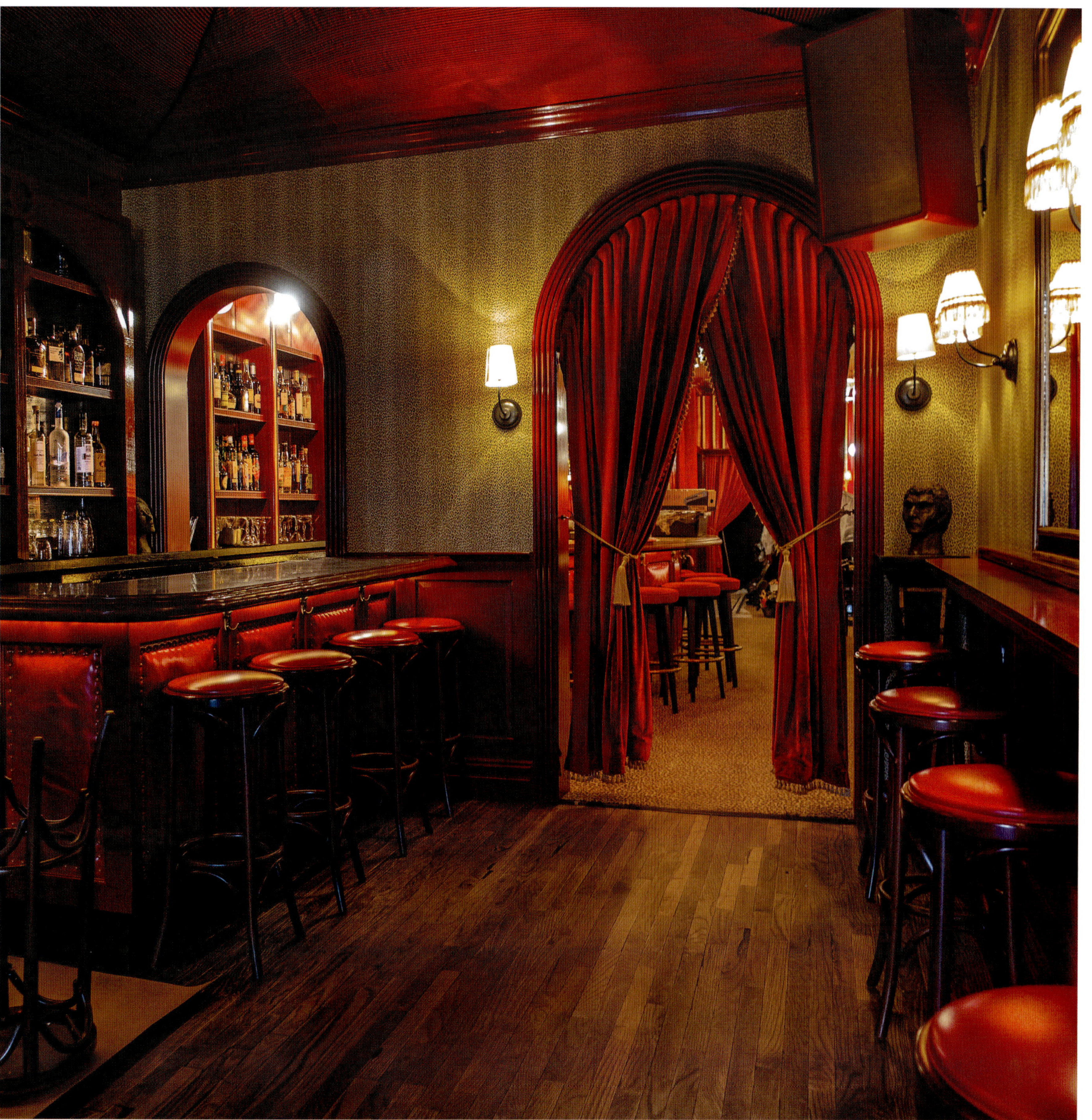

The Nines

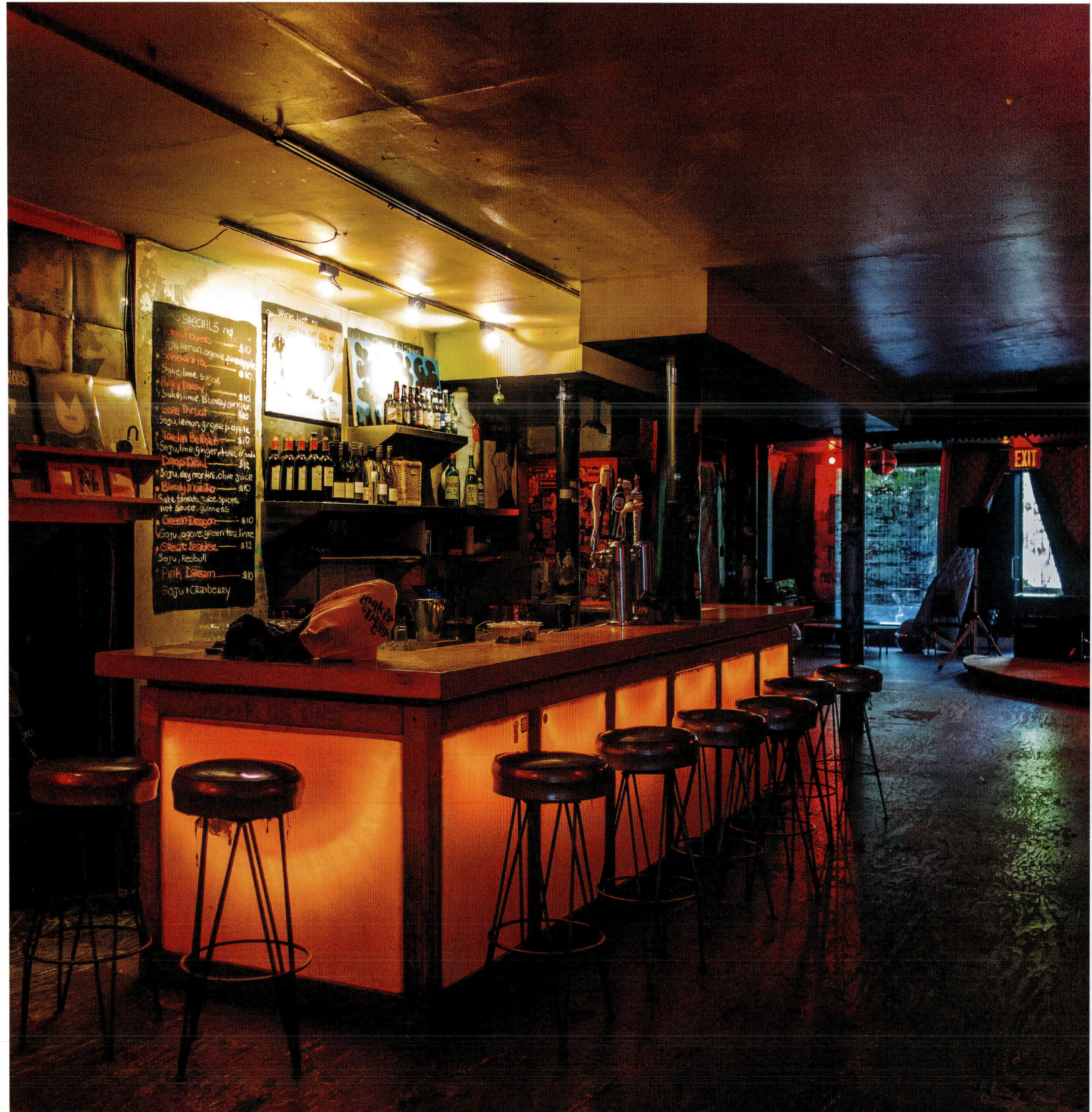

Nublu Classic

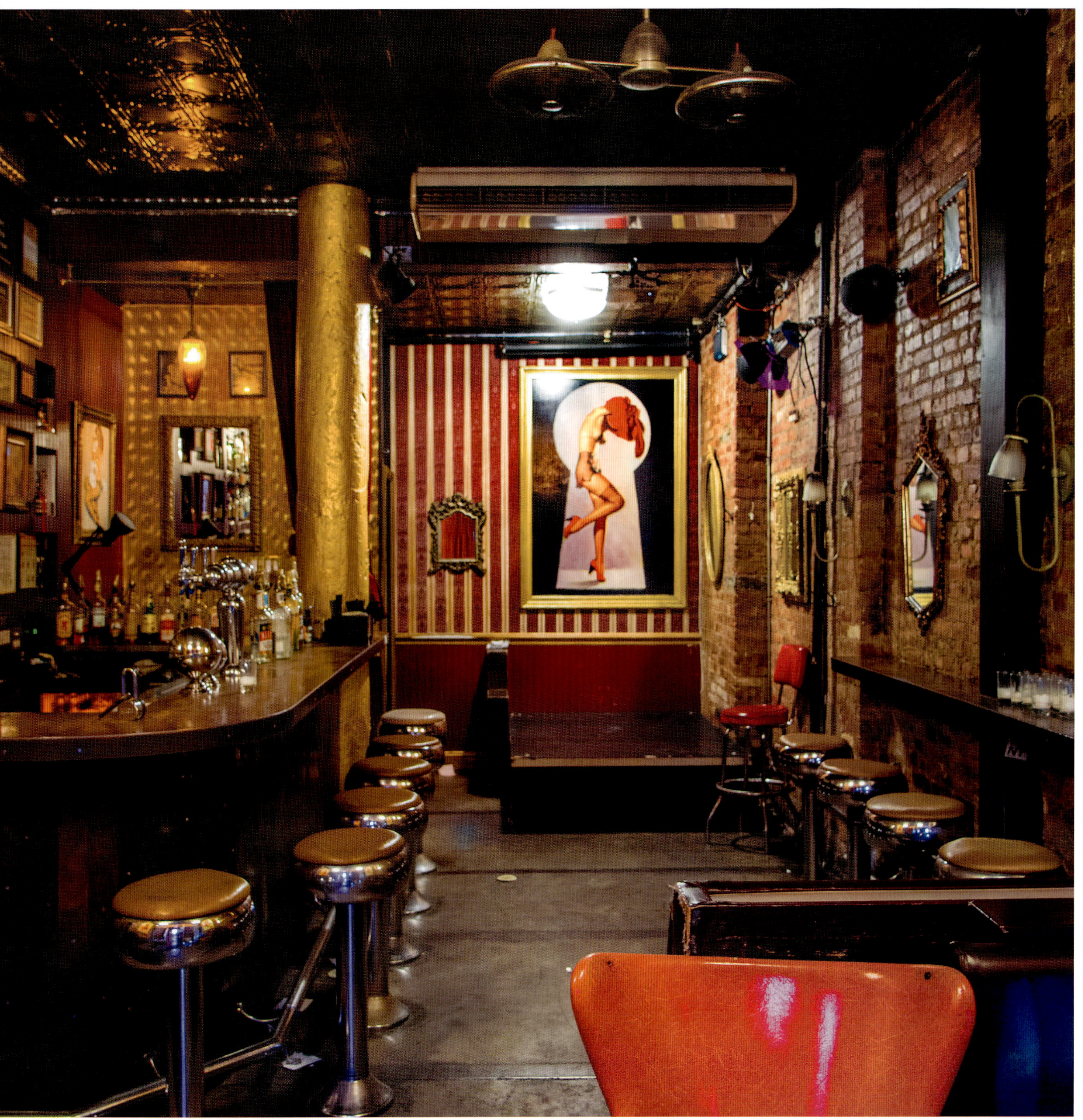

Nurse Bettie

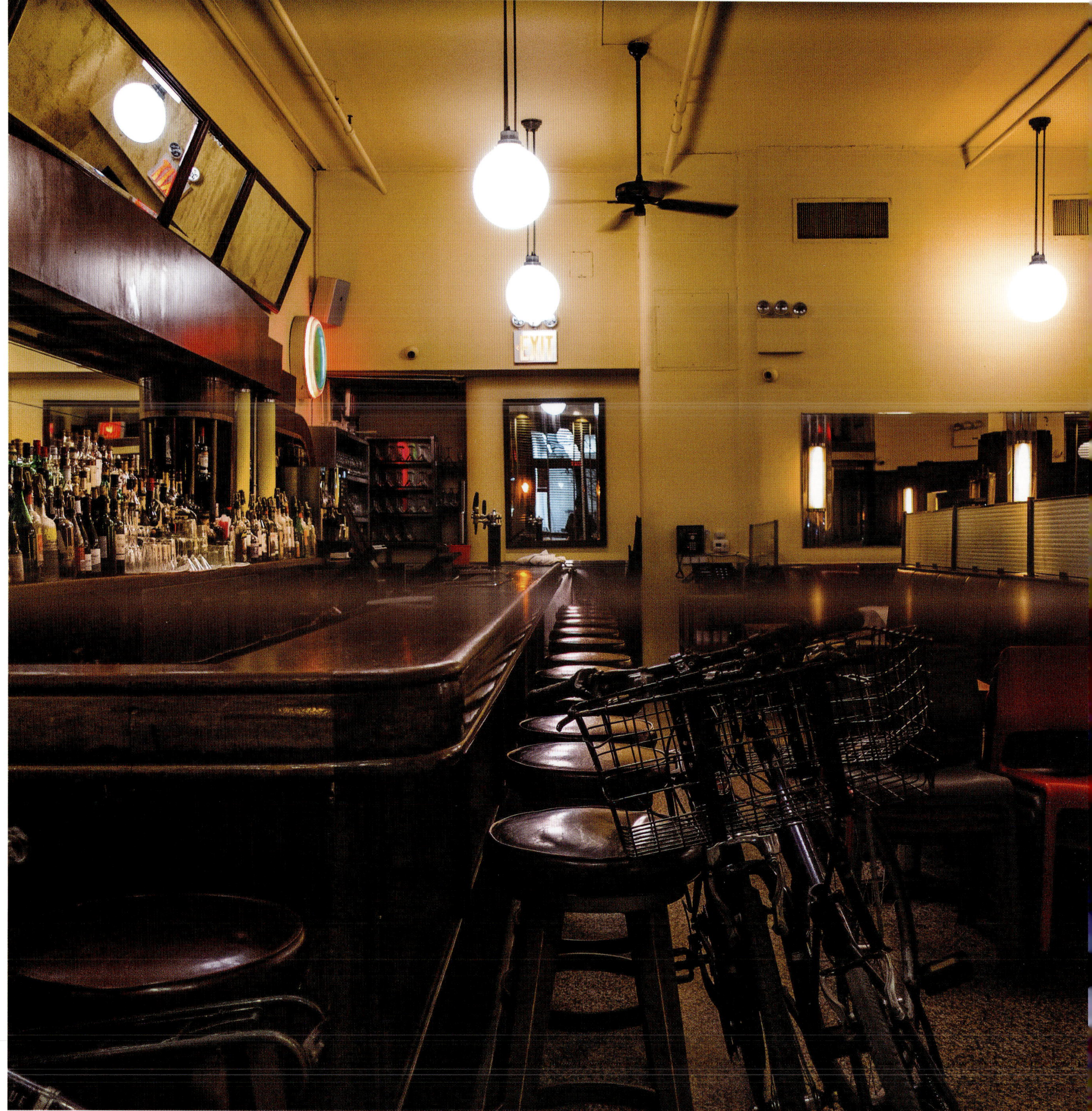

The Odeon

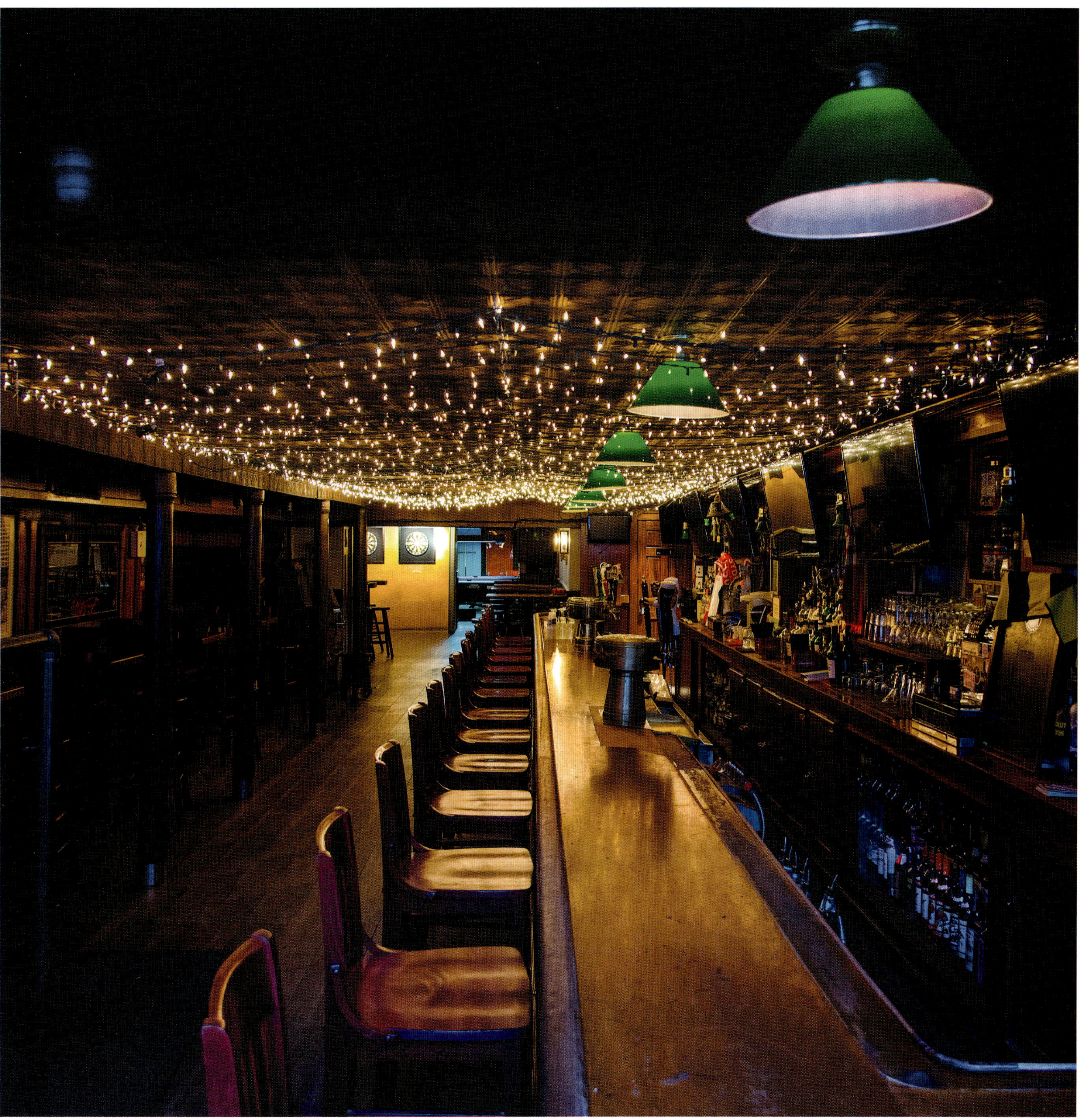

O'Hanlon's

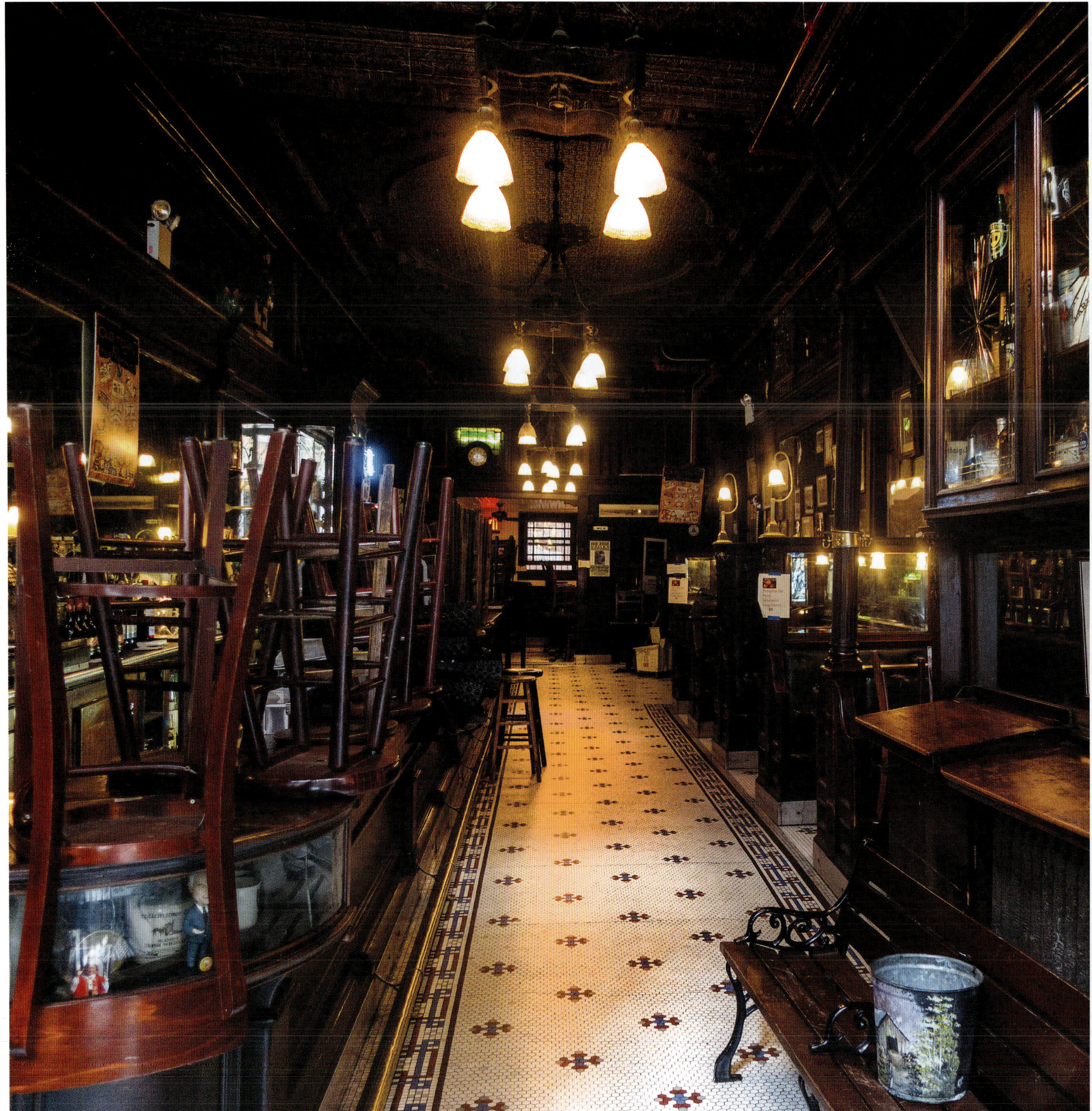

Old Town Bar

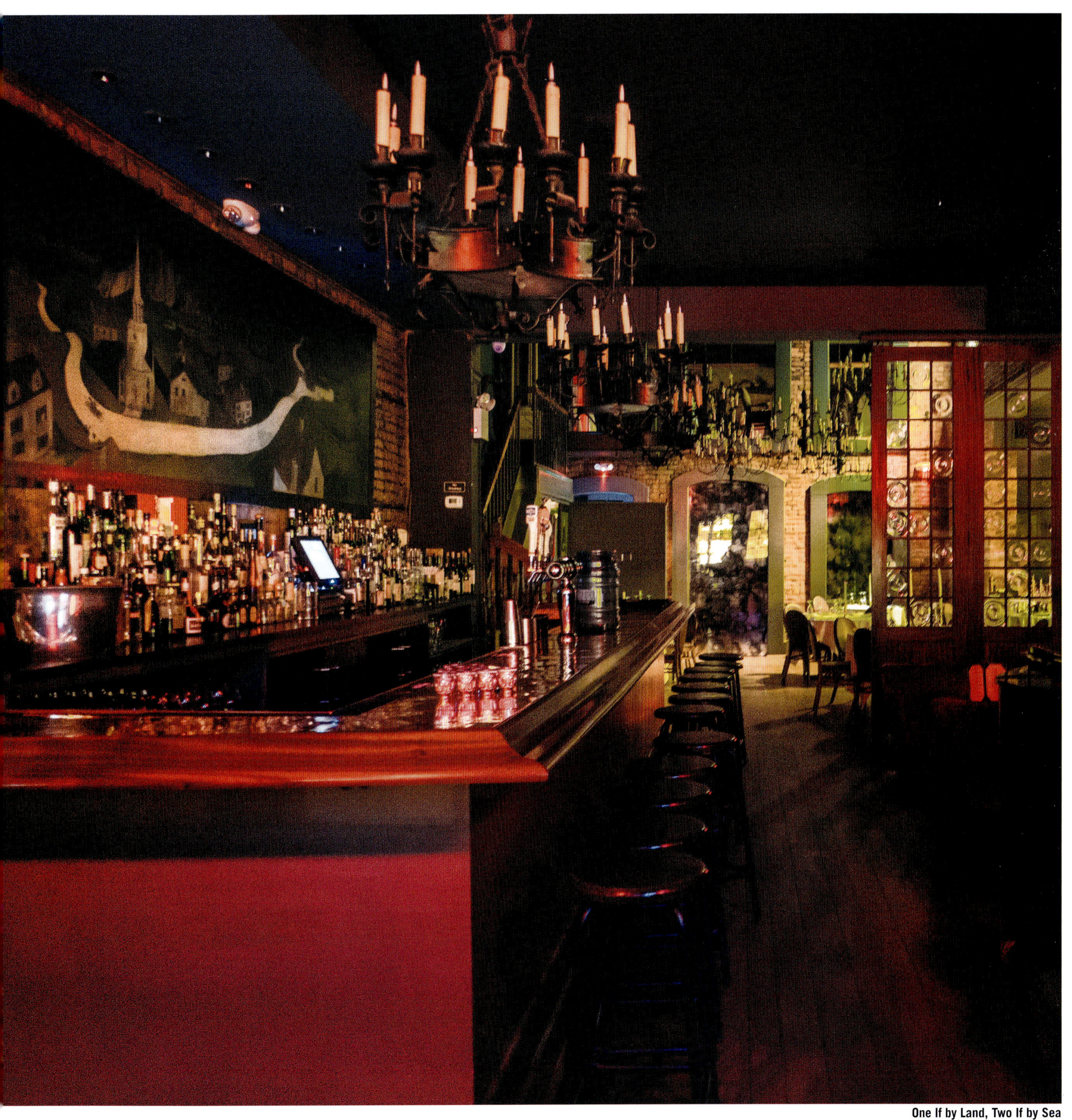

One If by Land, Two If by Sea

HAPPY HOURS
CHICKEN WINGS
FRIES
WELL DRINKS
RED & WHITE WINE
ALL DRAFTS
ALL DAY | MON
WINE 4 & DRAF
cheers
Dickel

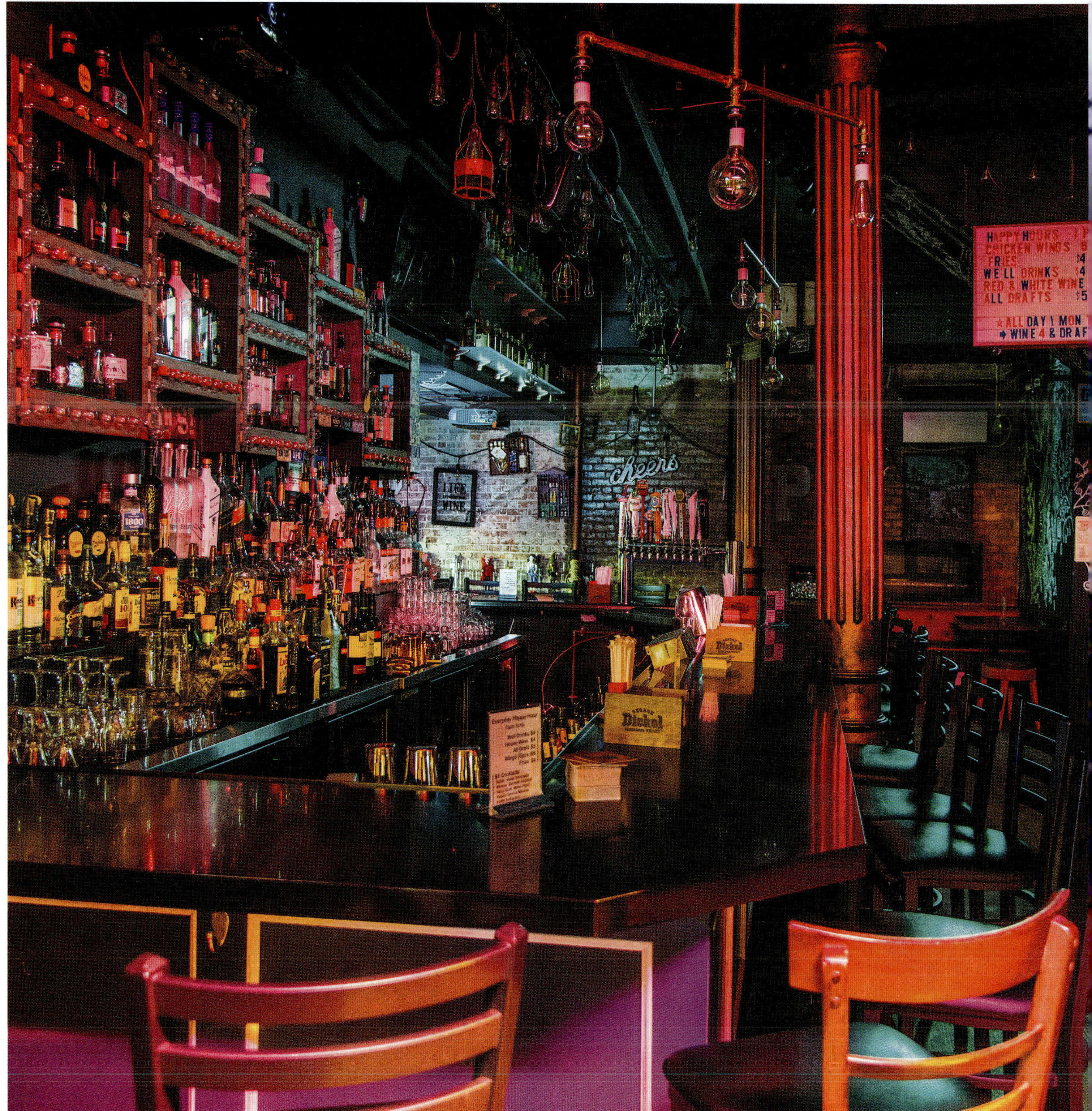

Oppa Bistro

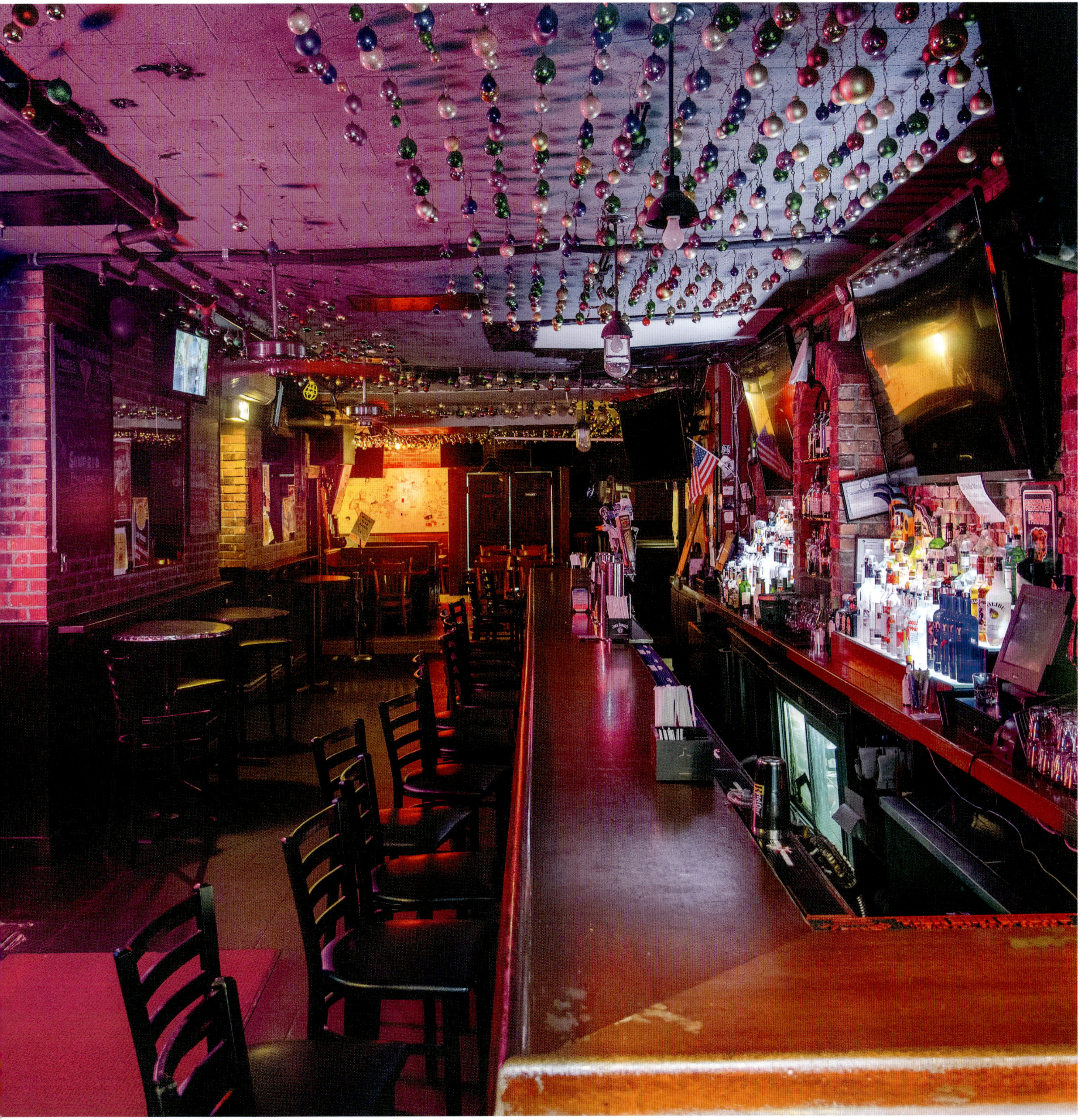

Overlook

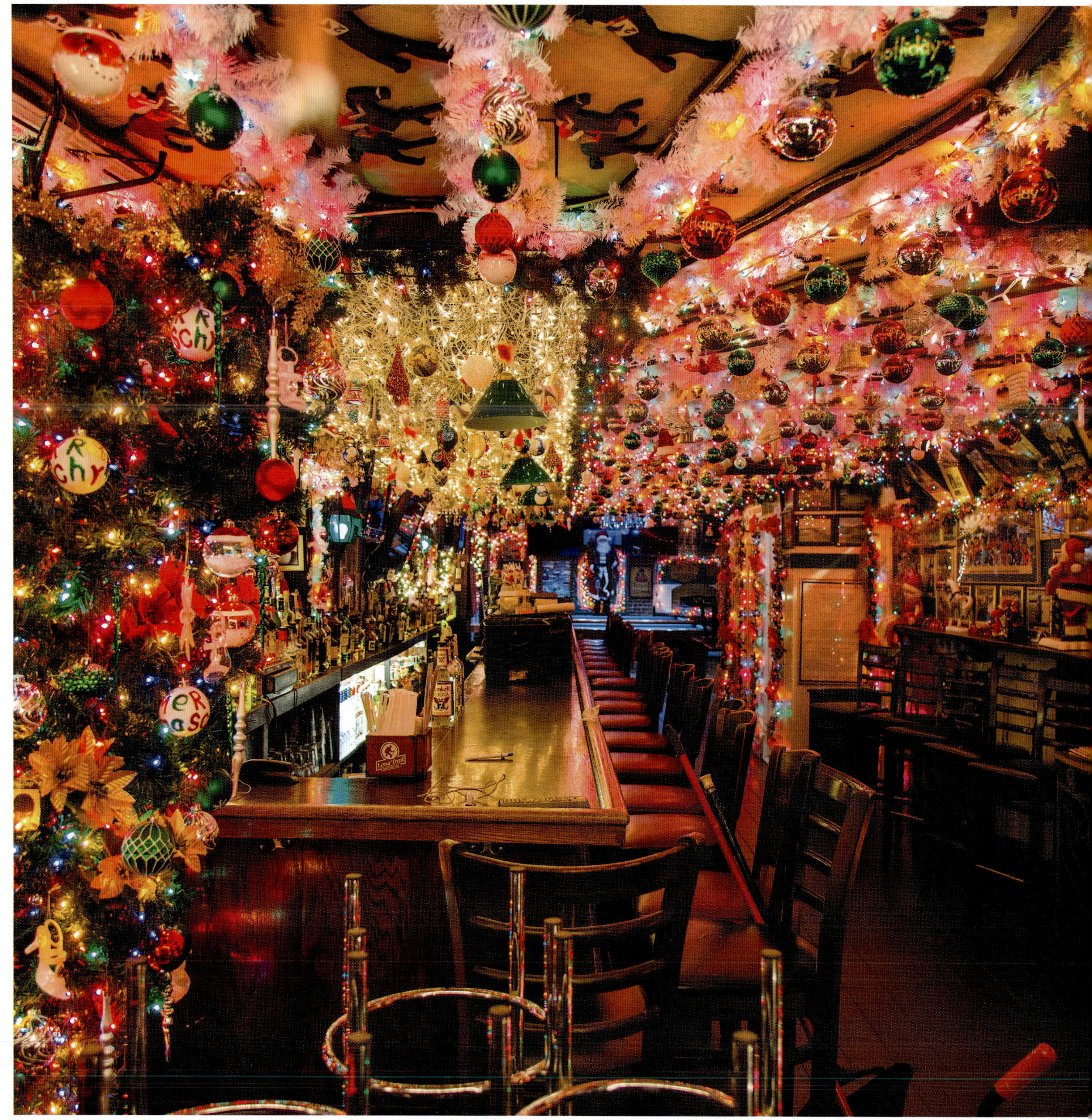
Paddy Maguire's Ale House

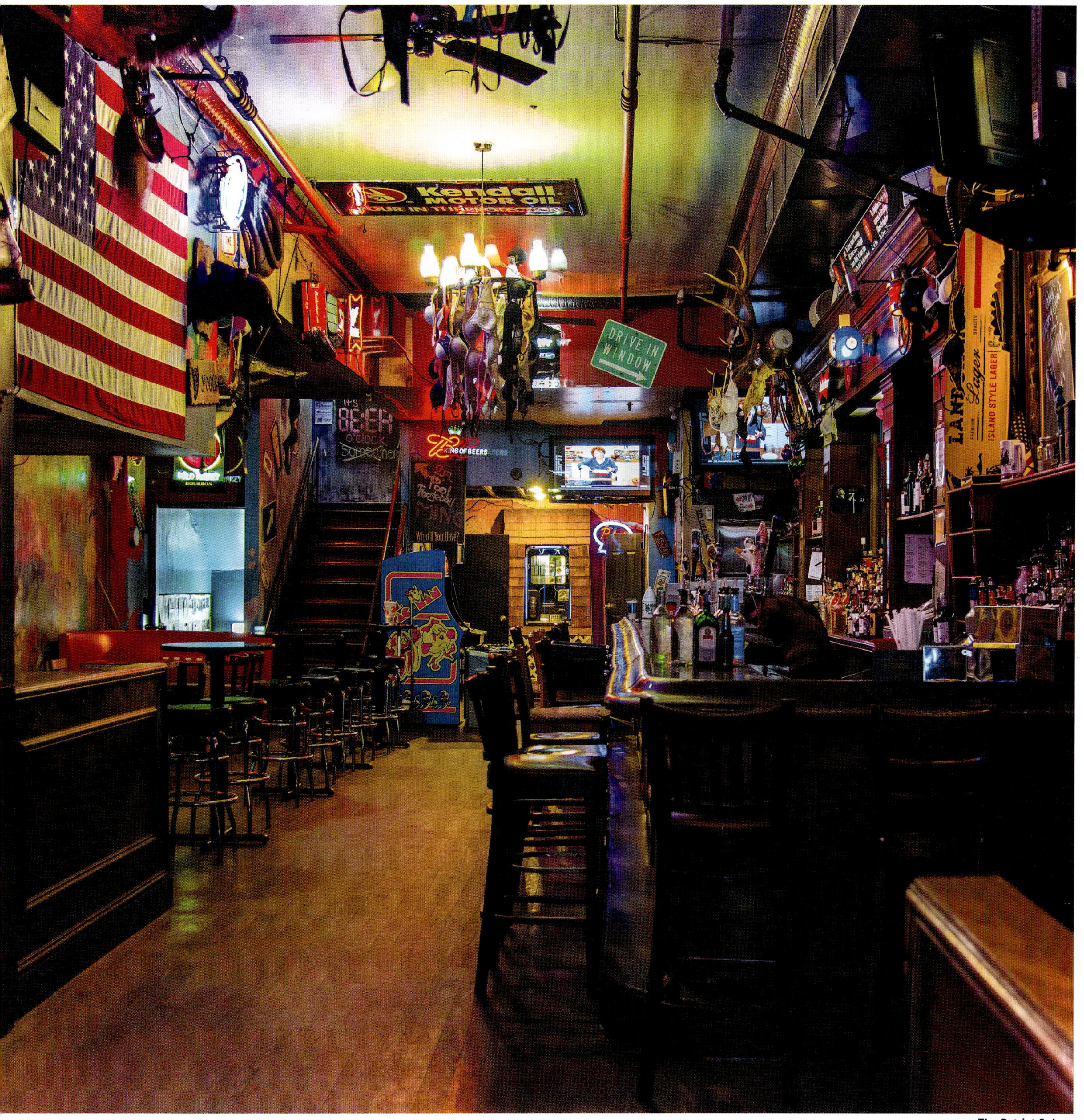

The Patriot Saloon

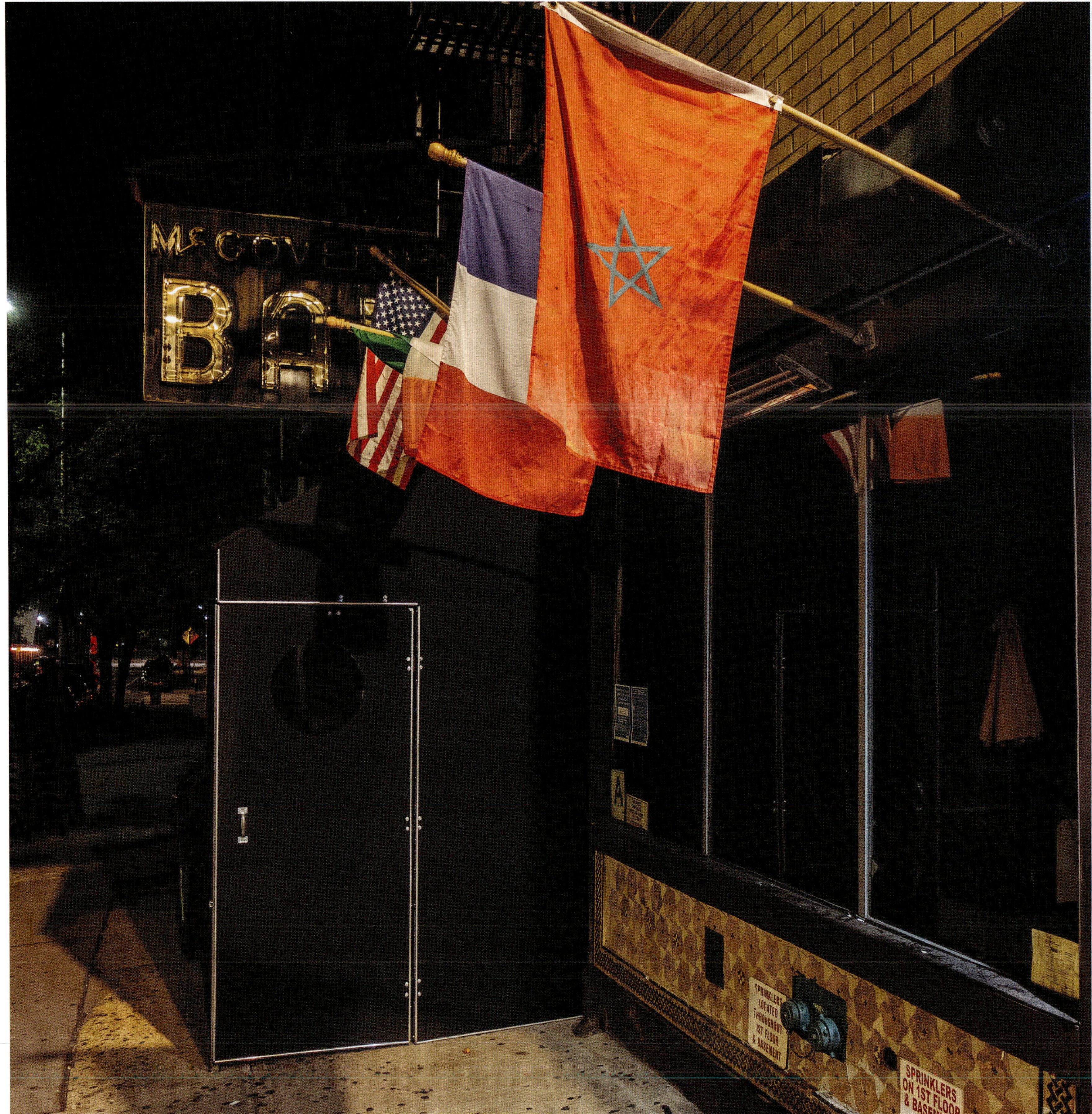

Paul's Casablanca

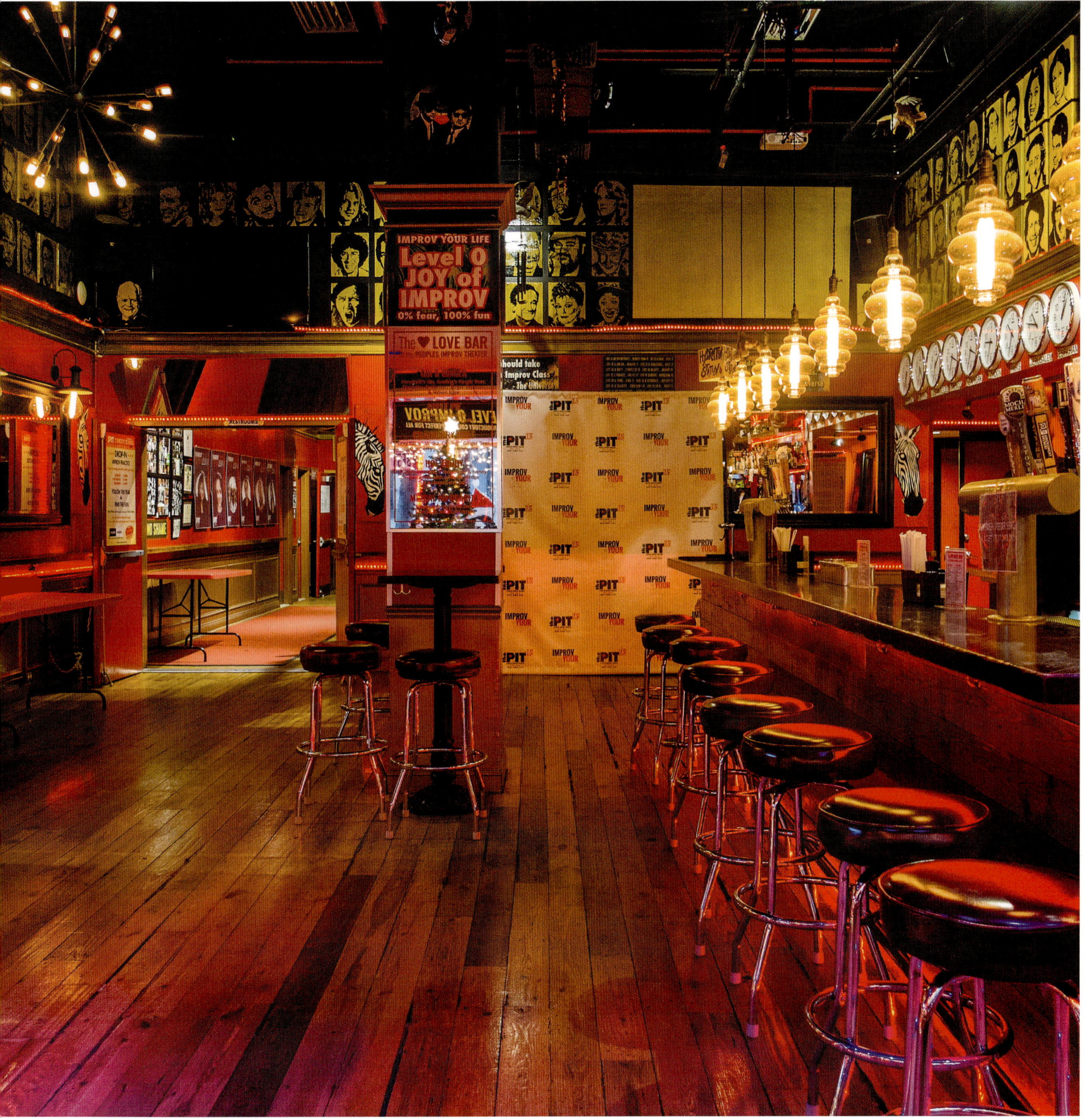

Peoples Improv Theater

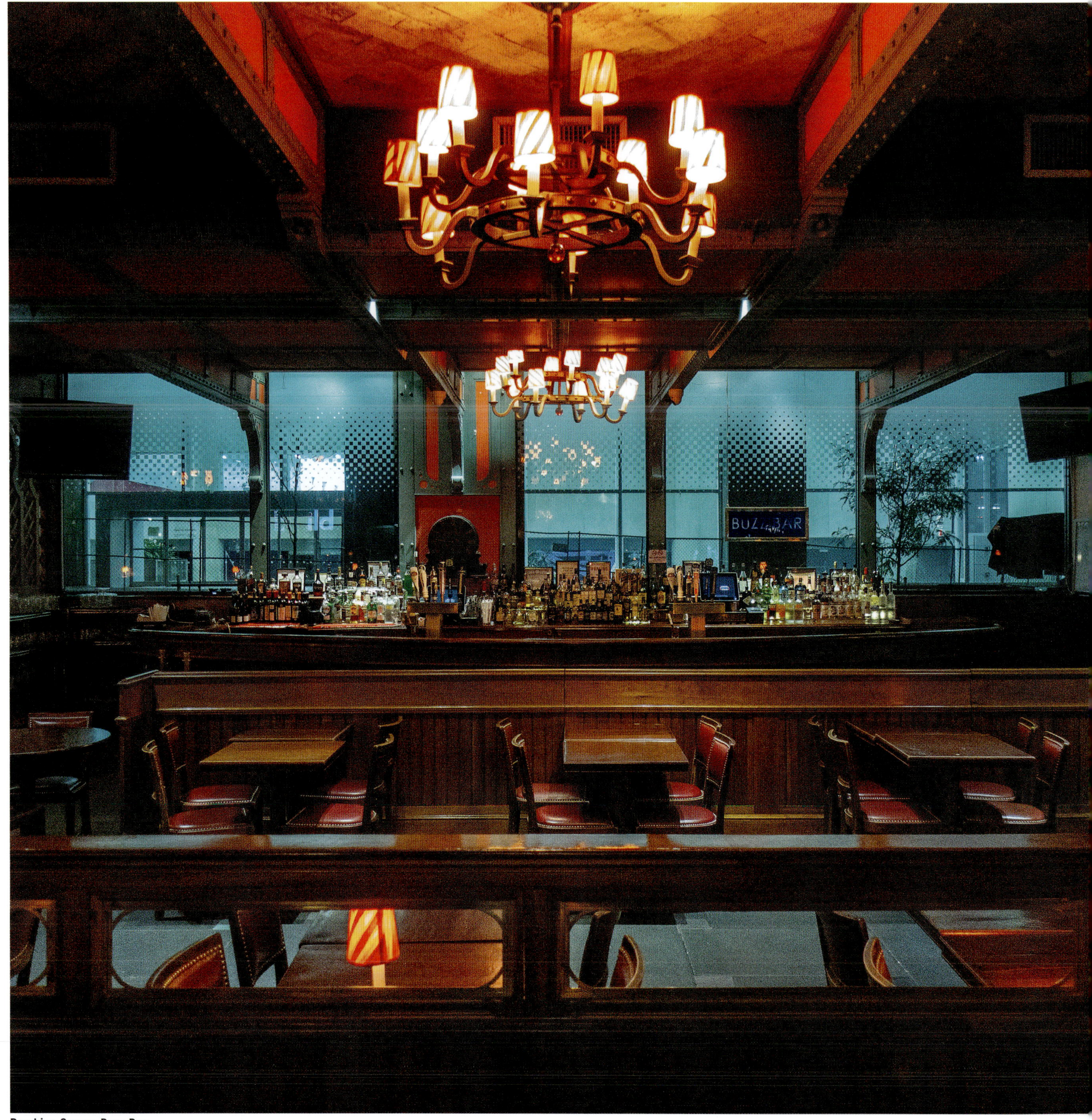

Pershing Square Buzz Bar

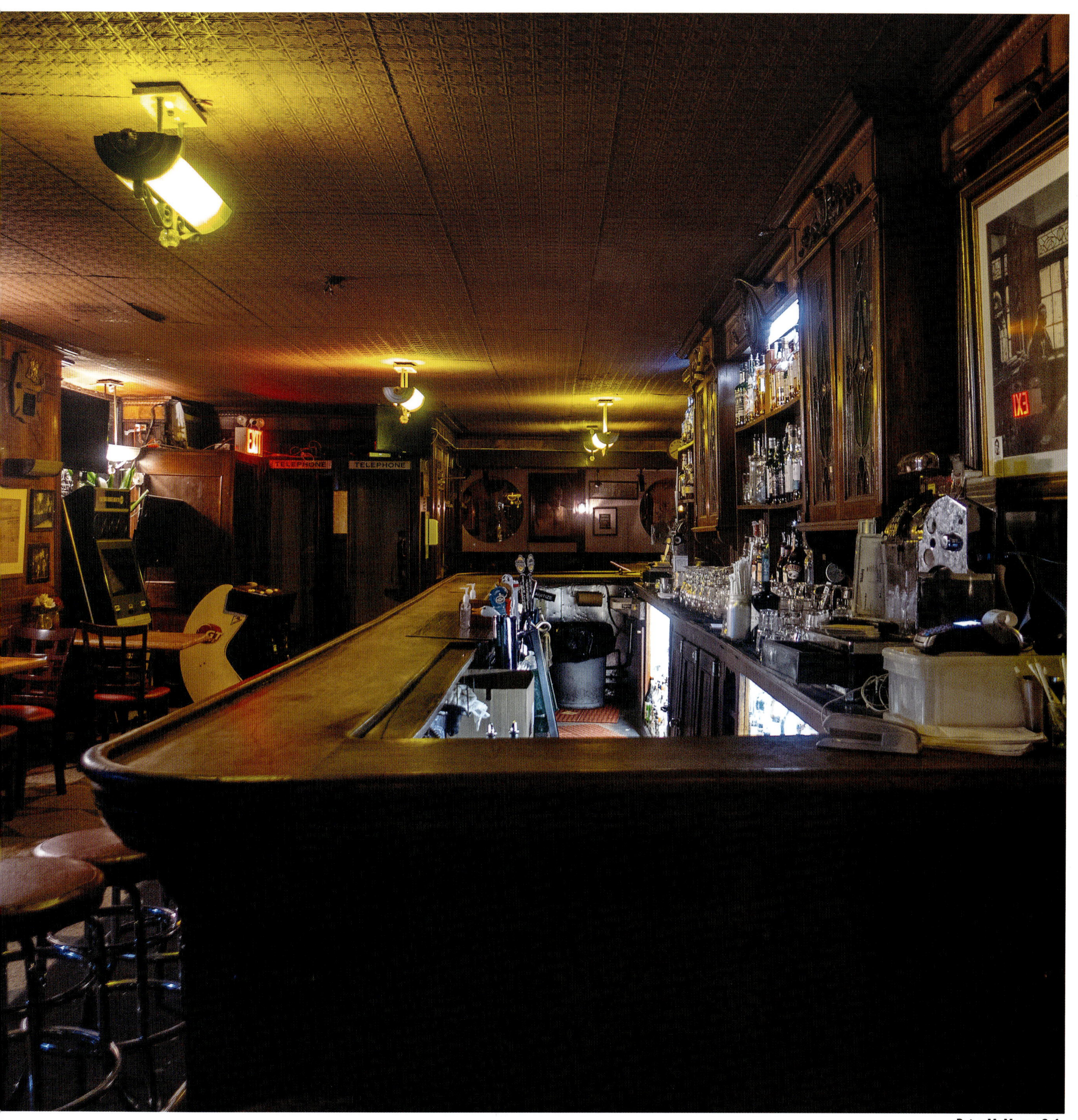

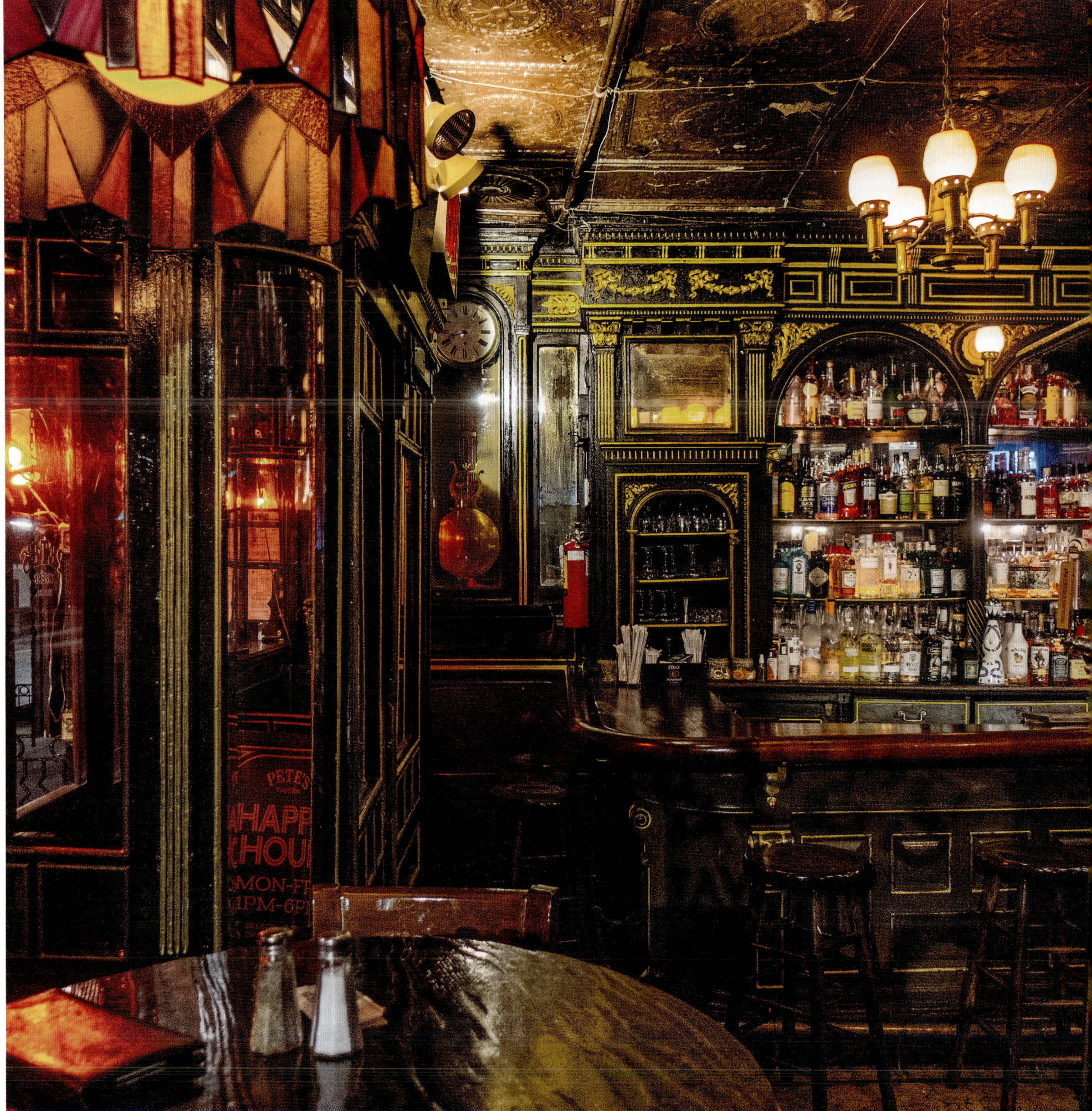

Pete's Tavern

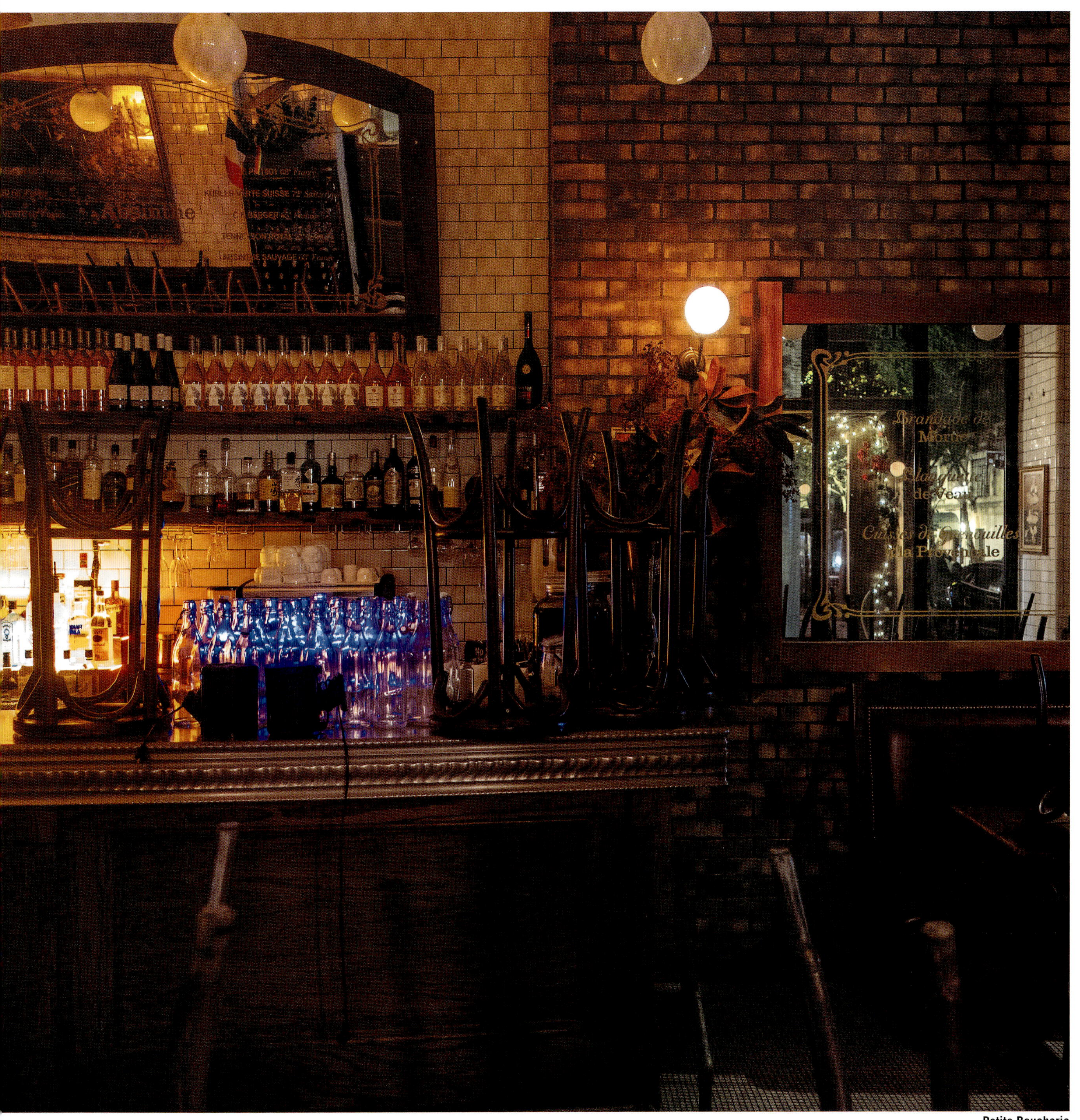

Petite Boucherie

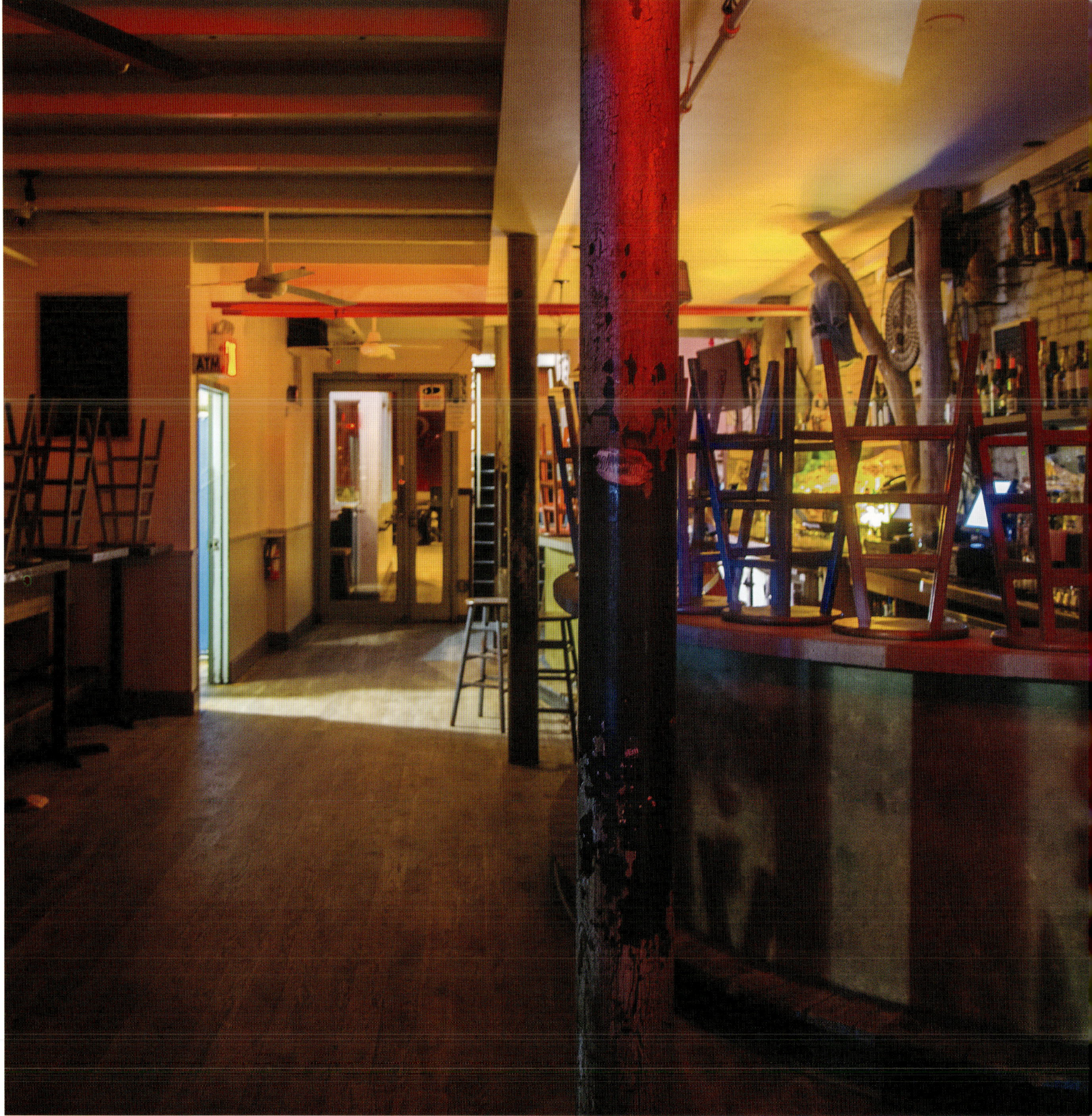

Pianos

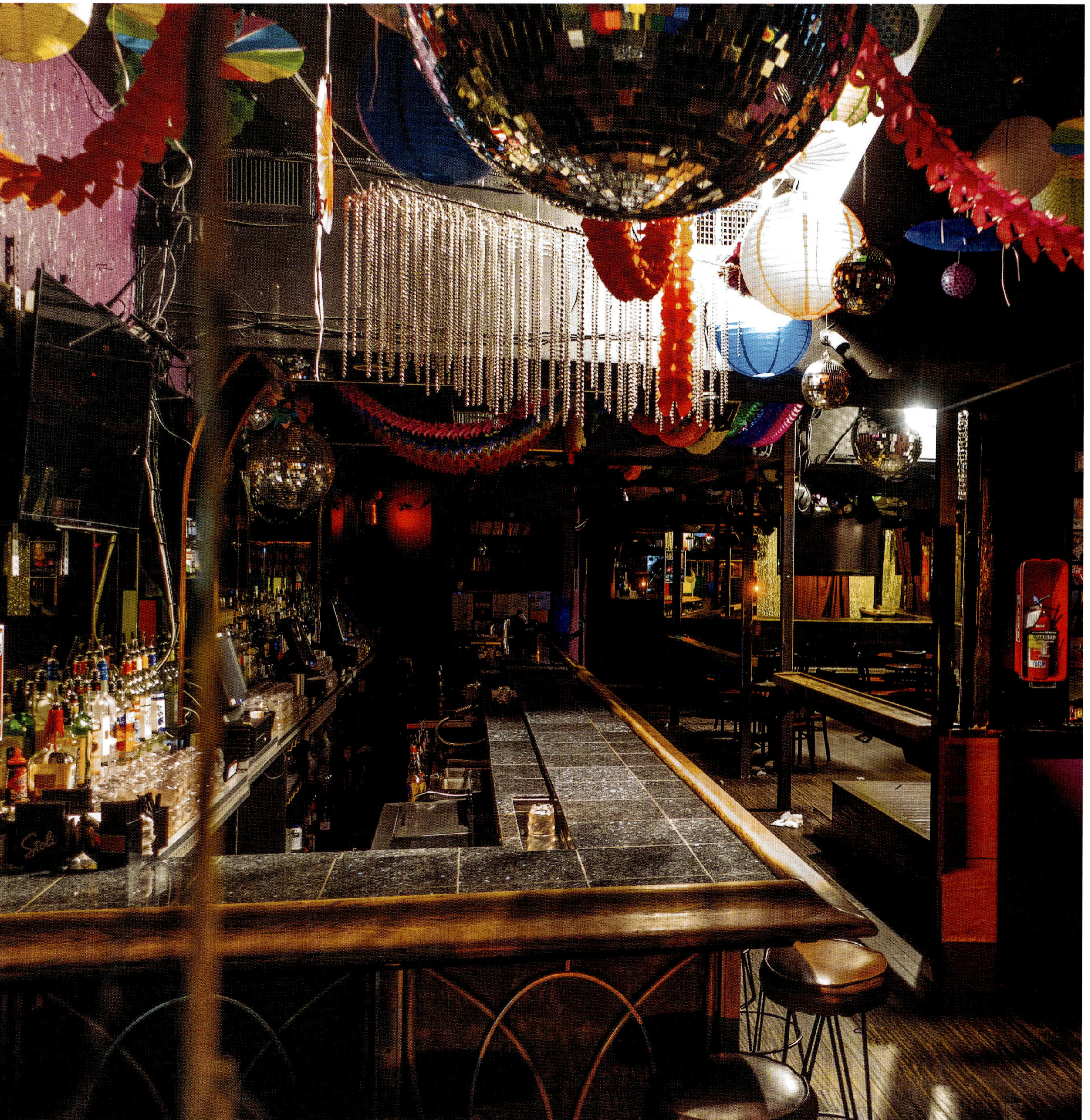

Pieces

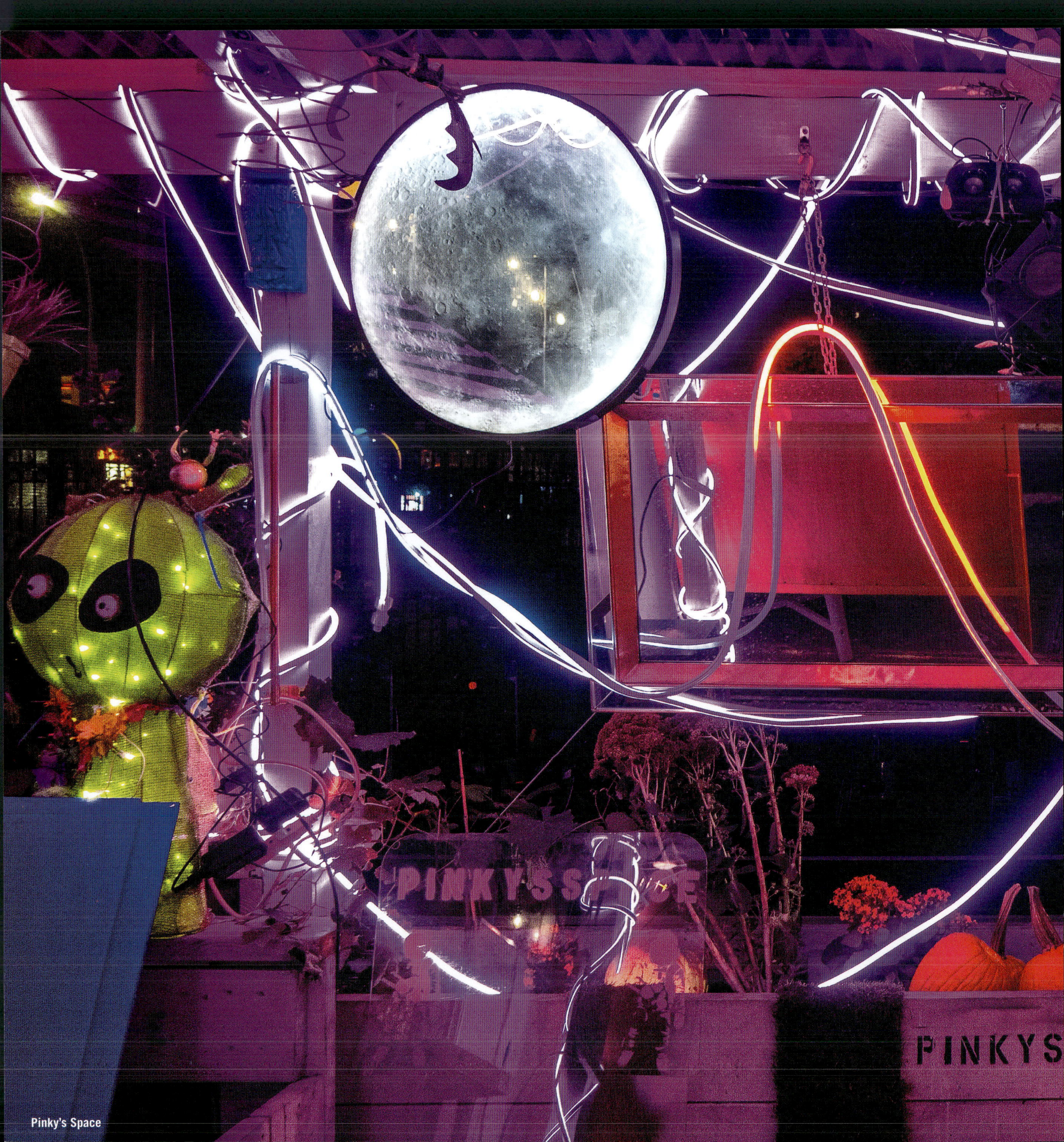

Pinky's Space

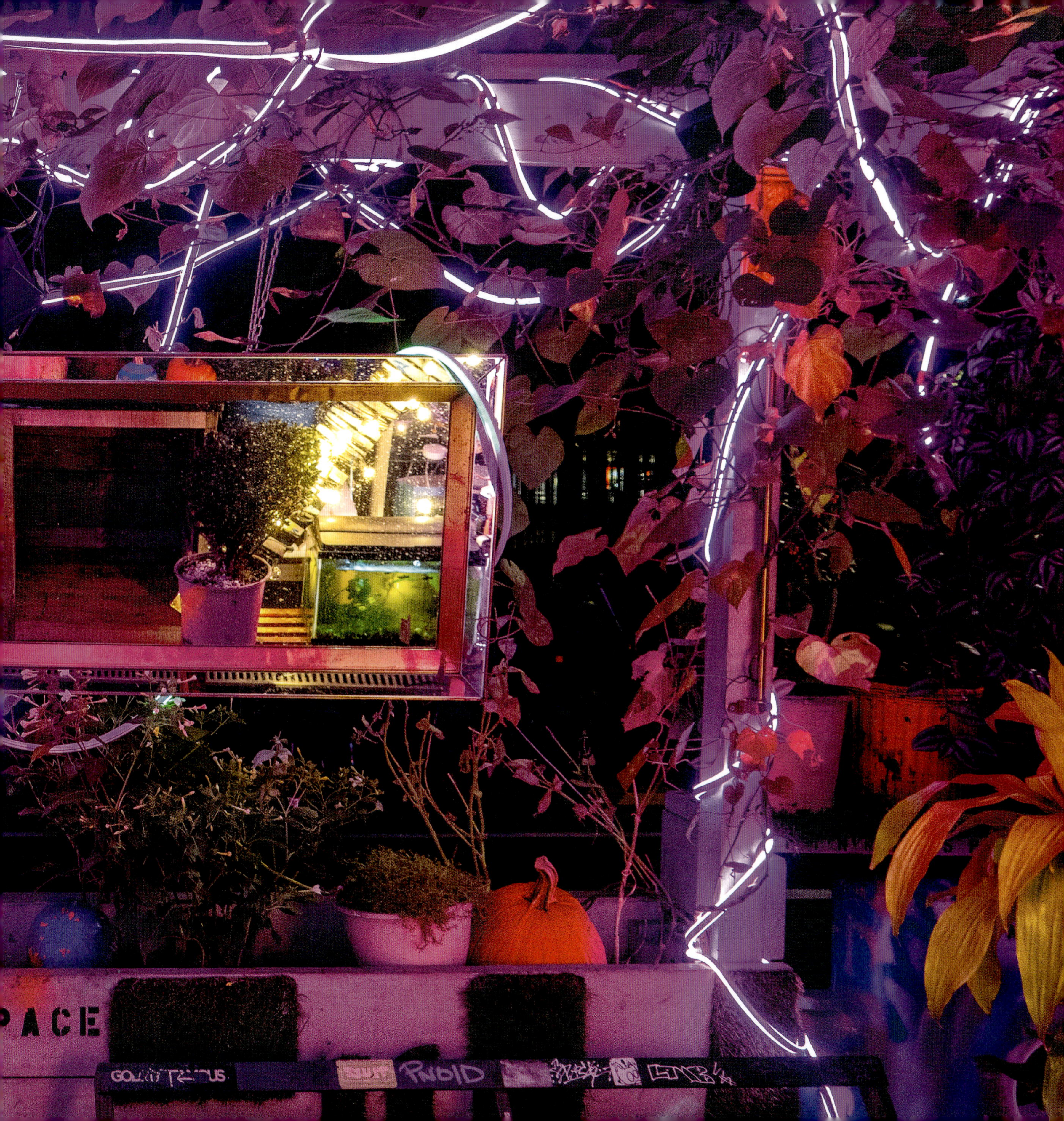

PACE
PNOID

EXIT
UN
WE BELIEVE
Not Responsible
for Personal Property
WARNING

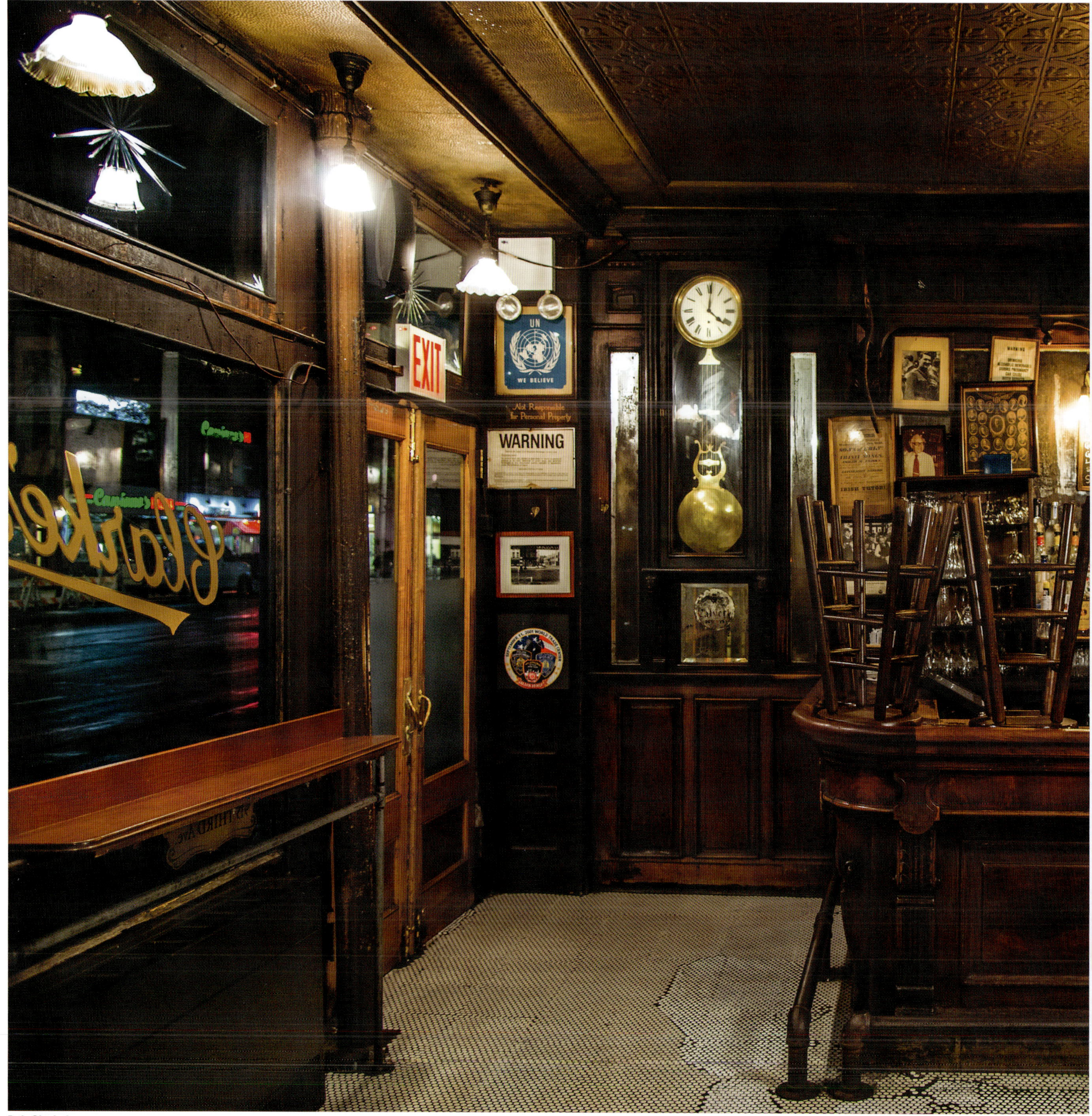

P. J. Clarke's

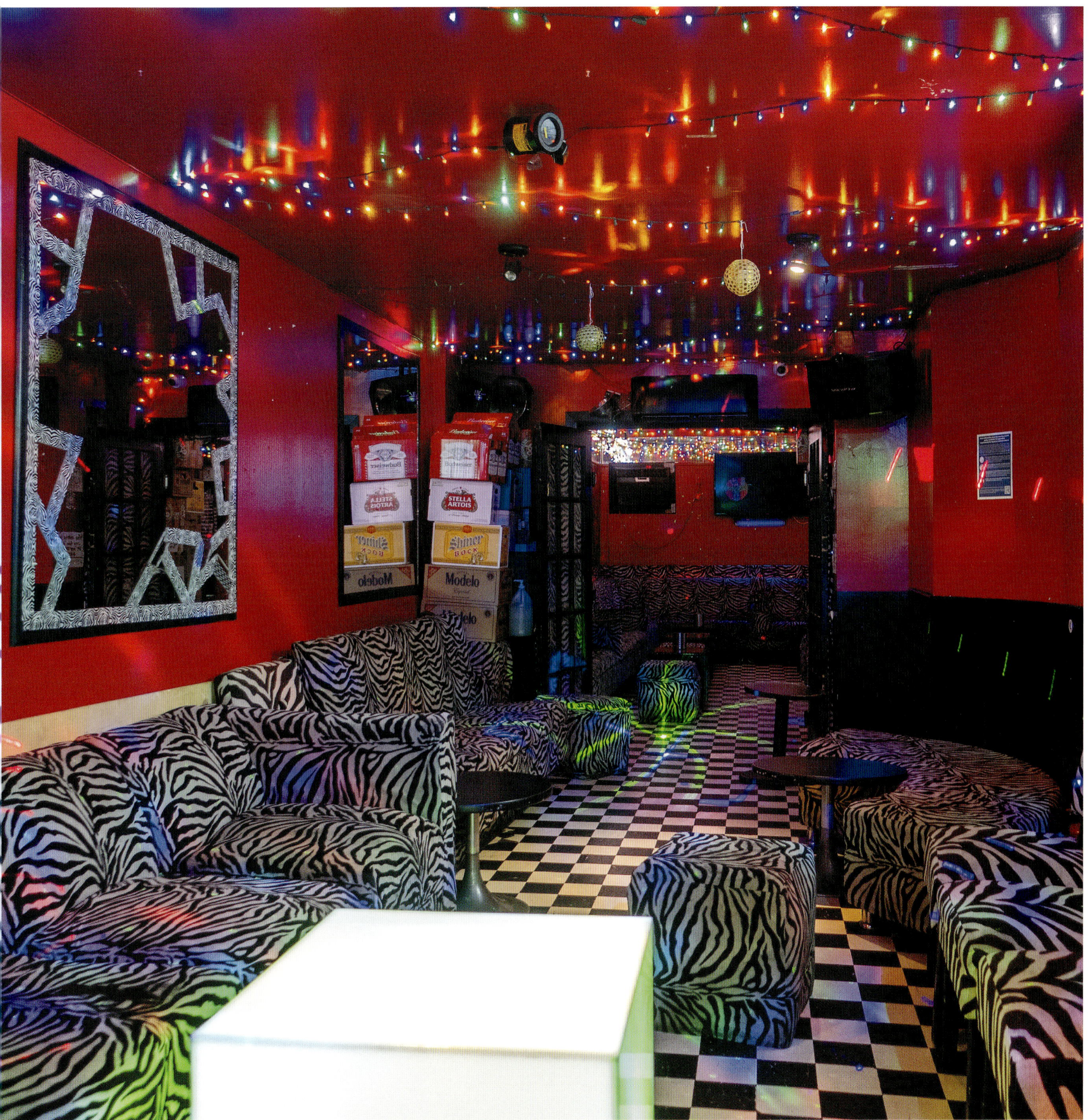

Planet Rose

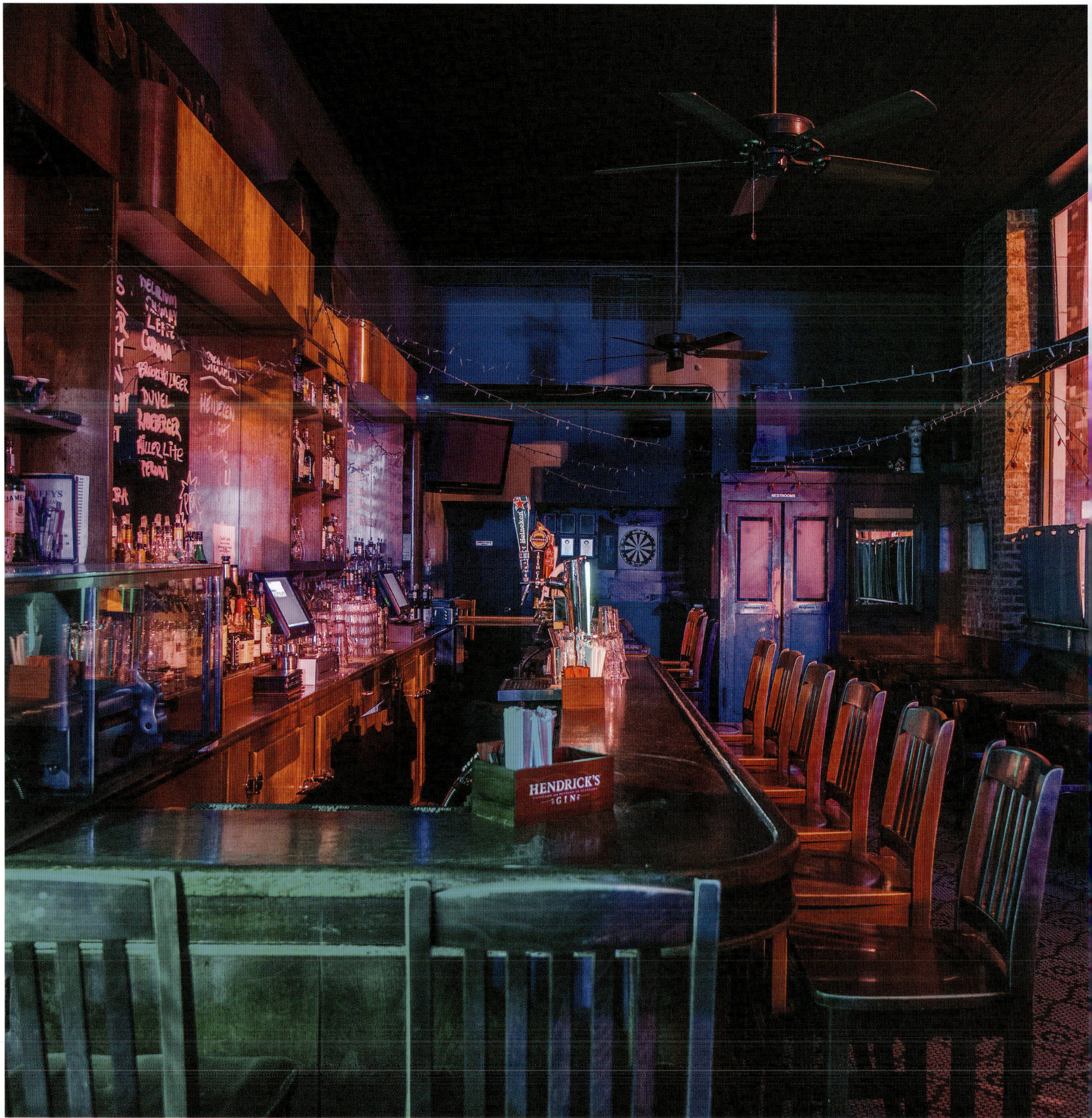

Puffy's Tavern

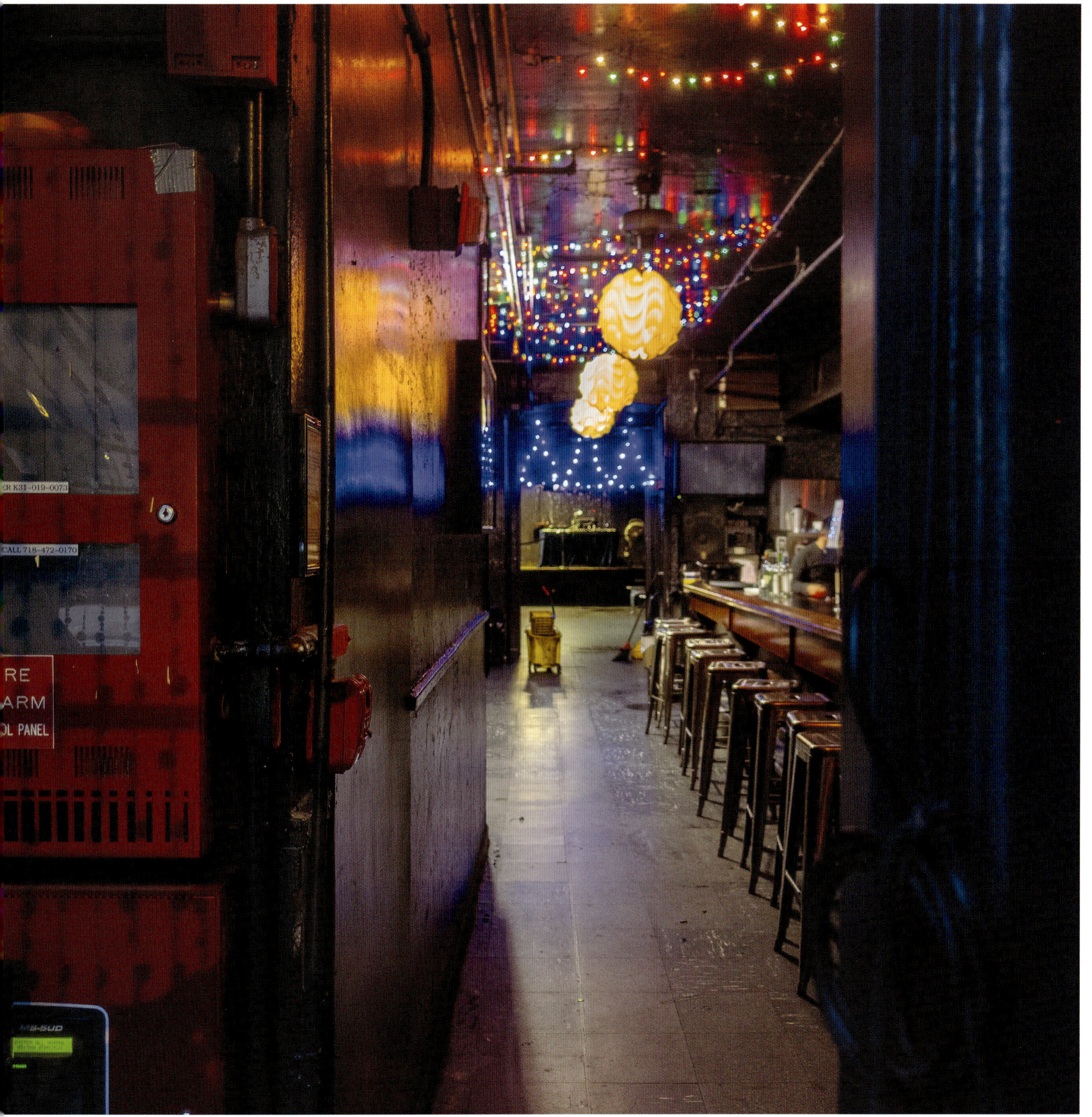

Pyramid Club

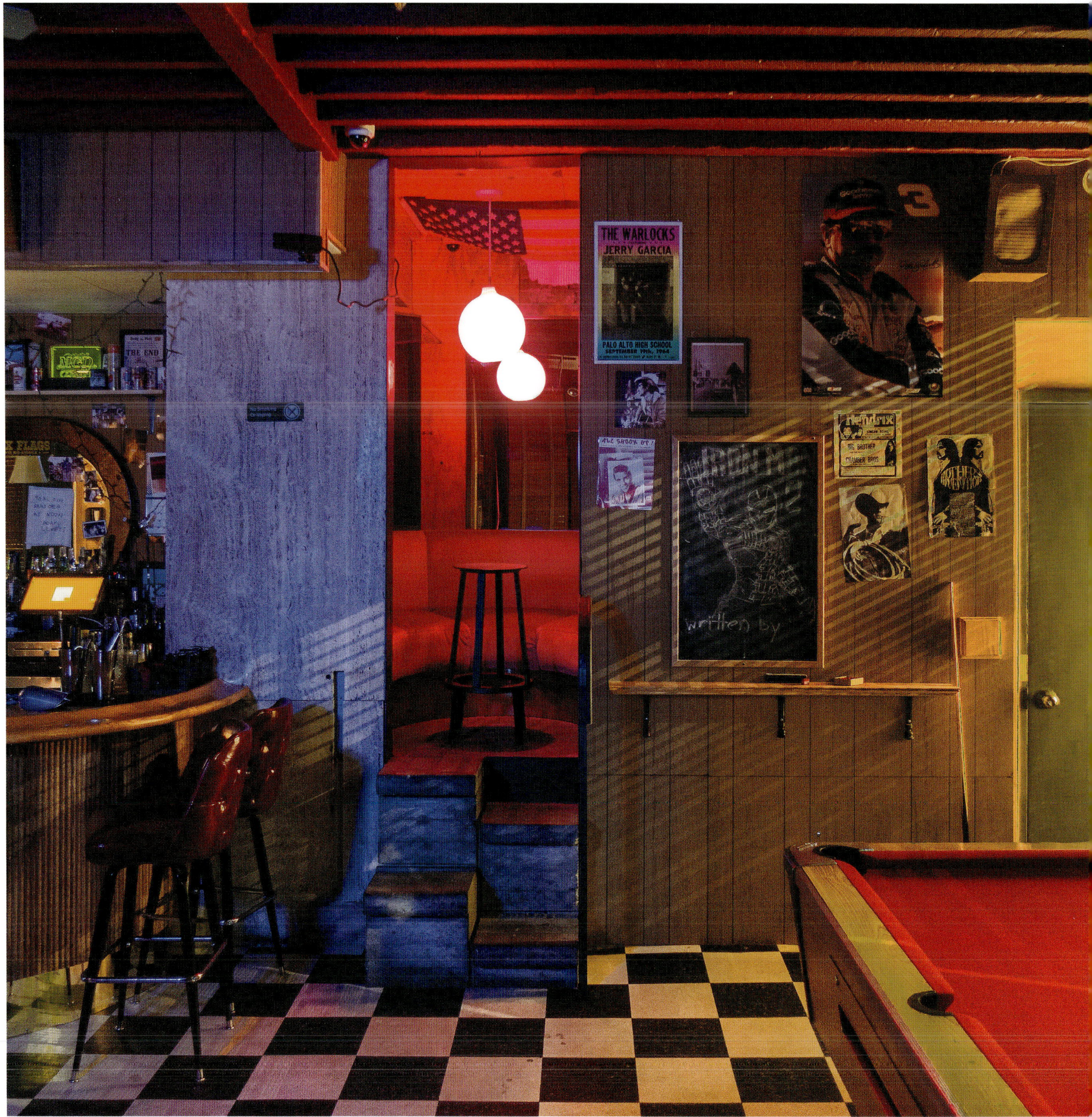

Ray's

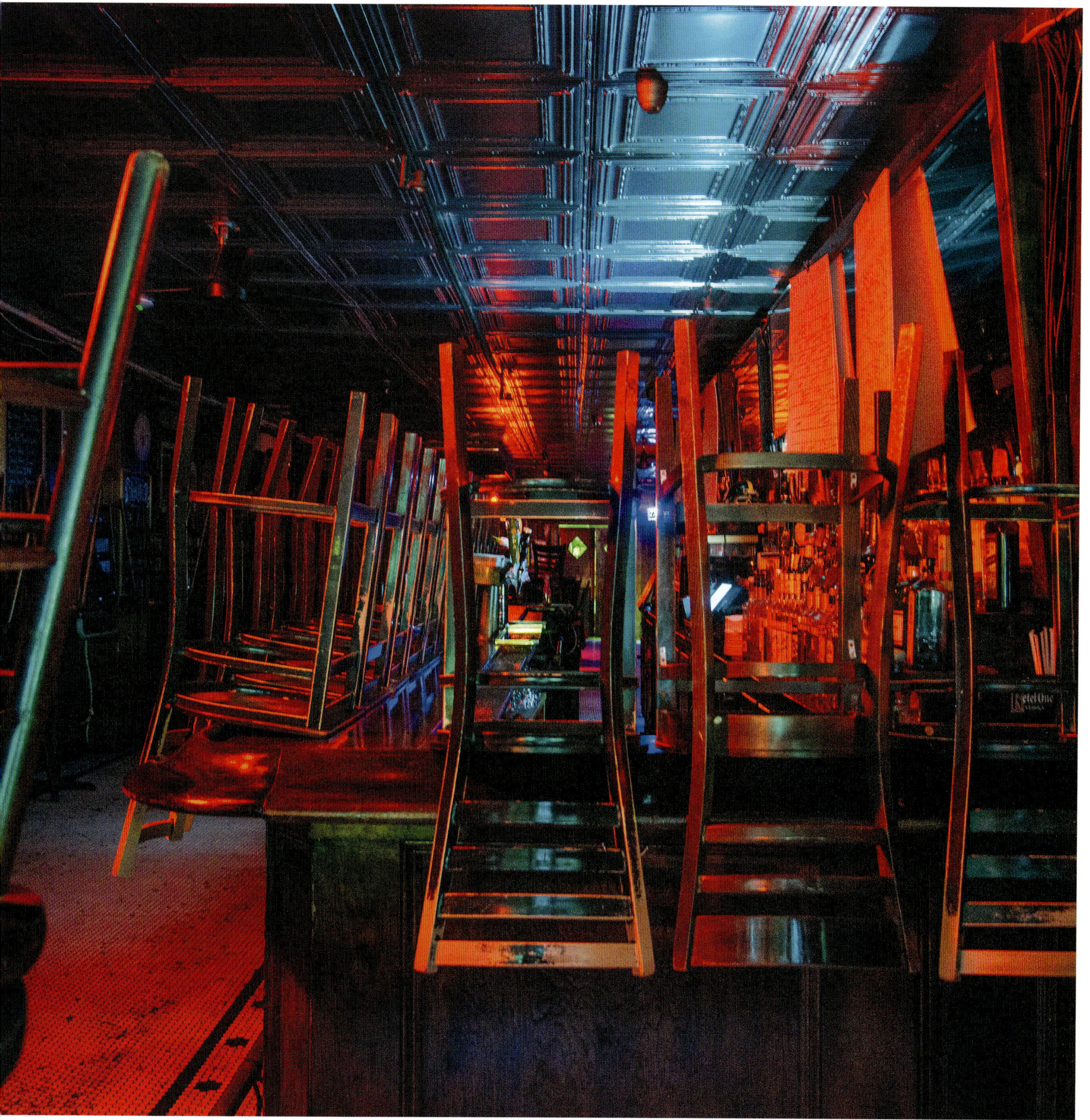

Reservoir

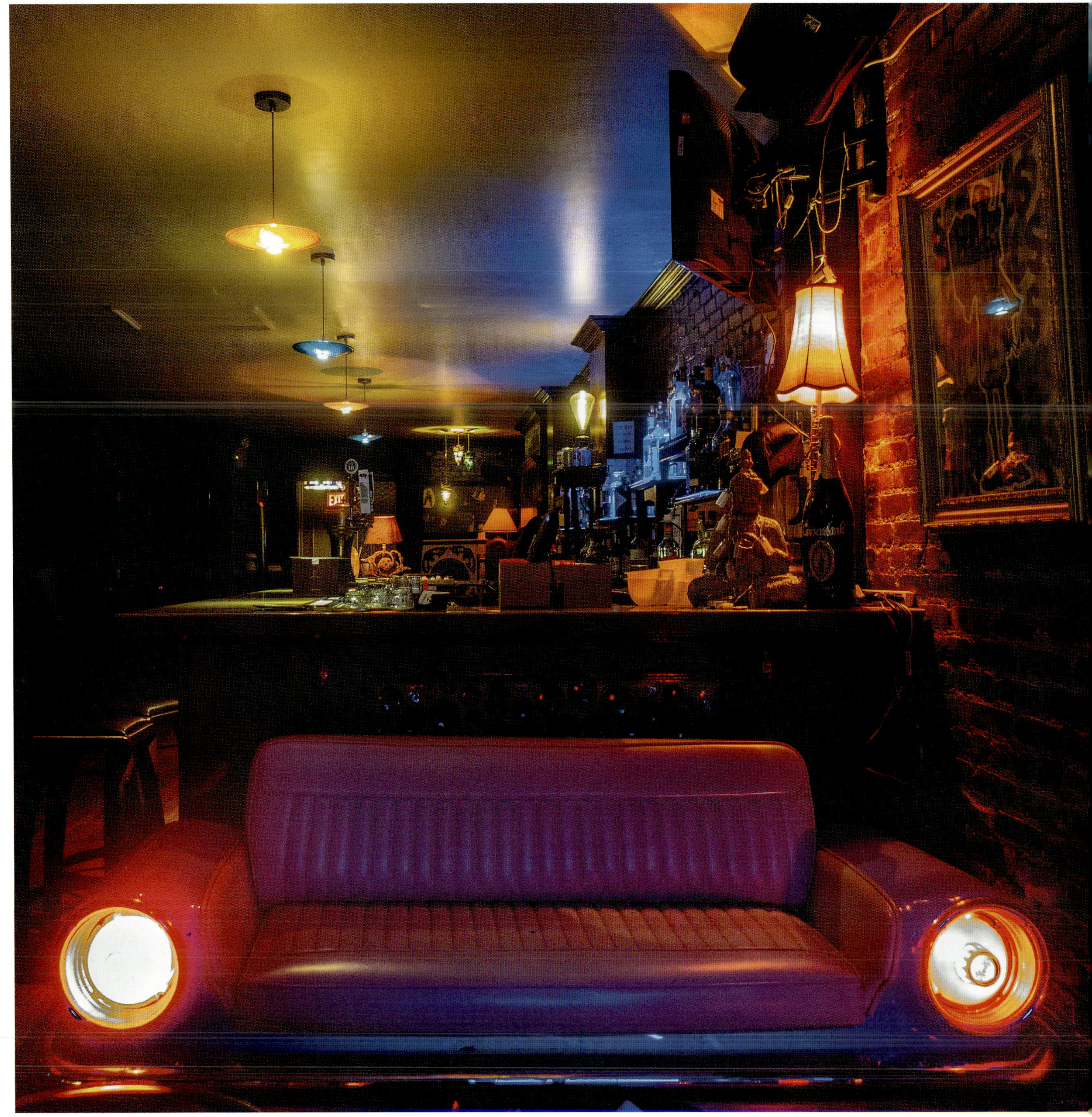

ReVision Lounge and Gallery

BUD LIGHT
BUD LIGHT
BUD LIGHT
ROCKBAR
NYC
WARNING
EMERGENCY
FIRST AID
AND
CPR KIT
NOTICE
WARNING
DRINKING
ALCOHOLIC
BEVERAGES
DURING
PREGNANCY
CAN CAUSE
BIRTH
DEFECTS
NO SMOKING
GOVERNMENT
WARNING:

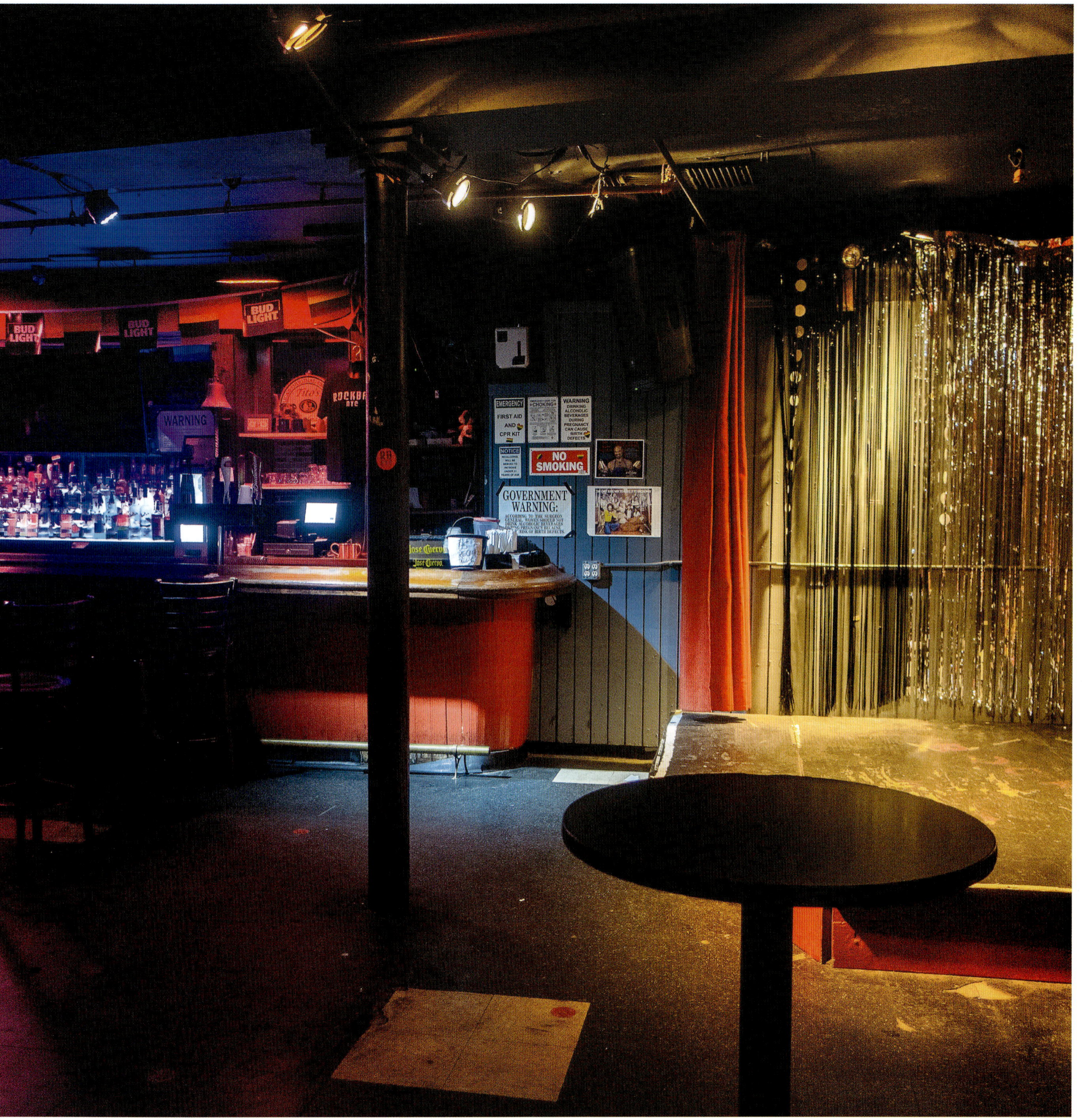

Rockbar

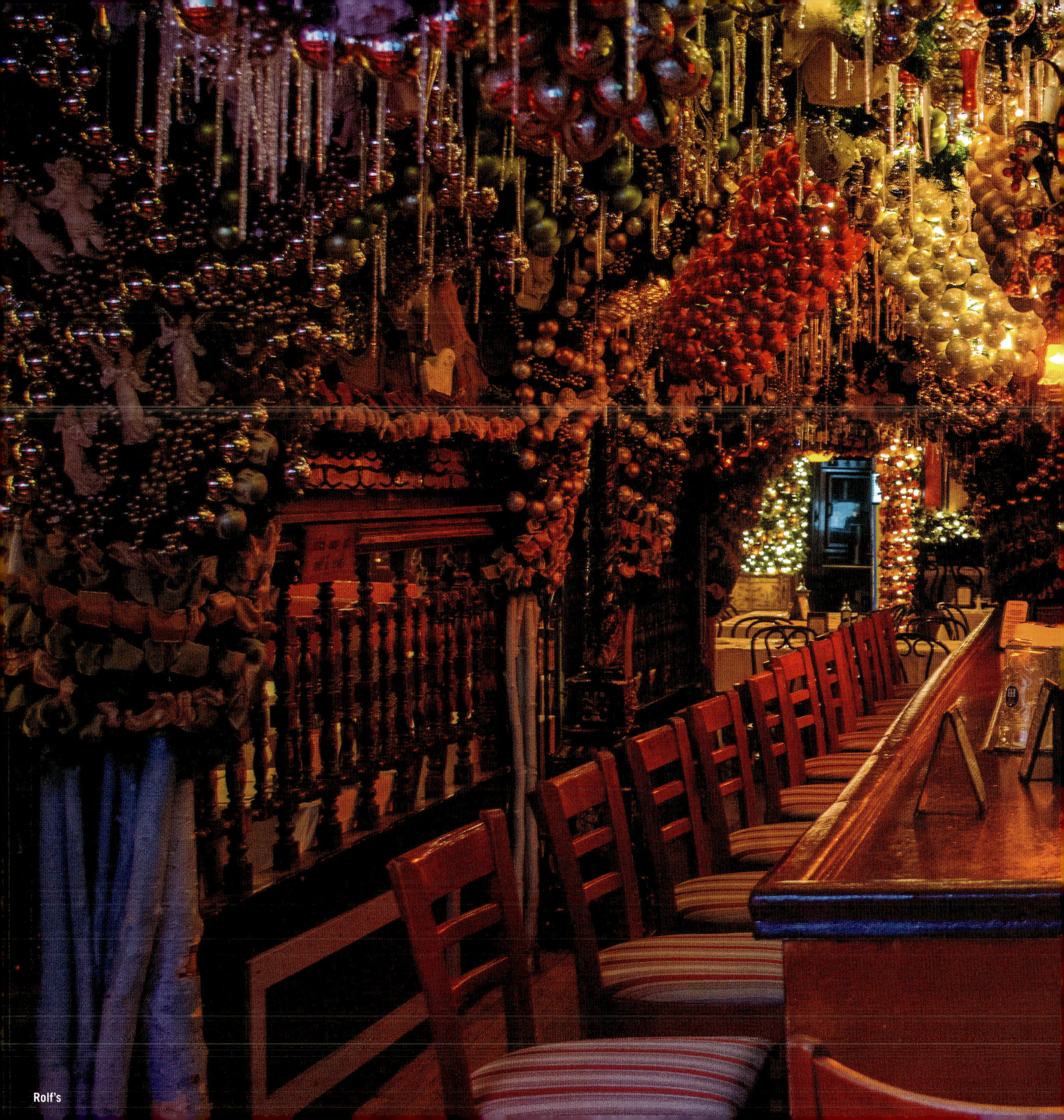

Rolf's

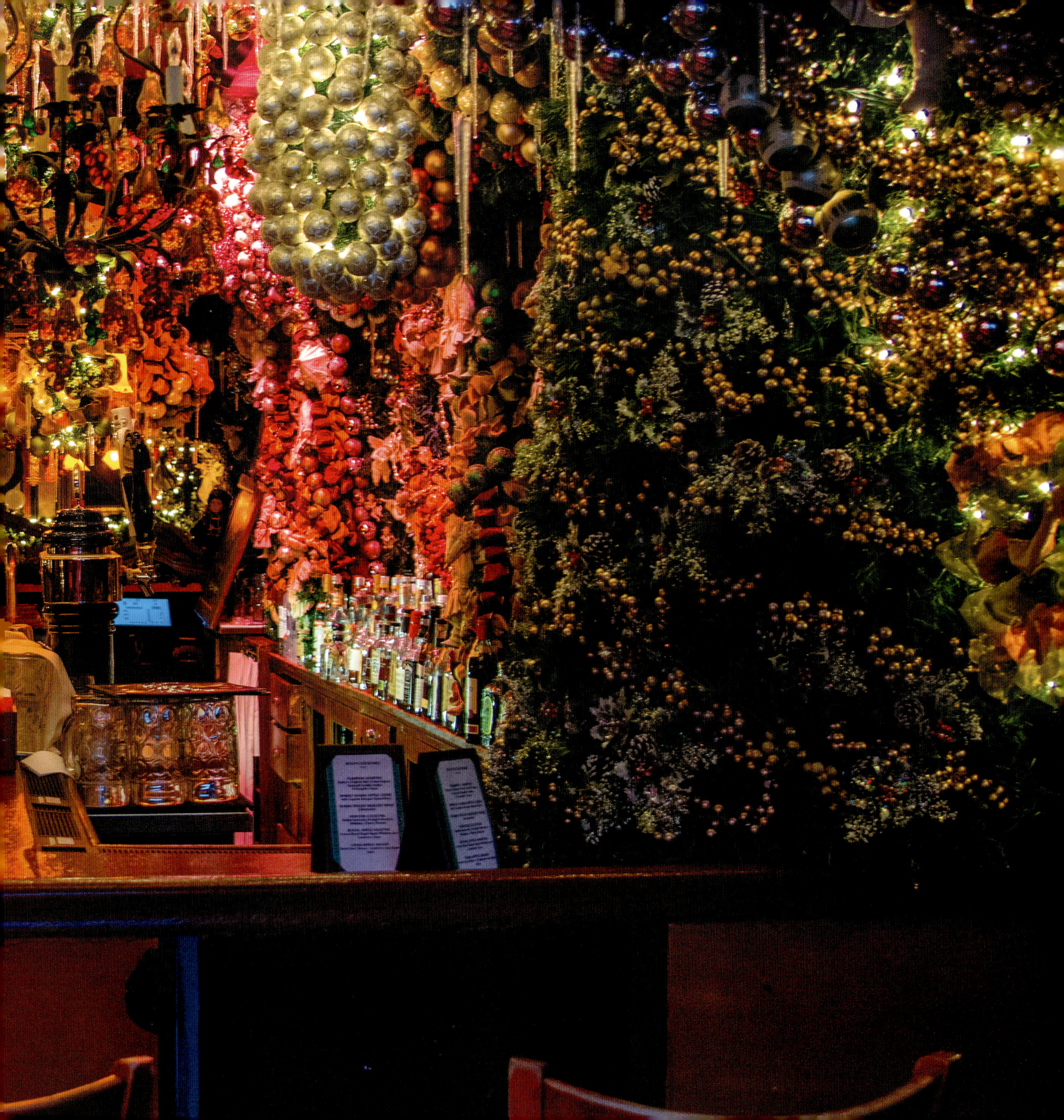

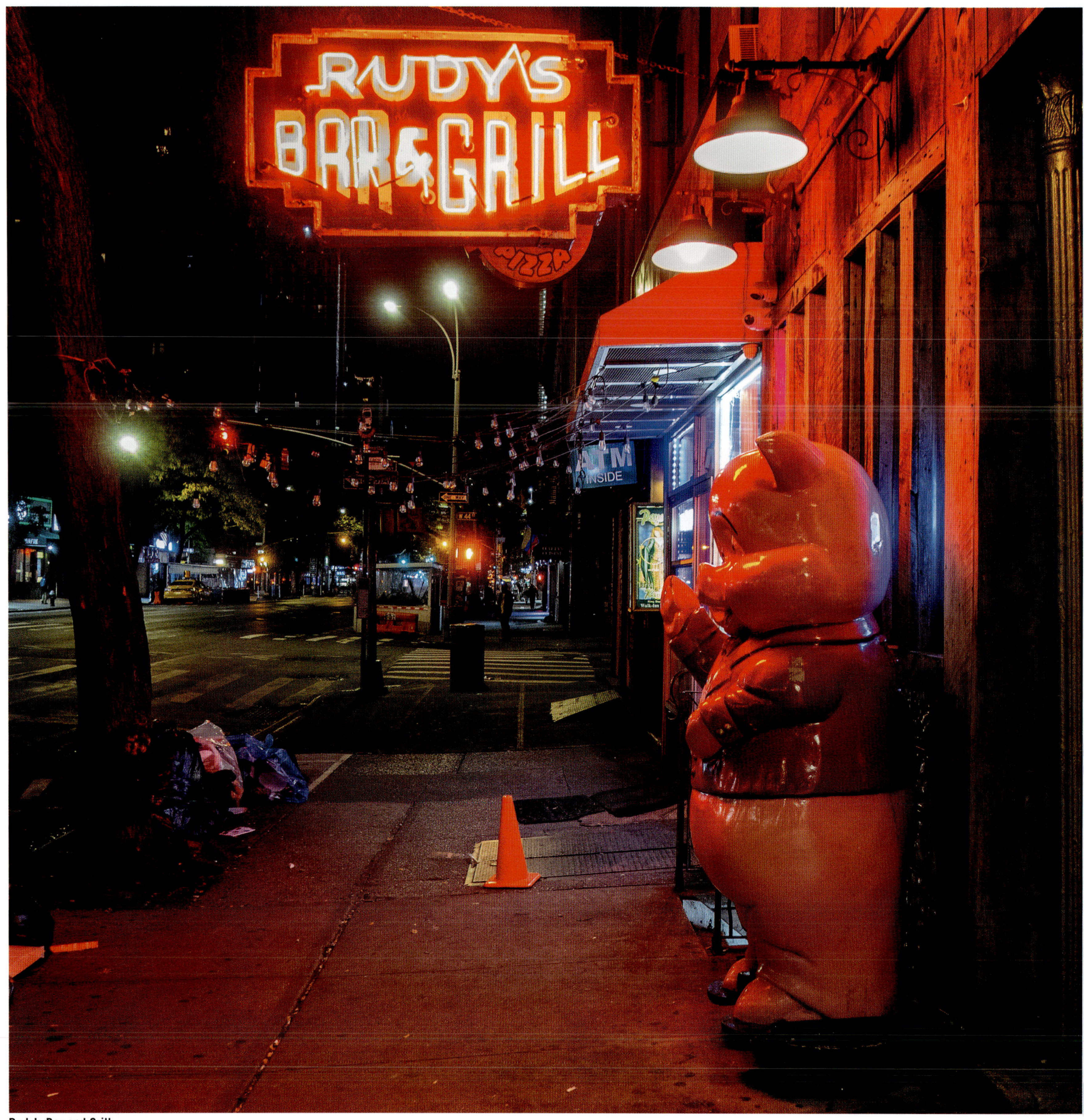

Rudy's Bar and Grill

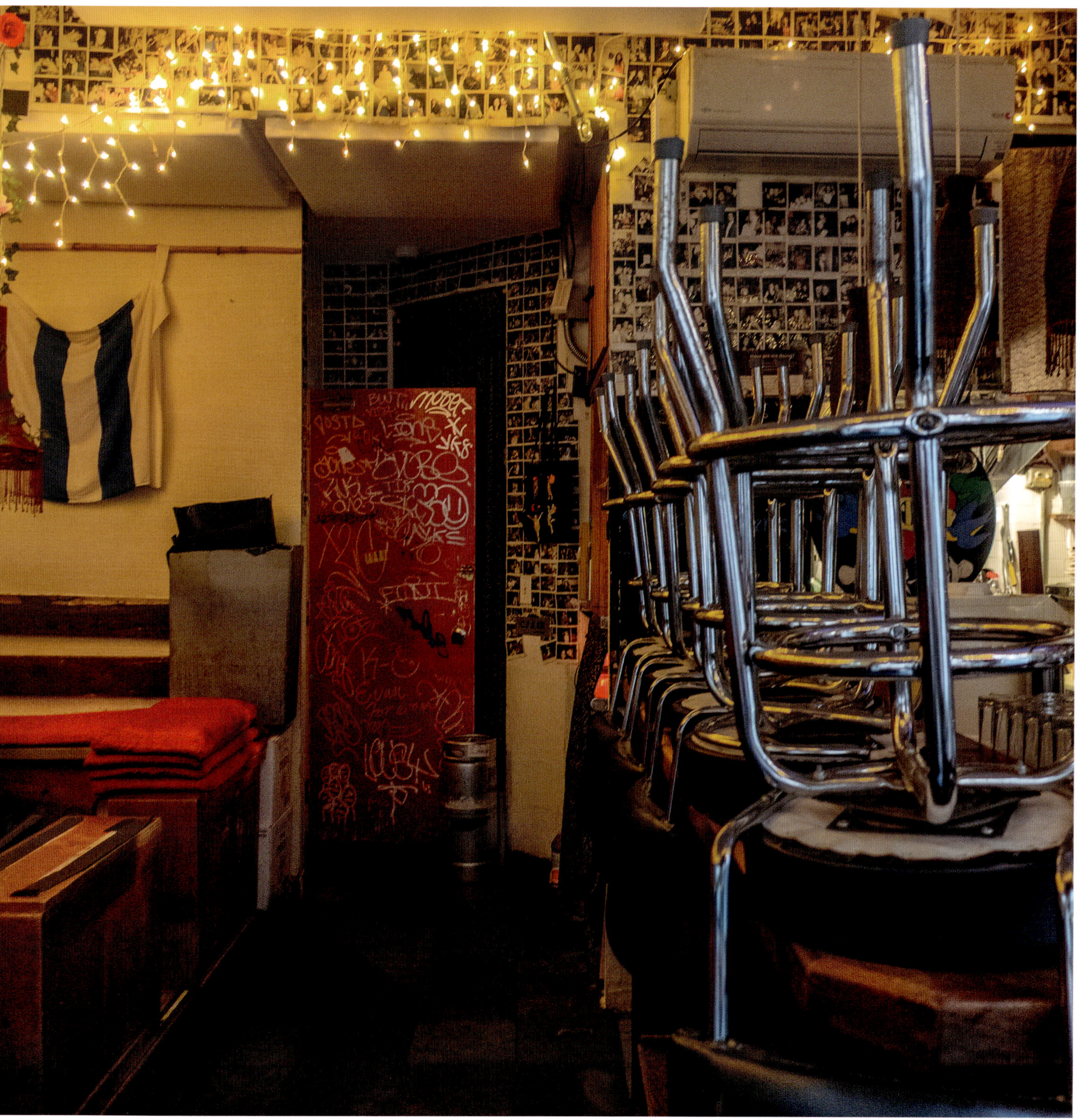

Sake Bar Satsko

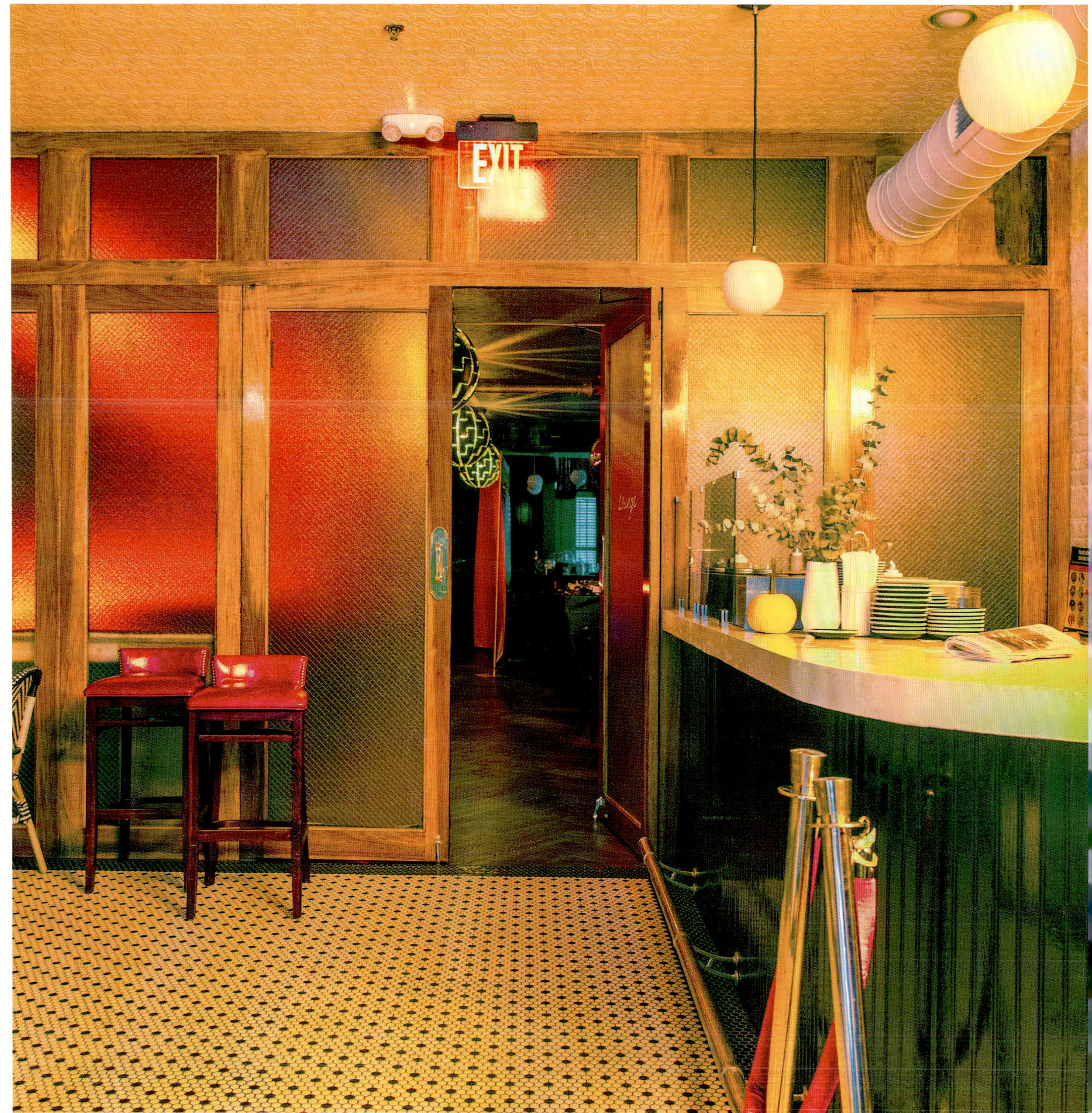

San Remo Cafe

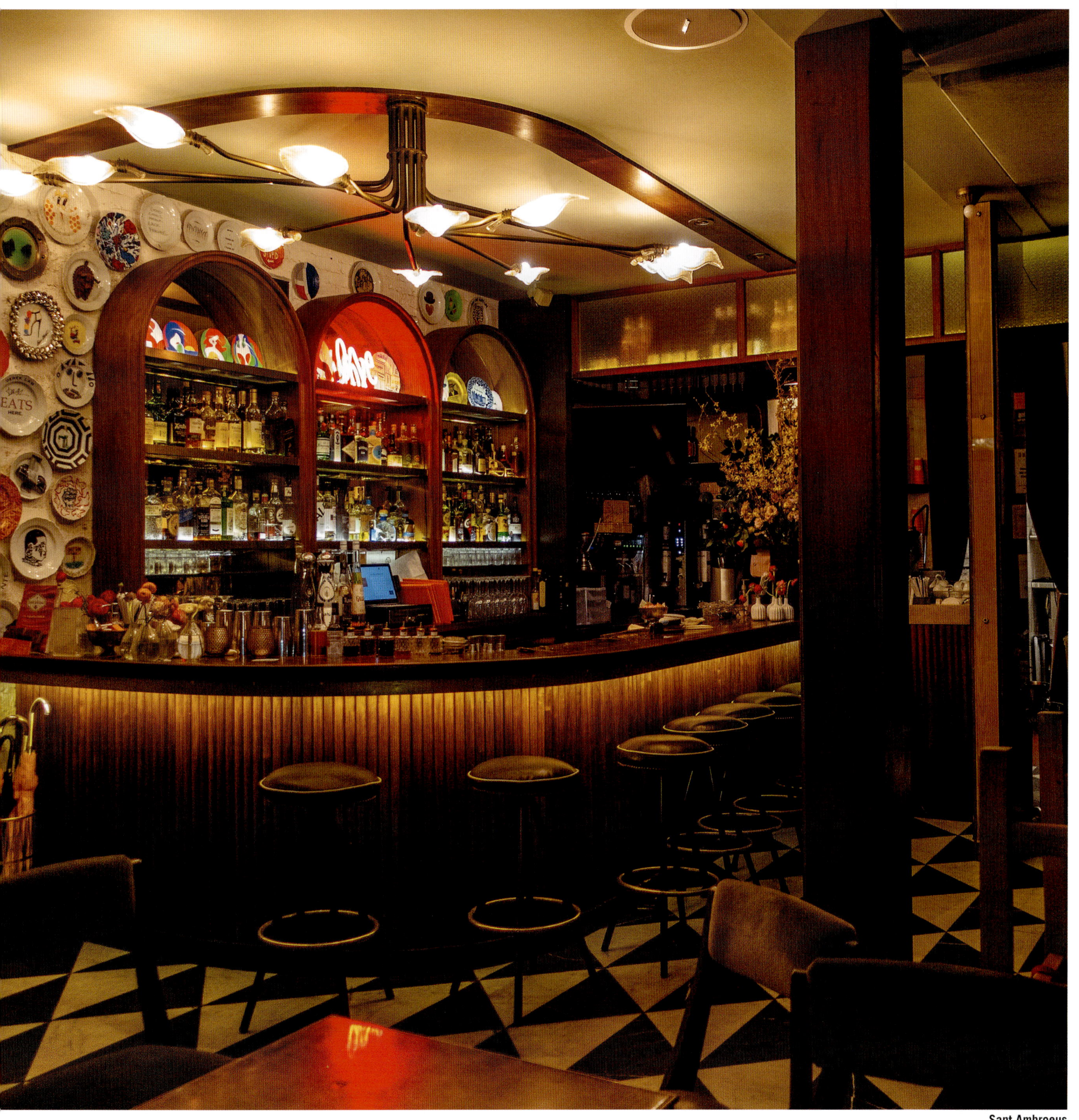

Sant Ambroeus

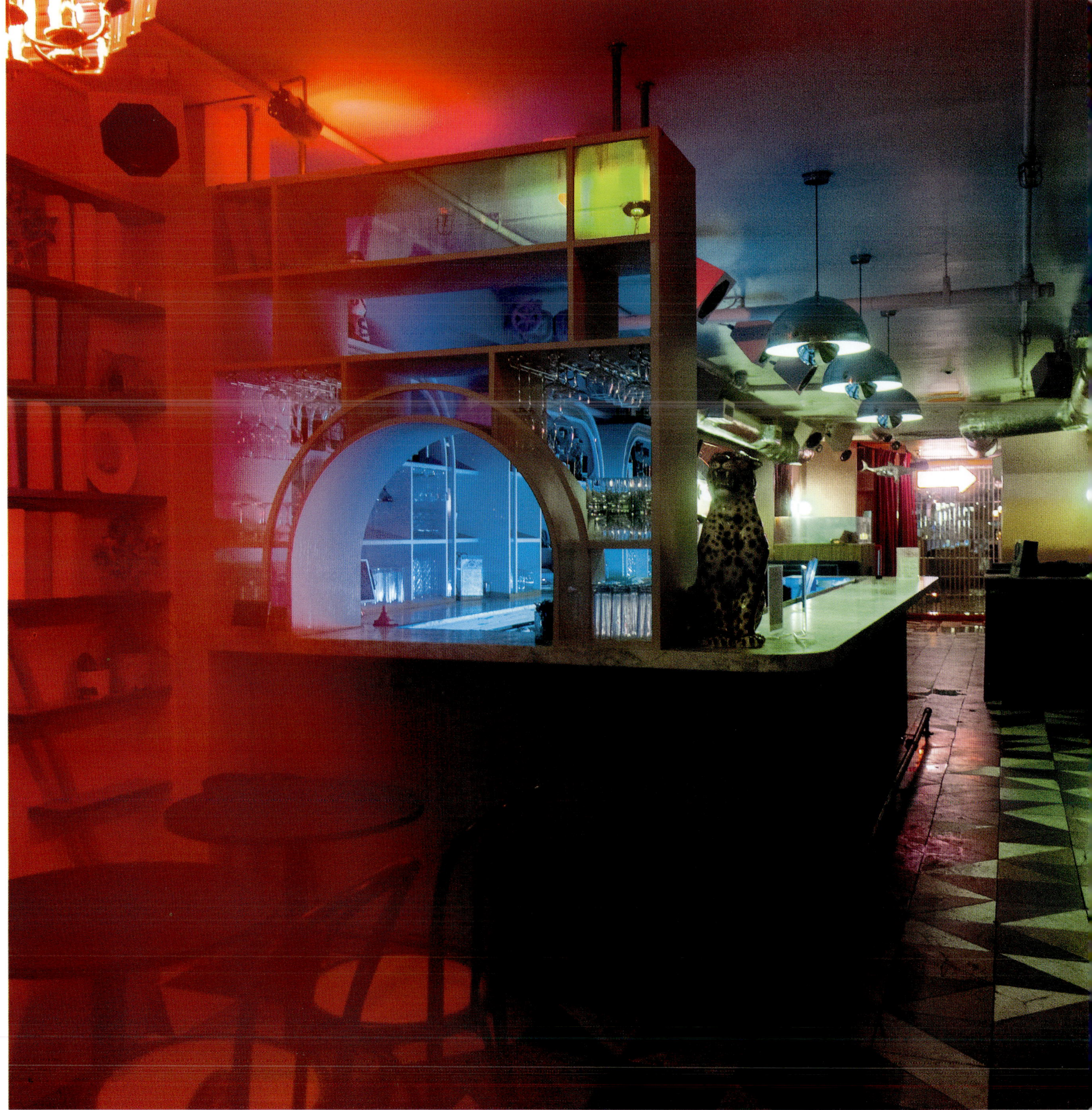

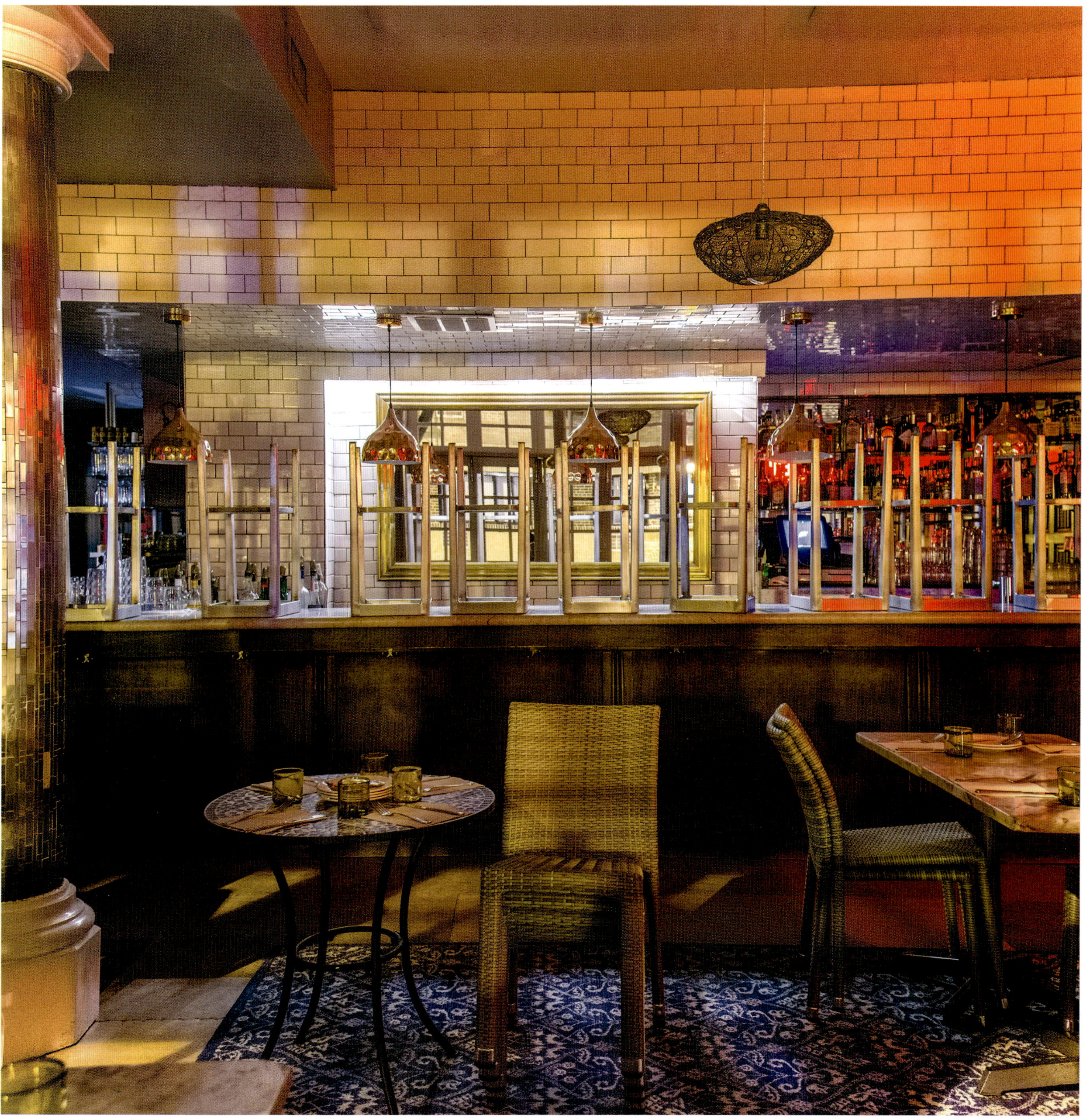

Shuka

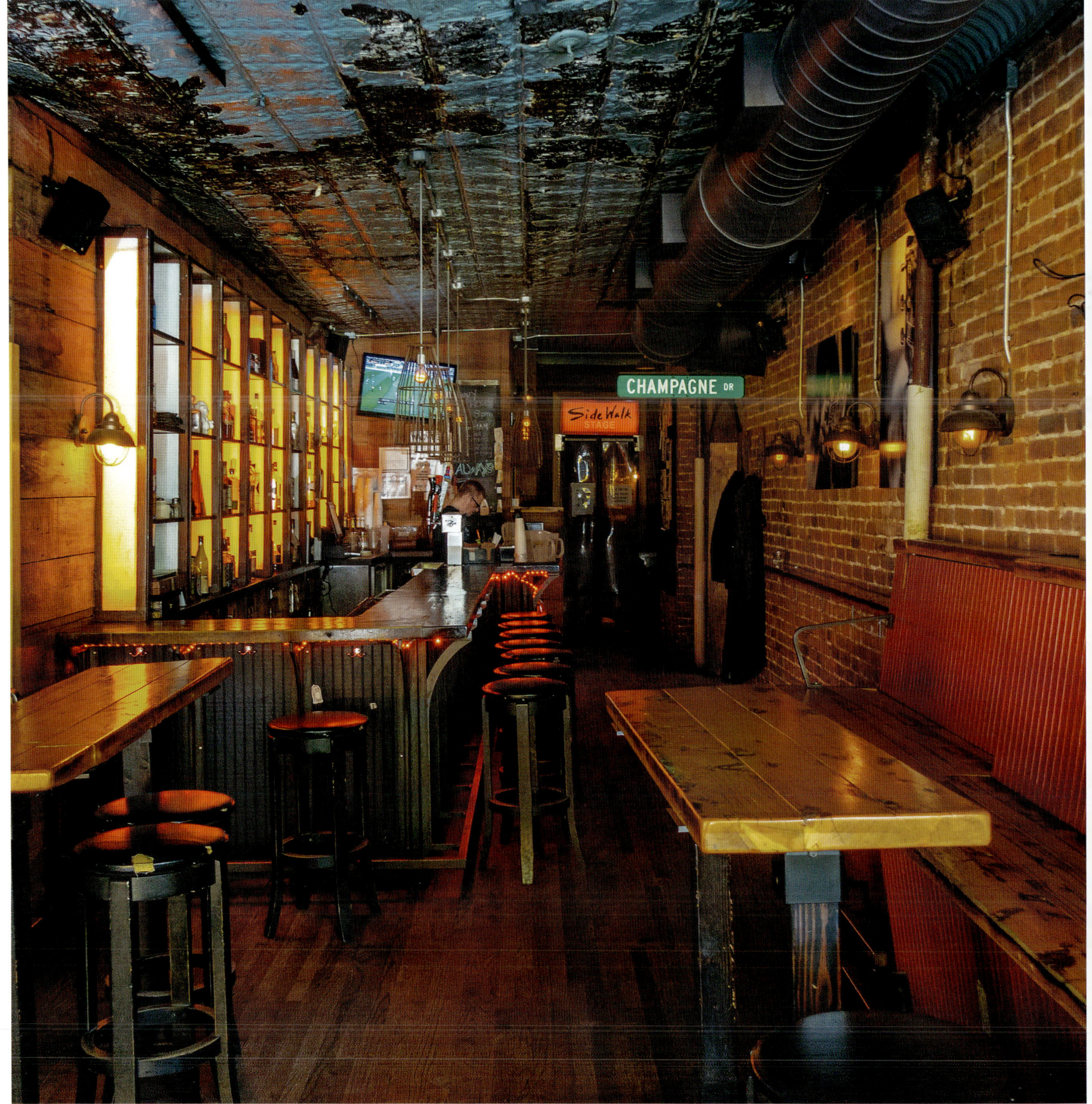
SideWalk Cafe

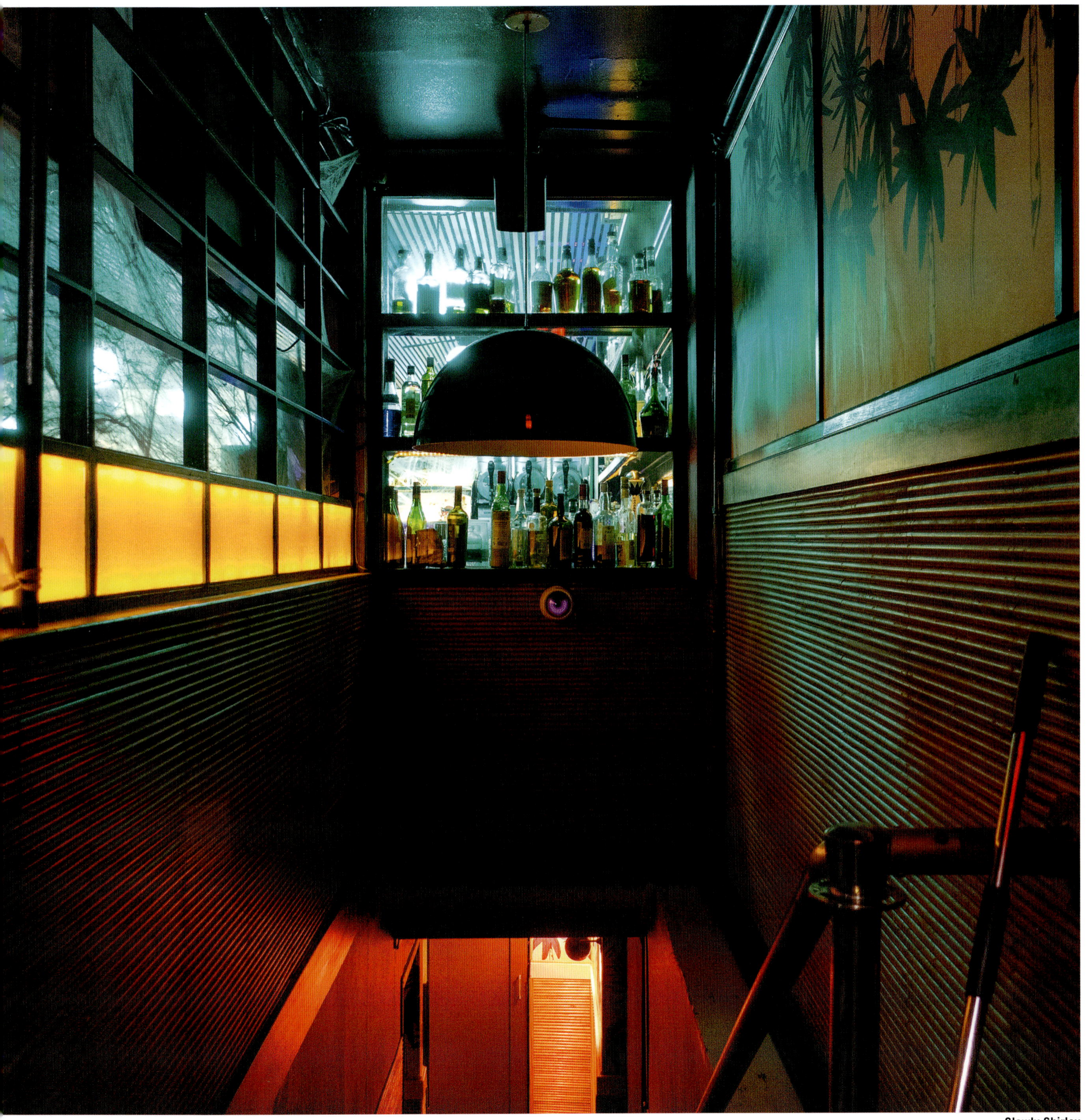

Slowly Shirley

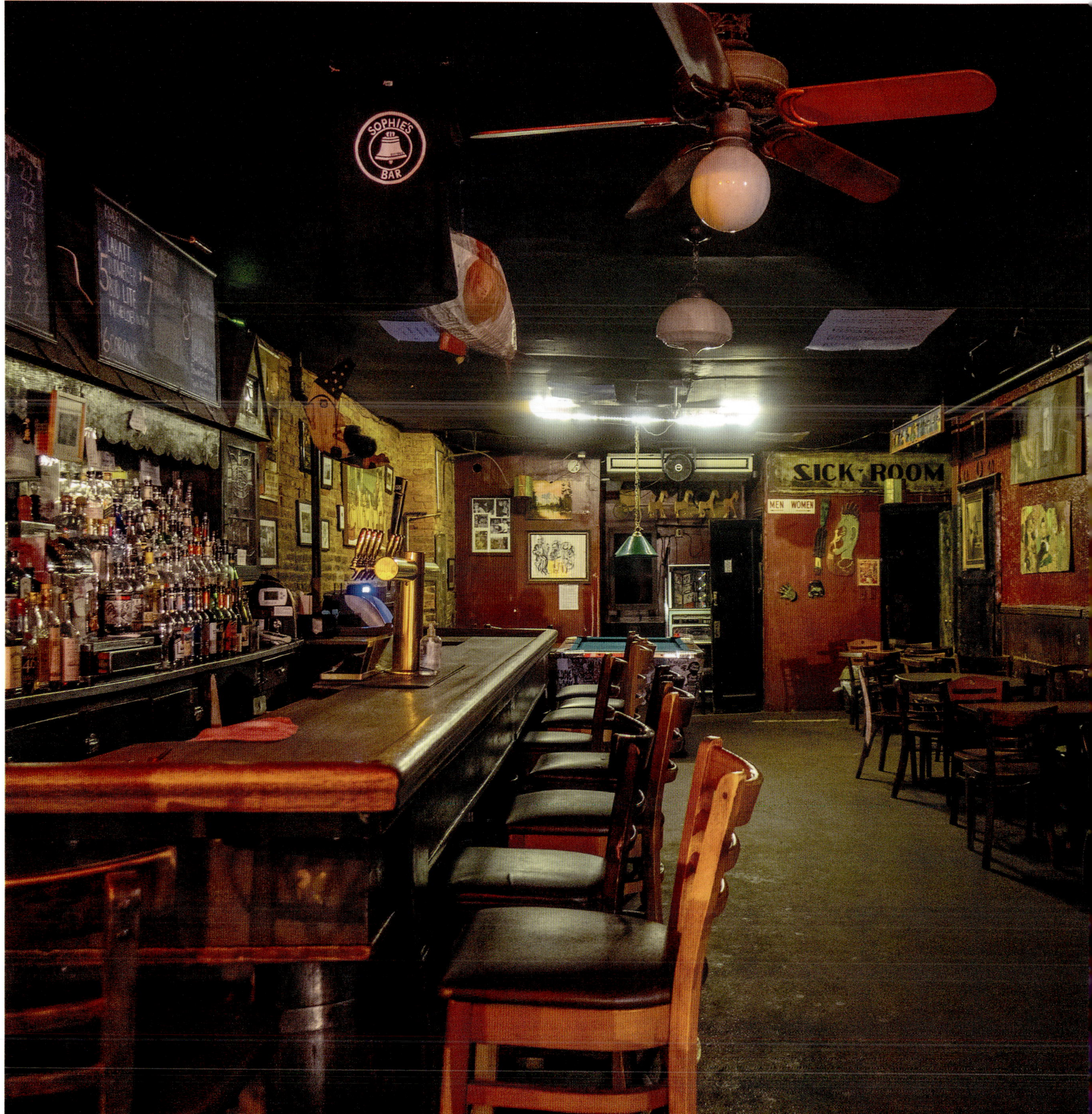

Sophie's

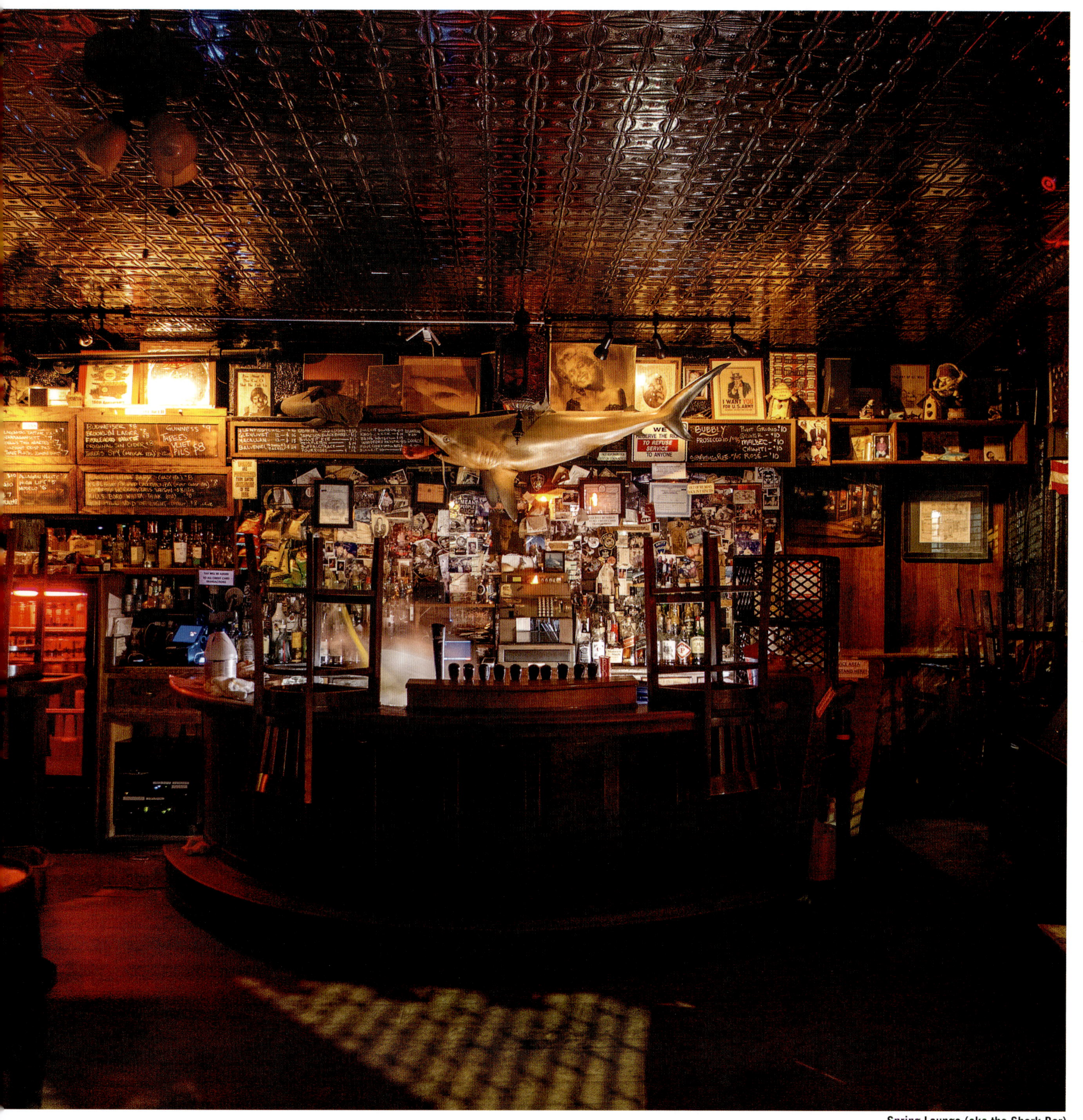

Spring Lounge (aka the Shark Bar)

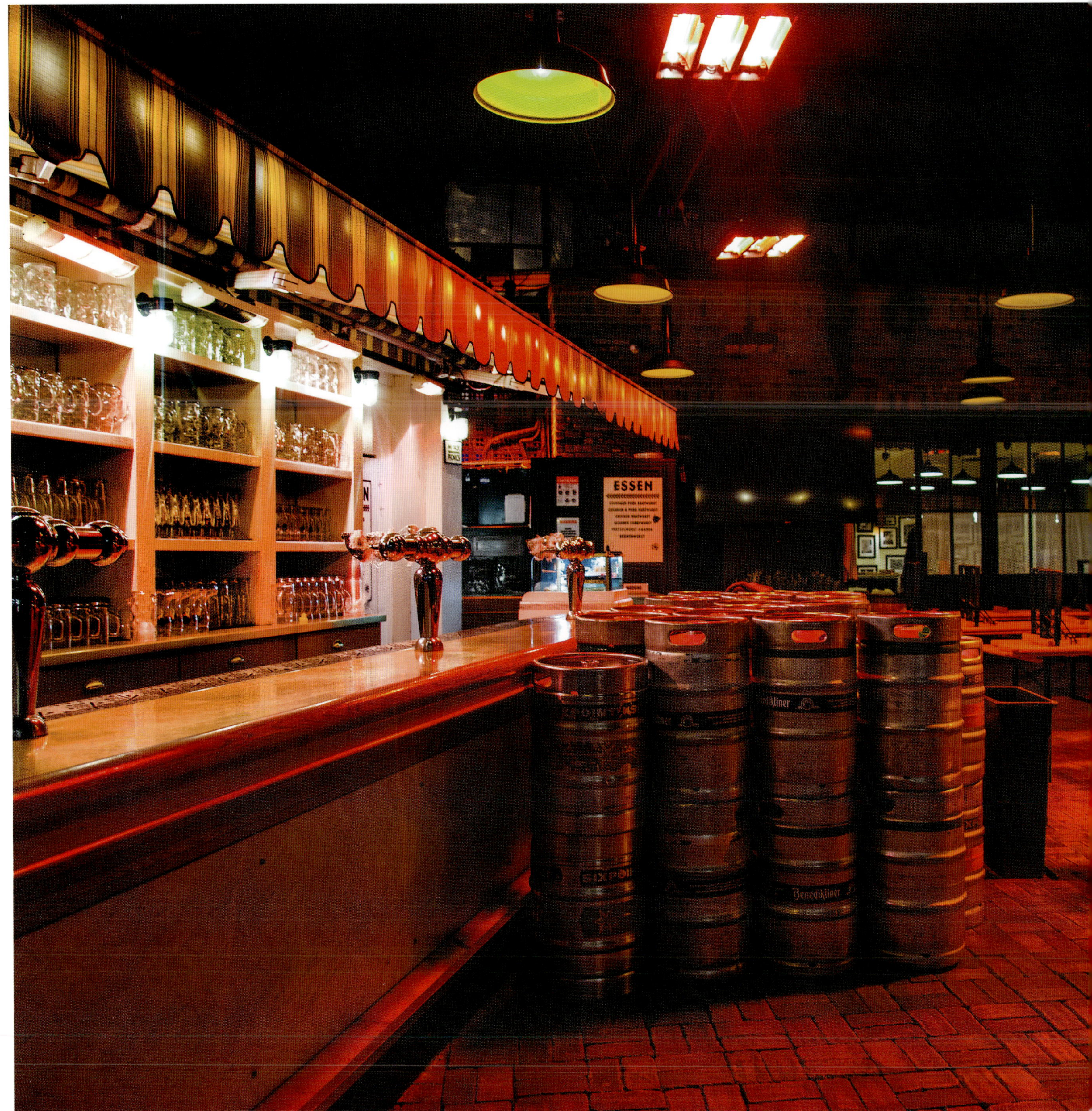

The Standard Biergarten

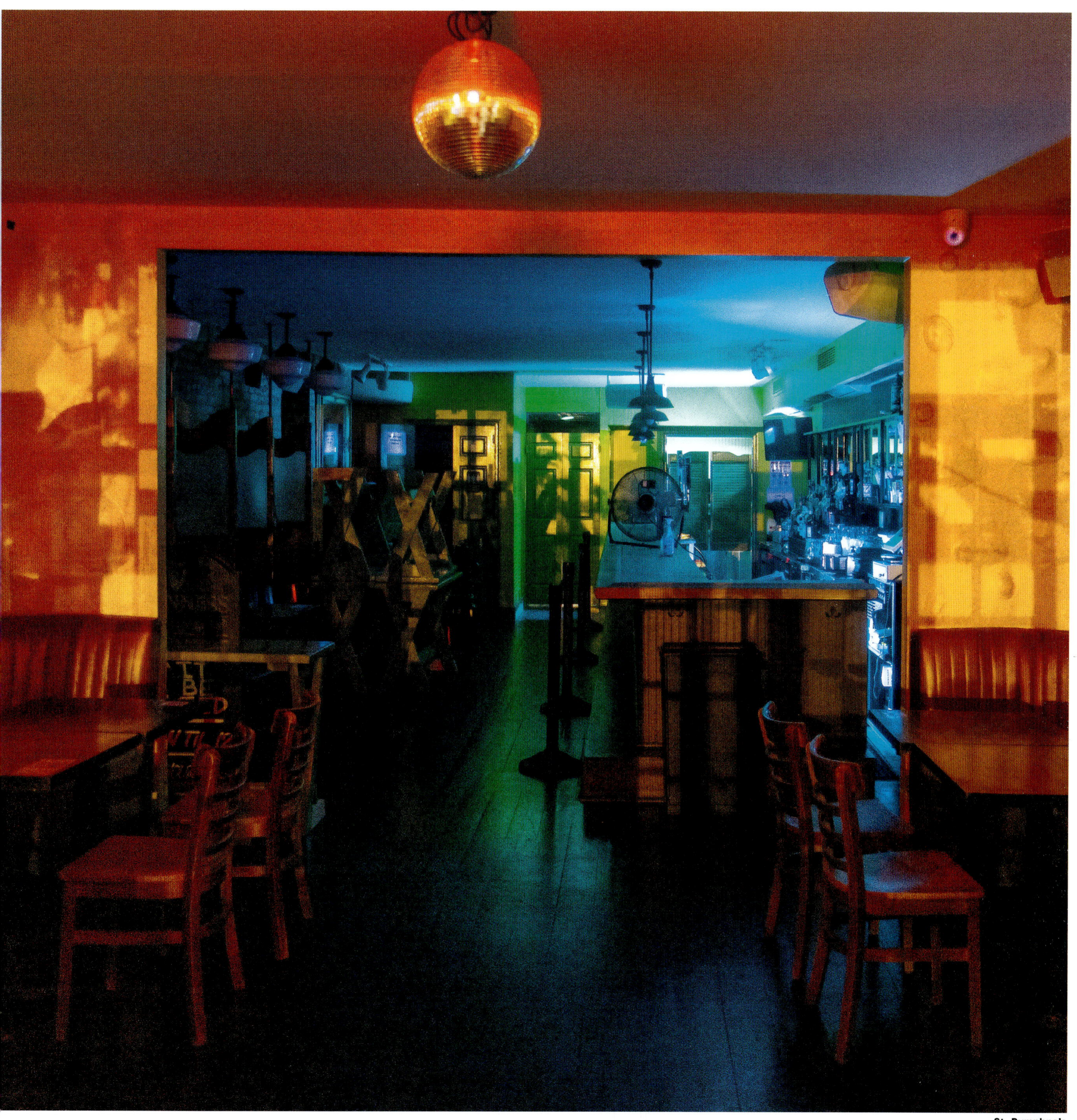

St. Dymphna's

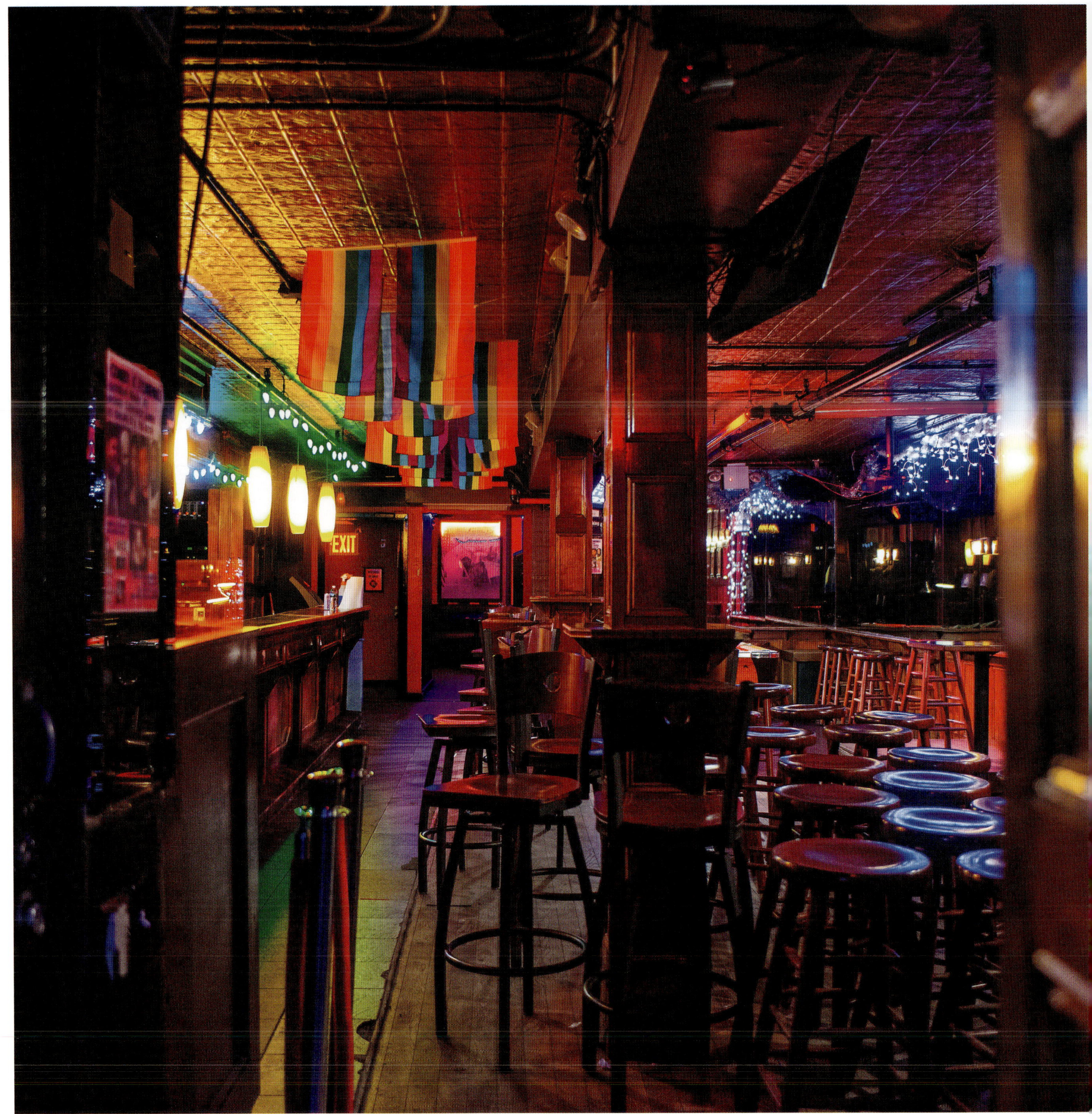

The Stonewall Inn

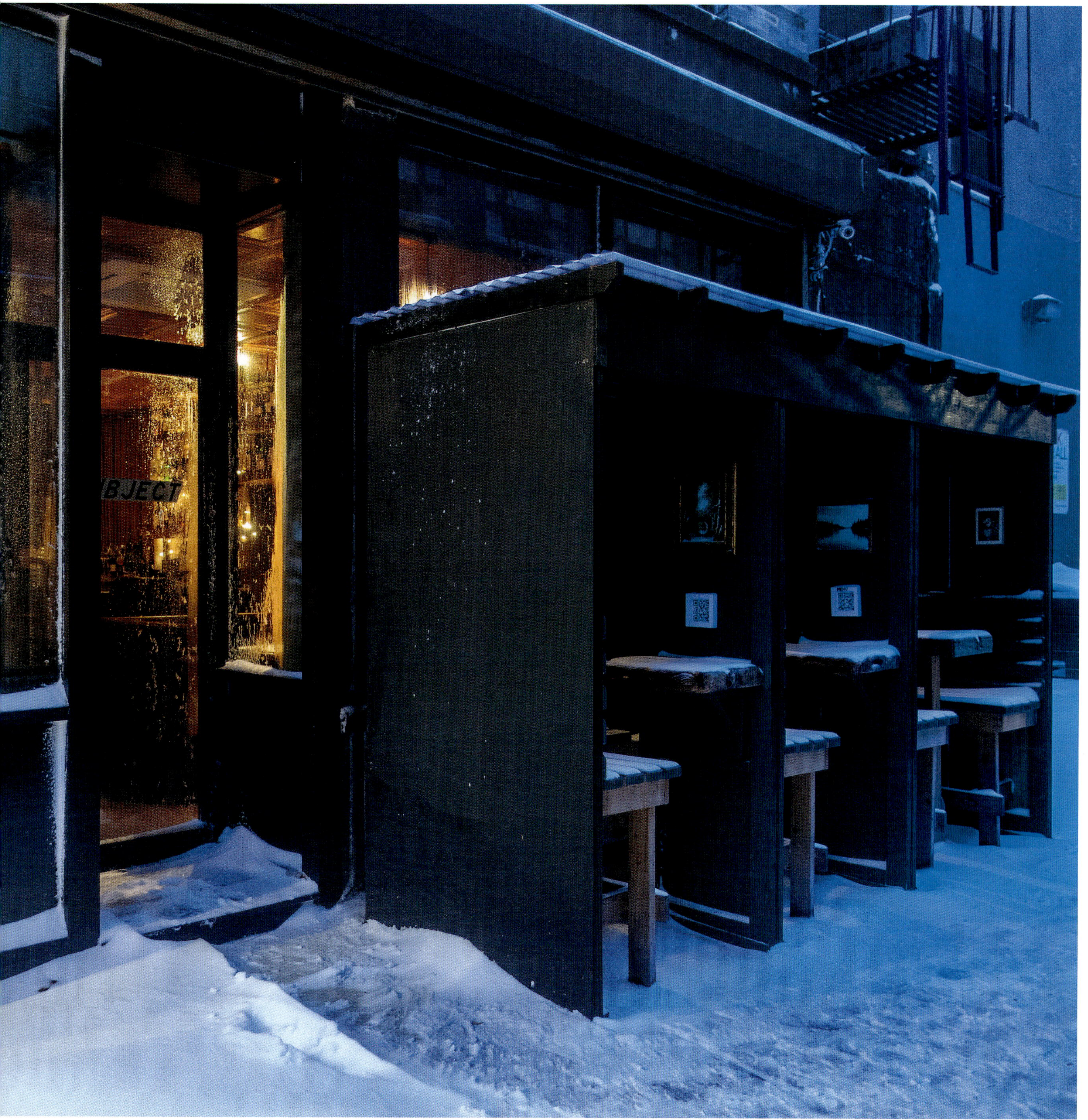

BJECT

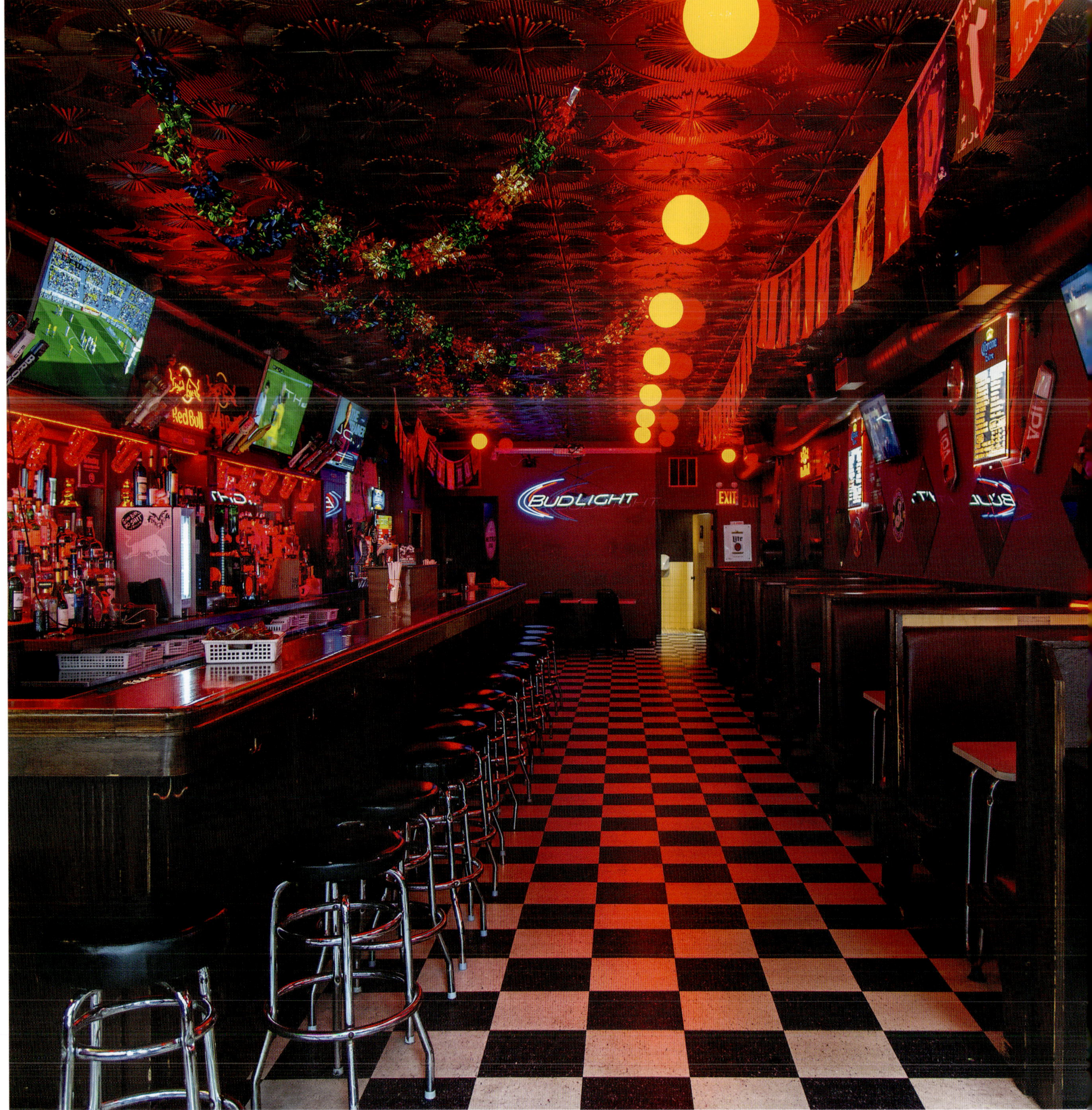

Subway Inn

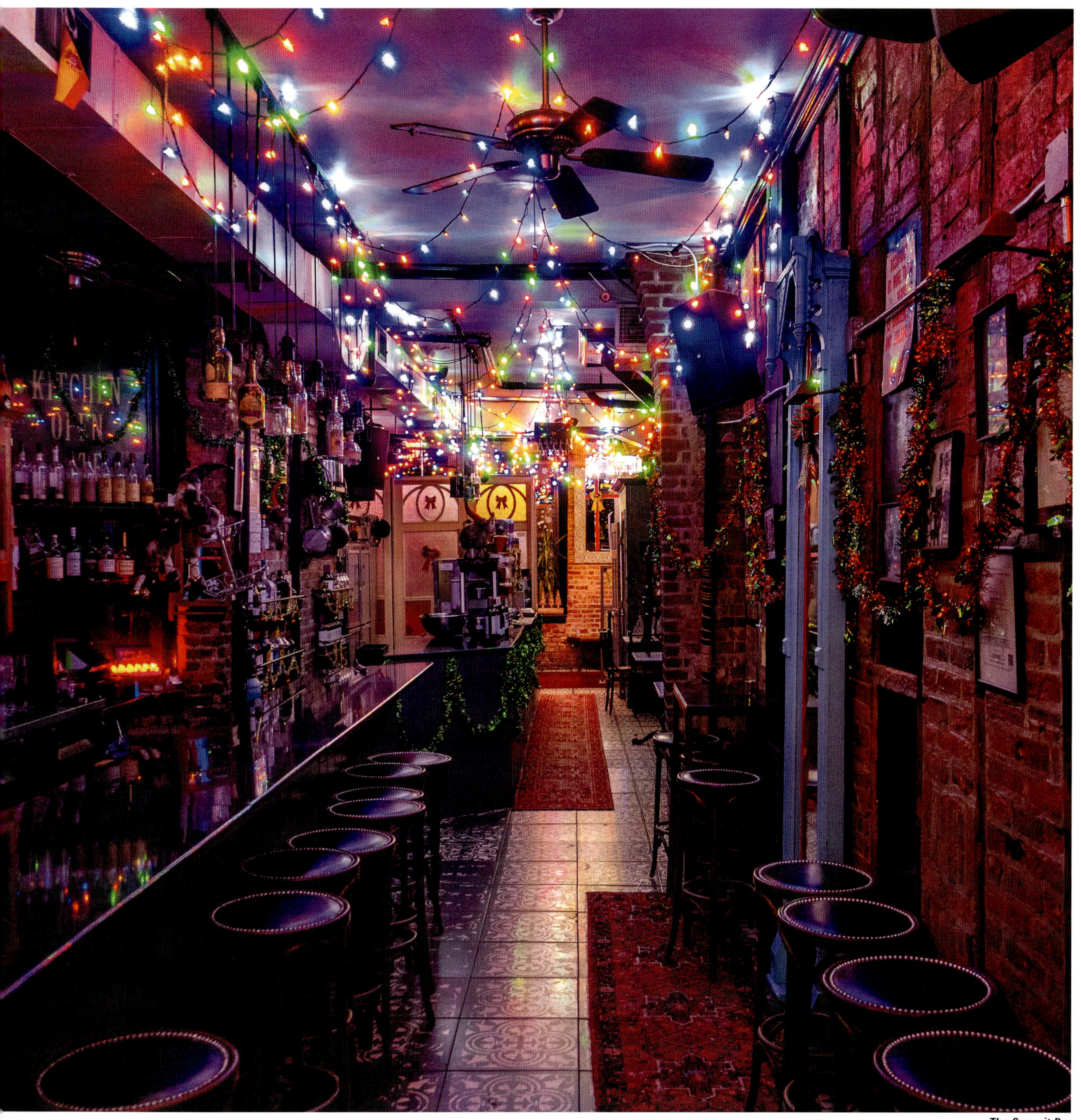

The Summit Bar

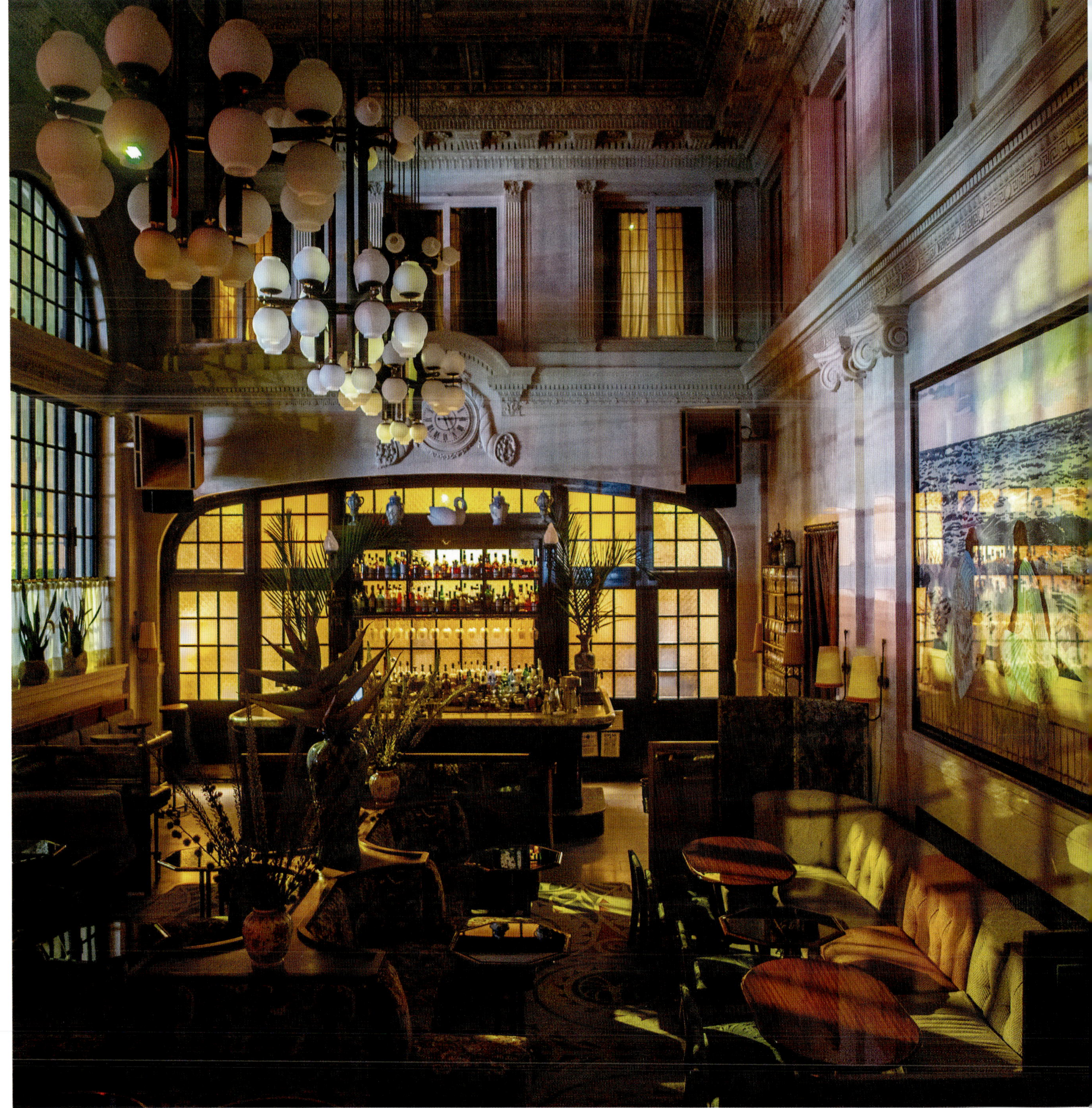

Swan Room

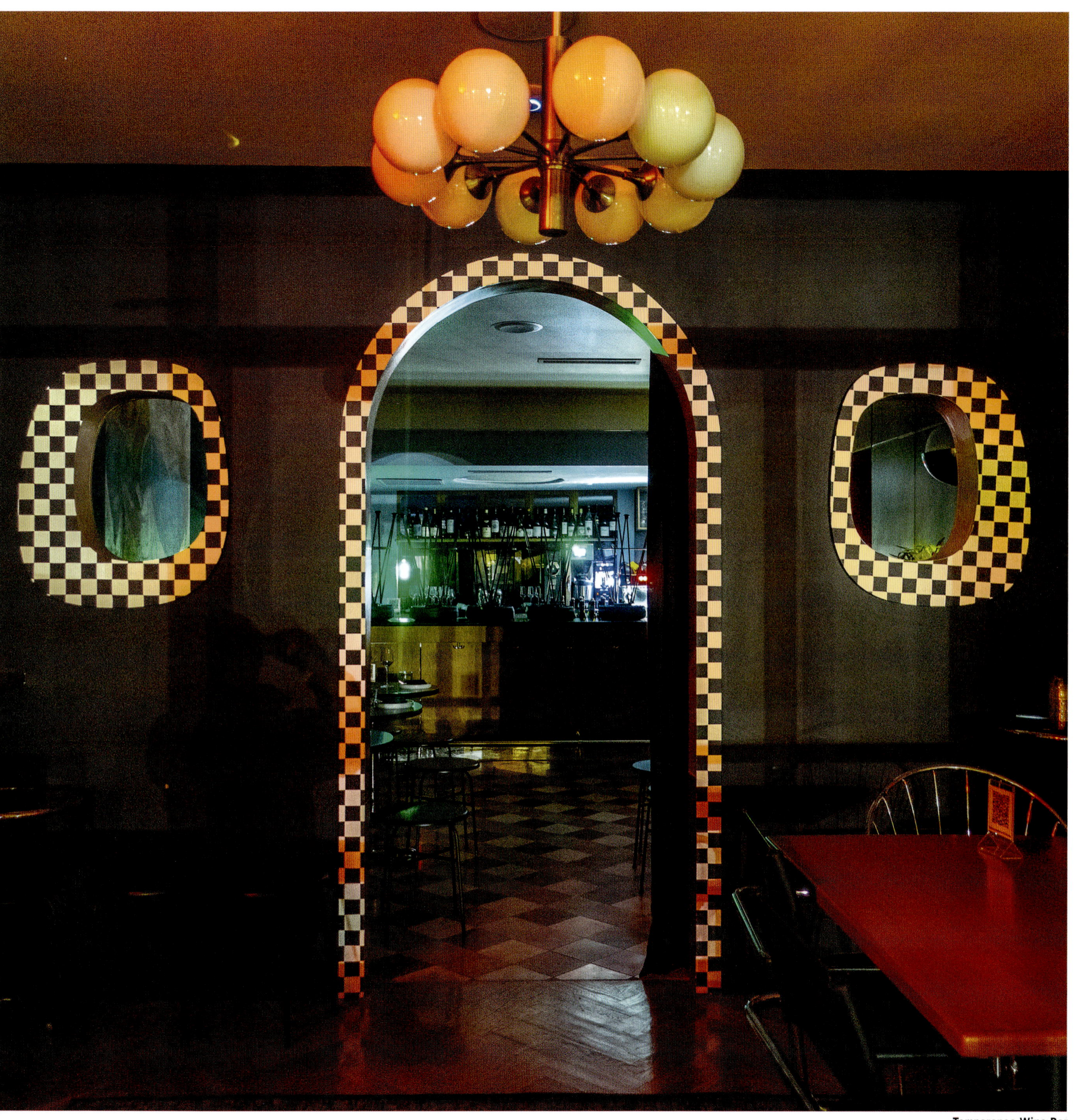
Temperance Wine Bar

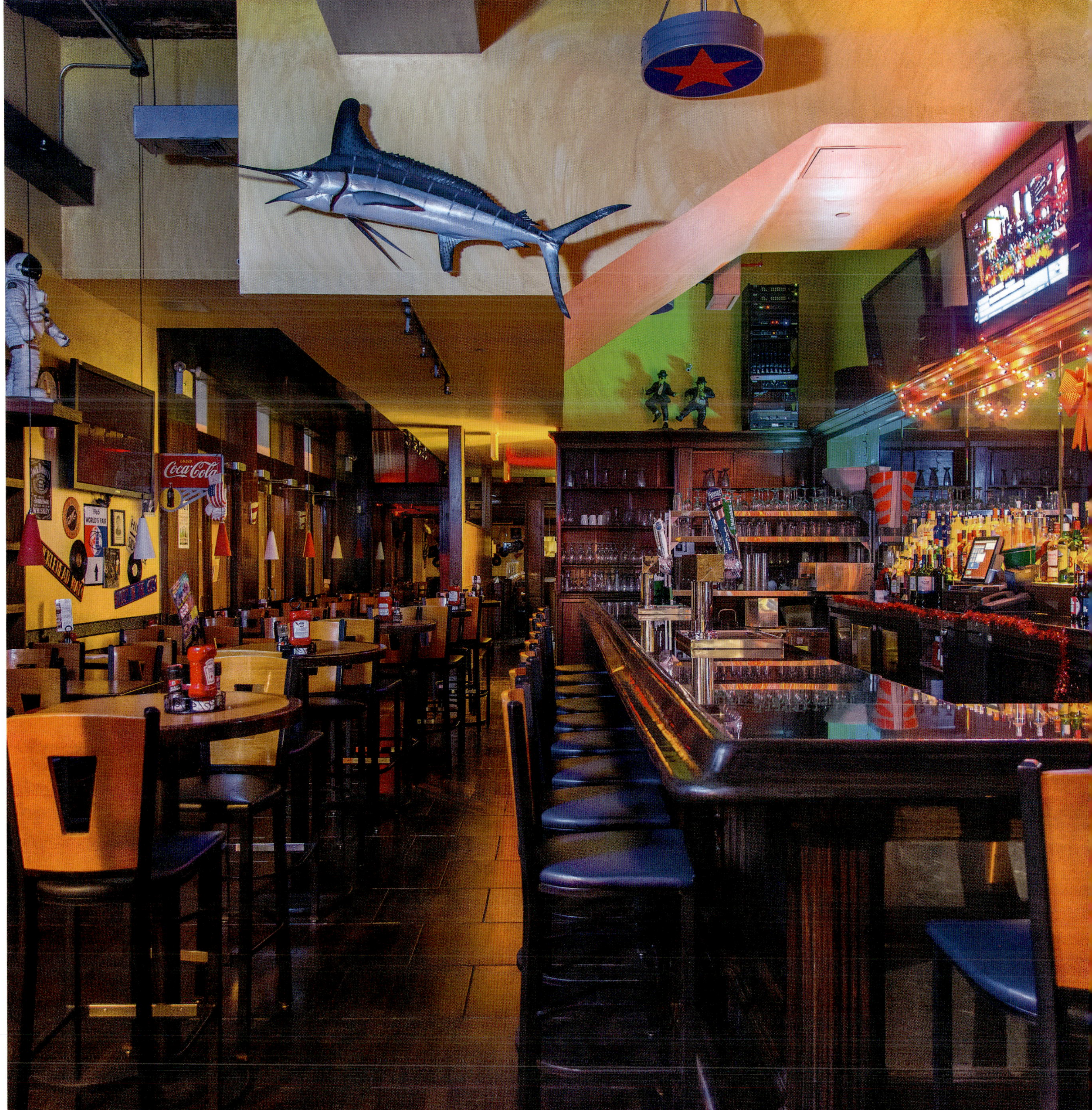

TGI Friday's

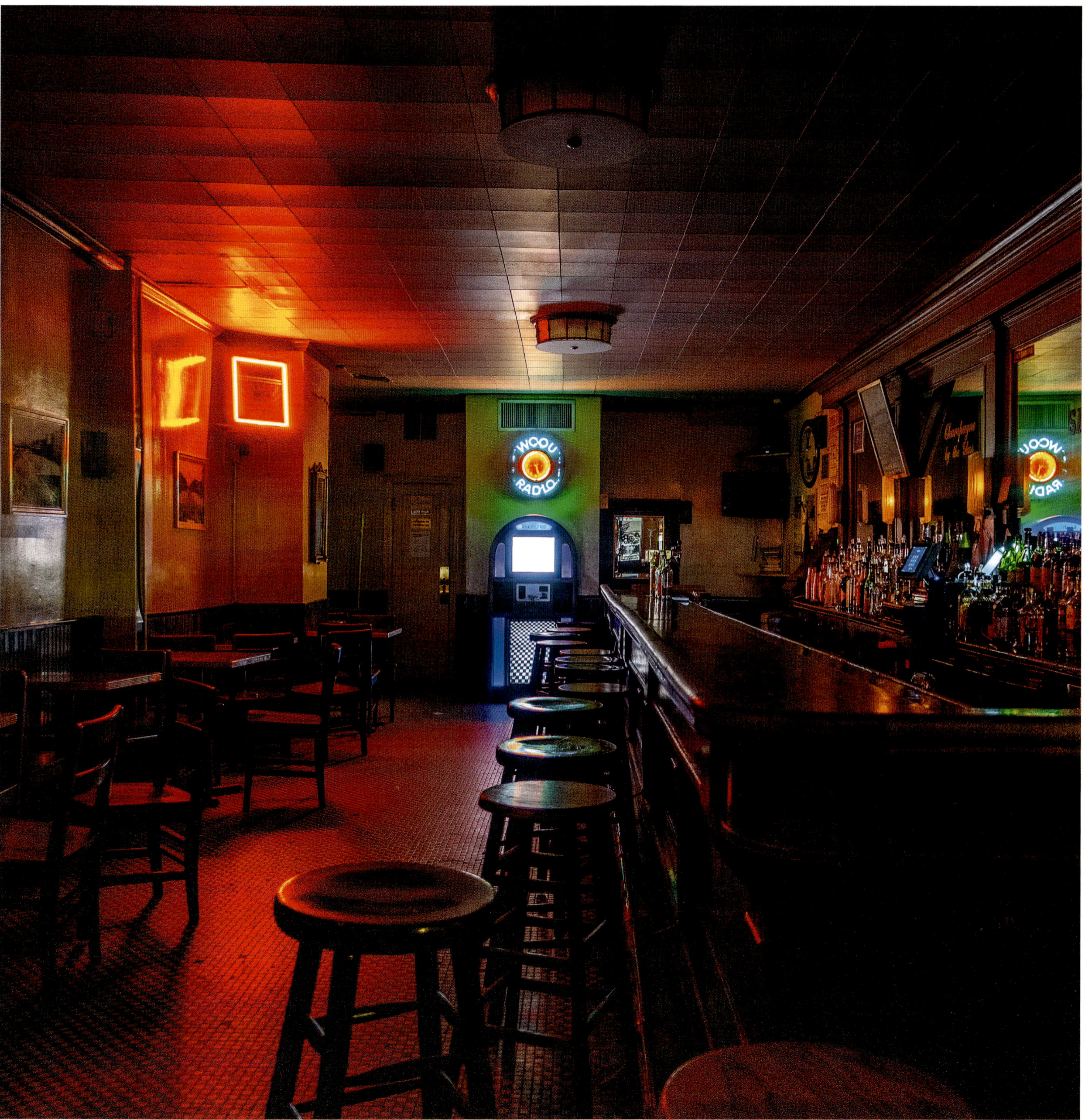

Tile Bar

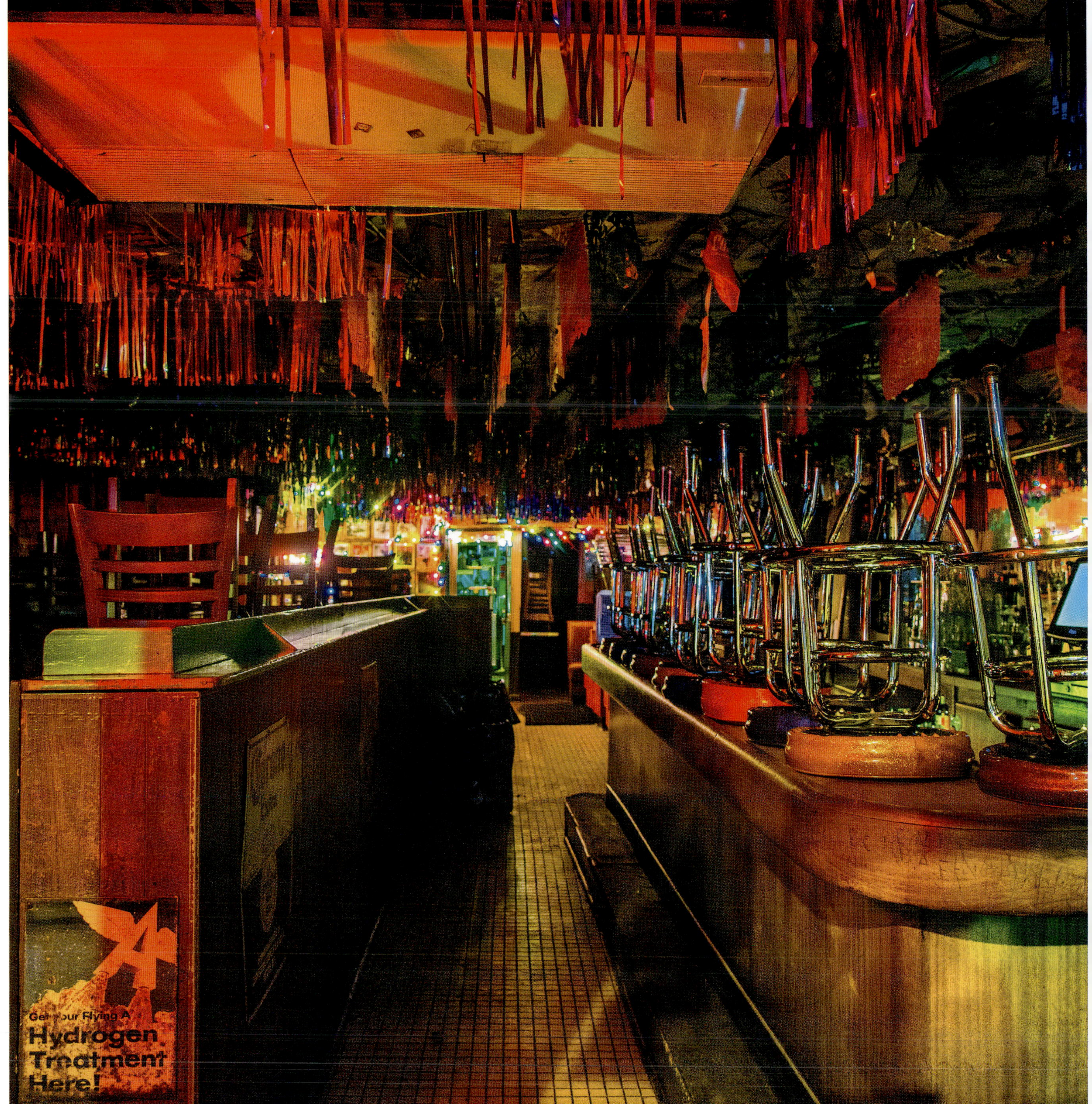

Tortilla Flats

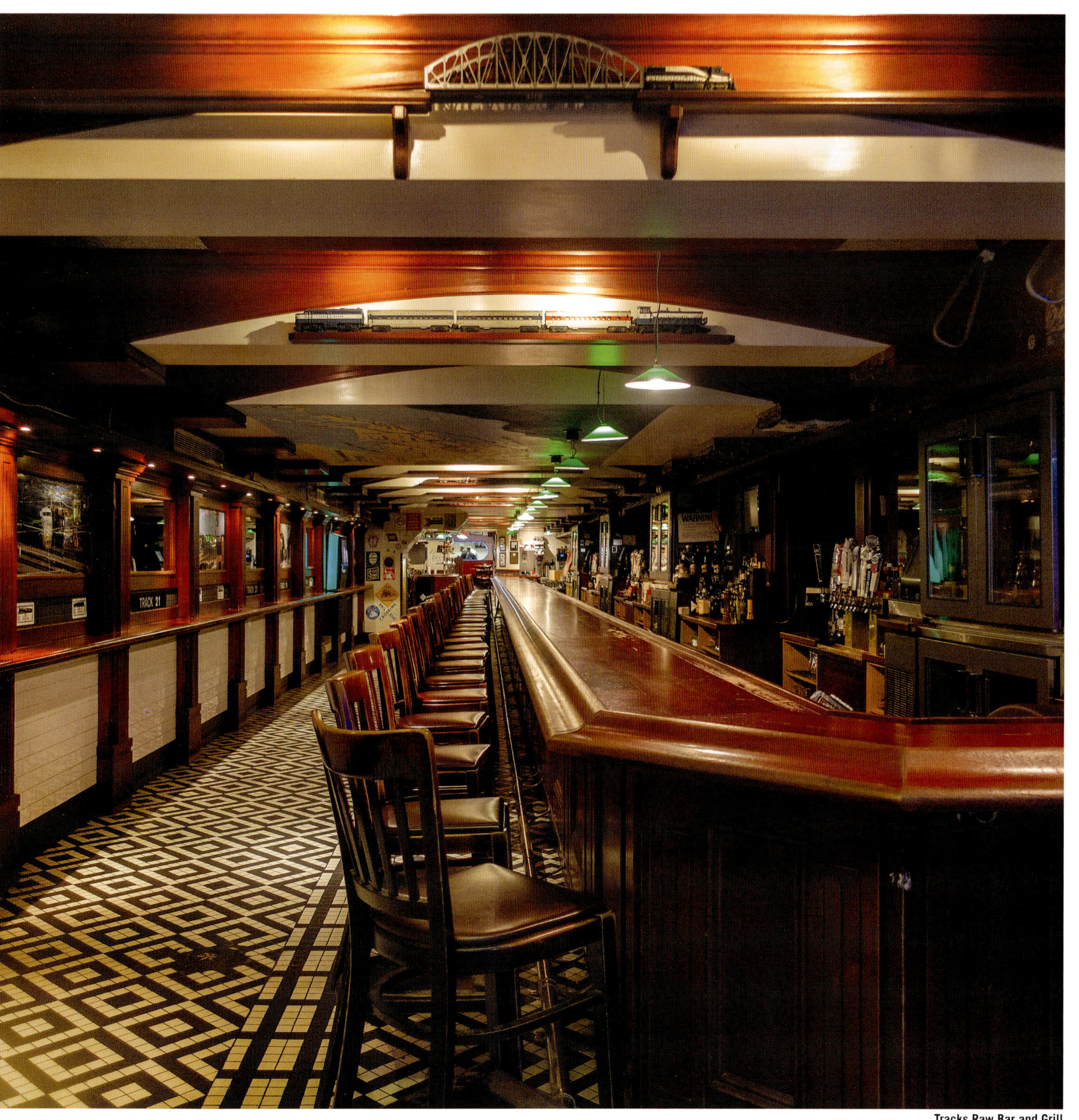

Tracks Raw Bar and Grill

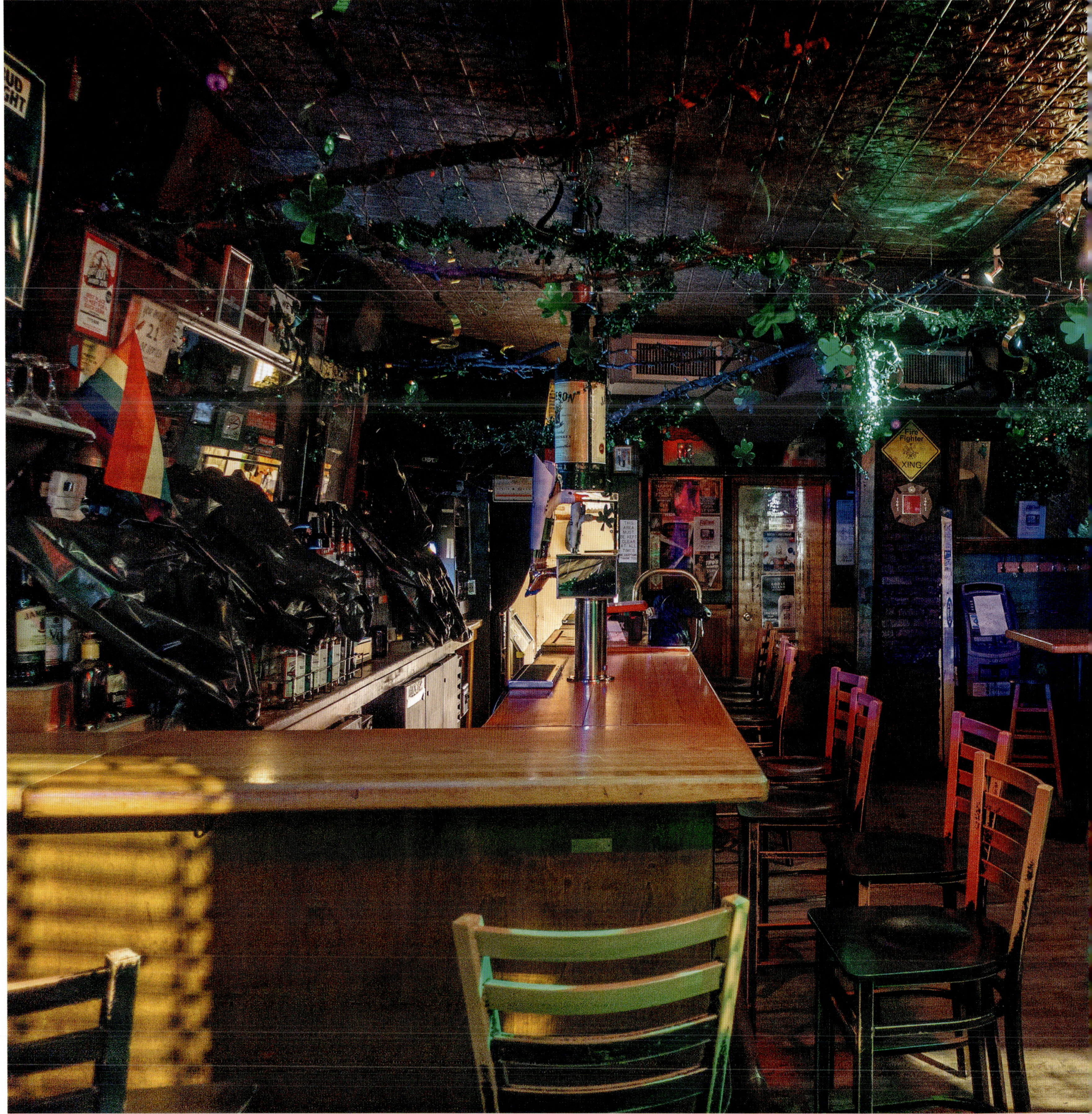

Ty's Bar

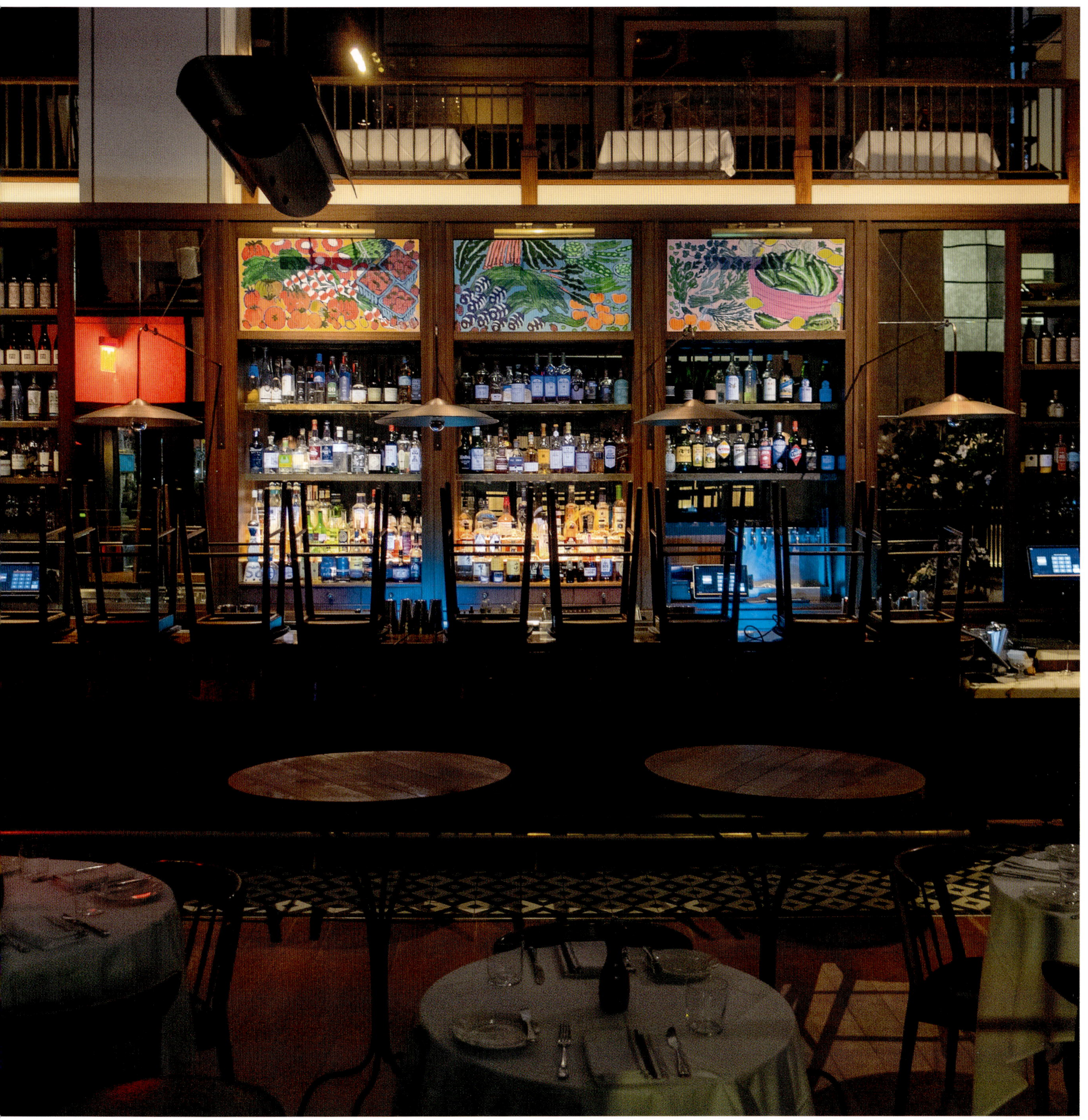

Union Square Cafe

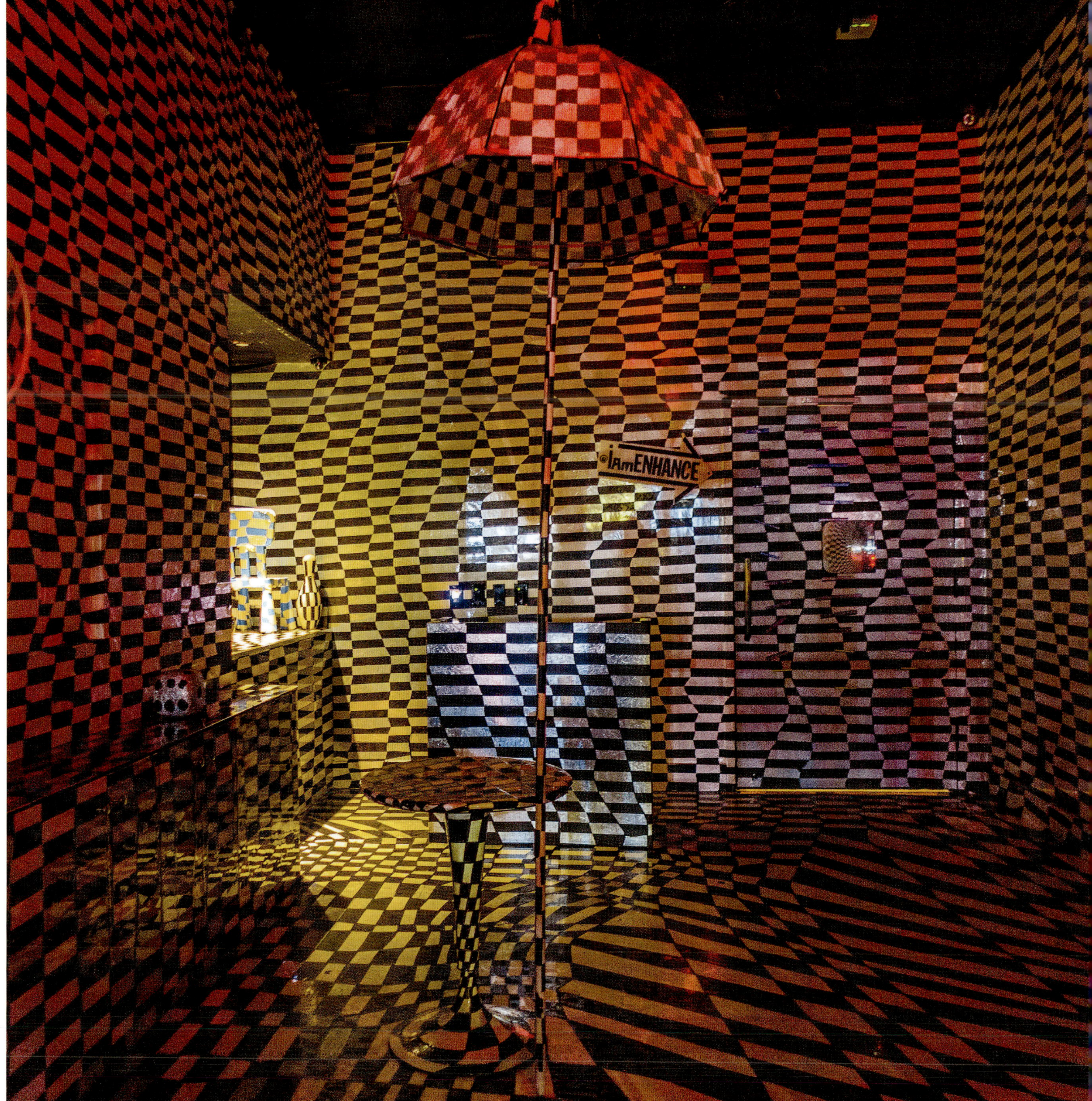

Vandal

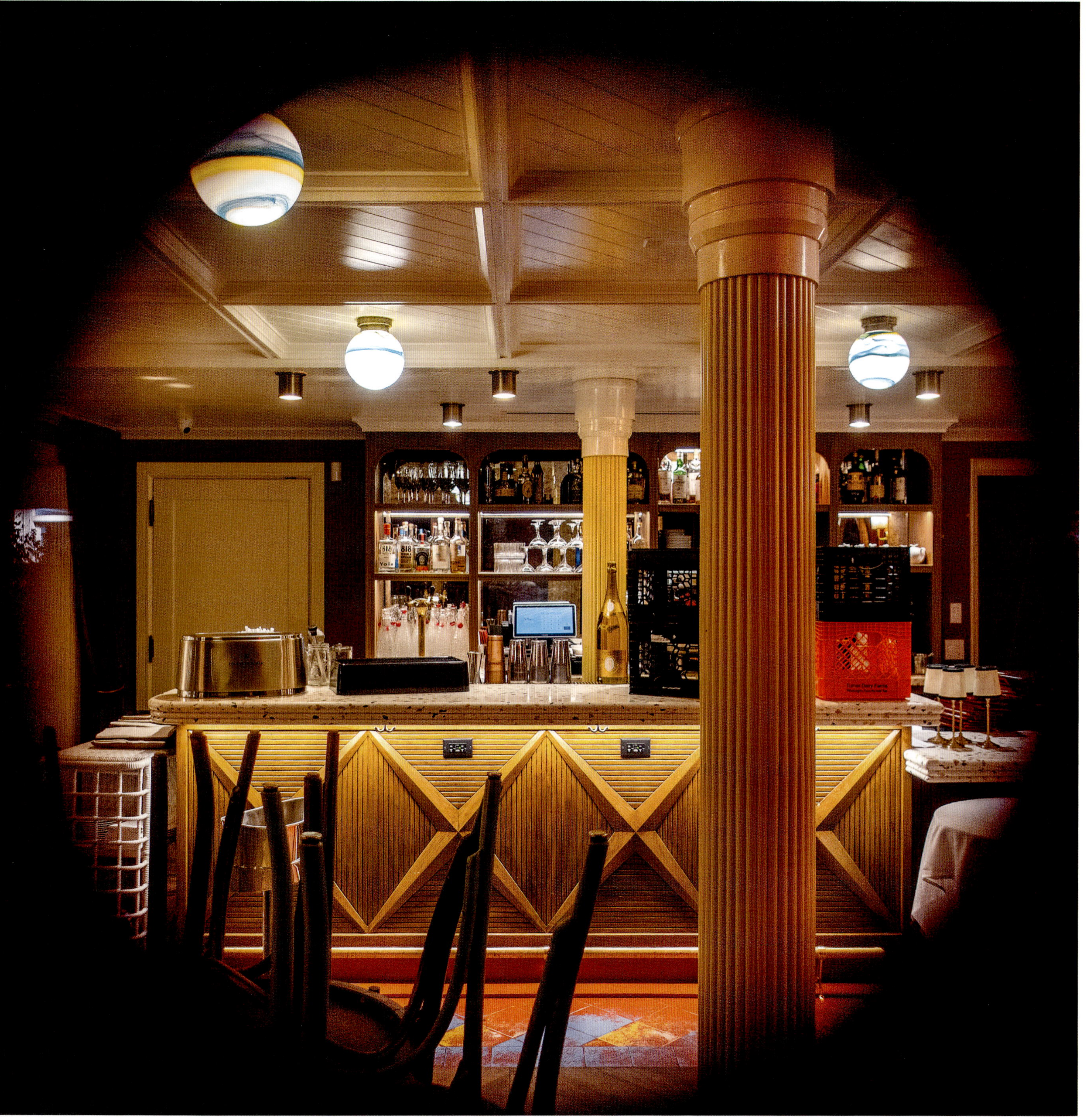

Venice Bar

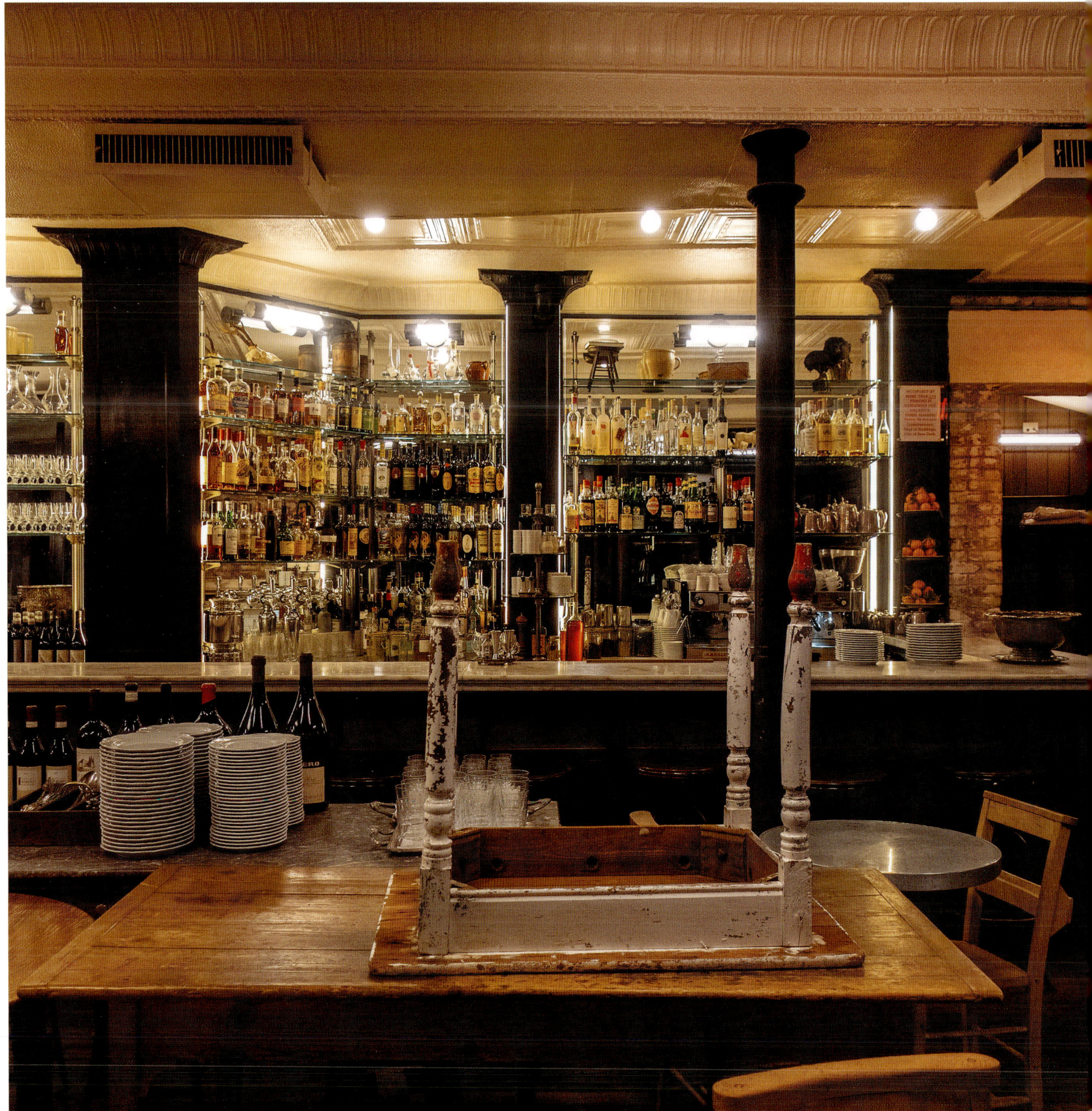

Via Carota

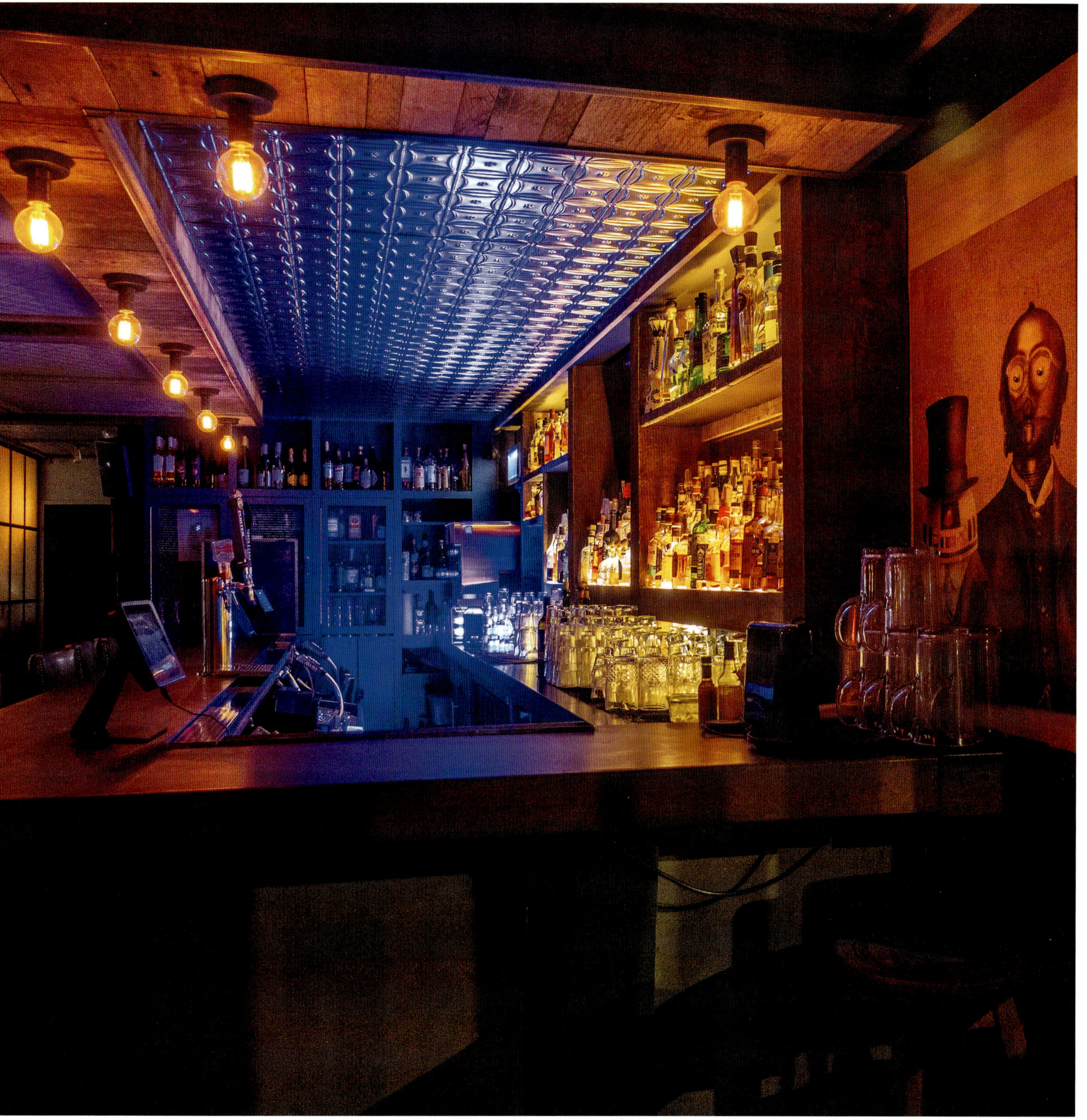

Vig Bar

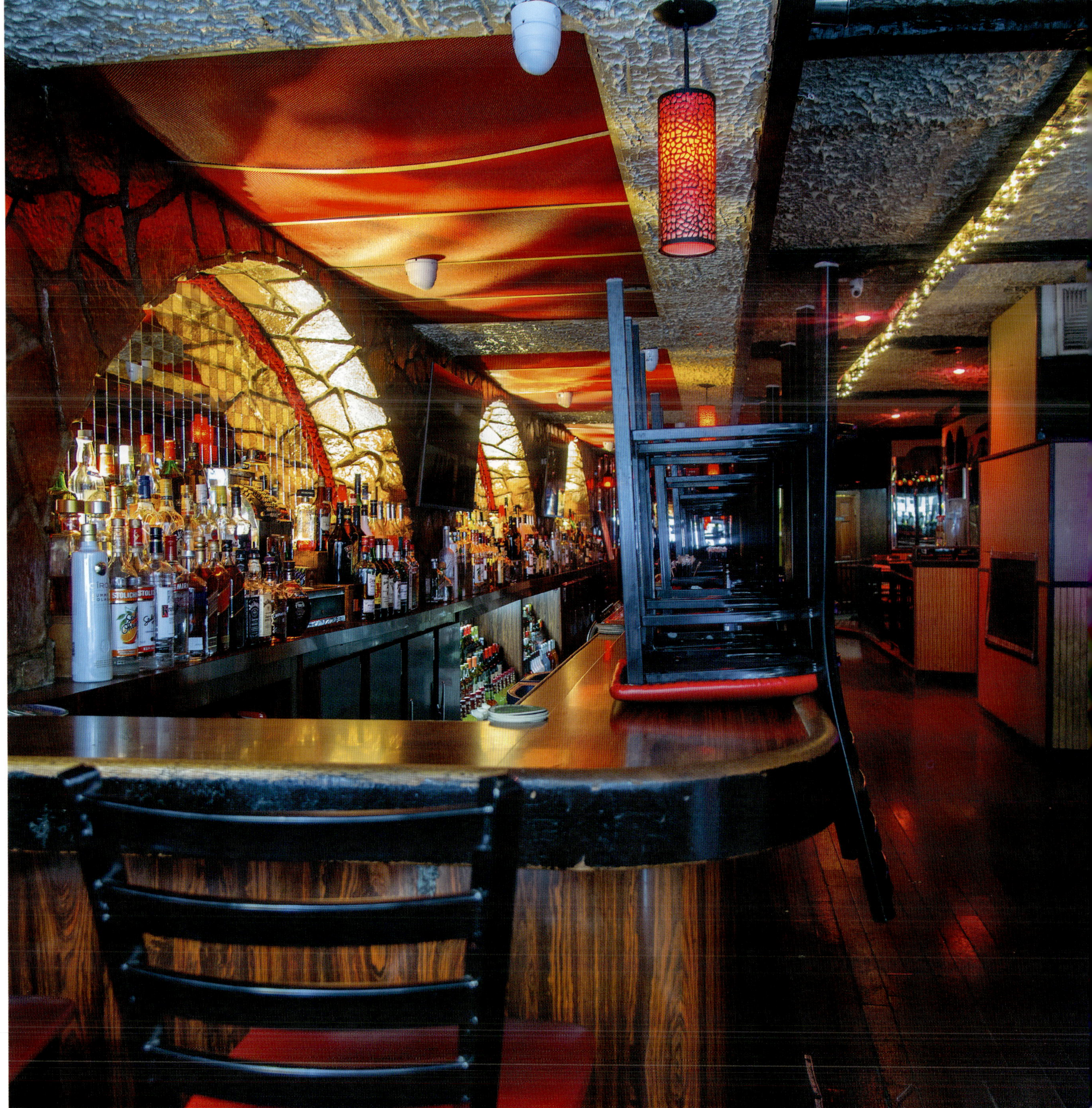

Wakamba

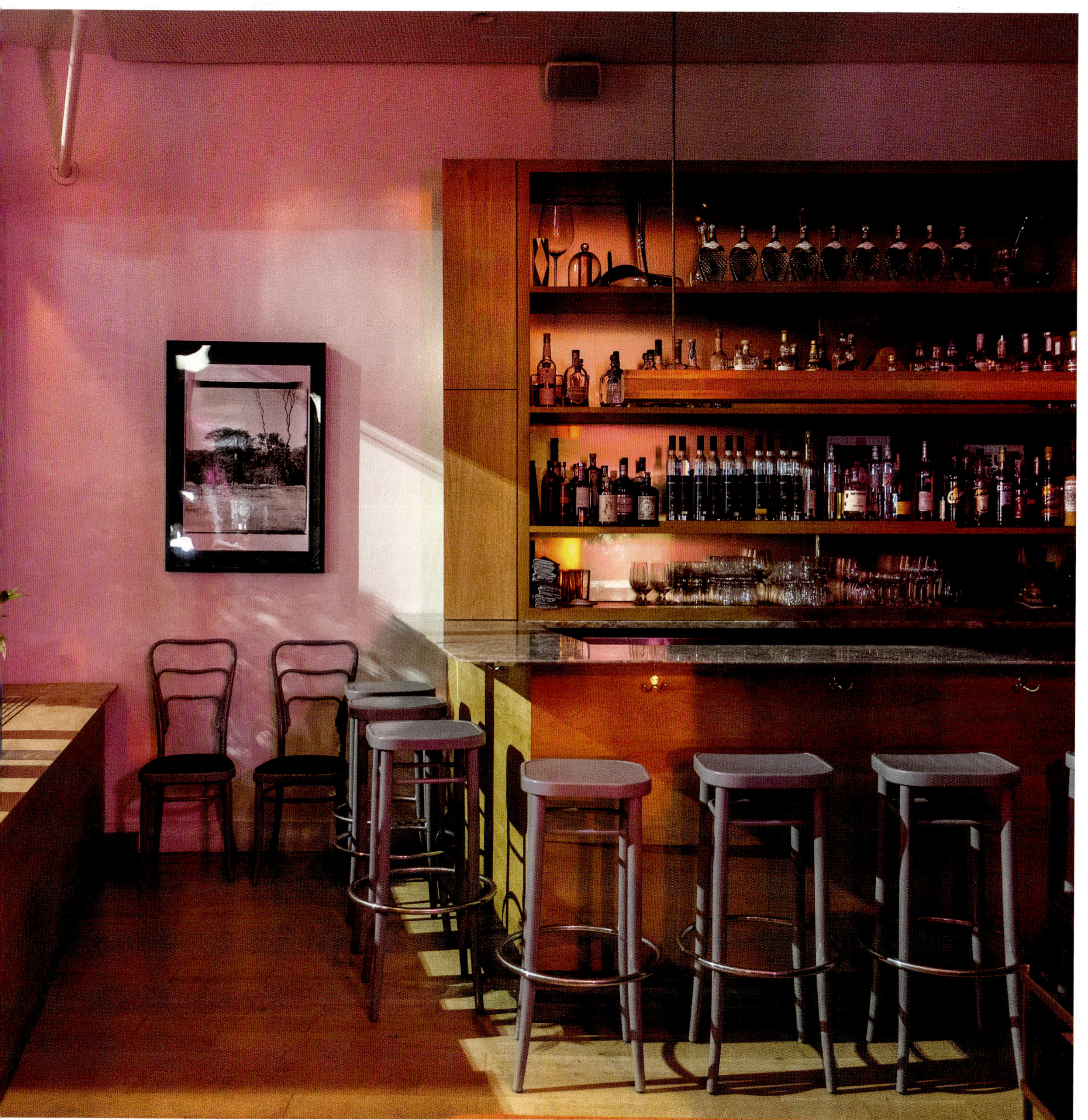

Wallsé

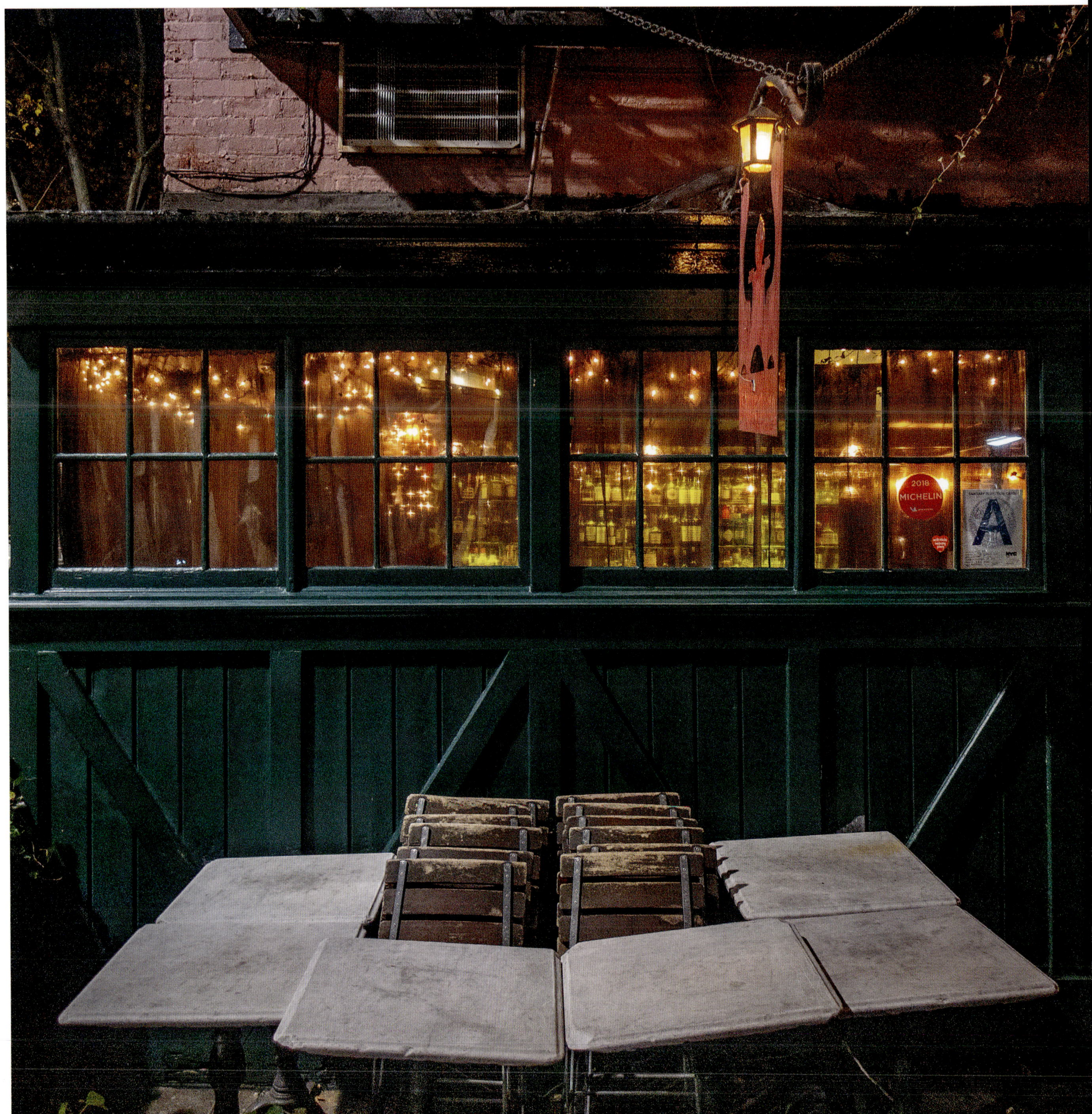

Waverly Inn

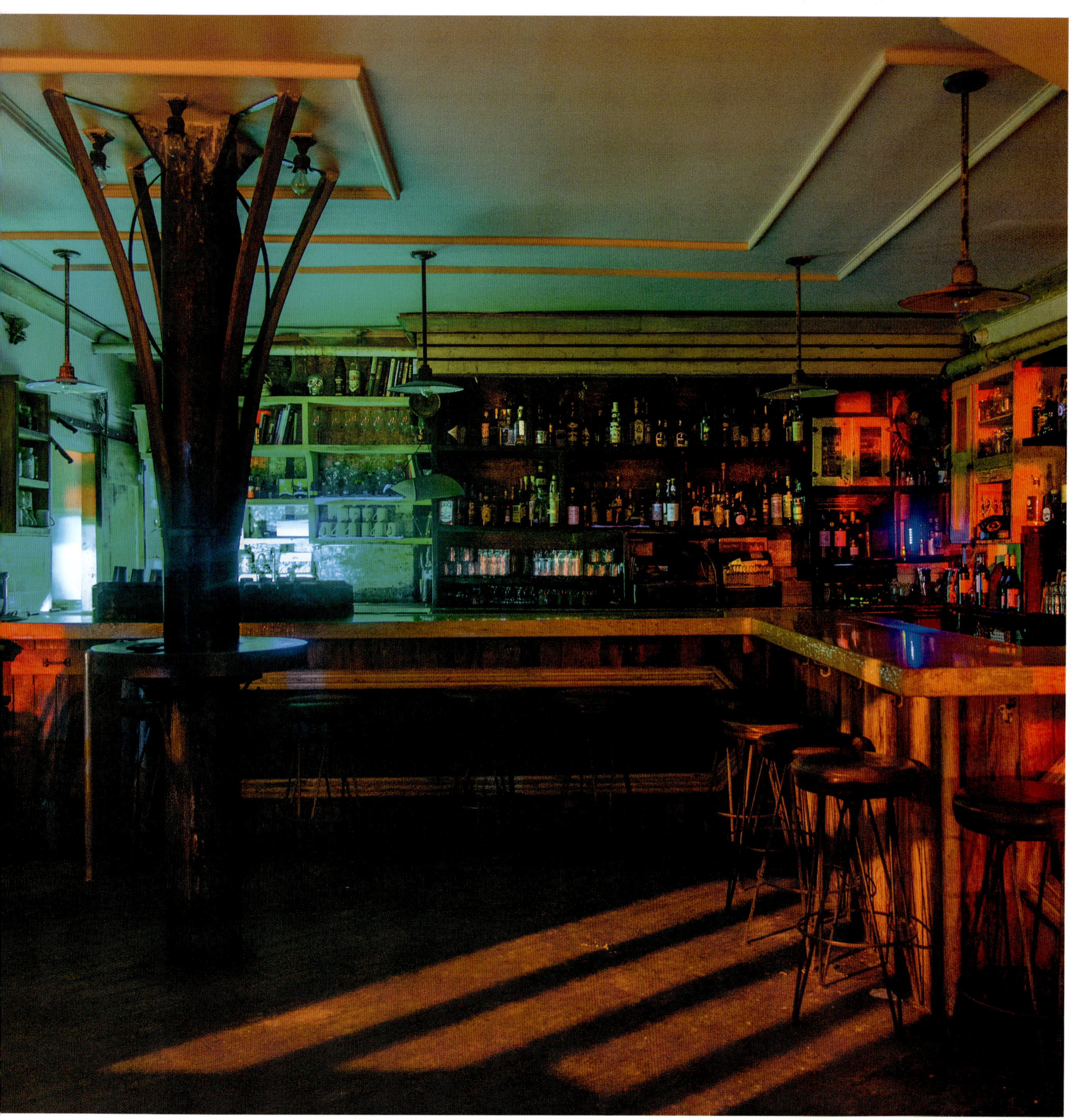

The Wayland

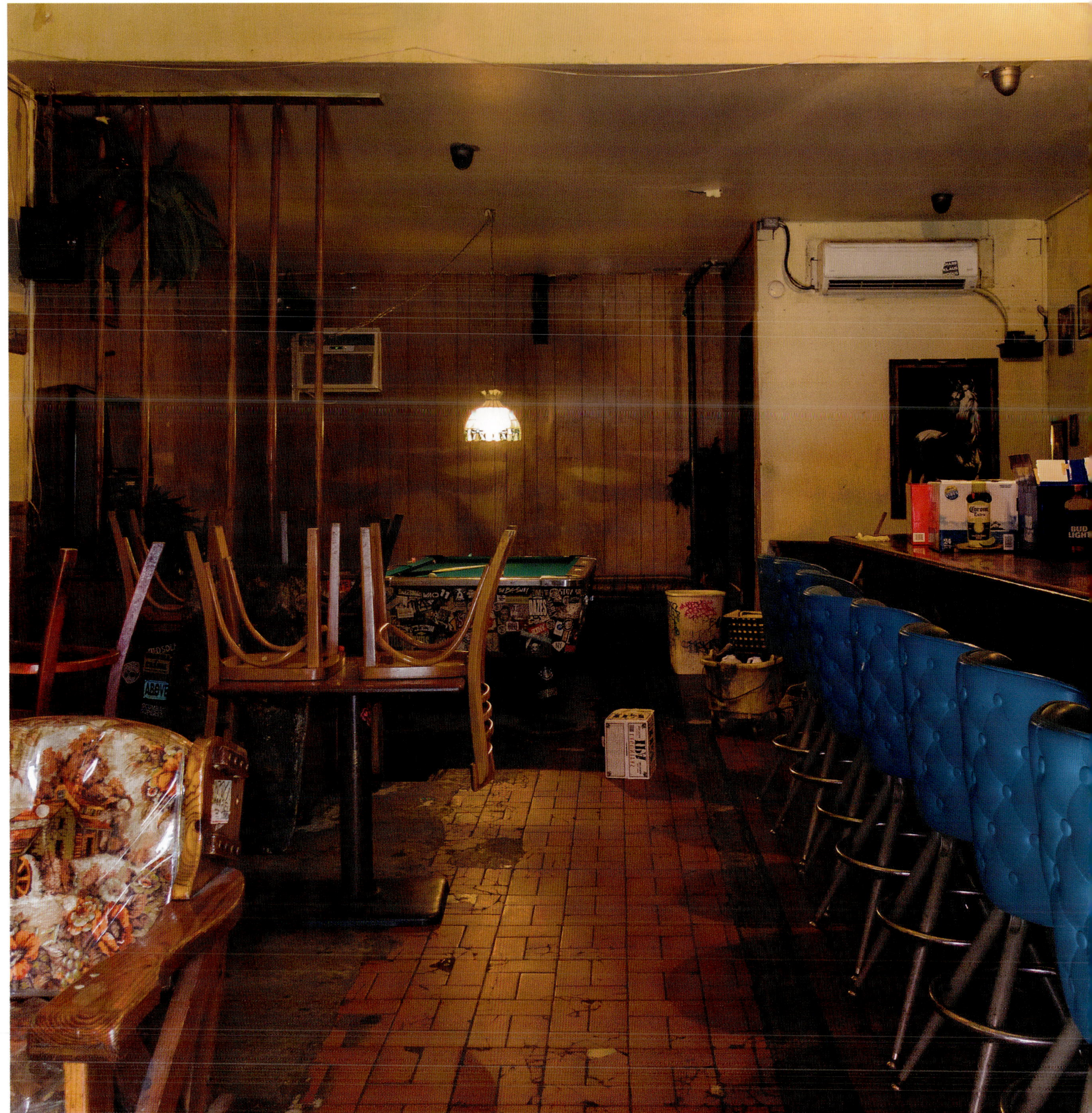

Welcome to the Johnsons

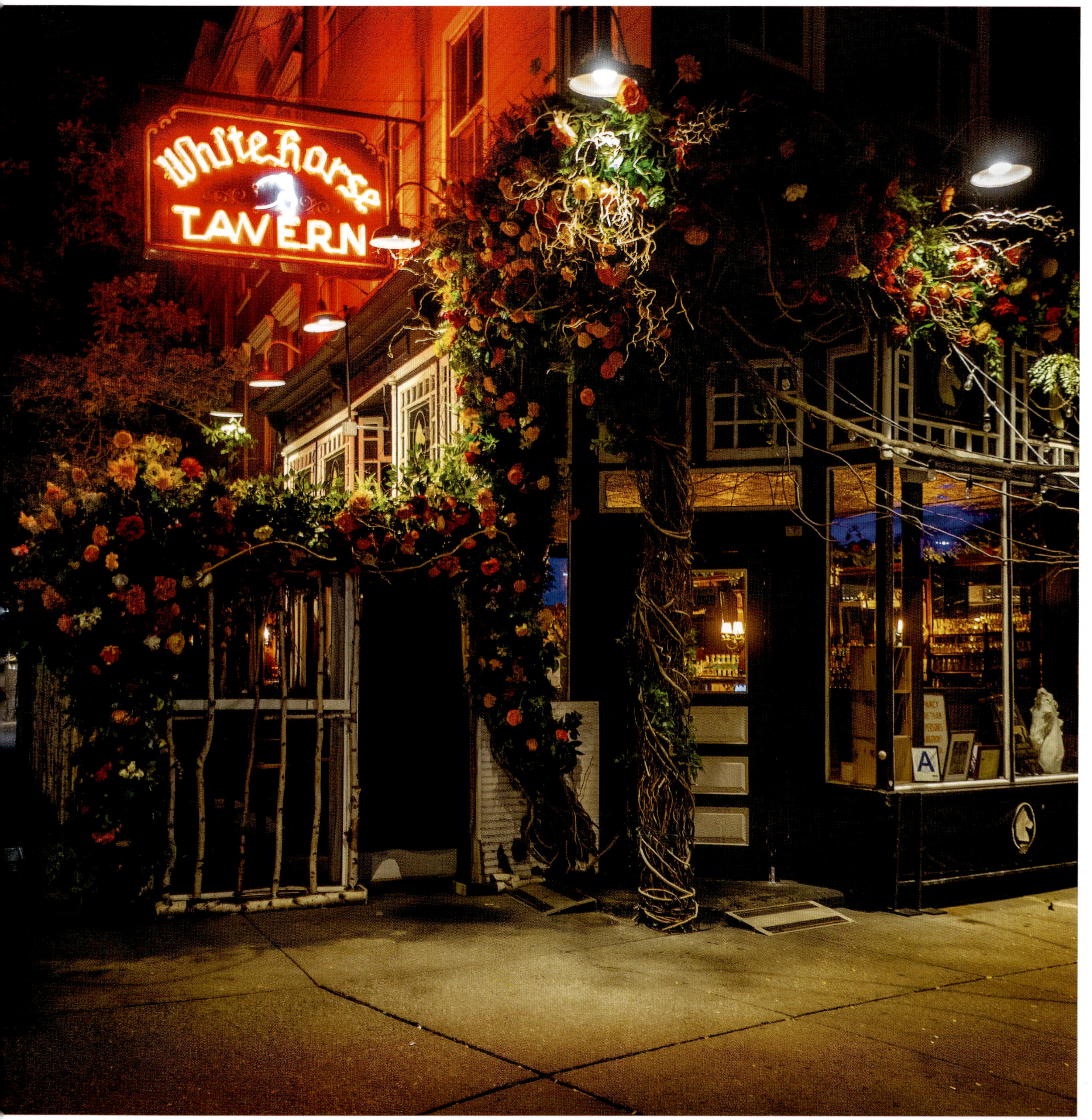

White Horse Tavern

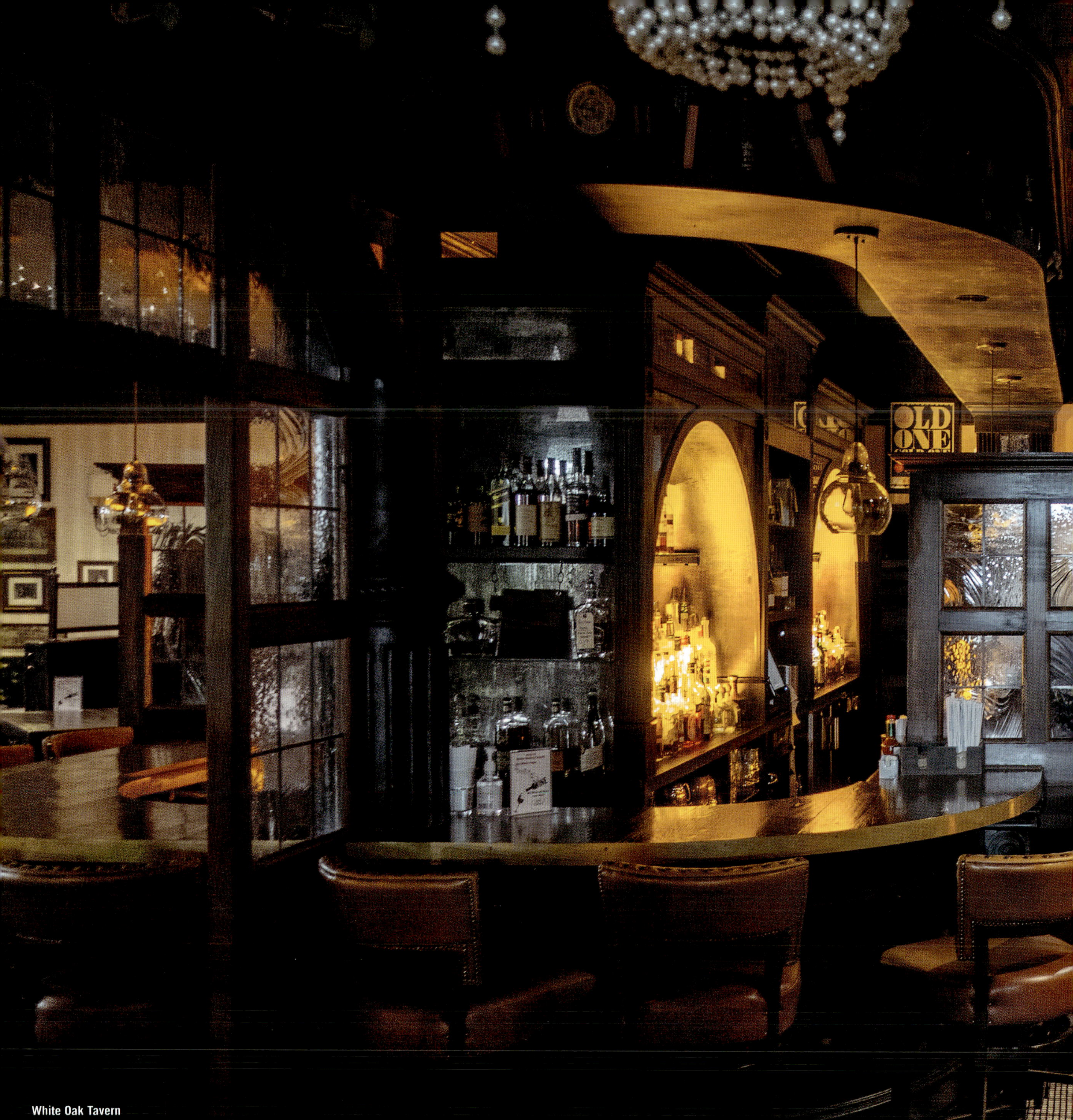

White Oak Tavern

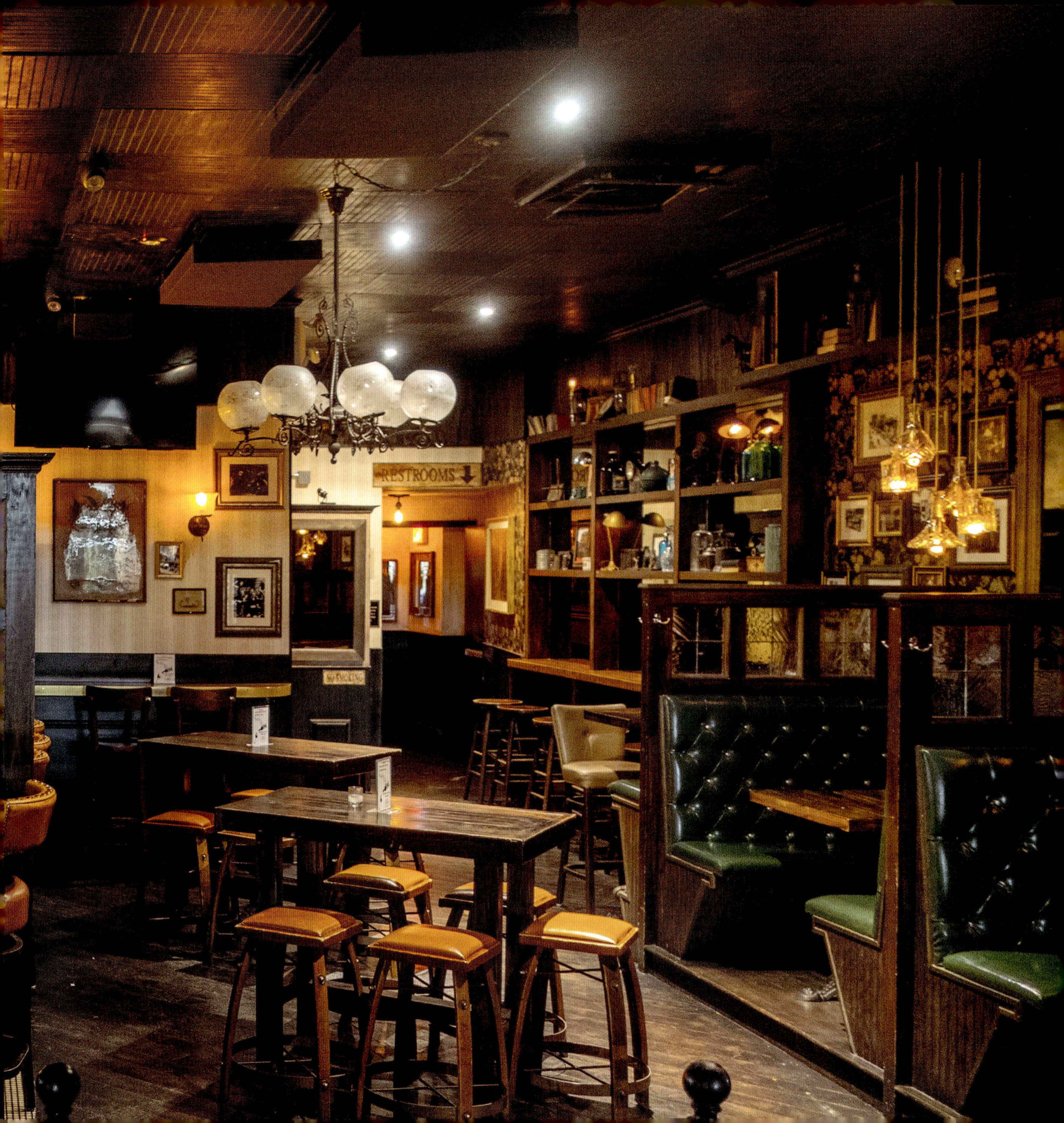
RESTROOMS

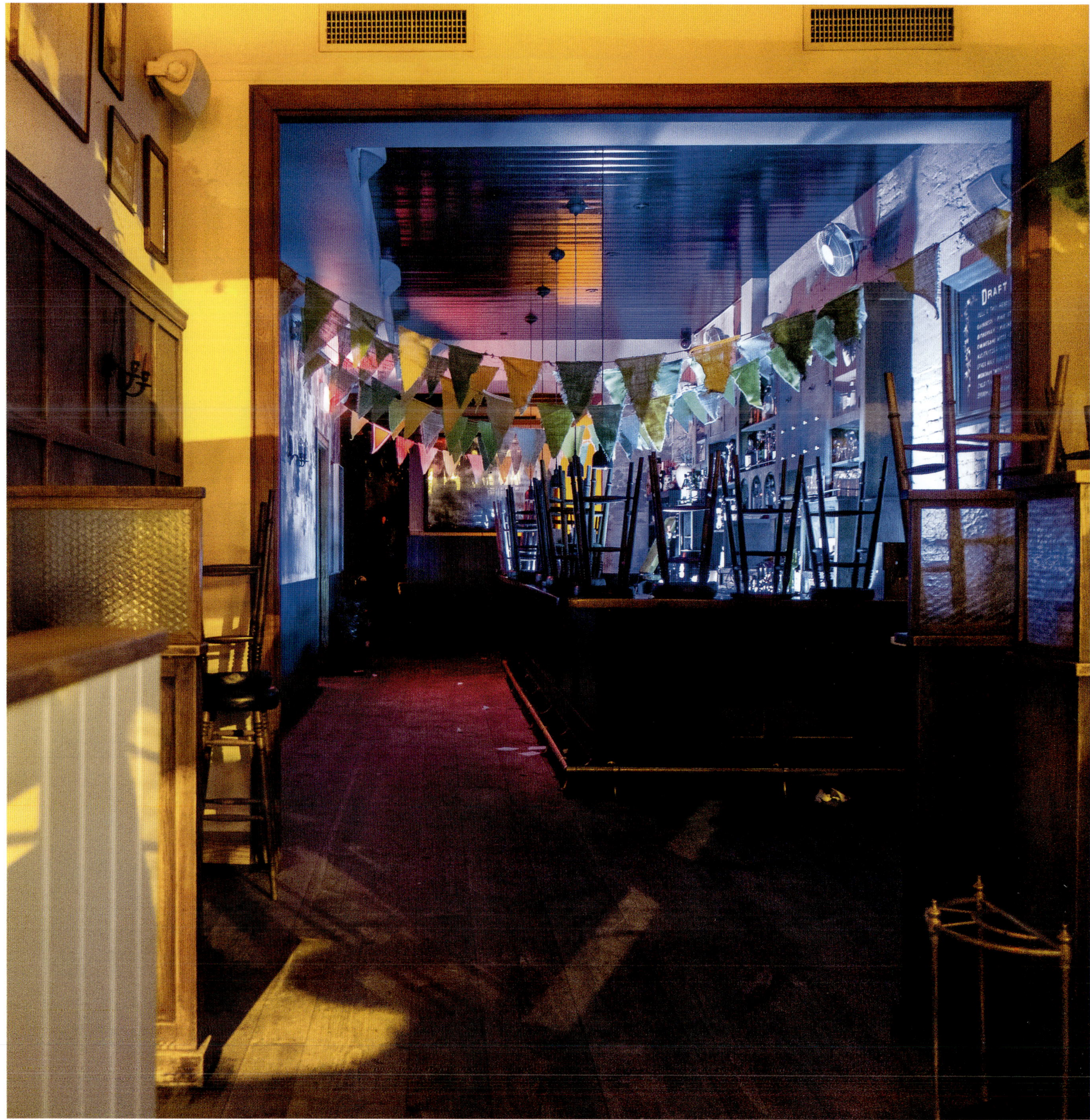

The Wren

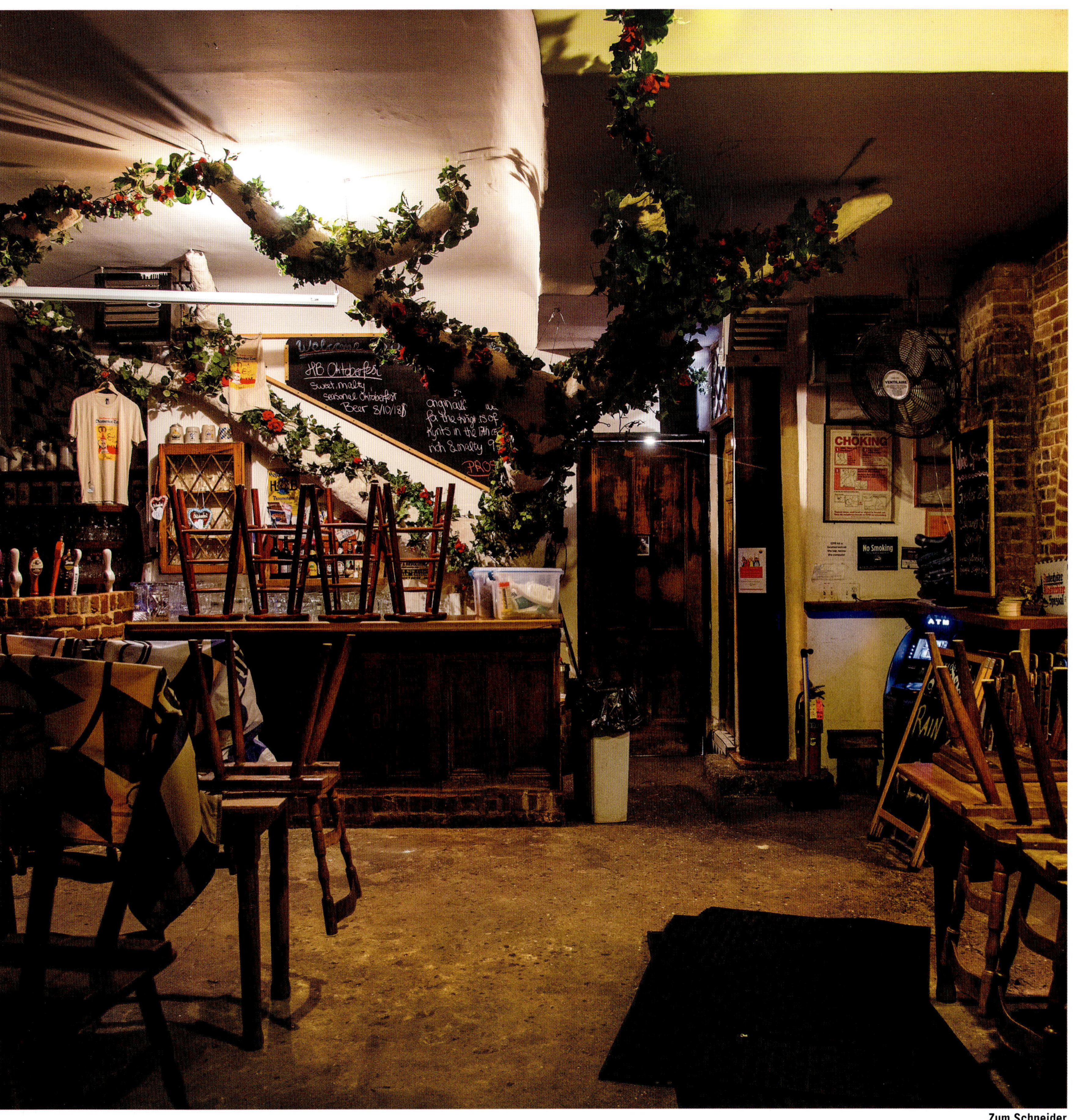

Zum Schneider

BAR ADDRESSES AND NOTES

Moves and closures are noted as of May 2023.

cover
**7B Horseshoe Bar,
aka Vazac's**
108 Avenue B

pages 2–3
Dirty French
180 Ludlow Street

page 6
Rosie's
29 East 2nd Street

page 10
Niagara
112 Avenue A
Previously King Tut's
Wah Wah Hut and before
that A7, an early hard-
core scene bar. The
first place I saw slam
dancing.

page 222
Leitao
547 Hudson Street

page 224
Goodnight Sonny
134 First Avenue

2A
25 Avenue A
Longtime neighborhood
spot.

169 Bar
169 East Broadway
Since 1916. Once known
as "the Bloody Bucket"
for the bar fights.

310 Bowery Bar
310 Bowery

519
519 Broome Street
Closed

Accidental Bar
98 Avenue C
Owned by *kikisake-shi*
(sake sommelier)
Austin Powers.

Alta
64 West 10th Street
Not sure about the
martini left by the door.
An overnight offering?
To whom?

**American Legion
Post 1212**
193 Prince Street
Same guy here every
morning getting things
straightened up for
the day.

Ampersand
294 Third Avenue

Añejo Tribeca
301 Church Street

Arlene's Grocery
95 Stanton Street
Music venue in old
bodega.

Art Bar
52 Eighth Avenue

Arthur's Tavern
57 Grove Street
Since 1937. Live jazz
since the '50s.

Arturo's
106 West Houston Street
Pizza and live jazz.

Attaboy
134 Eldridge Street
Behind a sign for M&H
Tailors and Alterations.

Automatic Slim's
733 Washington Street
Last bar on Washington
Street? The name is
from the lyrics of a Willie
Dixon song, "Wang Dang
Doodle."

Baar Baar
13 East 1st Street

Baby Grand
161 Lafayette Street
*Moved to
29 West 17th Street*

Balthazar
80 Spring Street
Steak frites and more
steak frites. Also sitting
next to Uma Thurman.

Bandits
44 Bedford Street
The old Daddy-O.

Bar Fedora
239 West 4th Street
Closed
Classic New York City
neon street scene.

Bar Pisellino
52 Grove Street

Bar Primi
325 Bowery
Jazz bar Tin Palace in
the '70s.

**The Bar Room at the
Beekman**
123 Nassau Street
An amazing nine-story
atrium.

Beatrice Inn
285 West 12th Street
Closed
Lacquered ceiling
reflecting.

Beauty and Essex
146 Essex Street
There is a bar back there

Beetle House
308 East 6th Street
A Tim Burton vibe.

Big Bar
75 East 7th Street

Billymark's West
332 Ninth Avenue
Dive bar, opens at 8 a.m.

The Bitter End
147 Bleecker Street
Music bar that everyone
seems to have played at
least once.

Blarney Stone
410 Eighth Avenue
Bar on left, steam table
on right.

Blind Barber
339 East 10th Street
Haircut up front,
bar in back.

Blue and Gold
79 East 7th Street
Since 1958.

Blue Note
131 West 3rd Street
Local jazz club,
now worldwide.

Botanica
47 East Houston Street

Boucherie Union Square
225 Park Avenue South

Bridge Cafe
279 Water Street
Closed
Opened in 1794 as
a "grocery and wine
bottler," closed by
Hurricane Sandy.
Bar, brothel, rat den.
In the mid-nineteenth
century, a jar of pickled
earlobes was on the bar.
They were bitten off
by the bouncer, a woman
named Gallus Mag.

Brother Jimmy's
416 Eighth Avenue
Closed
BBQ joint near
Penn Station.

Café Altro Paradiso
234 Spring Street

Caffè Vivaldi
32 Jones Street
Closed

The Campbell
15 Vanderbilt Avenue
In 1923, the financier
John W. Campbell turned
this space in Grand
Central into his office/
reception room.

Casa La Femme
140 Charles Street

Cherry Tavern
441 East 6th Street

Chinese Tuxedo
5 Doyers Street
One of the few remaining
street-level bars in
Chinatown.

Clockwork
21 Essex Street
Where the tagging
never stops.

Club Cumming
505 East 6th Street
The actor Alan
Cumming's bar.

The Cock
93 Second Avenue
The name says it all.

Coney Island Baby
169 Avenue A
Closed
One in a long line of mu-
sic bars at this location.
Brownies was a big one.

Corner Bistro
331 West 4th Street
The red glow to guide
you.

Cowgirl SeaHorse
259 Front Street
Hard by the
Brooklyn Bridge.

Cubbyhole
281 West 12th Street
One of two remaining
lesbian bars in town.

CUT by Wolfgang Puck
99 Church Street
High-end bar in the
Four Seasons.

Dante Seaport
89 South Street
Closed
Seaport outpost.

Dante West Village
551 Hudson Street
Outpost of Caffe Dante
on MacDougal Street.

The Dead Rabbit
30 Water Street
Named after a
Five Points gang.

Ding-A-Ling
116 Avenue C

Doc Holliday's
141 Avenue A

Don Angie
103 Greenwich Avenue

Double Down Saloon
14 Avenue A
Sister bar to the Las
Vegas location.

Downtime
25 Avenue B
The old basement of
Save the Robots.

Dr. Clark
104 Bayard Street
The swing sign is from
Winnie's Bar, as is
the ghost sign above
the door.

Dudley's
85 Orchard Street

The Duplex
61 Christopher Street
They change their out-
door lighting all the time.
Winners for best lighting.

Ear Inn
326 Spring Street
Est. 1817. Bar, brothel.
Before landfill it used to
be on the banks of the
Hudson.

East Village Social
126 Saint Marks Place

Extra Virgin
259 West 4th Street

Fairfax
234 West 4th Street

Fanelli Cafe
94 Prince Street
Saloon since 1863.

Fish Bar
237 East 5th Street

Fishmarket
111 South Street

Flats Fix
14 East 23rd Street
Closed at this location
AOC bartended at the
Union Square location.

FMN General Store
136 Division Street
Fastest pivot after Covid
hit. Forgetmenot bar to
FMN General Store (with
drinks to go) within a
month.

Fraunces Tavern
54 Pearl Street
Est. 1762. Where George
Washington bade farewell
to his officers after the
Revolution.

Freehold in the Park
20 Union Square West
*Moved to 145 East
39th Street as Freehold
Rooftop*

Frenchette
241 West Broadway

The Frying Pan
207 Twelfth Avenue/
Pier 66

**The Garden at the Standard
East Village**
25 Cooper Square
Changes looks with the
seasons.

Gemma
335 Bowery

Gitano Garden of Love
23 Grand Street
*Moved to Governors
Island*
Tulum-themed on a lot by
the Holland Tunnel.

Gramercy Tavern
42 East 20th Street

Grand Banks
Pier 25

Great Jones Cafe
54 Great Jones Street
Closed
Local favorite across the
street from Basquiat's
studio.

Grey Lady
77 Delancey Street

Heineken Riverdeck
Pier 17
Closed
Temporary summertime
bar on the pier.

Henrietta Hudson
438 Hudson Street
The other lesbian bar in
the city.

Holiday Cocktail Lounge
75 Saint Marks Place
W. H. Auden lived
upstairs and used the
bathroom at the bar when
it was a dive bar.

Holland Bar
532 9th Avenue
Closed
A proper Port Authority
dive bar.

Hudson Bar and Books
636 Hudson Street
Technically a cigar bar so
you can still smoke.

Iggy's Keltic Lounge
132 Ludlow Street
A late, late spot.

International Bar
120½ First Avenue
*Moved to 102 First
Avenue*
They used to open at
8 a.m.

Jack and Charlie's No. 118
118 Greenwich Avenue
That's West 13th Street
through the window.

Jeffrey's Grocery
172 Waverly Place

Jeremy's Ale House
228 Front Street
Bras on the ceiling type
of place.

Jimmy's Corner
140 West 44th Street
The last regular, small
bar in the Theater
District.

Joe's Pub
425 Lafayette Street
And the stage down
below.

Johnny's Bar
90 Greenwich Street
Your basic bar.

Josie's
520 East 6th Street
Another basic bar.

Joyface
104 Avenue C
Disco ball and waterbed.
What could go wrong?

Jules Bistro
65 Saint Marks Place
Closed

Julius
159 West 10th Street
Est. 1864. Historic gay
rights bar.

Kabooz's Bar and Grill
2 Pennsylvania Plaza
A commuter bar in
Penn Station.

Kenn's Broome Street Bar
363 West Broadway
Serving the SoHo artist
since the '70s.

Kettle of Fish
59 Christopher Street
Originally on MacDougal
Street and associated
with the Beats and
folk music, now on
Christopher Street.

Key Bar
432 East 13th Street

Ladybird
111 East 7th Street
The porter let me grab
a shot while the door
was open.

Le Coucou
138 Lafayette Street

Little Owl
90 Bedford Street

Loulou Speakeasy
176 Eighth Avenue
The door to the basement
speakeasy below Loulou.

Loverboy
127 Avenue C
Closed

Lovers of Today
132½ East 7th Street
A basement bar under
Niagara.

Lucien
14 First Avenue

Lucy's
135 Avenue A
Through the plexiglass.

M1-5
52 Walker Street
Closed

Macao Trading Company
311 Church Street

The Margarita Bar
4 South Street/
Whitehall Terminal
Commuter bar at the
Staten Island Ferry
terminal.

Marie's Crisis Cafe
59 Grove Street
A show tunes piano bar
since 1929. Named
after the original owner,
Marie DuMont, and
The American Crisis, a
series of pamphlets by
Thomas Paine. Paine was
living at this address at
the time of his death in
1809.

Marshall Stack
66 Rivington Street

McAnn's
625 Eighth Avenue/Port
Authority Bus Terminal
Another commuter bar.

**McNally Jackson Books
Seaport**
4 Fulton Street
Someone left the light on
overnight, once.

McSorley's Old Ale House
15 East 7th Street
Est. 1854. Light or
dark ale, those are the
choices.

The Mercury Lounge
217 East Houston Street
Live music venue with
drum kit visible onstage.

Milano's Bar
51 East Houston Street
Narrow/divey/nice.

Minetta Tavern
113 MacDougal Street
Old-school Italian turned
upscale restaurant,
with Cafe Wha? in the
background.

Mission Chinese
171 East Broadway
Closed
Long gone, but the
lighting!

The Monster
80 Grove Street
The butt-plug artwork
sets the tone.

Mr. Fong's
40 Market Street
The welcoming look of
Madison and Market
Streets at dawn.

Mulberry Street Bar
176 Mulberry Street
A Little Italy staple since
1908.

Nancy Whiskey Pub
1 Lispenard Street
Since 1967. Serving
Tribeca before it
was Tribeca.

Nassau Bar
118 Nassau Street

Nightingale
89 Greenwich Avenue
Closed

The Nines
9 Great Jones Street
The sign still says Acme,
but they've really done
up the place.

Nublu Classic
62 Avenue C
The original Nublu
location.

Nurse Bettie
106 Norfolk Street
Pinup-themed
burlesque bar.

The Odeon
145 West Broadway
Classic Tribeca.

O'Hanlon's
349 East 14th Street

Old Town Bar
45 East 18th Street
Nineteenth-century bar,
originally German and
named Viemeisters.

**One If by Land,
Two If by Sea**
17 Barrow Street
Candlelight, fireplaces,
piano!

Oppa Bistro
162 West 4th Street

Overlook
225 East 44th Street

**Paddy Maguire's Ale
House**
237 Third Avenue
Lighting for every holiday.
A lot of it.

The Patriot Saloon
110 Chambers Street
Closed

Paul's Casablanca
305 Spring Street
The sign still says
McGovern's.

Peoples Improv Theater
123 East 24th Street
*Moved to 154 West 29th
Street*

Pershing Square Buzz Bar
90 East 42nd Street

Peter McManus Cafe
152 Seventh Avenue

Pete's Tavern
129 East 18th Street
Still there since 1864.
O. Henry was a regular in
addition to many others.

Petite Boucherie
14 Christopher Street
From Gay Street, with
Christopher Street in
the mirror.

Pianos
158 Ludlow Street
Live music venue,
originally a piano store.

Pieces
8 Christopher Street

Pinky's Space
70 East 1st Street
Dining shed dismantled
A visual explosion most
welcome in the morning.

P. J. Clarke's
915 Third Avenue
Since 1884, with
Nat King Cole and Buddy
Holly as regulars.

Planet Rose
219 Avenue A
A festively lit karaoke
spot.

Puffy's Tavern
81 Hudson Street
In the '70s the local artists convinced the owner
to stay open into the
evening. Before that they
mainly served the truck
drivers delivering butter
and eggs.

Pyramid Club
101 Avenue A
Closed
Bar-top dancing,
Madonna, drag
shows, etc.

Ray's
177 Chrystie Street

Reservoir
70 University Place

**ReVision Lounge and
Gallery**
219 Avenue B

Rockbar
185 Christopher Street
Gay bar at Weehawken
Street.

Rolf's
281 Third Avenue
Where it's always
Christmas.

Rudy's Bar and Grill
627 Ninth Avenue
The human-size pig gives
it away. Also, the cheap
beer.

Sake Bar Satsko
202 East 7th Street
A sake bar pioneer this
far east (between B
and C).

San Remo Cafe
201 Lafayette Street
Closed

Sant Ambroeus
265 Lafayette Street

Short Stories
355 Bowery

Shuka
38 MacDougal Street

SideWalk Cafe
94 Avenue A
Closed
Home of Anti-folk music.

Slowly Shirley
121 West 10th Street
Closed
Basement spot below the
Happiest Hour.

Sophie's
507 East 5th Street
A regular bar.

**Spring Lounge
(aka the Shark Bar)**
48 Spring Street
During Prohibition it
was a "buckets of beer
to go" spot, then it was
Chappy's in the '40s and
Wilson's 10:30 (that's
when the craps game
started) in the '60s. Now
most know it as Shark
Bar for the stuffed sharks
about the place.

The Standard Biergarten
848 Washington Street
A beer garden for the
meat market set.

St. Dymphna's
117 Avenue A

The Stonewall Inn
53 Christopher Street
A police raid in 1969
started a riot that be-
came a turning point in
the gay rights movement.

Subject
188 Suffolk Street
In the days of dining
sheds and during a
snowstorm.

Subway Inn
1140 Second Avenue
*Moved to 1154 Second
Avenue*
Not the original location
but still a classic.

The Summit Bar
133 Avenue C

Swan Room
54 Canal Street
In the Nine Orchard
Hotel, the old
Jarmulowsky Bank.

Temperance Wine Bar
40 Carmine Street

TGI Friday's
34 Union Square East
Closed
Took the picture without
noting the name. Got
home and noticed the
Blues Brothers dolls and
then realized it was a
TGI Friday's.

Tile Bar
115 First Avenue
Once known as WCOU
for the clock on the back
wall.

Tortilla Flats
767 Washington Street
Closed
Long gone, long empty.

Tracks Raw Bar and Grill
Pennsylvania Station,
lower level
*Moved to 221 West 31st
Street*
Commuter bar in Penn
Station with one of the
longest bars in New York.

Ty's Bar
114 Christopher Street

Union Square Cafe
101 East 19th Street
With Devon Grimes
paintings above the bar.

Vandal
199 Bowery
Closed
A visually active entry.

Venice Bar
340 Bleecker Street
In Saint Theo's restaurant.
Photographed through the
cut-out hole of the *i* in
"Venice Bar" on the door.

Via Carota
51 Grove Street
Always crowded, so they
send you to their Bar
Pisellino (see above) across
the street.

Vig Bar
12 Spring Street

Wakamba
543 Eighth Avenue
Wonderful Eighth Avenue
dive.

Wallsé
344 West 11th Street
Austrian at Washington
Street.

Waverly Inn
16 Bank Street
A great four- or
five-stool bar.

The Wayland
700 East 9th Street

Welcome to the Johnsons
123 Rivington Street
Plastic couch covers
and all.

White Horse Tavern
567 Hudson Street
With all the history,
Dylan Thomas might
be mentioned the most.

White Oak Tavern
21 Waverly Place

The Wren
344 Bowery

Zum Schneider
107 Avenue C
Closed
They had proper beer and
knew how to serve it.

AFTERWORD

Lighting Corners

By Suzaan Boettger

*I am sick of "lighting candles," I want to know what the "darkness" is,
I don't "curse" it or praise it, but I know it is there.*
—Artist/essayist Robert Smithson to artist/theorist Gyorgy Kepes, 1969

Like Robert Smithson, Daniel Root is not a stranger to the dark. He too
seeks it, having for years risen dreadfully early to ramble in its last hours.
In the way-past-midnight intermission between nightfall and daybreak, he
has explored scenes near and beyond his neighborhood in far east downtown
Manhattan. Unlike Smithson, who lived across town and ruminated on "The
Iconography of Desolation," Root's obsession with darkness as it appears in
saloons and streets highlights that which defies desolation. He is drawn to
light, the electrified radiances that push shadows aside. Surveying these, he
has photographically captured—created—something like an iconography of
(artificial) illumination.

Root's act of going to darkness to focus on light is but one of his plays with
antipodes that make contemplation of his imagery fascinating. He works
in the dead of night, when most sensible—sober—souls are sound asleep,
but by the clock is strolling in the morning. Propelled by the sense of inde-
pendence afforded by unconfined solitude in quiet darkness, he is drawn to
gaudy color signaling raucous partying. Confined behind grates and windows,
he becomes a peeping Dan of watchfulness, photographically conjuring im-
mersion in environments otherwise unknown.

Bars are places of conviviality, release from constraints, and for some, descent into oblivion. But here they are evacuated of the buzz of good cheer, the beat of music and howls at stand-up. Empty of revelers and runaways from responsibilities, these taverns take on the silent solemnity of a museum's historical period room or the eeriness of a postapocalyptic tale where everyone has vanished. But if not the human species, these social spaces remain alive, animated by neon. Consider the ravishing Beatrice Inn. In the heart of a blood-of-Christ crimson *boîte* stands a veritable altar in aqua, fronted by acidic gold. Pray that the bartender knows how to make a sidecar.

Vivid hues lift the common pictorial mood in these otherwise shadowy dens away from melancholy toward the manic, countering alcohol's enervating effect. The lurid color and sites of wild abandon link Root's imagery to German Expressionist precedents of more than a century ago, Ernst Ludwig Kirchner's and George Grosz's decadent night crawlers in Berlin. His subject matter also relates to Edgar Degas's café scene of a bedraggled duo nursing a morning hangover (*Absinthe Drinkers*). But those artists' critiques of drunkenness, streetwalkers, and political corruption do not apply.

Root's locales are not all dives catering to the louche life. The salmon Louis XVI daybed before a mural painting of a Romantic landscape at twilight indicates Le Coucou's aspirations, confirmed by its website urging patrons to arrive "dressed their best." Well! In spirit Root's imagery is more akin to Edward Hopper's emphasis on light, structure, and solitude, as in *Early Sunday Morning* and *Nighthawks,* and the sharply glowing row of pendant globes reflected into doubleness in the nocturnal *Automat.* A related ancestor is Bernice Abbott's monochrome photographs of Greenwich Village architecture as studies in shadowy geometrics.

For those of us swept up and nourished by hues—who dress as much by color as occasion, paint our places in tones evoking emotion, and choose our destinations by visual atmosphere—this collection offers chromatic ecstasy. Yet Root's photographic strengths also encompass subtle drama, most eloquently in the focal point of the bronzy brown milieu of Cherry Tavern. Isolated in the murky distance, the luminous green triangular lamp shade over a pool table is reflected on the gleaming floor in chartreuse, with a kelly apex above the shimmering white core.

And *New York Bars at Dawn* becomes a wish book. On my list for future bar hopping are Jeremy's Ale House for its hanging brassieres (style tips more amusing than at Victoria's Secret) and the Beetle House, where its florid violet, fuchsia, and apple green envelopment will surely enhance cocktails' flavors. For afternoon tippling, I'll sink into the Swan Room's sofas below the curved mullioned window and clusters of lustrous globes, and for enchanted evenings with intimates dine within the embrace of Boucherie's expansive arches.

Like an inverted heliotrope, Root turns toward moonscapes for his creativity—that in-between time after bars close and before most of us open our window shades. The side of his visual equation that ignites a corner of your mind—garish color or shadowy gloom—will tell you as much about yourself as his work. In either case, Root exposes us to scenes we would not otherwise see, whether in life or in art.